THE CAMBRIDGE
MODERNIS

This Companion offers the most compre.
poetry, its forms, its major authors and its contexts. The first part explo..
historical and cultural contexts and sexual politics of literary modernism and the
avant garde. The chapters in the second part concentrate on individual authors
and movements, while the concluding part offers a comprehensive overview of
the early reception and subsequent canonisation of modernist poetry. As well
as insightful readings of canonical poets, the Companion features extended discussions of poets whose importance is now being increasingly recognised, such
as Mina Loy, poets of the Harlem Renaissance, British modernists and postcolonial poets in the Caribbean, Africa and India. While modernist poets are
often thought of as difficult, these essays will help students to understand and
appreciate their experimental and creative responses to contemporary social and
cultural change.

THE CAMBRIDGE
COMPANION TO
# MODERNIST POETRY

EDITED BY
## ALEX DAVIS
*University College Cork*

AND

## LEE M. JENKINS
*University College Cork*

CAMBRIDGE UNIVERSITY PRESS
Cambridge, New York, Melbourne, Madrid, Cape Town, Singapore, São Paulo

Cambridge University Press
The Edinburgh Building, Cambridge CB2 8RU, UK

Published in the United States of America by Cambridge University Press, New York

www.cambridge.org
Information on this title: www.cambridge.org/9780521618151

© Cambridge University Press 2007

First published 2007

Printed in the United Kingdom at the University Press, Cambridge

*A catalogue record for this publication is available from the British Library*

ISBN 978-0-521-85305-7 hardback
ISBN 978-0-521-61815-1 paperback

# CONTENTS

# CONTRIBUTORS

DAVID AYERS is Reader in Modernism and Critical Theory in the School of English at the University of Kent. His publications include *Wyndham Lewis and Western Man* (1992), *English Literature of the 1920s* (1999), *Modernism: A Short Introduction* (2004) and *Literary Theory: A Reintroduction* (2007).

BONNIE COSTELLO is Professor of English at Boston University and the author of many studies on modern and contemporary poetry, including, most recently, *Shifting Ground: Reinventing Landscape in Modern American Poetry* (2003). Her new book, *Planets on Tables: Poetry, Still Life and the Turning World*, will be published by Cornell University Press in 2007.

ALEX DAVIS is Senior Lecturer in Modern English at University College Cork. He is the author of *A Broken Line: Denis Devlin and Irish Poetic Modernism* (2000) and co-author of *Irish Studies: The Essential Glossary* (2003). He has co-edited two collections of essays on modernist poetry: with Lee M. Jenkins, *Locations of Literary Modernism: Region and Nation in British and American Modernist Poetry* (2000) and, with Patricia Coughlan, *Modernism and Ireland: The Poetry of the 1930s* (1995).

RACHEL BLAU DuPLESSIS, Professor at Temple University, is an American poet-critic. Her critical writing includes *Blue Studios: Poetry and Its Cultural Work* (2006), *The Pink Guitar: Writing as Feminist Practice* (2006) and *Genders, Races, and Religious Cultures in Modern American Poetry, 1908–1934* (2001). Earlier work includes *Writing Beyond the Ending: Narrative Strategies of Twentieth-Century Women Writers* (1985) and *H.D.: The Career of that Struggle* (1986), as well as an edition of *The Selected Letters of George Oppen* (1990). DuPlessis's ongoing long poem project is *Drafts* (2001, 2004, 2007).

ANNE FOGARTY is Professor of James Joyce Studies at University College Dublin and Director of the UCD Research Centre for James Joyce Studies. She is editor of the *Irish University Review* and President-elect of the International James Joyce Foundation. She has lectured and published widely on aspects of Irish modernism and on twentieth-century Irish women's writing. She is co-editor, with Timothy Martin, of *Joyce on the Threshold* (2005) and is currently completing a monograph entitled *James Joyce and Cultural Memory: Reading History in Ulysses*.

JASON HARDING is Lecturer in English Studies at the University of Durham. He is the author of *The 'Criterion': Cultural Politics and Periodical Networks in Inter-War Britain* (2002) and a co-editor of the collection of critical essays *T. S. Eliot and the Concept of Tradition* (2007). He is currently researching a book on Cold War cultural politics and editing a volume in the Faber *Collected Prose of T. S. Eliot*.

LEE MARGARET JENKINS is Senior Lecturer in Modern English at University College Cork. She has published widely on American and African-American literature and modern poetry and is the author of *Wallace Stevens: Rage for Order* (1999) and *The Language of Caribbean Poetry* (2004). With Alex Davis, she is the editor of *Locations of Literary Modernism: Region and Nation in British and American Modernist Poetry* (2000). She is currently researching a monograph on D. H. Lawrence and America.

SHARON LYNETTE JONES is Associate Professor of English at Wright State University in Ohio. She is the author of *Rereading the Harlem Renaissance: Race, Class, and Gender in the Fiction of Jessie Fauset, Zora Neale Hurston, and Dorothy West* (2002) and co-editor, with Rochelle Smith, of *The Prentice Hall Anthology of African American Literature* (2000). She has also contributed articles to journals such as *Langston Hughes Review* and *Social Alternatives*.

CRISTANNE MILLER is Edward H. Butler Professor of Literature and Chair of the English Department at University at Buffalo, SUNY. Her publications include *Cultures of Modernism: Marianne Moore, Mina Loy, Else Lasker-Schuler* (2005), *Marianne Moore: Questions of Authority* (1996), and she is a co-editor with Bonnie Costello and Celeste Goodridge of the *Selected Letters of Marianne Moore* (1997). She has also written extensively on Emily Dickinson and other US poets.

DREW MILNE is the Judith E. Wilson Lecturer in Drama and Poetry, Faculty of English, University of Cambridge. His critical publications include *Modern Critical Thought: An Anthology of Theorists Writing on Theorists* (2003). His books of poetry include *Bench Marks* (1998), *Mars Disarmed* (2001), *The Damage: New and Selected Poems* (2002) and *Go Figure* (2003).

PETER NICHOLLS is Professor of English and American Literature at the University of Sussex. His publications include *Ezra Pound: Politics, Economics and Writing* (1984), *Modernisms: A Literary Guide* (1995), and many articles and essays on literature and theory. He recently co-edited, with Laura Marcus, *The Cambridge History of Twentieth-Century English Literature* (2005) and his *George Oppen and the Fate of Modernism* will be published by Oxford University Press in 2007. He is editor of the journal *Textual Practice* and co-director of the Centre for Modernist Studies at Sussex.

PAUL PEPPIS is Associate Professor of English Literature and Culture at the University of Oregon. He is the author of *Literature, Politics, and the English Avant-Garde: Nation and Empire 1901–1918* (2000) and has published articles on a range of twentieth-century authors, including E. M. Forster, Ford Madox Ford, Wyndham Lewis, Mina Loy and Gertrude Stein. He is currently at work on a book entitled *Sciences of Modernism: Sexology, Psychology, and Anthropology*.

LAWRENCE RAINEY is Professor of Modern Literature at the University of York. He is the founding editor of the journal *Modernism/Modernity*, and his most recent books on T. S. Eliot – *Revisiting 'The Waste Land'* (2005) and *The Annotated Waste Land with Eliot's Contemporary Prose* (2005) – were jointly awarded the 2006 Robert Motherwell Book Prize for the best contribution to the study of modernism.

JAHAN RAMAZANI is Edgar F. Shannon Professor of English and Department Chair at the University of Virginia. He is the author of *Yeats and the Poetry of Death: Elegy, Self-Elegy, and the Sublime* (1990), *Poetry of Mourning: The Modern Elegy from Hardy to Heaney* (1994) and *The Hybrid Muse: Postcolonial Poetry in English* (2001). He co-edited the third edition of *The Norton Anthology of Modern and Contemporary Poetry* (2003) and the eighth edition of *The Twentieth Century and After* in *The Norton Anthology of English Literature* (2006).

MARK SCROGGINS is Associate Professor in the Department of English at Florida Atlantic University. He is the author of *Louis Zukofsky and the Poetry of Knowledge* (1998), *Anarchy* (poems, 2003), *The Poem of a Life: A Biography of Louis Zukofsky* (2007) and editor of *Upper Limit Music: The Writing of Louis Zukofsky* (1997).

# ACKNOWLEDGEMENTS

The editors would like, first and foremost, to thank the contributors to this Companion; it has been a privilege and a pleasure to bring together such a rich diversity of voices. Our thanks, as ever, to Ray Ryan of Cambridge University Press for his enthusiasm, his unfailingly wise counsel, his patience and good humour. For seeing the book into print, thanks to Jacqui Burton, Alison Powell, Maartje Scheltens and Nikky Twyman. We are also indebted to our students, both undergraduates and postgraduates, who have helped to inform our understanding of and love for modernist poetry. We are grateful to our colleagues in the Department of English and in the College of Arts, Celtic Studies and Social Sciences at University College Cork for fostering an academic environment conducive to and appreciative of research. Indeed, work on this Companion was greatly facilitated by sabbatical leave granted by the President of University College Cork. Our special thanks go to Anne FitzGerald and her marvellous colleagues, Jennifer Crowley, Elaine Hickey and Mary O'Mahoney, in the Department of English, for their administrative support. Other scholars, poets and friends who have offered us various encouragements and advice, and, perhaps most importantly, have cheerfully engaged in creative dialogue about modernist poetry and much else include: Graham Allen, George Bornstein, Kamau Brathwaite, Philip Coleman, Patricia Coughlan, David and Ros Cox, John Goodby, Hugh Haughton, Peter Howarth, Trevor Joyce, John Matthias, Peter Middleton, Clíona Ó Gallchoir, Lorenzo Thomas and Keith Tuma.

# CHRONOLOGY

| | |
|---|---|
| 1876 | Internal combustion engine developed. |
| 1890 | James Frazer, *The Golden Bough* (3rd edn, in 12 vols, 1906–1915).<br>William James, *Principles of Psychology*. |
| 1893 | Independent Labour Party founded in Britain. |
| 1895 | Invention of the motion picture.<br>Invention of wireless. |
| 1899 | Arthur Symons, *The Symbolist Movement in Literature*. |
| 1900 | Sigmund Freud, *The Interpretation of Dreams*.<br>George Santayana, *Interpretations of Poetry and Religion*. |
| 1901 | Death of Queen Victoria.<br>Edward VII accedes to the British throne.<br>Theodore Roosevelt elected to the US presidency. |
| 1902 | The *Times Literary Supplement* founded. |
| 1903 | W. E. B. Du Bois, *The Souls of Black Folk*.<br>*Camera Work* magazine founded.<br>Wright brothers' first aeroplane flight. |
| 1905 | George Santayana, *The Life of Reason: Reason in Art*.<br>Albert Einstein announces special theory of relativity. |
| 1907 | Picasso, *Les Demoiselles d'Avignon*.<br>Henri Bergson, *Creative Evolution*. |
| 1909 | Filippo Tommaso Marinetti, 'The Founding and Manifesto of Futurism'.<br>National Association for the Advancement of Colored People (NAACP) founded. |

1910    Filippo Tommaso Marinetti delivers 'Futurist Speech to the
        English' in London.
        First Post-Impressionist exhibition in London.
        Death of Edward VII.
        George V accedes to the British throne.

1911    Franz Boas, *The Mind of Primitive Man*.

1912    Edward Marsh (ed.), *Georgian Poetry* (vols II–V, 1915, 1917,
        1919, 1922).
        Filippo Tommaso Marinetti, 'Technical Manifesto of Futurist
        Literature'.
        T. E. Hulme, 'The Complete Poetical Works of T. E. Hulme'.
        Claude McKay, *Songs of Jamaica* and *Constab Ballads*.
        *Poetry* (Chicago) magazine founded.
        Arnold Schoenberg, *Pierrot Lunaire*.
        Sinking of the *Titanic*.

1913    Igor Stravinsky, *Le Sacre du printemps*.
        The New York Armory Show.
        Woodrow Wilson elected to the US presidency.

1914    *Blast* magazine founded (second and final issue 1915).
        *The Egoist* magazine founded (formerly *The Freewoman/The
        New Freewoman*, founded 1911).
        *Little Review* founded.
        Ezra Pound (ed.), *Des Imagistes*.
        Gertrude Stein, *Tender Buttons*.
        Irish Home Rule Bill passed by Parliament.
        Commencement of First World War.

1915    Ezra Pound, *Cathay*.
        D. W. Griffith, *Birth of a Nation*.
        *Others* magazine founded.

1916    H.D., *Sea Garden*.
        Albert Einstein, *General Theory of Relativity*.
        First Dada performances at the Cabaret Voltaire, Zurich.
        Easter Rising in Dublin.
        First Battle of the Somme.

1917    T. S. Eliot, *Prufrock and Other Observations*.
        Mina Loy, *Love Songs to Joannes*.
        Marcel Duchamp, *Fountain*.

Russian Revolution.

United States enters First World War.

1918    Tristan Tzara, *Dada Manifesto 1918*.

Van Wyck Brooks, 'On Creating a Usable Past'.

Lytton Strachey, *Eminent Victorians*.

Armistice (end of First World War).

Enfranchisement of women aged 30 and over in Britain.

Influenza epidemic.

1919    T. S. Eliot, 'Tradition and the Individual Talent'.

Ezra Pound, *Homage to Sextus Propertius*.

Oswald Spengler, *Decline of the West* (English translation).

Treaty of Versailles.

League of Nations created.

Prohibition Act passed by US Congress.

American Communist Party founded.

1920    T. S. Eliot, *The Sacred Wood*.

T. S. Eliot, *Ara Vos Prec*.

Ezra Pound, *Hugh Selwyn Mauberley*.

William Carlos Williams, *Kora in Hell: Improvisations*.

Lothrop Stoddard, *The Rising Tide of Color Against White World Supremacy*.

Jacques Maritain, *Art and Scholasticism*.

*Dial* magazine founded.

Nineteenth Amendment grants American women the vote (upheld by Supreme Court in 1922).

1921    Marcel Duchamp and Man Ray, *New York Dada* magazine founded.

1922    Thomas Hardy, *Late Lyrics and Earlier*.

T. S. Eliot, *The Waste Land*.

Claude McKay, *Harlem Shadows*.

James Weldon Johnson (ed.), *The Book of American Negro Poetry*.

Bronislaw Malinowski, *Argonauts of the Western Pacific*.

Ludwig Wittgenstein, *Tractatus Logico-Philosophicus*.

*Criterion* magazine founded.

British Broadcasting Corporation founded.

Creation of the Irish Free State.

| 1923 | William Carlos Williams, *Spring and All.* |

1923
William Carlos Williams, *Spring and All.*
Wallace Stevens, *Harmonium.*
Jean Toomer, *Cane.*
D. H. Lawrence, *Birds, Beasts and Flowers.*
Mina Loy, *Lunar Baedecker.*
Mina Loy, *Anglo-Mongrels and the Rose.*

1924
Marianne Moore, *Observations.*
André Breton, *Manifesto of Surrealism.*
First Labour government elected in Britain.
Indian Citizenship Act passed in USA.

1925
Alain Locke (ed.), *The New Negro.*
Ezra Pound, *A Draft of XVI. Cantos.*
Hugh MacDiarmid, *Sangschaw.*
Alfred North Whitehead, *Science and the Modern World.*
Sergei Mikhailovich Eisenstein, *Battleship Potemkin.*
Scopes trial, Tennessee.

1926
Langston Hughes, *The Weary Blues.*
*FIRE!!* magazine founded.
Hugh MacDiarmid, *A Drunk Man Looks at the Thistle.*
T. E. Hulme, *Speculations.*
Louis Zukofsky, 'Poem beginning "The"'.
General Strike in Britain.

1927
*transition* magazine founded.
Wyndham Lewis, *Time and Western Man.*
Laura Riding and Robert Graves, *A Survey of Modernist Poetry.*
Martin Heidegger, *Being and Time.*
Alan Crosland, *The Jazz Singer.*
Fritz Lang, *Metropolis.*
Charles Lindbergh flies *The Spirit of St Louis* from New York to Paris.

1928
W. B. Yeats, *The Tower.*
Enfranchisement of women over 21 in Britain.
Television broadcasts commence in USA.

1929
Eugene Jolas et al., 'Revolution of the Word'.
Edith Sitwell, *Gold Coast Customs.*
Wyndham Lewis, *Paleface: The Philosophy of the Melting Pot.*

Museum of Modern Art in New York opens.
Wall Street Crash.
Censorship of Publications Act (Ireland).

1930 Hart Crane, *The Bridge.*
T. S. Eliot, *Ash Wednesday.*
W. H. Auden, *Poems.*
Allen Tate et al., *I'll Take My Stand.*
Sigmund Freud, *Civilization and its Discontents.*
Samuel Beckett, *Whoroscope.*
Ezra Pound, *A Draft of XXX Cantos.*
William Empson, *Seven Types of Ambiguity.*

1931 E. E. Cummings, *Viva.*
Britain leaves the Gold Standard.

1932 Louis Zukofsky (ed.), *An 'Objectivists' Anthology.*
Sterling A. Brown, *Southern Road.*
T. S. Eliot, *Selected Essays.*
Michael Roberts (ed.), *New Signatures.*
F. R. Leavis, *New Bearings in English Poetry.*
*Scrutiny* magazine founded.

1933 Wyndham Lewis, *One-Way Song.*
W. B. Yeats, *The Winding Stair and Other Poems.*
Adolf Hitler becomes Chancellor of Germany.
Franklin Delano Roosevelt elected to the US presidency.
Federal Emergency Relief Act passed in USA.

1934 T. S. Eliot, *After Strange Gods.*
Hugh MacDiarmid, *Stony Limits and Other Poems.*
Thomas MacGreevy, *Poems.*
George Oppen, *Discrete Series.*

1935 Marianne Moore, *Selected Poems.*
Samuel Beckett, *Echo's Bones and Other Precipitates.*
William Empson, *Poems.*
Ezra Pound, *Jefferson and/or Mussolini.*
Wallace Stevens, *Ideas of Order.*
Italy invades Abyssinia.

1936 Michael Roberts (ed.), *The Faber Book of Modern Verse.*
Dylan Thomas, *Twenty-Five Poems.*
W. B. Yeats (ed.), *The Oxford Book of Modern Verse.*
Charlie Chaplin, *Modern Times.*

John Maynard Keynes, *General Theory of Employment, Interest and Money.*
Death of George V.
Edward VIII abdicates.
George VI accedes to the British throne.
Spanish Civil War begins.
BBC television commences broadcasting.

1937    David Jones, *In Parenthesis.*
Wallace Stevens, *The Man with the Blue Guitar.*
Denis Devlin, *Intercessions.*

1938    Ezra Pound, *Guide to Kulchur.*
Brian Coffey, *Third Person.*
Cleanth Brooks and Robert Penn Warren, *Understanding Poetry.*
Munich crisis.
House UnAmerican Activities Committee founded in USA.

1939    W. B. Yeats, *Last Poems and Two Plays.*
Louis MacNeice, *Autumn Journal.*
Second World War commences.

1940    Charlie Chaplin, *The Great Dictator.*
British evacuation at Dunkirk.

1941    John Crowe Ransom, *The New Criticism.*
James Agee and Walter Evans, *Let Us Now Praise Famous Men.*
Japanese attack Pearl Harbor.

1942    Wallace Stevens, *Notes Toward a Supreme Fiction.*

1943    Hugh MacDiarmid, *Lucky Poet.*

1944    T. S. Eliot, *Four Quartets.*
H.D., *The Walls Do Not Fall.*
Lynette Roberts, *Poems.*
Carl Gustav Jung, *Psychology and Alchemy.*

1945    H.D., *Tribute to the Angels.*
End of Second World War in Europe and Far East.
Foundation of the United Nations.

1946    William Carlos Williams, *Paterson* Book I (Books II–V published 1948, 1949, 1951, 1958).

H.D., *Flowering of the Rod*.
Lorine Niedecker, *New Goose*.

1947   India achieves Independence.

1948   Ezra Pound, *The Pisan Cantos*.

1949   Formation of the Republic of Ireland.

1950   Charles Olson, 'Projective Verse'.

1951   Lynette Roberts, *Gods with Stainless Ears*.

1952   David Jones, *The Anathemata*.

1953   Melvin B. Tolson, *Libretto for the Republic of Liberia*.

1955   Hugh MacDiarmid, *In Memoriam James Joyce*.

1960   Charles Olson, *The Maximus Poems* (two further vols, 1968, 1975).

1965   David Gascoyne, *Collected Poems*.

1966   Louise Bennett, *Jamaica Labrish*.
       Basil Bunting, *Briggflatts*.

1969   J. H. Prynne, *The White Stones*.
       Ezra Pound, *Drafts & Fragments of Cantos CX–CXVII*.
       Okot p'Bitek, *Song of Lawino*.

1971   Hugh Kenner, *The Pound Era*.

1973   (Edward) Kamau Brathwaite, *The Arrivants*.

1987   Kamau Brathwaite, *X/Self*.
       Agha Shahid Ali, *Half-Inch Himalayas*.

1999   Inaugural conference of the Modernist Studies Association.

ALEX DAVIS AND LEE M. JENKINS

# Introduction

In 1921, T. S. Eliot declared that 'poets in our civilization . . . must be *difficult*'.[1] The publication in the following year of *The Waste Land* served to confirm the truth of this pronouncement: Eliot's bristlingly allusive poem, and its seven pages of accompanying notes, insists that 'difficulty' is a *sine qua non* of the modernist artwork.[2] For other practitioners of modernist poetics, like William Carlos Williams, the learnedness of Eliot's poem returned poetry to the classroom: arguably, however, Williams's democratic model of modernist poetry requires as much exegesis for the twenty-first-century reader as Eliot's elitist masterpiece. After all, critics have expended as much ingenuity in surmising *what* depends on Williams's red wheelbarrow, in his sixteen-word poem of that title, as they have in pursuing the meaning of Tarot cards and the Holy Grail in Eliot's pocket epic. Between the polar extremes represented by Eliot and Williams we find a heterogeneous array of modernist poetries. The broad church of poetic modernism includes Wallace Stevens's post-Arnoldian idea of poetry as a substitute for religion; the avant-garde '*écriture feminine*' of H.D. (Hilda Doolittle) and Mina Loy; and the cultural nationalisms of African-American and certain Irish and Scottish poetry of the period.

Modernist poetry involves recuperations of history *and* Futurist and Dada abandonments of tradition; arcane *and* demotic registers of language; elitist *and* populist forms of literature. The rich diversity of modernist poetries, no less than the particular difficulties presented by *The Waste Land*, inevitably necessitates the kind of 'classroom assistance' Williams believed the 'new art' was on the point of escaping.[3]

We might date the periodisation of modernism, as an historical epoch, to the death of the critic Hugh Kenner, author of the hugely influential *The Pound Era* (1971). Kenner's death in 2003 can be seen as having marked the passing, figuratively and largely literally, of an entire generation of scholars and readers for whom modernist poetry, or Williams's 'new art', was contemporary poetry. For the overwhelming majority of twenty-first-century readers, modernism belongs as much to literary history as does romantic literature.[4]

While from one angle the modernist era has come into focus as a period, viewed from another its historical parameters are hazy. As this Companion demonstrates, the temporal boundaries of the modernist era are permeable: hence the discernible difficulty literary historians have in assigning dates to modernism. Since Frank Kermode's *Romantic Image* (1957), modernism's roots in the poetry of the 1890s has become ever more apparent. Christopher Ricks's edition of Eliot's early poetry, *Inventions of the March Hare* (1996), is vivid testimony to the importance of fin-de-siècle symbolism to high modernism. Indeed, Marshall Berman's *All That Is Solid Melts Into Air* (1982) dates the beginnings of modernism to the mid-nineteenth century, to the thought of Karl Marx and the poetry of Baudelaire. At the other end of the modernist timeline, Marjorie Perloff contends that we find in certain contemporary poets (J. H. Prynne, Susan Howe and others) a twenty-first-century modernism that circles back to the restless experimentation of the historical avant garde in the early years of the twentieth century. Inheritors of modernist tendencies, such as the Objectivists (George Oppen, Carl Rakosi, Louis Zukofsky, Lorine Niedecker and Charles Reznikoff), and the Black Mountain poets associated with Charles Olson, may also be considered proponents of a 'late' or 'new' modernism. Certainly, modernism has not reached its expiry date for certain postcolonial poets. Kamau Brathwaite's creolised Caribbean modernism illustrates the 'uneven development' of avant-garde poetries between what we might term First and Third World modernisms. Brathwaite's poetry demonstrates that modernism and postcoloniality are not mutually exclusive categories, as some theorists of the postmodern would have us believe. Indeed, as Michael North has observed, 1922, the year of the publication of *The Waste Land* and of James Joyce's *Ulysses*, also saw the birth of the Irish Free State and the emergence of Egyptian self-determination, thus signalling 'the beginning of the postcolonial era'.[5]

In this respect as in others, the concept of postmodernism has shown itself to be overly reliant on a caricatured 'straw man' notion of modernism, of the kind presented in Ihab Hassan's *The Dismemberment of Orpheus: Toward a Postmodern Literature* (1971). However, it is significant that one of the earliest proponents of the 'post-modern', Charles Olson, did not construe the relationship between modernism and postmodernism as a binary division.[6] Contemporaneous with the growing valorisation of 'postmodernist' literature, and the accompanying downgrading of modernist texts, was the rise of literary theory during the 1970s and 1980s. The reappraisal of romantic literature by, among others, the Yale Critics (in particular, Paul de Man,

Geoffrey Hartman and Harold Bloom) proved to be detrimental to the reputation of certain modernists, especially Eliot and Pound, loftily dismissed by Bloom as the Cleveland and Cowley of their age. (Doubtless, Eliot and Pound's frequently hostile and, in Eliot's case, highly influential interpretations of romantic writers played a part in the relative marginalisation of modernist poetry at this time.) Only modernists recuperable to a late romantic paradigm, such as Wallace Stevens, thrived during the heyday of theory. Not coincidentally, the present waning of interest in Stevens has gone hand in hand with the rise of a newly historicised critical attention to Eliot.

Recent years have seen a remarkable renaissance in the study of modernist literature in general; at the centre of this has been renewed attention to modernist poetry in particular, both that of the established canon, and the work of poets who have until now been marginalised in modernist studies. An example and a catalyst of this rejuvenation of the discipline is the Modernist Studies Association and its influential journal, *Modernism/Modernity*. The new modernist studies departs from the New Critical version of modernism canonised in the 1940s, with its emphasis on the text as an autonomous entity,[7] in its attention to, among other topics, the historical conjuncture in which modernism emerged, the material culture of modernity, and race and gender. Major reassessments of established reputations are currently under way – witness the lively controversy surrounding Eliot and the subject of anti-Semitism.[8] This rejuvenation of interest in modernist literature is to be welcomed; though it is important that issues of poetic form – so crucial to modernist texts – are not inadvertently sidelined in the current historicisation of the discipline.

An encouraging sign that the quiddity of the modernist text is still respected is the emergence of a growing number of reliable scholarly editions, though Ezra Pound's *The Cantos* is a significant exception, and perhaps an irresolvable one.[9] Carcanet's multi-volume edition of Hugh MacDiarmid's poetry and prose, and the works of W. B. Yeats under the general editorship of Richard J. Finneran and George Mills Harper, offer two instances of modernist authors who have received the kind of editorial attention previously reserved for writers of earlier eras.

Complementing this, the modernist canon has been significantly expanded, to represent the contribution to modernist poetry of, for instance, the Harlem Renaissance and pioneering women writers such as H.D. and Mina Loy. As George Bornstein has pointed out, the seminal anthology of the Harlem Renaissance, *The New Negro* (1925), is 'deliberately biracial', deploying a 'hybrid racial politics' apparent, for example, in the prominence, in the text, of illustrations by Winold Reiss.[10] The recovery of the London-born Loy is an instance of the growing interest shown in British modernist poetry, of which Keith Tuma's *Fishing by Obstinate Isles* (1999) is an important instance. Indeed, the very title of Peter Nicholls's *Modernisms* (1995) is testimony to our more capacious comprehension of this literary era. The chapters included in *The Cambridge Companion to Modernist Poetry* reflect the recent transformation of the discipline, a sea-change increasingly manifested in the academic curriculum.

Recent groundbreaking studies of modernist poetry include Lawrence Rainey's *Institutions of Modernism* (1998), Michael North's *Dialect of Modernism* (1994), and Marjorie Perloff's many interventions in the field. This Companion complements such specialised monographs in offering an up-to-date overview of the spectrum of modernist poetry, its contexts and its formal demands. Although there are several excellent introductions to modernism, including Michael Levenson's *Cambridge Companion to Modernism* (1999) and Malcolm Bradbury and James McFarlane's still indispensable *Modernism* (1976), this Companion remedies the singular lack of a corresponding text devoted solely to modernist *poetry*.

*The Cambridge Companion to Modernist Poetry* is composed of three Parts. Firstly, four chapters address those contexts that are essential to the comprehension of modernist poetry, providing a balance between necessary historical information and attention to the formal demands of the modernist poem. Secondly, eight chapters provide advanced introductions to the work of a range of Anglophone modernist poets and movements. Thirdly, the final chapter assesses the critical reception of modernist poetry. The Companion is framed by a chronology of key events and publication dates and an up-to-date Bibliography.

In the first chapter, David Ayers introduces the philosophical and political contexts out of which modernism emerged and developed. From the vantage point of the reader in the twenty-first century, the increasingly remote intellectual milieu of the period of modernism requires a comprehensive appraisal for its poetry to be accurately and adequately appreciated. To that end, Ayers explores the history of ideas to which modernism responds.

The three chapters that follow deal with specific dimensions of modernist poetry. Modernist poetry is not a homogeneous entity: Paul Peppis's chapter details the miscellaneous modernist schools that comprise Anglo-American and continental European poetry, discriminating between the many 'isms' and avant gardes – Imagism, Vorticism, Surrealism, Dada, Futurism – that comprise the modernist movement from before the First World War to the 1930s. The focus of this chapter is on Anglophone movements in the broader context of continental European modernisms. (Post-Second World War avant gardes are considered in chapters 10 and 12 of the *Companion*, which consider American poetry in the 'Williams tradition' and Anglophone modernisms from the Caribbean, Africa and India respectively.)

Peter Nicholls's chapter analyses the challenge posed by experimental form faced by all readers of modernist poetry. Nicholls provides an overview of the various techniques and devices deployed by modernist poets, including dialogue between tradition and the new, discontinuous form, fragmentation, personae, an emphasis on poiesis or poetic 'making', the modernist use of irony derived from the French poet Jules Laforgue, self-reflexivity, and the mythic method deployed by Eliot and Pound and denounced by Williams.

The sexual politics of modernist poetry are extreme, reactionary and subversive in equal measure. Cristanne Miller's chapter analyses the representation and role of gender and sexuality in both male and female-authored modernist poetry. Miller considers the historical context of debate about gender relations and sexuality in the period of modernism, re-reading modernist treatments of gender and sexuality as problematic and productive. Women's contribution to modernist poetry has until recently been relatively neglected, regardless of the fact that women writers and publishers were instrumental in the modernist movement from its earliest stages, particularly in the context of the 'little magazines' of modernism. This chapter addresses the careers of women poets (H.D., Gertrude Stein, Marianne Moore, Loy and Amy Lowell) who were crucial to the modernist project and whose work was shaped in often terse dialogue with their male peers. Miller also analyses the representation of sexuality and of women in male-authored modernist poetry (Pound, Eliot, Jean Toomer, Hart Crane and Langston Hughes).

The second Part of this Companion focuses on specific authors, collaborations and groupings. This Part begins with an extended analysis by Lawrence Rainey of Ezra Pound and T. S. Eliot, arguably the most influential of modernist poets, the impact of whose poetic practice and cultural assumptions on poets writing in their wake is immense. Rainey's analysis of the poetics of Pound and Eliot is complemented by an interpretation of these major modernists as cultural catalysts for their era, and addresses the critical interpretations of their respective legacies. Rachel Blau DuPlessis's chapter complements Rainey's in its analysis of the increasingly acknowledged significance of the work of H.D. and its relationship to the male pantheon of modernist poets. H.D. is read in relation to her major male modernist contemporaries, her mythopoetic poems making a revisionary intervention into the 'masculine' mythic method of Pound and Eliot.

This second Part of the Companion continues with Anne Fogarty's consideration of W. B. Yeats's relationship with the modernist movement. Although belonging to an earlier generation, Yeats's contribution to modernism is immense. Indeed, the Irish Literary Revival, of which Yeats was a major orchestrator, has been regarded as prefiguring other movements within Anglo-American and European modernism. Fogarty's chapter considers the ways in which Yeats's project is imbricated in the evolution of modernism, his lyric mode, developed in the late nineteenth century, increasingly subjected to the pressures of modernity. Drew Milne's chapter constitutes an appraisal of British modernist poets, considering the important contribution made to modernist poetry by its Scottish, English and Welsh practitioners, including MacDiarmid, Loy, Basil Bunting, William Empson, John Rodker, Nancy Cunard, David Jones and Lynette Roberts. The chapter examines the relative critical neglect of British modernism, which has often been seen as peripheral in dominant critical accounts, especially in the wake of the anti-modernism of the Movement writers (Philip Larkin, Kingsley Amis and, in a far more complex form, Donald Davie). Milne also explores connections between regionalism and internationalism with reference to the work of MacDiarmid, Bunting and Jones, and discusses the British Surrealist aesthetic developed by Charles Madge, Dylan Thomas and David Gascoyne.

The following two chapters are devoted to the seminal significance, and internal diversity, of North American poetic modernisms. Bonnie Costello explores a dominant strain in the bifurcated tradition of American modernist poetry: the invention of the American modernist lyric, as manifested in the work of Marianne Moore and Wallace Stevens. Costello investigates Moore and Stevens's creation of a poetic idiom appropriate to the America in which both poets chose to remain, unlike their expatriate contemporaries Pound and Eliot. Costello also explores the rich diversity of linguistic textures and lexical range in Moore and Stevens, the American renovation of the image undertaken by both poets, and their meditations on the function of the imagination in relation to religion. Mark Scroggins's chapter maps the 'other tradition' in American modernist poetry – that of Williams, Louis Zukofsky and Olson – which both derives and diverges from the example of Pound. This chapter assesses a nativist-modernist American poetics written in opposition to the Eurocentric imagination of Eliot and that celebrates, instead, the local American scene in innovative and disjunctive epic forms.

Our understanding of American poetic modernisms is complemented and extended in Sharon Lynette Jones's chapter on the poetry of the Harlem Renaissance, which discusses the work of a number of poets, including Langston Hughes, Claude McKay, Countee Cullen, Jean Toomer, Alice Dunbar-Nelson, Helene Johnson, Georgia Douglas Johnson and Angelina Weld Grimké. Jones discusses the contested relationship between modernism and the Harlem Renaissance, arguing that the Harlem Renaissance is essential, if not wholly assimilable, to a properly inclusive understanding of poetic modernism. Jahan Ramazani's chapter examines the heretofore underexplored cross-culturality of modernist poetry, focusing on the strategies of (re)appropriation and revision that characterise the work of Caribbean, African and Indian poets. Ramazani discusses a range of Anglophone modernisms, including the vernacular language of poetry deployed by the Jamaican Louise Bennett and Barbadian Kamau Brathwaite's experimental poetics of a Caribbean 'Little Tradition', to the deployment of ethnography in the work of the African Okot p'Bitek and Kashmiri-American Agha Shahid Ali.

Part III of the Companion comprises Jason Harding's detailed survey of modernist poetry and the canon. Harding assesses modernism's evolution within and ambivalent response to the swiftly altering literary marketplace of the late nineteenth and early twentieth centuries, and draws our attention to the centrality of the 'little magazine' to the dissemination and reception of modernist writing. Harding analyses the way in which modernist poetry was absorbed by the academy, attaining a central place within the burgeoning 'profession' of university literary studies. Harding concludes his summary of the critical reception and fate of modernist poetry with reference to the vigorous and exciting re-evaluations of modernist poetry at the present moment, a debate to which *The Cambridge Companion to Modernist Poetry* itself contributes.

## NOTES

1. T. S. Eliot, *Selected Essays*, 3rd edn (London: Faber and Faber, 1951), p. 289. In his controversial appraisal of the period, *The Intellectuals and the Masses: Pride and Prejudice Among the Literary Intelligentsia, 1880–1939* (London: Faber and Faber, 1992), John Carey attributes modernist 'difficulty' to a wilful attempt on the part of the 'intellectuals' to exclude the increasingly literate 'masses'.
2. In its magazine publication, in the October 1922 issue of the *Criterion* and in the November 1922 (which appeared in October) issue of the *Dial*, *The Waste Land* had no notes; these were added to the Boni and Liveright text on its publication in December of that year.
3. William Carlos Williams, *The Autobiography of William Carlos Williams* (New York: New Directions, 1967), p. 174.
4. For a provocative account of 'modern poetry', in which modernism is viewed as one element within a wider 'modern movement', see Chris Baldick, *The Oxford English Literary History*, vol. X, *1910–1940, The Modern Movement* (Oxford University Press, 2004). For a nuanced reappraisal of a number of 'non-modernist' poets of the Edwardian and Georgian eras, see Peter Howarth, *British Poetry in the Age of Modernism* (Cambridge University Press, 2005).
5. Michael North, *Reading 1922: A Return to the Scene of the Modern* (New York: Oxford University Press, 1999).
6. George F. Butterick (ed.), *Charles Olson and Robert Creeley: The Complete Correspondence*, vol. VII (Santa Rosa: Black Sparrow Press, 1987), p. 75.

7. For an authoritative account of the New Criticism and its relation to modernism, see A. Walton Litz, Louis Menand and Lawrence Rainey (eds), *The Cambridge History of Literary Criticism,* vol. VII, *Modernism and the New Criticism* (Cambridge University Press, 2000).
8. See Anthony Julius, *T. S. Eliot, Anti-Semitism and Literary Form,* 2nd edn (London: Thames and Hudson, 2003), and the replies made by Ronald Schuchard and others in *Modernism/Modernity* 10.1 (2003).
9. See the essays collected in Lawrence Rainey (ed.), *A Poem Containing History: Textual Studies in 'The Cantos'* (Ann Arbor: University of Michigan Press, 1997).
10. George Bornstein, *Material Modernism: The Politics of the Page* (Cambridge University Press, 2001), pp. 4, 152. As the title of his book suggests, George Hutchinson's *The Harlem Renaissance in Black and White* (Cambridge, Mass.: Belknap Press of Harvard University Press, 1995) offers a similarly inclusive version of the Harlem movement.

# PART I
# Contexts

# I

## DAVID AYERS

# Modernist poetry in history

## I

The discussion of modernist poetry in history seems at first glance to allow for a model in which poetry, in a specific phase of its development marked as 'modernist', will be situated in the wider context of a series of histories – the 'material' history of events, technologies and relations of production; and the 'cultural' history of ideas, artistic practices, science, education, and so on. In the context of the analysis of the social situation of modernist poetry, however, the term 'history' itself requires unpacking.

A specific poem may be judged 'modernist' in terms of its advanced technical features or in terms of the modernity of outlook of the producing poet or implied readership. Underlying such a judgement is something more than the notion that a poem or poet is 'modern' in the sense of 'recent'. The notion of modernism in the arts seems implicitly to rest upon a broader notion of modernity in society. This model – modernism in the arts corresponding to modernity in society – already seems conveniently to present something of which a history might be written, a promising set of correspondences between social realities and artistic practices. The cultural historicism of contemporary scholarship will commonly present accounts which depend in one way or another on this paradigm. However, history too belongs to modernity and is a product of it. History can be set alongside poetry and need not be granted instant analytic priority as something which contains poetry, or to which poetry in some simple sense belongs.

The relationship of poetry to history can be viewed under a variety of rubrics. Setting aside questions of reception, these include the poet, the poetic oeuvre (a poem or poems), and poetry itself as the speculative category in which the possibilities of this art and these works are mapped in terms of their social situation. It is plain that the speculative category 'poetry' will produce a notion of the social situation of poetry which may never have been available to any particular poet, and which might never have been plainly articulated, or even obscurely implied, by any particular poetic work. Certainly, the ability of any given work to rise to the occasion of a possible poetry – and thereby to anything like a condition of truth – is obviously limited by individual talent, the technical state of poetry, and by the demands of marketplace and reception. Poetry which is thought of as modernist has generally been acutely aware of all these potential limitations and has sought to overcome them, making a cult of the poetic producer, embracing technical innovation and cultivating a coterie rather than a popular readership. However, the question of the possible scope of poetry goes beyond these questions of organisation – questions which only the most focused of authors showed any sign of addressing – to a broader field. To see poetry in terms of its social situation does not mean, straightforwardly, to look at the immediate specifics of the social situation of the producers of poetry as artists, or of the dynamics of circulation and reception of poetic works, but to attend to poetry in terms of its social situation as one which is different from that in which poetry first emerged. Such an analysis begins to describe what it is that calls for poetry, what a poetry might need to be like in order to answer that call. This analysis will inevitably be prompted by actually existing poetry. At the same time, it will recognise that even poetry in its most historically and philosophically self-conscious forms will have struggled to grasp its own calling and meet the demands which it has identified, with the result that a gap between speculative ideal and actual poetic product will appear at every turn. Indeed it is the object of such analysis to articulate and indicate this gap in a process which will both serve to actualise historical accomplishment and performatively produce the aporia of a task or calling – 'poetry' – which can never properly, finally and fully accomplish itself.

History too is susceptible to division into things that have happened and the account of things that have happened. In other words, the term 'history' can be taken to mean either the actuality of events or the representation of those events. For the analysis of modernist poetry in history, this distinction adds considerably to the potential methodological complexity. We will of course wish to account for the impact of events and developments on the poets and on the society to which they belong. We will also wish to discuss modernist literature in terms of the historiography and philosophy of history which was historically available to it, in terms of the implicit and explicit approach to history of poets and poetic works, and in terms of our own attitude to the philosophy of history and our own constructions of the historical- and social-theoretical *zeitgeist* of modernism. In addition, we will wish to recall that poetry has its own history which constitutes its self-consciousness as an art of ancient origin.

There is of course a rich tradition in speaking of poetry as such which goes back to ancient Greece and to a time when history and poetry could be set alongside each other as textual forms without giving priority to history as the metalanguage governing the existence of poetry. Aristotle famously claimed that poetry was 'more philosophic and of graver import than history' (1451b). The Greeks regarded actual historical events as ephemeral, but the writing of history had in common with poetry the aim of providing images or examples of that which was eternal, of permanent importance in a transient world. History and poetry – which included the epic, the dramatic and the lyric – are strongly related as discursive forms, although poetry is considered philosophically purer, less conditioned by the contingency of what actually happens than history, and therefore of 'graver import'.

In modern times, this priority of poetry begins to be dislocated in two ways: first, by the growing primacy of science as truth-telling discourse; second, by the growing awareness of history as a process of change, and not merely as a random selection of events dictated by destiny or chance. In modern thought, attempts to award any primacy to poetic discourse are few. Giambattista Vico's *Princìpi di scienza nuova* (1725) was unusual in being an attempt to demonstrate the importance of poetic understanding for the development of modern society. Vico claimed that the history of a nation could be grasped as a process of development akin to that from infancy to maturity in the individual. 'All the histories of the gentile nations had their origin in fable', Vico wrote: 'the first men of knowledge were poet theologians'.[1] Vico's approach gives him the means to interpret ancient texts as the symbolic embodiment of philosophical understanding in all areas of human knowledge – metaphysics, logic, morality, and so on. Vico's text locates the poetic past not as simple error awaiting its correction by philosophical or scientific truth, but as the very stuff of the understanding which has made that greater truth possible. As such, the *Scienza nuova* is a powerful vindication of the poetic basis of human understanding. The impact of Vico on thought about poetry was not immediate. It remained substantially indirect until his work was taken up by W. B. Yeats and James Joyce, whose works incorporated a Viconian understanding of the interpretation of poetic trope and his corresponding account of the cyclical nature of human history. While Yeats and Joyce discovered in Vico a way of restoring poetry to the level of history, Vico's influence on the theory of history in his own time and outside his own immediate circle was slight.

The modern rethinking of history and human culture was prompted in large part by Jean-Jacques Rousseau's *Discourse on the Origin and Foundations of Inequality Amongst Men* (1755), which demonstrates, among other things, that man is a historical being, separated from nature by virtue of his own internal and social development. Rousseau presented the separation from nature as a narrative of degeneration, but in parallel developments, eighteenth-century historicists such as Vico, Herder and Condorcet sought to demonstrate the reality of man's historical progress from ancient to modern times. Stemming from Rousseau, questions regarding man's independence from nature and the relationship between freedom and necessity provoked the intense development of German philosophy which led from Kant to Hegel. This development tended to present history and philosophy as the discourses which must govern the investigation of human nature, a convergence confirmed by the presentation of the history of philosophy as intertwined with the development of human understanding and society in Hegel's ambitious speculative text, *Phenomenology of Spirit* (1807).

While Aristotle could regard poetry as more important than history for its philosophical nature, Hegel can offer poetry any regard only as an earlier and superseded form of human understanding. In Hegel's system, poetry is the highest of the arts, but the arts as a whole are only a step on the way to religious understanding, first, and then to the philosophical understanding – reason, which is the final form of the human spirit. In his *Lectures on Fine Art* (delivered in the 1820s and posthumously published in 1835), Hegel argues that 'art's vocation is to unveil the *truth* in the form of sensuous artistic configuration. . . . For other ends, like instruction, purification, bettering, financial gain, struggling for fame and honour, have nothing to do with the work of art as such, and do not determine its nature.'[2] Like Kant, Hegel asserts the autonomy of the artwork. Modern art, termed by Hegel 'romantic art', is said to go beyond classical art in that its true content is 'absolute inwardness', and its form embodies 'spiritual subjectivity with its grasp of its independence and freedom'. Of all the arts, it is lyrical poetry which, beyond even music, succeeds in communicating inwardness, because in the lyric 'spirit and heart strive to speak, through every one of their productions, to the spirit and the heart.'[3] However, in Hegel's terms there is a tension between appearance and truth. All forms of art deal in appearance, even where their content is inwardness, and the materials of art, since they *are* material, are secondary to the truths which they bear and which, on this argument, transcend them. Art is transcended by modes of engagement with the real which are simply more true – religion, and then philosophy. Art is no longer the highest form of truth: 'we may well hope that art will always rise higher and come to perfection, but the form of art has ceased to be the supreme need of the spirit'.[4] On the one hand, Hegel clearly believes that art can go no further, but on the other he admits that art continues to exist. In Hegel's description, art has arrived at a supremely self-conscious mode which he, using the term given currency by Schlegel in 1797, calls irony.

Hegel rejects irony, which he considers to be a false position that glorifies the ego. The ego celebrates its own genius and mastery over matter, and in doing so mistakes the nature of reality: 'this virtuosity of an ironical artistic life apprehends itself as a divine creative genius for which anything and everything is only an unsubstantial creature, to which the creator, knowing himself to be disengaged and free from everything, is not bound, because he is just as able to destroy it as create it'.[5] Although Hegel rejects the ironic stance as one-sided, his description of the final mode of romantic art – as opposed to his description of the stance of the artist – seems to anticipate many of the later developments which we now call modernism. In the last stages of romantic art, art has lost its necessary relationship to reality:

> Bondage to a particular subject-matter and a mode of portrayal suitable for this material alone are for artists today something past, and art has therefore become a free instrument which the artist can wield in proportion to his subjective skill in relation to any material of whatever kind. The artist thus stands above specific consecrated forms and configurations and moves freely of his own account. . . . No content, no form, is any longer immediately identical with the inwardness, the nature, the unconscious substantial essence of the artist; any material may be indifferent to him if only it does not contradict the formal law of being simply beautiful and capable of artistic treatment. . . . In this way every form and every material is now at the service and command of the artist whose talent and genius is explicitly freed from the earlier limitation to one specific art-form.[6]

Although Hegel is hostile to this mode of 'genius', it is striking that this description anticipates the notion of artist as formal arranger which was popularised by post-Impressionist painters and influenced modernist literature in English via the writings of Roger Fry, Clive Bell and Wyndham Lewis. It also anticipates the late twentieth-century celebration of 'postmodern irony' stimulated by critics such as Fredric Jameson in 'Postmodernism: or, The Cultural Logic of Late Capitalism' (1984) – a celebration which, as reference to Hegel reveals, tended to over-emphasise the novelty of the ironic situation of the artist.

Hegel provides a suggestive theoretical articulation to a situation which could be expressed simply; art is no longer necessary for a society's self-understanding, because philosophical and scientific understanding has advanced further than art can. The artist stands at an ironic distance from his materials because he already knows better than art can know, since he has already been furnished with the knowledge of his society. All that is left to the artist is to adopt the stance of genius and celebrate his own cleverness as a manipulator of materials. Humanity must be understood, as Rousseau

showed, not as a part of nature, but in terms of the history of its own development, a development which, as Hegel showed, was the development of
inwardness. This inwardness, which was the progressive complicating and
authenticating of the encounter of mind with the real, was no longer the
privileged terrain of art, not even of poetry which, in Hegel's view, was the
highest form of art because it was the most able to objectify inwardness.

## II

The view that poetry has been superseded by the history of human development is not inevitably correct. Already Hegel's own description of the last
phase of romantic art allows for a continuation of art beyond its necessity to
historical progress. Yet accounts of human realities which emerged during
the nineteenth century dissent from the optimistic view of progress which
informs Hegel's thinking, and create spaces in which poetry can redefine its
purposes.

The impact of the thought of Karl Marx on modernist poetry in English
lay more in its eventual outcomes than in its intellectual content, although
the direct impact of Marx's thought on poets such as Ezra Pound, Louis
Zukofsky and the Auden group is itself an important sub-history. The
thought of Karl Marx was intertwined with the salient social fact of the
modernist period, industrial development. Of course, Marx was not responsible for the technological and social changes which he theorised, but he
was responsible for creating a way of thinking about capitalism which had a
direct social and political impact, an influence disseminated by such works
as *The Communist Manifesto* (1848) and the first volume of *Capital* (1867).
Marx denied that the final stage of history had been reached in bourgeois
society, as Hegel had tended to affirm, and described social progress in terms
of a series of class conflicts which would ultimately result in a classless, communist society. The final class conflict between proletariat and bourgeoisie
was still in process, and the tenor of Marx's work was to argue, polemically
and philosophically, that just as the concentration of wealth as capital had
been necessary for the increase in productivity which made society more
wealthy, so too the concentration of wealth must appear increasingly illog-
ical as human productivity increased and made it possible for humanity to
free itself of the bonds of nature. Human nature itself was distorted by the
capitalist division of labour, and the reality of human freedom was something that could only be partially anticipated from the standpoint of the
present. In contrast to Hegel's claim that the modern bourgeois state was the
final form that society would adopt, Marx, in common with other socialist
and utopian thinkers of the nineteenth century, postulated a further stage

of human development beyond capitalism, one in which not only existing social relations, but also human nature itself would be changed in ways that were not fully predictable.

Marx's attempts to predict the human existence of the future remain suspiciously rudimentary, receiving their fullest exposition in this famously brief passage:

> As soon as the division of labour comes into being, each man has a particular, exclusive sphere of activity, which is forced upon him and from which he cannot escape. He is a hunter, a fisherman, a shepherd, or a critical critic, and must remain so if he does not want to lose his livelihood; whereas in communist society, where nobody has one exclusive sphere of activity but each can become accomplished in any branch he wishes, society regulates the general production and thus makes it possible for me to do one thing today and another thing tomorrow, to hunt in the morning, fish in the afternoon, rear cattle in the evening, criticise after dinner, just as I have a mind, without ever becoming hunter, fisherman, shepherd or critic.[7]

The reference to the 'critical critic' is an in-joke, the occupations of hunting, fishing and sheep-herding unhelpfully pre-capitalist, but the substantial inference can be taken not only that culture as it currently exists ('critical criticism') is given its shape by the division of labour, but that in the future it will form a part of every human existence, albeit in an as-yet-unanticipated form. In contrast to Hegel's notion that history is in effect complete, Marx and Engels offer the vision of an incomplete history and emergent future. Indeed they counter Hegel by referring to the present as the 'prehistory' of a humanity which is yet to come into being. The future society will be transformed not simply in terms of wealth distribution, but in terms of all social relations. Engels's *The Origin of the Family, Private Property and the State* (1884) is the most theoretically developed account of the family unit itself as a product of history, and opens the way to grasping human sexuality and eventually pleasure itself as historically shaped and disciplined.

Marx and Engels provide several elements of a theory of culture, but their work does not fully develop such a theory. Modernist poetry in one of its guises presents itself as avant garde, an anticipation of the aesthetic and social future akin to the political avant garde of the pre-revolutionary communist party. Those pages of Marx which famously evoke the idea of a 'poetry of the future' express the thought that the imagination must anticipate the actuality of social change, rather than read the future as a version of the past.[8] However, Marx's theory of consciousness does not allow that reflection in any of its forms will shape the future, but claims that consciousness is predominantly a disguised reflection of material circumstances:

> In studying [social] transformations it is always necessary to distinguish between the material transformation of the economic conditions of production, which can be determined with the precision of natural science, and the legal, political, religious, artistic or philosophic – in short, ideological forms in which men become conscious of the conflict and fight it out. Just as one does not judge an individual by what he thinks about himself, so one cannot judge such a period of contradiction by its consciousness, but, on the contrary, this consciousness must be explained from the contradictions of material life.[9]

Marx's theory of consciousness does not allow poetry the role of anticipating the future, nor does it allow the poet any claim of special sensibility or privileged perspective.

Marx's claim that consciousness generally reflects existing social conditions rather than forming them should be seen more generally in the context of a century in which the dominant ideas really were very clearly formed to serve the commercial, material interests which were at all points running up against traditional ideas and traditional institutions. The idea of progress was a dominant theme of the nineteenth century and was evidenced on all sides in the form of rapid economic change, social unrest, and the attendant political and ideological conflicts. The poet and educationalist Matthew Arnold registered the situation of poetry in *Culture and Anarchy* (1869). This text was prepared in the wake of the Reform Act of 1867, which extended the franchise, doubling the size of the electorate. Although introduced by the Conservative government, this Act represented a triumph of commercial interests and Liberal politics, and also encouraged the supporters of socialism. *Culture and Anarchy* characterised the aristocratic, established church, Conservative interests as 'Barbarian', the commercial, nonconformist, Liberal interests as 'Philistine', and the workers and socialists as 'the Populace'. Arnold asserts the importance of culture in offsetting the tendency to anarchy embodied in the individualism of Philistines and the mass demonstrations of the Populace. In particular, the nonconformist Philistines are identified with 'Hebraism', on the grounds that they have overdeveloped their sense of religious individualism. The defective character of Hebraism appears when it is set against the rounded character of 'Hellenism', which is oriented toward truth – 'seeing things as they are'. Arnold develops a bold cultural narrative in terms of the ancient opposition of anti-establishment Hebraism and establishment Hellenism and the tripartite class structure of Barbarian, Philistine and Populace. The Hebraism of the Philistines is a one-sided human development which must be offset by culture. While a single established church could provide a unified context for individual development, churches divided between nonconformist and episcopalian can no longer provide such a context, and culture, to be disseminated in the education of the Philistines, must furnish the balanced inner human development which will offset anarchy. Culture is 'the study of perfection' and 'goes beyond religion' in that its approach to truth is more complete, passing through art, science, poetry, philosophy and history, as well as religion. Culture, Arnold states, 'is of like spirit with poetry, follows one law with poetry'; 'the idea of beauty and of a human nature perfect on all its sides, which is the dominant idea of poetry, is a true and invaluable idea'.[10] Arnold later wrote: 'The future of poetry is immense, because in poetry, where it is worthy of its highest destinies, our race, as time goes on, will find an ever surer and surer stay.'[11] Poetry in Arnold is a synecdoche for culture, which in its turn stands for a process of educating the middle classes which will help preserve national unity as the grip of the aristocracy is loosened by democracy:

> The course taken in the next fifty years by the middle classes of this nation will probably give a decisive turn to its history. . . . They will rule it by their energy, but they will deteriorate it by their low ideals and want of culture.[12]

This class will not learn to produce cultural artefacts but to know them. For this reason, the criticism of poetry receives far more emphasis than its creation. Arnold does not wish to turn the middle classes into a new rank of poetic producers. It is perhaps unsurprising that the influence of Arnold in the early twentieth century is found far more in the field of criticism than in that of poetic practice. His influence on the development of English as a university subject is of course great. Arnold recognised that British society was defined by the shifting of class interests and sought to claim a central role for poetry in the educational development of a 'culture' designed to preserve the totality of nation by overcoming the imperfect perspectives of class. Yet there seems to be little in modernist poetic practice which is designed to correspond to Arnold's programme, and it is plain that modernist poets had other objectives for their art.

Aestheticism and its successor movement, Decadence, represented an alternative to Arnold's mode of adapting to the social situation of art. Walter Pater's *Studies in the History of the Renaissance* (1873), subsequently issued as *The Renaissance: Studies in Art and Poetry* (1877), was a key document of the Aesthetic movement. The change in title denotes a refusal of the priority of the term 'history'; appropriately so, since Pater's writing celebrated 'perception', 'sensation', 'vision' – the modes of apprehension of the vivid but fleeting moment. The 'Conclusion' to *The Renaissance* describes the mind as being at the centre of a constant flux of force which lies outside it. This is the world described by science, the 'combination of natural elements to which science gives their names'. The impression of the moment is beyond analysis: 'It is with this movement, with the passage and dissolution of impressions, images, sensations, that analysis leaves off.' The human spirit must 'be present always at the focus where the greatest number of vital forces unite in their purest energy. . . . To burn always with this hard, gem-like flame, to maintain this ecstasy, is success in life.'[13] Pater's emphasis on the aesthetic quality of experience, and many aspects of his vocabulary, stand behind several strands of the Anglo-American modernist project. Pater's influence on Yeats, Pound and Stevens is notable. The specific formulations of the 'Conclusion' seem intended to allow a priority to a historical world undifferentiated from nature inasmuch as it is composed of Newtonian forces, while reserving a place for the subject as a zone of highly refined affect. Although this moment of ecstasy appears to have something in common with the Wordsworthian 'spots of time', the contrast with characteristic romantic ideas of the imagination is fairly pronounced. Wordsworth emphasised the role of memory and reflection, the process of moral development, and natural objects as a source of the intimation of a higher spirit. Coleridge, understanding the contours of the German romantic reaction against Kant, emphasised the creative function of imagination, and was prepared to find in nature not merely a congruence of forces but the immanence of God. Hegel, himself part of the reaction against Kant, had developed a model of the relationship between mind and nature which was rationalist, even if it tended to meet the romantic goal of restoring the identity of mind and nature. The model which Pater suggests is different from all of these. Sensation and perception, in Pater, are not the means of approaching 'nature'; indeed, cultural objects are preferred over natural ones. The notion of personal 'development' is present in Pater, but only in a form which suggests the refinement of mind for its own sake. Mind is not in a dialectic with nature; its role is mostly passive, such activity as it displays being dedicated to positioning itself better for reception and consumption. The position of the aesthete which derives from Pater is a very particular case of the artist as ironist described by Hegel; it also very clearly begins to develop the consequences of the Kantian notion of the autonomy of art into a theory about the nature of the artist and, especially, the art consumer.

Aestheticism, on the one hand, can be seen as a specific mode of the consumer in capitalist and imperialist society, the consummation of a process of refinement that borders on Decadence. Indeed, Aestheticism develops briefly into Decadence in a process that involves the internalisation of this possible critique in a moment of both self-mastery and dissolution. On the other hand, Aestheticism can be grasped as the product of alienated social relations which has the potential for certain kinds of self-knowledge and resistance. While Kant and Hegel alike emphasised the art object and its relationship with judgement or understanding, Aestheticism creates a space for pleasure and internal autonomy. Interior space is in one sense simply bourgeois, the corollary of the bourgeois interior which is described by Adorno and Benjamin as one of the principal productions of developed capitalism. Interior space is also the alienated production of capitalism, the space in which the subject might choose not, simply, to consume or enjoy its own differentiation from the society which claims it, but in which it might recognise its alienation and construct strategies not merely of adaptation but of confrontation. A consequence of this for poetry is the emphasis on persona or mask, found in an early and already highly developed stage in the poetry of Tennyson and Browning, and a recurrent feature of modernist irony. Another consequence is the aesthetic development of the person of the poet himself or herself in terms of lifestyle, the type of the alienated artist. Baudelaire's *Le Peintre de la vie moderne* (1863) described the way of life of the Dandy. Dandyism was characterised by leisure and money, by the ecstatic, the beautiful, the original, and by a 'cult of oneself'. The notion allies the appreciation of beauty to the consumption of wealth and leisure and to the formation of oneself according to aesthetic criteria. Baudelaire sees it as the final appearance of heroism in the midst of decadence. For modernist poets, decades later, Dandyism remained a part of the modern tradition, a model for the bohemian artist, an active way of both confronting and inhabiting bourgeois values, to be both adopted and questioned.

Baudelaire was not initially well known in England, although the poet A. C. Swinburne attempted to introduce English readers to his work, but the French influence in the last decades of the nineteenth century was significant for the brief florescence of English Decadence. The moment of Decadence corresponds to a waning in confidence in the ideals or ideology of progress, not least following the dissemination of the ideas of Charles Darwin, whose theory of evolution seemed to confirm that blind forces, rather than progressive human enlightenment, were the motive forces of historical change. Herbert Spencer's *First Principles* (1862) extrapolated from the claims of Darwin's *Origin of Species* (1859) regarding biological species to argue that 'survival of the fittest' was also the driver of racial/cultural change. Although few would have recognised it in these terms, this intellectual background created conditions under which egotistical theories with an implicitly or explicitly biological rationale could gain legitimacy, and modernist poetry stands at a confluence of, on the one hand, the legacy of Decadence in England, and, on the other, the legacy of the reaction against Kant in Germany which led to the development of philosophies of will or ego in the work of Arthur Schopenhauer, Max Stirner and Friedrich Nietzsche.

The texts of English Decadence are few: Oscar Wilde's *The Picture of Dorian Gray* (1891) and poet Arthur Symons's *The Symbolist Movement in*

*Literature* (1899) are the two principal documents. Wilde's text is notable for its moral criticism of the tenets of Decadence, which is embodied in the novel by Dorian Gray's obsession with a 'yellow book' which we understand to be J.-K. Huysmans's *À rebours* (1884). While Symons's 'The Decadent Movement in Literature' (1893) had celebrated the perversity of Huysmans's hero, Des Esseintes, only a few years later he privileged the idea of Symbolism and rejected Decadence: 'no doubt perversity of form and perversity of matter are often found together, and, among the lesser men especially, experiment was carried far, not only in the direction of style. But a movement which in this sense might have been called Decadent could but have been a straying aside from the main road of literature.'[14] In renouncing Decadence and asserting the category of Symbolism, Symons very carefully distances himself from the former as a hybrid category which combines questions of lifestyle and aesthetics. In Symons as in Wilde, sexual 'perversity' is the content of Decadence, and art becomes the zone in which all forms of perversity marginalised by the rules of the upper-class Victorian marriage can make their embarrassing appearance.

Decadence then is the form of Aestheticism under which sexual pleasure and 'perversity' become available to the modernist not only as a content for art but as a lifestyle in which art and life exist in a complementary state. This is important not least because it gives fresh social significance to the artistic priority of mapping inner states. As a development it coincides with the work of Freud, whose conditioning of modernism was significant but also diffuse. Freud's *The Interpretation of Dreams* (1900) not only made available the notion of the unconscious as a force driving behaviour, but also provided a way of mapping the unconscious which, as in effect a poetics of dreaming, was profoundly literary. Yet Freud's impact on modernist poetry in English was initially limited. While the development of psychoanalysis became a topic for bohemian conversation, it is clear that real knowledge of Freud's work among writers was slow in developing, even though in the aftermath of the First World War it became relatively well known for its application to 'shell shock' as a form of hysteria, and even though the English translations of Freud were published in the heart of literary London by Leonard and Virginia Woolf's Hogarth Press. The poet H.D., who had sessions with Freud in 1933–4 that influenced her subsequent poetic work, described how 'the late war-intellectuals gabbled of Oedipus across tea-cups or Soho café tables; it was not Vimy or Loos they talked of'.[15] This is a retrospective view, but seems to confirm that in bohemian circles Freud was a topic more for conversation than for serious investigation. It was left to the poet André Breton and his collaborators in the Surrealist movement in France to develop an art intended to access unconscious contents for politically liberative purposes, as outlined in Breton's Surrealist manifestoes of 1924 and 1930.

Although psychoanalysis would have given legitimacy to modernist poetry's interest in psychology it is only a general point of reference in the period of Anglo-American high modernism. As a science, psychoanalysis is in important respects a branch of biology, an exploration of psychological function with surprising findings concerning the complexity and relative autonomy of supposedly functional mechanisms. It expands its field fairly rapidly from the practical goal of individual adaptation (health) to the speculative goal of describing the role of adaptive processes in collective cultural development. Although it resembles a poetics, and although its potential for grasping psychic formation as both development and mutilation promises rich content to the project of poetry, the theory of the unconscious tends to be sidelined in favour of the assertion of conscious will by many Anglo-American modernists. The theory of will as it is found in early German romantics is a response to the absence in the Kantian system of an adequate theory of action. Max Stirner's *The Ego and His Own* (1844), which was roundly derided by Marx and Engels in *The German Ideology*, obtained a belated influence among modernist poets when it was published in English in 1912 and advocated by the editor Dora Marsden, whose journal *The Egoist* published work by Pound, Eliot and Joyce among others. Interest in an anarchic egoism was confluent with the writings of Friedrich Nietzsche, whose influence at this time was, like that of Freud, only occasionally direct, but whose texts sustained an assertion of the individual artist against the herd, and romantically asserted a 'transvaluation of all values' in which conventional social morality would be recognised as a passive, adaptive behaviour and abandoned by the minority of 'free spirits' able to separate themselves from the mass.

## III

At the turn of the twentieth century, the legitimacy of poetry had become limited and tangential, fostered in coteries that stood at the end of a set of traditions which only with some difficulty could maintain the claims of the artistic sensibility against the realities of commerce, history and science. The major historical events of the early twentieth century offered even further challenges to the tenuously egoistic stance of the modernist. The First World War demonstrated the priority of the collective over the individual in dramatic ways. It was not simply a question of military demands and the large scale of casualties, but also of the social reorganisation which accompanied the war, characterised by direct state control of key industries and the growth

of trades union influence. Although our own view of the Great War is generally refracted through war poetry and images of the trenches, social changes
in the direction of centralised mass society were dominant facts for modernist
artists, whose aspiration to cultural leadership seemed further eclipsed by a
new social dispensation, in which an expanded electorate was addressed
directly by a hectoring press and the nuances of the cultivated sensibility
seemed to be marginal. The success of the Russian Revolution served only to
confirm, in the minds of the Anglo-American high modernists, the inevitable
onset of a global mass society in which individuality would be secondary –
an opinion which would be substantially revised by the English poets of the
1930s. Capitalist and imperial development could present itself as a constant progress, while socialism and feminism could harness the vocabulary
of progress to promise the dawn of a new humanity. The generation conditioned by Aestheticism and ironic egoism felt itself charged with the cargo
of rich interiority, differentiated by its social and sexual attitudes, but only
in uneasy and sceptical relationship with any ethos of historical progress,
whether bourgeois, socialist or feminist.

The poetry and essays of Ezra Pound define practices of writing poetry
and being a poet which are highly conscious of the historical claims of a
progress guided by commerce and science. Pound's work up to the 1920s
is characterised by a tension between the Symbolist celebration of internal
states and the naturalist insistence on impersonal objectivity. Pound tends to
affirm the necessity of objectivity, but his emphasis on mood remains a powerful Symbolist residue. *Hugh Selwyn Mauberley* (1919, 1920) is a sequence
of poems published in the aftermath of the First World War which presents
the social situation of the poet and his inherited resources partly as autobiography and partly as the biography of an imaginary Aesthete and Dandy
whose aesthetic predilections have many elements in common with Pound's
own. Pound/Mauberley's values are represented as being marginalised by
external events and by the publishing dominance of newspapers and fiction. The rhetoric of the newspapers is presented in inverted commas in the
poem as the journalistic phrase 'the march of events' which bypasses the
aesthetic poet. The tendency of the press to speak loudly on behalf of irre-
sistible universality is dramatised in the claim that 'The age demanded an
image / Of its accelerated grimace' and not 'the obscure reveries / Of the
inward gaze'. Progress is characterised by the grimace, and the 'age' is the
governing notion that the shape and trajectory of a culture, both as a history of events and of cultural forms, dominates the individual. The phrase
'age demanded' appears in inverted commas as a reminder of the press which
gives articulation to history, in doing so hijacking both language and democracy by leading and linguistically forming the collective will which it claims

to represent. In a section of the poem dealing with the novelist and reviewer 'Mr Nixon', who resembles Arnold Bennett, the link between 'age', press and the writer are framed in Nixon's advice to the poet to 'take a column', ingratiate himself with reviewers, and 'give up verse, my boy / There's nothing in it.' 'Nothing' is both a question of remuneration and perceived content. As well as defining the demands on poetry as framed by the publishing industry, Pound's poem acknowledges that subjective content is marginalised not merely by the fictive 'age' but also by the reality of the recent war and the 'hysterias' and 'trench confessions' which it produced. Pound's portrait of Mauberley satirises his 'mildness', apathy and, finally, almost inarticulate immersion, against the background of 'neo-Nietzschean clatter' of his art-world contemporaries.[16] Aestheticism cannot survive either the 'age' or the robustness of the aggressive egoism of the Vorticist brand of bohemianism, although Pound's sequence allows Mauberley an artful if limited triumph in its concluding section, 'Medallion'.

Pound described Mauberley's dilemma in order to escape it. His self-construction as a poet is characterised by continued acknowledgement of the discursive priority of history and science, along with the attempt to harness poetry to both. The poet is a variety of artist, never just a verbal specialist. 'Artists are the antennae of the race', Pound asserted, claiming that literature has a diagnostic function and quoting Flaubert's assertion that 'If they had read my *Education Sentimentale*, this sort of thing [the Franco-Prussian war of 1870] wouldn't have happened.'[17] In essays such as 'The Serious Artist' (1913), Pound developed the claim that the poet was a type of scientist, having a moral prescience given authority only by the precision of his 'report' and commitment to truth. In 'The Serious Artist' this makes of the poet a psychological naturalist, a complementary figure to Zola or Gissing. However, Pound's *Cantos* (1917–76) utilise modes of textuality which go beyond the tenets of Aestheticism and situate the poet as a reader and presenter of alternative histories. *The Cantos*, Pound announced, would be a 'poem containing history', reversing, we might say, the priority of history over poetry. The writer of *The Cantos*, who presents himself in the manner of an impersonal scribe ('*ego scriptor cantilenae*'), will combine intuition and objectivity in an attempt to recover eclipsed moments of political virtue, with the intention of restoring equity and justice in the state along lines suggested by John Adams (President of the United States 1797–1801) and Confucius, among others. Pound's support for Mussolini, whom he likened to Thomas Jefferson, was confirmed in the anti-Semitic propaganda broadcasts which he made for Rome Radio between 1941 and 1943. Pound had left behind the posture of the ironic artist as defined by Hegel. No longer an ironic manipulator of materials, Pound's poetic practice defined him as an educator, his poetry increasingly conceived as a digest presenting 'luminous details' and advocating a curriculum of reading. Pound's career as a poet catapulted him into history in an almost unprecedented way when he surrendered himself to American forces in Italy in the closing stages of the Second World War in order to answer charges of treason. This stage produced *The Pisan Cantos* (1948), which combine fragments of text recalling the London literary world of the 1910s, and a host of other aesthetic references, alongside material derived from Pound's concern with economics and justice. Pound depicts himself in the ruined fascist state as an anonymous worker now without purpose – 'a lone ant on a broken anthill' – while continuing to assert the validity of his Symbolist vision of the polis – 'the city of Dioce whose terraces are the colour of stars'[18] – as well as his commitment to the linguistic objectivity of the 'precise definition'.

Pound's career and oeuvre offer only one example, albeit a major one, of modernist poetry's attempt to rise to its own occasion. It seems that Pound, in asserting the seriousness of art against the ironic, may have ended in error – his own belief. Yet the transaction between the ironic and serious in poetry is a complex one and other modernist poetics would investigate further the truth-telling potential of irony in ways that suggestively produce or represent inward contents in the complexity of their awkward relationship with an objectivity to which they can never properly belong. We might well regard as modernist any poetry which refuses to accept its place in history.

## NOTES

1. Giambattista Vico, *New Science*, ed. Anthony Grafton, trans. David Marsh (London: Penguin, 1999), p. 361.
2. G. W. F. Hegel, *Aesthetics: Lectures on Fine Art*, vol. I, trans. T. M. Knox (Oxford: Clarendon Press, 1975), p. 55.
3. Hegel, *Aesthetics*, pp. 519, 528.
4. Hegel, *Aesthetics*, p. 103.
5. Hegel, *Aesthetics*, p. 66.
6. Hegel, *Aesthetics*, pp. 605–6.
7. Karl Marx and Friedrich Engels, *The German Ideology*, ed. and trans. S. Ryazanskaya (Moscow: Progress Publishers, 1968), p. 53.
8. Karl Marx, *Surveys from Exile: Political Writings*, vol. II, ed. David Fernbach (Harmondsworth: Penguin, 1973), pp. 146, 149.
9. Karl Marx, *A Contribution to the Critique of Political Economy*, ed. Maurice Dobb, trans. S. W. Ryazanskaya (Moscow and London: Progress Publishers/Lawrence and Wishart, 1971), p. 21.
10. Matthew Arnold, *Culture and Anarchy*, ed. J. Dover Wilson (Cambridge University Press, 1960), pp. 45, 47, 48, 54.

11. Matthew Arnold, 'The Study of Poetry' (1880), in Christopher Ricks (ed.), *Selected Criticism of Matthew Arnold* (New York and Scarborough, ON: New American Library, 1972), p. 171.
12. Matthew Arnold, 'Education and the State' (1864), in Ernest Rhys (ed.), *On the Study of Celtic Literature and Other Essays* (London: Dent, 1976), p. 188.
13. Walter Pater, *The Renaissance: Studies in Art and Poetry*, ed. Adam Phillips (Oxford University Press, 1986), pp. 150, 152.
14. Arthur Symons, *The Symbolist Movement in Literature* (New York: Dutton, 1947), p. 4.
15. H.D., *Bid Me to Live* (London: Virago, 1984), p. 8.
16. Ezra Pound, *Personae: The Shorter Poems*, ed. Lea Baechler and A. Walton Litz (New York: New Directions, 1990), pp. 186, 190, 191.
17. Ezra Pound, 'Henry James' (1918), in T. S. Eliot (ed.), *Literary Essays of Ezra Pound* (London: Faber, 1954), p. 297.
18. Ezra Pound, *The Cantos*, 4th edn (London: Faber and Faber), pp. 472, 439.

# 2

## PAUL PEPPIS

# Schools, movements, manifestoes

Reading modernist poetry today, we usually sit in classrooms, holding literary anthologies or volumes of collected or selected poems. Such encounters, mediated by institutions of publication and the academy, minimise modernist poetry's original social and institutional contexts. But many poems now considered canonically modernist were first produced in the early twentieth-century milieu of social and artistic experiment in which a generation of young artists and writers endeavoured to cross the 'great divide' between 'art' and 'life' and remake both. Converging in major cities, these would-be modernists collaborate and compete for cultural attention in the world of modern print capitalism. They initiate a phenomenon today termed the 'historical avant garde', an unprecedented irruption across the West of oppositional artistic movements, experimental art and writing, little magazines and alternative presses, unconventional performances, and spectacular happenings. During the first thirty years of the century, scores of these groups, works and events proliferate. New schools and movements spring up across Europe and America, a plethora of new 'isms' vying for attention: Cubism, Futurism, Imagism, Vorticism, Surrealism, Dada.

Peter Bürger has influentially argued that the avant-garde ambition to cross the divide between art and life praxis is ultimately thwarted by the inherent aestheticism of the institution of art under bourgeois capitalism.[1] Yet modernism's major writers and artists are born and raised during the closing decades of the nineteenth century. They come to adulthood amid profound political, technological, social and scientific transformations commonly identified with 'modernisation': spreading industrialisation, growth of the bourgeoisie and democracy, increasing literacy, invention of new sciences, a proliferating print culture, expansion of commodity capitalism and modern imperialism. Raised in this rapidly transforming modernity, as alive to technological modernisation and the market economy as to artistic and social experiment, these artists and writers take up the tools of print capitalism to promote their artistic and literary schools and movements. Bürger's argument notwithstanding, no amount of will or effort could detach modern art and literature from praxis.

Indeed, this thing we think of when we think 'modernist poetry' was constituted out of the artistic, social and political ferment of the avant garde. Many modernist poets were affiliated with avant-garde groups. Many modernist poems first appeared in avant-garde little reviews. Many books of modernist poetry were first published by small, alternative presses. Like modernism in general, modernist poetry's original production was collaborative and contentious, multifarious and dynamic – born out of the turbulent life of the modernising city, entangled with the modalities and technologies of print capital, especially modern publishing and advertising. Modernist poetry was always manifestly a part of modern life.

What modernist poetry would become in the 1920s emerges just before the First World War, forged in numerous competitive and collaborative encounters between poets, poetry and the schools and movements of the avant-garde moment. Modernist poets and poetry react especially productively to the period's pre-eminent modes of avant-garde experimentation: manifestoes and the leading techniques of modernist visual art, collage and abstraction. Responding to and reinventing these avant-garde discourses and practices – not in any conventional sense poetic – twentieth-century poets derive modernist poetry's signal formal techniques: free verse, montage, juxtaposition, intertextuality and linguistic abstraction.

### Definitions and contexts

To understand how and why schools, movements and manifestoes are important for modernist poetry, it's necessary first to define these key terms. In his seminal *The Theory of the Avant Garde* (1962), Renato Poggioli describes the 'school concept' as the dominant paradigm for organising western artists and writers since the Greeks. Poggioli emphasises in particular two defining characteristics of schools: they stress 'techniques, training, and apprenticeship' and depend on 'a master and a method, the criterion of tradition and the principle of authority'.[2] This emphasis on tradition, authority and technique helps account for the endurance of the paradigm. As Poggioli notes, the school concept enjoys relatively uncontested influence as a way of conceptualising groups of western writers and artists until the late eighteenth century.[3]

But the revolutionary period challenges monarchies *and* ancient regimes of literature and art. The revolutionary *zeitgeist* inspires the romantics to present their works as integral to their age's political transfigurations and to fashion themselves as a revolutionary cultural movement bent on changing social and political relations as well as literary and artistic technique. Following romanticism, ambitious young artists have tended to join together in *movements*, committed, as Poggioli puts it, to pass 'beyond the limits of art'.[4] Such movements reject traditions and academies, casting their art as activist, interventionist and oppositional. Thus the movements of the later nineteenth century, like their romantic forebears, produce revolutionary art and literary works, issue manifestoes promoting their principles, provoke heated discussion and resistance in the press and earn distinctive, sometimes derogatory monikers: Transcendentalism, Aestheticism, Impressionism, Symbolism.

In the first decades of the twentieth century, young writers and artists modernise the movement idea, embracing – with varying enthusiasm – the techniques and technologies of modern advertising, mass-producing 'isms'. Arguably, no avant-garde group plays a greater role in this modernisation of movements than Italian Futurism, led by the poet, promoter and impresario Filippo Tommaso Marinetti. Marinetti makes the fervent celebration of modernity and its defining manifestations – speed, machines, violence – the content of Futurist theory and art. Polemics like 'Destruction of Syntax – Imagination without Strings – Words-in-Freedom' (1913) articulate Marinetti's elaborate, esoteric and experimental technical principles for Futurist literature. The manifesto calls for disregarding 'punctuation and the right adjectives' and 'brutally destroying' syntax.[5] It advocates a 'Typographical revolution', 'Free expressive orthography' and the uncompromising literary use of verbs in the infinitive, onomatopoeia and mathematical signs.[6] These technical innovations depend on and are shaped by Marinetti's embrace of modern advertising and marketing methods; his genius is to place these modes of commerce at the heart of modern art and letters. He adopts the techniques of modern publicity to promote Futurism in part because they epitomise the modernity he worships. But Marinetti also believes them necessary to win a mass audience for Futurism; he dreams of an avant-garde movement for the masses.

Crucial to the publicising of Futurism were its numerous and provocative manifestoes. These tracts adapt to the cause of modernism a traditionally political genre, associated with the enlightenment heritage of political revolution and feminist agitation.[7] They draw on the political manifestoes of the revolutionary period, the literary manifestoes of romanticism and the American renaissance, and the philosophical manifestoes of modern Europe's most rebellious thinkers (Nietzsche, Bergson, Sorel). Inspired as well by modern publicity methods, the Futurist manifestoes ramp up the rhetoric of militancy, exaggerating even to the point of absurdity the genre's distinctive traits – enumeration of principles, grievances and demands; telegraphic and declarative rhetoric; use of capitalisation and white space for emphasis.[8] Typical are the following declarations on poets and poetry from the 'Manifesto of Futurism':

> 6. The poet must spend himself with ardour, splendour and generosity, to swell the enthusiastic fervour of the primordial elements.
> 7. Except in struggle, there is no more beauty. No work without an aggressive character can be a masterpiece. Poetry must be conceived as a violent attack on unknown forces, to reduce and prostrate them before man.[9]

Epitomising this overblown rhetoric of masculinist militancy, the manifesto concludes with an image of elevated, ejaculatory defiance: 'Erect on the summit of the world, once again we hurl defiance to the stars!'[10]

Futurist manifestoes aggressively pursue avant-garde imperatives to cross conceptual divides enshrined in Enlightenment discourse between aesthetics and praxis, high art and mass culture, genres and arts. Drawing as much on politics as aesthetics, on advertising as literary tradition, on gesture as substance, Futurist manifestoes play a crucial part in the development of what Marjorie Perloff calls 'the new technopoetics of the twentieth century', a poetics of collage, generic rupture, and verbal abstraction.[11]

## Modernist poetry's anti-movement

Lawrence Rainey argues that Futurism confronted modern poetry with a disturbing possibility: 'there was no longer a meaningful distinction between poetry and the most ephemeral of commodities, the daily newspaper'.[12] To survive in this modern marketplace, poetry would need to compete with the products and performances of movements like Futurism, whose greatest achievements were generally non-poetic, often non-literary. Imagism, the first major 'ism' of modernist poetry in English, clarifies how this competition helps solidify commitments among Anglo-American poets to reaffirm by various means poetry's privileged status within capitalist culture, even while 'modernising' poetry's form using techniques perfected by the Futurists in their polemics and visual artworks.

As Rainey shows, in the spring of 1912 London is gripped by political crises of coal miners striking and suffragists smashing windows. Both actions prompt alarmed reporting in the press. At the same time, the Futurists storm London, promoting the first English exhibition of Futurist paintings. Goaded by manifestoes translated in the exhibition catalogue (including the 'Manifesto of Futurism'), and the Futurists' relentless advertising efforts and publicity schemes, the press responds vociferously, sometimes showing as much shock as it does over the miners and suffragists. A major event in the

Futurists' tour is a lecture Marinetti gives on 19 March, which subjects the English to a full Futurist assault ('a nation of sycophants and snobs, enslaved by old worm-eaten traditions, social conventions, and romanticism').[13] That same day, the young American expatriate Ezra Pound delivers a lecture on the Troubadour poet Arnaut Daniel at the London home of an aristocratic patron. The second in a series of lectures Pound gives on medieval poetry in an intimate, aristocratic venue, the talk provokes no scandalised reportage. Even Pound's fiancée, Dorothy Shakespear, disregards his lecture: she attends Marinetti's performance instead.[14]

Within a month, Pound christens Hilda Doolittle and Richard Aldington 'Imagistes', initiating the first 'ism' of modernist poetry in English. Pound deems H.D. and Aldington Imagistes because they write in ways compatible with the anti-romantic aesthetics he was concocting under the influence of T. E. Hulme and Ford Madox Ford (then Hueffer).[15] But the invention of Imagism also represents a powerful response to Futurism, especially the Futurists' celebration of modernity and attack on passéist literature. In September, the avant-garde weekly The New Age begins publishing Pound's essays on America, 'Patria Mia' (September–November 1912). While the 'Manifesto of Futurism' promises to 'free this land from its smelly gangrene of professors, archaeologists . . . and antiquarians', and 'destroy the museums, libraries, academies of every kind', 'Patria Mia' calls for the founding of 'an efficient college of the arts' in America.[16] As the Futurists dream of liberating Italy from the stifling legacy of the Italian renaissance, Pound dreams of initiating an 'American Risorgimento'.[17] Pound and those closest to him react against Futurism's fanatic hostility to passéism and idolisation of modernity by insisting that making poetry new requires 'reconnecting it to a valued cultural tradition'.[18]

Imagist polemics evoke a new modernist poetry movement, even as they resist Futurism's example by insisting that the Imagists constitute only a poetic school, devoted to study, craft and tradition. The first Imagist polemic, a Note on 'Imagisme' by F. S. Flint published in Poetry Magazine (March 1913), admits that, while the Imagists are 'contemporaries of the Post Impressionists and the Futurists', those latter groups have 'nothing in common' with the Imagists. The Imagists have 'not published a manifesto' and are not 'revolutionary'. Their 'only endeavor' is 'to write in accordance with the best tradition'.[19] Imagist polemics resolutely disregard the Futurist call to pass 'beyond the limits of art'. They oppose the movement imperative with a renovated concept of the school, refusing to make Imagism anything other than an esoteric poetic doctrine shared by a small group of like-minded poets.

Technical treatises of a modern poetic school, Imagist polemics offer themselves as anti-manifestoes of an anti-movement. They anticipate Imagist poetics rhetorically in their brevity, their refusal of Futurist excess. Imagism's essential technical principles are rigorous and few:

1. Direct treatment of the 'thing' whether subjective or objective.
2. To use absolutely no word that does not contribute to the presentation.
3. As regarding rhythm: to compose in the sequence of the musical phrase, not in sequence of a metronome.[20]

These principles articulate a free-verse poetic of linguistic concision and metaphoric condensation, epitomised in poems like Pound's 'In a Station of the Metro': 'The apparition   of these faces   in the crowd   : / Petals   on a wet, black   bough.'[21] Having dispensed with verbs, rhyme, fixed metre and the lyric I, the poem as first published, in *Poetry* (March 1913) and the *New Freewoman* (August 1913), uses white space within lines to highlight its visual and aural dimensions and alert readers to its 'underlying phrasal rhythm'.[22] By condensing poetry to basics, Imagism throws language's materiality into relief – an early contribution to linguistic abstraction.

Despite their anti-rhetorical rhetoric and disregard for commerce and the non-poetic, Imagist polemics nonetheless market their austere poetry. The title of Pound's 'A Few Don'ts By an Imagiste' may stress its difference from the positive declarations of Futurist polemic. But Pound's polemic sells Imagism's strict poetics of juxtaposed images, shorn of linguistic connective tissue, by promoting the poetic Image as 'that which presents an intellectual and emotional complex in an instant of time'.[23] Imagism's innovation of a poetics of juxtaposition is an important early step in the derivation of modernist collage poetics, a process also inspired by Futurist manifestoes, with their reduction of discursivity and linguistic connective tissue, and the visual collage methods of Cubist and Futurist visual art.

Despite assertions of difference from the Futurists, however, the Imagists could neither deny nor avoid the economic, institutional and technological changes Marinetti and the Futurists had exposed and embraced. Both Futurism's acceptance of print capitalism and its conception of modernist art and art movements as commodities force the Imagists to confront, as Rainey argues, 'the role of new institutions of mass culture and assess their bearings on the place of art in a cultural marketplace' where 'distinctions between art and commodity' are collapsing.[24] In part as a result of his confrontation with this new reality, Pound shortly abandons Imagism in favour of Vorticism, England's first fully fledged (though short-lived) avant-garde movement. That alliance would intensify modernist poetry's interactions with avant-garde discourses and practices.

## Advertising the avant garde, visualising the word

Less than a year after christening H.D. and Aldington *Imagistes*, Pound grows frustrated with the Imagist credo of brevity and condensation and his battle for control of the movement with Amy Lowell, America's most committed and influential Imagist. Pound shortly concedes the struggle, henceforth dismissing the school under the derisive pun 'Amygism'. Striving to come to terms with the place of poetry in the modern marketplace, increasingly inspired by developments in modern visual art, Pound allies with painters and sculptors pursuing modes of visual abstraction – especially Wyndham Lewis and the expatriate French sculptor Henri Gaudier-Brzeska. Provoked and antagonised by Marinetti's conquest of London's emerging modernist milieu, Lewis nationalistically leads his fellows in the formation of Vorticism as an explicitly 'Anglo-Saxon' reaction to Marinetti's 'Latin' group. Pound eagerly joins the movement.

If Imagism opposes Futurism by refusing its invitation to cross divides between art and life, high art and mass culture, Vorticism resists Futurism by turning Futurist tools against it. In the early summer of 1914, the first issue of the Vorticist journal, *Blast*, proclaims the arrival of the group (a second and final issue, the 'War Number', appears in July 1915). *Blast* takes up Marinetti's techniques to publicise Vorticism as a specifically English movement distinct from and superior to Futurism and the other influential 'Latin' avant gardes, Impressionism and Cubism. 'The Modern World is due almost entirely to Anglo-Saxon genius', *Blast*'s third manifesto proclaims. The 'new possibilities of expression' should thus be 'more the legitimate property of Englishmen than of any other people in Europe'.[25]

Using advertising techniques – especially those of posters and sandwich boards – *Blast*'s manifestoes promote Vorticism as the most authentic and significant modernist movement.[26] They present Lewis's boisterous declarations and arguments, by turns antagonistic, esoteric, hilarious and obscure in visually striking form: nearly newspaper-sized pages, covered with black block letters, composed to maximise visual impact and explore language as a visual medium and the printed page as compositional field. Lewis's polemics enumerate aesthetic and philosophical principles; they BLESS those the Vorticists identify as suitably modern, rebellious and experimental, and BLAST those they deem retrograde, sentimental and feminised.[27] *Blast*'s manifestoes arguably surpass Marinetti's in mingling art and advertising. They make words on a page into modernist visual art – a significant example for later modernist poetry.

In addition to its manifestoes, *Blast* features a variety of visual and literary artworks. The visual art manifests most clearly the aesthetic experimentalism articulated in the polemics. These works share a commitment to visual abstraction and together constitute important artefacts of the brief but energetic English abstractionist painting movement just before the First World War.[28] *Blast*'s literary contributions are more varied in technique and tone. The most important are the opening chapters of Ford Madox Ford's novel in progress, 'The Saddest Story', which would eventually become *The Good Soldier*, and Rebecca West's radical feminist parable, 'Indissoluble Matrimony'. Both these texts pursue distinct experimental fictional aesthetics: Ford's use of an unreliable and epistemologically challenged narrator to deconstruct the English comedy of manners and articulate modernist doubt; West's satirical use of a limited third-person narrator to deflate middle-class English masculinity and promote a vital feminist fiction. But neither takes its experiments to the point of deconstructing fiction's traditional commitments to narrative and representation. Only Lewis's pseudo-play, *The Enemy of the Stars*, matches the pyrotechnic experimentalism of Vorticist visual art. In a series of manifesto-like pages, Lewis's play strives to abstract the language and conventions of drama, drawing on the design and promotional practices of modern advertising to stress the linguistic medium and interrogate traditional literary imperatives of communication and representation. The text even begins with an '<u>ADVERTISEMENT</u>' that sets the 'SCENE', describes the '<u>CHARACTERS</u>' and their 'DRESS', and subversively concludes with a comical evaluation of the play that follows ('VERY WELL ACTED BY YOU AND ME').[29]

As for canonical modernist poetry, however, the first issue of *Blast* contains none. Thirteen poems – all by Pound – are included. Most are satiric and polemical. They have been judged minor at best, terrible at worst. None appears in poetry anthologies today. Pound's Imagist collaborators, Lowell, Aldington and Flint, offended by his defection from Imagism and abandonment of Imagist aesthetics, predictably criticised the *Blast* poems. Lowell called them 'too indecent to be poetical'. They filled Aldington with 'regret'. Flint derided the 'charlatanry of Vorticism' and chided Pound for betraying Imagism: 'you spoiled everything by some native incapacity for walking square with your fellows; you have not been a good comrade'.[30] Flint's avant-gardist rhetoric failed to win Pound's return. He had quit school and joined a movement.

But if, for Lowell, Aldington and Flint, Pound's abandonment of Imagist standards signals an aesthetic failure, for us, Pound's turn towards satirical and polemical poetry confirms his engagement with the discourses of the avant garde. Pound's *Blast* poems, 'Salutation the Third', 'Monumentum Aere, Etc.' and 'Fratres Minores' show modernist poetry contending with the imperatives and successes of the manifesto. Written under the manifesto's sway and in its shadow, they actively engage and adapt its characteristic modes and tropes, defending freedom and the new, enumerating grievances, attacking foes in extravagant terms and militant tones. 'Salutation the Third' begins:

> Let us deride the smugness of 'The Times':
> GUFFAW!
>    So much the gagged reviewers,
> It will pay them when the worms are wriggling in their vitals;
> These were they who objected to newness,
> HERE are their TOMB-STONES.[31]

On evidence like this, we may agree that Pound's *Blast* poems are 'among the dreariest he ever produced'.[32] But the characteristics that arguably under-mine the poems' aesthetic value – their polemical rhetoric, contemptuous and intemperate tone, relative disinterest in figurative language – also demon-strate Pound's poetic engagement with the manifesto and participation in the promotional and partisan discourses of the avant garde. Polemically speaking, these poems attempt to give *Blast*'s manifestoes a run for their money.

But *Blast*'s poems also contend with the manifesto aesthetically by deploying its characteristic techniques: epigrammatic declarations (princ-iples, demands and grievances), condemnation of oppressors and manipula-tion of white space and capitalisation for stress. Insofar as these techniques emphasise the linguistic medium, Pound's poems join with Lewis's mani-festoes to prioritise, visualise and analyse language itself. Thus, despite their critical disrepute, Pound's *Blast* poems participate in the formulation of a poetic abstraction that might contend with Cubist and Futurist painting. At the same time, the poems contribute to the invention of poetic montage. As the art manifesto conjoins the discourses of politics and aesthetics, *Blast*'s manifesto poems mingle the genres of poetry and polemic. By making poetry polemical and polemics poetic, Pound's *Blast* poems challenge the manifesto for the role of pre-eminent genre of avant-garde proclamation, even as they anticipate the experimental techniques of *Hugh Selwyn Mauberley* and *The Cantos*.

Rainey concludes that *Blast* fails to provide a viable solution to the prob-lem Futurism had exposed: how to sustain the privileged status and critical force of art and literature, especially poetry, in the context of commodity capitalism.[33] But *Blast*'s manifestoes and poems contribute to solving that problem by encouraging poets to bring into poetry non-poetic discourses (polemic, advertising) and by rendering language a visual as well as verbal medium. The following section considers how two other modernists, both intimately involved with leading avant-garde movements, address this challenge with ambitious and determinedly experimental poetic texts that adapt defining innovations of modernist visual art – abstraction, collage – into modes of modernist poetry.

## Versifying abstraction and collage

Though they pursue distinct poetic paths, Gertrude Stein and Mina Loy make defining contributions to the invention of poetic abstraction and montage poetics. Stein and Loy derive these verse modes in response to close encounters with leading European avant-garde movements – Cubism in Stein's case, Futurism in Loy's. Their early poetic texts – especially Stein's *Tender Buttons* (written 1912, published 1914) and Loy's *Love Songs to Joannes* (1915–17) – offer groundbreaking efforts to translate into poetic form the abstractionist and collage techniques innovated by Cubist and Futurist painters.

Stein's efforts to translate visual modernism into literary form are well noted. *The Autobiography of Alice B. Toklas* (1933) tells readers that her first published literary work, *Three Lives* (1909), was composed under the 'stimulus' of a Cézanne portrait she owned.[34] Critics have followed the lead, analysing Stein's experiments with narrative and characterisation in *Three Lives* as efforts to translate Cézanne's techniques into verbal form.[35] As Stein's intimacy with modernist painters and painting increases, her literary experiments evolve. In 1908, she completes her immense, experimental novel, *The Making of Americans* (published in 1925), which elaborates, on an epic scale, the repetitive sentence structure and concern with psychological types first innovated in *Three Lives*.

The increasing influence and success of the Cubist painters prompts Stein to begin a series of experiments in verbal portraiture. Two of the earliest, on Matisse and Picasso, are published in the August 1912 issue of Alfred Stieglitz's celebrated New York little magazine, *Camera Work* (a key source for Stein's influence on other American modernist poets). These portraits apply Stein's wandering, repetitive prose style to the task of 'trying to describe' Matisse and Picasso. Although stylistically similar to *Three Lives*, slowing narrative through repetition with slight variations, 'Matisse' and 'Picasso' represent crucial steps in the development of Steinian poetics. They intensify Stein's experimentation with description, objects and, especially, the poet's materials – 'rhythms, sonorities, and grammatical norms'.[36]

During 1912–13, in Paris and on a sojourn in Spain, Stein writes her first important poetic texts, *Tender Buttons*, and the portrait poems 'Susie Asado' (on a famous flamenco dancer), 'Guillaume Apollinaire' (on the French poet and defender of Cubism) and 'Preciosilla' (on a popular Spanish singer). These texts pursue Stein's stylistic experiments in poetic abstraction and collage. The first published and most ambitious, *Tender Buttons*, strikes readers initially for its generic hybridity and discursive elusiveness. Described best, but inadequately, as prose poetry, it combines prose's interest in description, narrative and reportage with (modern) poetry's interest in concision, repetition and sound effects. A series of verbal portraits of objects, food and rooms, most of these 'portraits' dissolve into opacity almost as soon as they begin coming into focus. Like an analytical Cubist painting, Stein's *Tender Buttons* is more concerned to analyse the linguistic medium than to 'describe' the things it allegedly represents. *Tender Buttons* relentlessly interrogates language and its conventions, tinkering with sentences, violating grammatical rules, playing with sound.

At times, Stein's sentences become so telegraphic and perplexing that they yield to wordplay, even the dissolution of words into syllabic fragments:

*Eating*
Eat ting, eating a grand old man said roof and never never re soluble burst, not a near ring not a bewildered neck, not really any such bay.
It is so a noise to be is it a least remain to rest, is it a so old say to be, is it a leading are been. Is it so, is it so, is it so, is it so is it so is it so.
Eel us eel us with no no pea no pea cool, no pea cool cooler, no pea cooler with a land a land cost in, with a land cost in stretches.
Eating he heat eating he heat it eating, he heat it heat eating. He heat eating.[37]

These techniques take readers seeking straightforward meaning on an interpretive roller-coaster ride, as fleeting moments of comprehension and connection yield to opacity. But even resistant or dismissive readers cannot read *Tender Buttons* without experiencing a heightened, sensual awareness of the linguistic medium itself – grammar, words, syllables, sounds and marks on the page.

*Tender Buttons* is significant for our account as well because it uses montage techniques to organise its verbal portraits. Like synthetic Cubism's juxtaposition of painted canvas and pieces of 'life' (newspaper clippings, wallpaper, calling cards), or Imagism's juxtaposition of different poetic images, Stein juxtaposes her portraits to each other with no transitions, no connective tissue. Readers must make sense of the individual portraits *and* how they relate to each other. In contrast to the sonnet sequence, which also strings individual poems together, *Tender Buttons* lacks a conventional (male) lyric speaker whose obsession with a beloved makes the sequence cohere. Anticipating later modernist collage poems like Pound's *Hugh Selwyn Mauberley* and Eliot's *The Waste Land*, the collage methods of *Tender Buttons* erode the single, stable speaker of lyric poetry. As the prompting objects, food and rooms and their relations dissolve amid the text's repetitions, elisions and digressions, the speaker's attitudes toward the things she 'describes' become correspondingly elusive. These effects accumulate with the portraits, eliding not only the speaker's relations to the things she describes, but (her) subjectivity itself. If we think of *Tender Buttons'* individual 'poems' as Cubist portraits of objects in verse, the text's erosion of lyric subjectivity can be compared to a Cubist self-portrait, fragmenting its artist-subject beyond recognition.

As Stein pursues the investigations that produce *Tender Buttons'* Cubistic still-life prose poems, another unconventional and ambitious expatriate modernist is engaged in her own experiments in close proximity to a leading European avant-garde movement. Mina Loy's literary innovations, in the genres of the manifesto and lyric, yield another important modernist poetry of abstraction and collage. But if Stein's poetry looks to and learns from Cubist paintings, Loy's learns from and reacts against Futurist manifestoes. She writes many of her early poems in response to intimate relations with the Futurists at the height of their success (she had had love affairs with Marinetti and Giovanni Papini, the philosopher of the Florentine wing of the movement). But, while best known for a series of aggressively modernist poems satirising the Futurists and her relations with them, Loy also crafts two of the period's most striking manifestoes. These polemics imitate and critique Futurist examples, clarifying how Loy's distinctive modernist poetry develops in response to Futurism and its manifestoes.

Loy's first publication is not a poem, but a manifesto. Like Stein's portraits of Matisse and Picasso, Loy's 'Aphorisms on Futurism' first appears in Stieglitz's *Camera Work* (January 1914). As its title suggests, the manifesto owes much to Futurist examples and resembles them in form and content. It shares with Marinetti's polemics a militant speaker, declaiming Futuristic slogans on art and life. It varies typesize and uses white space to emphasise its claims and visualise its enthusiasm. It urges readers to 'ACCEPT the tremendous truth of Futurism', fantasises profound social and aesthetic change, attacks opponents, and at times echoes the theatrically aggressive rhetoric of Futurist polemics: 'TO your blushing we shout the obscenities, we scream the blasphemies, that you, being weak, whisper alone in the dark.'[38]

Yet some of Loy's 'Aphorisms' are more restrained, distanced from Futurism and its most aggressive polemicising. Futurist manifestoes characteristically declaim in the first-person plural voice, the insistent 'WE' embodying the movement's collective voice. But Loy's aphorisms speak primarily in the second person (only one 'Aphorism' uses the Futuristic 'we'): 'MAY your egotism be so gigantic that you comprise mankind in your self-sympathy';

'LET the universe flow into your consciousness, there is no limit to its capacity, nothing that it shall not re-create'. Twice, Loy's aphorisms refer to 'THE Futurist' not Marinetti's preferred 'We Futurists'.[39] These deviations from Futurist practice make 'Aphorisms' more evocative and less commanding than other Futurist manifestoes, opening ironic distance between the speaker and the movement her aphorisms putatively defend. The series of poetic satires Loy produces over the next five years confirm that her alienation from the movement intensified as she confronted the hypocrisy of the Futurists' sexual politics.[40] As Loy discovered, their 'revolutionary' attack on established institutions might permit women to enjoy 'free love', but did not include dethroning male privilege, either in the bedroom, in literature and art, or in the salons of the avant garde.

But, while Loy's second and more original polemic, 'Feminist Manifesto', is more sceptical of Futurist sexual politics than 'Aphorisms', defending a rebellious avant-garde feminism, it is, paradoxically, more Futurist in tone and rhetoric:

> Women if you want to realise yourselves – you are on the eve of a devastating psychological upheaval – all your pet illusions must be unmasked – the lies of centuries have got to go – are you prepared for the Wrench – ? There is no half-measure – NO scratching on the surface of the rubbish heap of tradition, will bring about Reform, the only method is Absolute Demolition.[41]

Given the rhetorical violence of the gender critique in passages like this, there's little wonder Loy's manifestoes often are cited to illuminate her dissident feminist politics and poetics. For us, they are important for two additional reasons. First, they confirm that Futurist manifestoes help alert Loy to language's materiality and the visual aspects of poetic composition. To perform visually their heated arguments, Loy's manifestoes exploit the tools of modern typesetting and advertising – capitalisation, font size, underlining, bold-face type, dashes, white space. Second, their embrace of the genre's excision of discursive transitions anticipates and facilitates the collage composition of Loy's most ambitious and important early poetic work, *Love Songs to Joannes*.

*Love Songs* establishes Loy instantly as a poetic contender. The poem's striking opening four sections appear in the inaugural issue of Alfred Kreymborg's celebrated New York little magazine of new verse, *Others* (July 1915); two years later, Kreymborg devotes an entire issue to the full poem (April 1917). The poem's (in)famous opening sections, with their fiercely anti-romantic portrait of Eros as 'Pig Cupid   his rosy snout / Rooting erotic garbage' and their deflating comparison of the male beloved to 'The skin-sack/In which a wanton duality/Packed', provokes critical controversy for its graphic language and imagery (according to Kreymborg, it prompted 'a small sized riot' and 'drove ... critics into furious despair').[42] But the poem's ironic and sexually explicit free-verse rewriting of the sonnet sequence and its traditions of romantic love lyric also displays a wealth of modernist virtues: technical innovation, intellectual rigour, engagement with psychology and sexuality, and an ironic and traumatised tone. The poem's individual sections, portraits not of objects but emotional states, rank *Love Songs*, with Eliot's *The Waste Land*, as one of modernism's major poems of psychological trauma and sexual dysfunction.

More important, Loy's *Love Songs* is among the earliest modernist poems consistently to explore language's visual capacities and adopt montage compositional methods. Like a manifesto, *Love Songs* manipulates lineation and white space to advance its sexually provocative argument:

> Today
> Everlasting   passing   apparent   imperceptible
> To you
> I bring the nascent virginity of
> – Myself   for the moment
> No love   or the other thing
> Only the impact of lighted bodies
> Knocking sparks off each other
> In chaos[43]

Loy's jagged free verse, punctuated only with white space, vividly captures a modernist sexual encounter, alienation and ecstasy mingled weirdly throughout. Yet the poem is as striking visually as verbally; its white spaces evoke absence and distance even as they invite attention and interpretation. *Love Songs* is a major modernist (love) poem in part because it is as interested in exploring the materiality of the poetic medium as it is in rendering modern love into lyric form.

*Love Songs* earns recognition as a major modernist poem as well because it uses montage composition to solve the Imagist problematic. James Longenbach suggests that the Imagists' aggressively 'diminished' poetics exposes a serious problem: 'how can a diminished aesthetic – one that eschews discursive breadth for obsessive precision, radical condensation, minute objects – produce a long poem' that can 'speak meaningfully of contemporary culture'?[44] Taking formal cues from Futurist manifestoes, Loy's *Love Songs* solves this problem by collaging thirty-four brief lyrics together into a sequence. Five years before Pound's *Hugh Selwyn Mauberley* (1920), seven years before Eliot's *The Waste Land* (1922), Loy's *Love Songs* joins Stein's *Tender Buttons* in offering contemporaries a formidable example of how collage composition could be used to make modernist poetry ambitious, even epic. *Love Songs* is an epic deconstruction of lyric subjectivity, a modernist anti-fairy-tale that dismantles bourgeois gender ideals and the gender of literary love, a broken lyric that renders and plumbs the shattered modernist subject. Dense, fragmented and difficult, *Love Songs* provides an example for later poets of a modernist collage poetics, attentive to the materiality of the word, which could contend poetically not only with the technical innovations of Futurist manifestoes and Cubist painting, but also with what Eliot would famously term the 'immense panorama of futility and anarchy' of a shell-shocked postwar modernity.[45]

Writing from the margins of high modernism, Stein and Loy remake modernist poetry. They respond to the imperatives, discourses and practices of the avant garde by innovating influential examples of collage poetics and poetic abstraction. The following section considers how, during the later 1920s, another group of authors, writing from the margins of modernism, further transform modernist poetry by adapting the lessons of the avant garde. These 'Younger Negro Artists' racialise the manifestoes and poetry of modernism even as they modernise the polemics and poetry of the Harlem Renaissance.

## Racialising manifestoes and modernist poetry

In Harlem in 1926, a group of African-American writers and artists calling themselves 'Younger Negro Artists' grows frustrated with the politics and aesthetics of their elder African-American mentors. Taking cues from avant-garde movements like Futurism and Vorticism, they form a fully-fledged 'Negro' avant-garde movement and crank out a party journal, *FIRE!!* (November 1926), 'devoted to' the incendiary work of Aaron Douglas, Langston Hughes, Zora Neale Hurston, Richard Bruce Nugent and Wallace Thurman. Consistent with the tendency of avant-garde polemics to sacrifice subtle distinctions in favour of rhetorical force, the polemics of the Younger Negro Artists tend to caricature and simplify their antagonists. Older Harlem Renaissance writers – 'Talented Tenth' intellectuals like W. E. B. Du Bois, Jessie Fauset, James Weldon Johnson – held a wide and dynamic range of political and aesthetic views; thus, for example, while Du Bois at times defended ideals of aesthetic propriety offensive to younger writers with modernist sympathies, his classic *The Souls of Black Folk*, with its mingling of different genres and media, its techniques of juxtaposition and defamiliarisation, is arguably proto-modernist. Nonetheless, around 1926 the Younger Negro Artists begin portraying their elders as a doctrinaire, close-minded and old-fashioned school, too beholden to the moral and aesthetic proprieties of the white middle class. Hughes calls them the 'Nordicized Negro intelligentsia' in his famous polemic, 'The Negro Artist and the Racial Mountain' (June 1926).[46] Disregarding white and black approval, 'The Negro Artist' proclaims, 'We younger Negro artists who create now intend to express our individual dark-skinned selves without fear or shame.'[47] The poetry of *FIRE!!* manifests in verse form this declaration of Afro-Modernist independence.[48]

The Younger Negro Artists' first manifesto, 'The Negro Artist and the Racial Mountain', adapts the conventions of the avant-garde manifesto to explicitly racial ends, joining modernist radicalism and racial critique. While Hughes's tone and argument are consistently more serious, discursive and essayistic than the telegraphic outrages of Futurist or Vorticist manifestoes, 'The Negro Artist' nonetheless assails bourgeois propriety in art and life, promoting a radical new aesthetic and ethics. In the context of Harlem Renaissance debate, the race critique 'The Negro Artist' offers is unconventional, modernist. The 'Racial Mountain' the manifesto seeks to overcome is not white racism, but the black internalisation of white values, what the polemic calls the 'urge within the race toward whiteness, the desire to pour racial individuality into the mold of American standardization, and to be as little Negro and as much American as possible'.[49]

To reinject African-American life into Harlem Renaissance art, 'The Negro Artist' calls for a new New Negro aesthetic inspired by the life and traditions of 'low-down folks, the so-called common element':

> These common people are not afraid of spirituals, as for a long time their more intellectual brethren were, and jazz is their child. They furnish a wealth of colorful, distinctive material for any artist because they still hold their own individuality in the face of American standardization.[50]

We might note that this celebration of plain black folk offers evidence that black modernists were not immune to the lure of racial exoticism that hooked a number of white modernists – Stein, Pound, Eliot. More interesting, the polemic's admiration for 'individuality in the face of . . . standardization' expresses a quintessentially modernist ethic, consistent with other period affirmations of artistic freedom and independence.

But if race consciousness leads 'The Negro Artist' to racialise modernism's antagonism to standardisation, its commitment to individual artistic vision modernises New Negro aesthetic standards. Hughes's manifesto scorns both blacks who urge, '"Oh, be respectable, write about nice people, show how good we are,"' and whites who advise, '"Be stereotyped, don't go too far, don't shatter our illusions about you, don't amuse us too seriously. We will pay you."' 'The Negro Artist' calls for a new art of individual African-American expression, 'racial in theme and treatment', antagonistic to black bourgeois respectability, New Negro aesthetic timidity and white bribery.[51] 'The Negro Artist and the Racial Mountain' ends, like Marinetti's 'Manifesto of Futurism', looking to the future, with an image of defiant, elevated, self-sufficiency: 'We build our temples for tomorrow, strong as we know how, and we stand on top of the mountain, free within ourselves.'[52] Having surmounted the racial mountain and freed themselves from the shackles of psychological racism, the Younger Negro Artists stand ready to create a new Negro modernism. *FIRE!!* presents key works of this Afro-Modernism.

The Younger Negro Artists' frustration comes to a boil over the publication of Carl Van Vechten's Harlem-themed novel, *Nigger Heaven* (1926). According to David Levering Lewis, it drives 'much of literate Afro-America into a dichotomy of approval and apoplexy over "authentic" versus "proper" cultural expression'.[53] Du Bois condemns it, memorably, for portraying Harlem life as 'just one damned orgy after another, with hate, hurt, gin and sadism'.[54] Firmly rejecting aesthetic propriety, fiercely defending artistic freedom, the Younger Negro Artists publish *FIRE!!*. An avowedly vanguard magazine, *FIRE!!* proclaims the formation of a distinctly African-American avant-garde movement – antagonistic, experimental, race-conscious.

Two components of *FIRE!!* are of particular relevance: its polemical-poetic 'Foreword' and its poetry selection. The former illuminates how the Younger Negro Artists revise the avant-garde manifesto to speak for African Americans; the latter clarifies their efforts to develop Afro-Modernist poetics. Incantatory and imagistic, the Foreword to *FIRE!!* brings racial consciousness to the manifesto-poem.

> *FIRE ... flaming, burning, searing, and penetrating far beneath the superficial items of the flesh to boil the sluggish blood.*
> *FIRE ... a cry of conquest in the night, warning those who sleep and revitalizing those who linger in the quiet places dozing.*[55]

The repetition and separation of the word '*FIRE*' might be cited as a visual evocation of the call-and-response tradition of black song and rhetorical forms, recalling Hughes's argument that modern Negro artists should look to the traditions of 'low-down folks, the so-called common element'. More important, however, the Foreword invokes the genre of the avant-garde manifesto in its manipulation of capitalisation and white space, its rhetorical energy, and its striking and violent imagery. Conjuring a military command, the word 'Foreword' itself suggests the Younger Negro Artists' commitment to advance African-American life and art. Most important, like many early-century manifestoes, *FIRE!!*'s Foreword perpetuates a popular prewar vision of violence as cleansing and revitalising (Marinetti's infamous motto 'war – the world's only hygiene' crystallises this prewar complex).[56] In the wake of the First World War's trauma, devastation and death, however, *FIRE!!*'s celebration of violence is provocative. And, in the context of New Negro discourse, the Foreword's insistent reliance on the imagery of lynching – burning flesh, boiling blood – is especially inflammatory. Typically, lynching appears in Harlem Renaissance writing as the ultimate racist atrocity. But *FIRE!!* provocatively resignifies the imagery of racism, conjoining New Negro images of burning flesh and boiling blood with avant-gardist images of violence as cleansing, even beautiful: '*Beauty? . . . flesh on fire – on fire in the furnace of life blazing. . . .*'[57]

At its centre, *FIRE!!* features ten poems by 'Younger Negro' poets. The section title, 'Flame From the Dark Tower', comes from the opening poem, Countee Cullen's sonnet, 'From the Dark Tower'. The inclusion of Cullen's sonnet in *FIRE!!* is somewhat surprising because Hughes's polemic in 'The Negro Artist and the Racial Mountain' begins with a critique of an unnamed poet, generally held to be Cullen, whom Hughes describes as epitomising the black internalisation of white values, the urge 'toward whiteness' that Hughes condemns. 'From the Dark Tower' resists such accusations by turning the traditions of the Italian sonnet to the task of protesting racism. 'We shall not always plant while others reap', the sonnet opens biblically; 'We were not made eternally to weep', its octave concludes. The sonnet rewrites the traditional sonneteer's posture of unrequited love in racial terms. Cullen's speaker expresses a heady mix of hope, waiting and pain worthy of a Renaissance sonneteer, but his feelings result from the sufferings of his race: 'we hide the heart that bleeds, / And wait, and tend our agonizing seeds.'[58] Despite the evident radicalism of making the quintessential love poetry genre a medium for racial protest, Cullen's poem is a sonnet, and as such declines the pyrotechnic experimentalism of most canonical modernist poems. Political critique notwithstanding, other poems in *FIRE!!* share this formal restraint. Formally speaking, most do not appear particularly modernist: many are rhymed and in metre; none uses the collage techniques associated with high modernist poems like *Hugh Selwyn Mauberley*, *The Waste Land* and *The Cantos*.

Nonetheless the *FIRE!!* poems of Hughes, Helene Johnson and Lewis Alexander deserve recognition as important modernist verse because they make key forms of earlier modernist poetry – free verse, imagism and dramatic monologue – into modes of racial critique. Johnson's 'A Southern Road' presents an anti-lynching poem in imagistic *vers libre*: 'A blue-fruited black gum, / . . . Bears a dangling figure, – / . . . A solemn, tortured shadow in the air.'[59] Hughes's 'Railroad Avenue' brings race consciousness to the alienated landscape and disaffected tone of Eliot's post-symbolist 'Preludes' (first published in *Blast 2*). Alexander's four-line 'Streets' draws on Imagism and Eliot's quatrain poems to evoke the suffering of urban African Americans: 'Avenues of dreams / Boulevards of pain / Moving black streams / Shimmering like rain'.[60] Most interesting, both Alexander's 'Little Cinderella' and Hughes's 'Elevator Boy' rescript the modernist dramatic monologue to voice the alienation not of educated white men like J. Alfred Prufrock, but of working-class African Americans. In the 'common' dialect of 'low-down folks', Hughes's 'Elevator Boy' makes his complaint:

> I got a job now
> Runnin' an elevator
> In the Dennison Hotel in Jersey,
> Job aint no good though.
> No money around.
>   Jobs are just chances
>   Like everything else.
>   Maybe a little luck now,
>   Maybe not.[61]

Countering the racist tones of the title's use of 'Boy' to characterise the black worker, Hughes's elevator operator turns plain vernacular speech into an articulate medium of social critique. The speaker's fatalistic ruminations mimic the monotonous ups and downs of the elevator, creating a rhetorical structure that manifests the numbing, go-nowhere shape of his existence. Even the ostensibly positive fact of employment ('I got a job now') makes little difference given the dehumanising, repetitive monotony of the work itself.[62]

The 'Elevator Boy's' protest also challenges the preferences of older Negro artists. Some elder writers disapproved of the use of the vernacular in modern African-American literature, concerned that it evoked minstrelsy and might be cited to substantiate racist mythologies of black inferiority.[63] 'Elevator Boy' and 'Little Cinderella' disregard such concerns and give common African Americans and their speech a place in modern poetry. Such poems demonstrate that the black vernacular can express modern African-American and human experience with eloquence, complexity and force. *FIRE!!*'s dialect poems also modernise New Negro poetry, not only by rejecting prejudices of the 'Nordicized Negro intelligentsia', but also by defamiliarising poetic language, heightening readers' consciousness of language as a medium that mediates meaning. So, while *FIRE!!* may not include a major Afro-Modernist montage poem, like Sterling Brown's 'Cabaret'

(1932), it does participate in modernist experiments with the linguistic medium, emphasising the mediating materiality of the word. These achievements earn the poems of *FIRE!!* a key part in the Younger Negro Artists' invention of an Afro-Modernist poetics that adapts the lessons of modernism to the task of creating an African-American literature as committed to artistic individuality and independence as to race consciousness and radical racial politics.

Anglo-American modernist poetry and its distinctive technical innovations develop in relation to the activities and innovations of the schools, movements and institutions of the early twentieth-century avant-garde moment. Whether in London and Paris just before the First World War, Florence and Manhattan between 1915 and 1918, or Harlem in the later 1920s, modernist poetry collaborates and competes with avant-garde movements and their defining productions, especially manifestoes and modernist visual art. Neither modernism's ambitious, later poems – Pound's *Hugh Selwyn Mauberley*, Eliot's *The Waste Land*, Moore's 'An Octopus', Loy's *Anglo-Mongrels and The Rose*, Stein's *Patriarchal Poetry*, Crane's *The Bridge*, Brown's 'Cabaret', H.D.'s *Trilogy*, Williams's *Paterson*, Hughes's *Montage of a Dream Deferred* – nor its characteristic poetic techniques – free verse, juxtaposition, collage, intertextuality, linguistic abstraction – would have developed as they did without the lessons learned from the avant-garde movements and their aesthetic innovations. This is not to deny the influence on modernist poetry's development of other precursor poets, poetic schools and movements (Sappho, Hopkins, Yeats, Hulme, haiku, Noh theatre, French Symbolism, to name a few). But the schools, movements and manifestoes of the avant-garde moment also play a constitutive role: they too belong in the genealogy of modernist poetry and its characteristic forms. Acknowledging them, we appreciate better modernist poetry's genesis out of the teeming, boisterous life of early twentieth-century modernity.

## NOTES

1. Peter Bürger, *Theory of the Avant Garde*, trans. Michael Shaw (Minneapolis: University of Minnesota Press, 1984), pp. 53–4.
2. Renato Poggioli, *Theory of the Avant Garde*, trans. Gerald Fitzgerald (1962; Cambridge, Mass.: Harvard University Press, 1968), pp. 18, 20.
3. Poggioli, *The Theory of the Avant Garde*, p. 19.
4. Poggioli, *The Theory of the Avant Garde*, p. 18.
5. F. T. Marinetti, 'Destruction of Syntax – Imagination without Strings – Words-in-Freedom' (May–June 1913), in Umbro Apollonio (ed.), *Futurist Manifestos*, trans. R. W. Flint et al. (New York: Viking, 1973), p. 98.
6. Marinetti, 'Destruction of Syntax', pp. 103–6.

7. See Janet Lyon, *Manifestoes: Provocations of the Modern* (Ithaca: Cornell University Press, 1999), pp. 9–45.
8. See Peter Nicholls, *Modernisms: A Literary Guide* (Basingstoke: Palgrave Macmillan, 1995), pp. 85–6.
9. Marinetti, 'The Founding and Manifesto of Futurism' (20 February 1909), in Apollonio (ed.), *Futurist Manifestos*, p. 21.
10. Marinetti, 'The Founding and Manifesto of Futurism', p. 24.
11. Marjorie Perloff, *The Futurist Moment: Avant Garde, Avant Guerre, and the Language of Rupture* (University of Chicago Press, 1986), p. 115.
12. Lawrence Rainey, *Institutions of Modernism: Literary Elites and Public Culture* (New Haven: Yale University Press, 1998), p. 32.
13. *Daily Chronicle*, 20 March 1912; quoted in Rainey, *Institutions*, p. 28.
14. See Rainey, *Institutions*, pp. 28–9.
15. Chris Baldick, *The Oxford English Literary History*, vol. X, *1910–1940, The Modern Movement* (Oxford University Press, 2004), p. 95.
16. Marinetti, 'The Founding and Manifesto of Futurism', p. 22; Ezra Pound, 'Patria Mia,' *Selected Prose 1909–1965*, ed. William Cookson (New York: New Directions, 1973), p. 128.
17. Pound, 'Patria Mia', p. 111.
18. Nicholls, *Modernisms*, p. 167.
19. F. S. Flint, 'Imagisme', *Poetry* 1.6 (March 1913), 199.
20. Flint, 'Imagisme', 199.
21. Pound, 'In a Station of the Metro', *New Freewoman* 5.1 (15 August 1913), 88.
22. Peter McDonald, 'Modernist Publishing: "Nomads and Mapmakers"', in David Bradshaw (ed.), *A Concise Companion to Modernism* (Oxford: Blackwell Publishing, 2003), p. 233.
23. Pound, 'A Few Don'ts By an Imagiste', *Poetry* 1.6 (March 1913), 200.
24. Rainey, *Institutions*, pp. 38–9.
25. Wyndham Lewis (ed.), *Blast 1: Review of the Great English Vortex* (1914; Santa Barbara: Black Sparrow, 1981), pp. 39, 41.
26. Perloff, *The Futurist Moment*, p. 181.
27. Lewis's use of the BLAST/BLESS structure in *Blast* also relies on Guillaume Apollinaire's 'L'Antitradition futuriste', a 1913 manifesto that both imitates and parodies Futurist polemics. On Apollinaire's text, see Perloff, *The Futurist Moment*, pp. 96–101.
28. See Richard Cork, *Vorticism and Abstract Art in the First Machine Age*, 2 vols (London: Gordon Fraser, 1976).
29. Lewis (ed.), *Blast*, 55; see Mark Morrisson, *The Public Face of Modernism: Little Magazines, Audiences, and Reception, 1905–1920* (Madison: University of Wisconsin Press, 2001), pp. 116–32.
30. Lowell, Aldington and Flint quoted in William Wees, *Vorticism and the English Avant Garde* (University of Toronto Press, 1972), p. 130.
31. Lewis (ed.), *Blast*, 45.
32. Rainey, *Institutions*, p. 38.
33. Rainey, *Institutions*, p. 38.
34. Gertrude Stein, *Writings 1903–1932*, ed. Catharine R. Stimpson and Harriet Chessman (New York: The Library of America, 1998), p. 690.

35. For example, James Mellow, *Charmed Circle: Gertrude Stein and Company* (New York: Avon, 1975), p. 94.
36. Jahan Ramazani, 'Introduction', *Norton Anthology of Modern and Contemporary Poetry*, 3rd edn, ed. Jahan Ramazani, Richard Ellmann and Robert O'Clair (New York: Norton, 2003), p. lv.
37. Stein, *Writings 1903–1932*, p. 342.
38. Mina Loy, *The Lost Lunar Baedeker*, ed. Roger L. Conover (New York: Farrar, Straus and Giroux, 1996), p. 152.
39. Loy, *Lost Lunar Baedeker*, pp. 150, 151, 150.
40. These satires are collected under the title 'FUTURISM X FEMINISM: THE CIRCLE SQUARED', in Loy, *Lost Lunar Baedeker*, pp. 1–50. 'The Effectual Marriage', the most cited and important of these, epitomises Loy's poetic critique of Futurist gender politics.
41. Loy, *Lost Lunar Baedeker*, p. 153.
42. Loy, *Lost Lunar Baedeker*, p. 53; Arthur Kreymborg, *Troubadour: An Autobiography* (New York: Liveright, 1925); Arthur Kreymborg, *Our Singing Strength* (New York: Coward-McCann, 1929) – both are quoted by Roger Conover, 'Notes on the Text', in Loy, *Lost Lunar Baedeker*, pp. 188–9.
43. Loy, *Lost Lunar Baedeker*, pp. 58–9.
44. James Longenbach, 'Modern Poetry', in Michael Levenson (ed.), *The Cambridge Companion to Modernism* (Cambridge University Press, 1999), pp. 106, 107, 108.
45. T. S. Eliot, *Selected Prose of T. S. Eliot*, ed. Frank Kermode (London: Faber and Faber, 1975), p. 177.
46. Langston Hughes, 'The Negro Artist and the Racial Mountain', *Nation* (June 1926), in David Levering Lewis (ed.), *The Portable Harlem Renaissance Reader* (New York: Penguin, 1994), p. 94.
47. Hughes, 'The Negro Artist', p. 95.
48. I borrow the useful term 'Afro-Modernist' from Mark Sanders, *Afro-Modernist Aesthetics and the Poetry of Sterling A. Brown* (Athens: University of Georgia Press, 1999).
49. Hughes, 'The Negro Artist', p. 91.
50. Hughes, 'The Negro Artist', p. 92.
51. Hughes, 'The Negro Artist', p. 94.
52. Hughes, 'The Negro Artist', p. 95.
53. Lewis, 'Introduction', *The Portable Harlem Renaissance Reader*, p. xxx.
54. W. E. B. Du Bois, 'Critique of Carl Van Vechten's *Nigger Heaven*', in Lewis (ed.), *The Portable Harlem Renaissance Reader*, p. 107; Du Bois's critique originally appeared in *Crisis*.
55. *FIRE!!: A Quarterly Devoted to Younger Negro Artists* 1.1 (1926), 1; ellipses in the original.
56. Marinetti, 'Manifesto of Futurism', p. 22.
57. *FIRE!!*, 1; ellipses in the original.
58. *FIRE!!*, 18.
59. *FIRE!!*, 17.
60. *FIRE!!*, 23.
61. *FIRE!!*, 20.
62. These observations have benefited from the insights of Karen Ford.

63. James Weldon Johnson, 'Preface', *The Book of American Negro Poetry* (1922; New York: Harcourt, Brace and Company, 1959), p. 45, for example, argues that 'Negro dialect is at present a medium that is not capable of giving expression to the varied conditions of Negro life in America, and much less is it capable of giving the fullest interpretation of Negro character and psychology. This is no indictment against the dialect as dialect, but against the mould of convention in which Negro dialect in the United States has been set.' On relations between race, dialect and modernism, see Michael North, *The Dialect of Modernism: Race, Language and Twentieth-Century Literature* (New York: Oxford University Press, 1994).

# 3

## PETER NICHOLLS

# The poetics of modernism

'Said Yo-Yo: / "What part ob yu iz deh poEM?".'[1] Tucked away in one of
the late *Cantos* that Ezra Pound wrote during his thirteen-year incarceration
in St Elizabeths hospital, this question from a fellow inmate is offered as
light relief in a passage which has already praised Adolf Hitler as a leader
'furious from perception'. In such a context, readers are unlikely to linger
over Yo-Yo's question, cast as it is in a damaged idiom that serves only to
reinforce the apparent obtuseness of its underlying assumption: Pound is a
poet, ergo his poem must exist somewhere in his person. The association is
silly, of course, though it has a certain irony when proposed in a place where
bodies are hardly at their best. But, whether or not it is recorded here for
that reason, Yo-Yo's question does remind us that, while a modernist poetics
seems to emerge from a distrust of earlier conceptions of poetry as ethereal
and disembodied, it is also founded in a partial and strategic dissociation
of the poet from the poem. In light of this, to ask where the poem 'is' –
to wonder which part of the poet's person it might seem to occupy – might
prompt us to ask where it comes from in the first place, a question of a rather
different order and one which may shed more light on modernist poetics than
Yo-Yo could have suspected.

Traditional answers to the conundrum frequently appeal to the function
of memory, especially the Platonic form of recollection, and in practice, of
course, especially in periods before our own, poetry did have close ties to
memory, not least through the common practice of learning by heart. Here
something paradoxical is at work, as Jacques Derrida has observed, for this
learning by heart entails a kind of double movement: on the one hand, it
interiorises the poem, giving it an 'intangible singularity' as it is assimilated
to the inner life of the self (one may think of those heterogeneous materials
that have 'carved the trace in the mind' in Pound's *Pisan Cantos*; at the same
time (this too is a feature of that sequence), the very act of possession recalls
us to the otherness or foreignness of those words that poets find themselves
remembering and rewriting, the heart now 'traversed', says Derrida, 'by the

dictated dictation'.[2] We may possess the words of others, then, but the fact of this ownership opens a kind of cleavage in the self, revealing otherness where one might have expected to find the impress of the author's own identity.

Derrida's reference to 'dictation' also alludes, of course, to a long and rich tradition of thinking about poets' own poems as verbal messages that seem to arrive in the mind from somewhere else. The location of that other place is variously specified, but from Homer to the Surrealists the mysterious advent of the poem, as something inexplicable in terms of the poet's thoughts alone, has been a prominent feature of the literary tradition. While modernist poetry is often described in holistic terms, as the expression, for example, of 'the radiant world' where the intelligence and the senses work as one (Pound), of the 'undissociated' sensibility (T. S. Eliot), of the 'whole personality' (Wallace Stevens),[3] this is complicated by an underlying sense of the new as something other that originates from 'outside', and is either conceived as a kind of literal dictation or is grasped intuitively as a structural and stylistic imperative that impels poetry toward unfamiliar regions of expression (the exemplary modernist poem deliberately invites the question 'Is it poetry?').[4]

Yeats's interest in automatic writing is an example of the first way with the new and is symptomatic of an age in which seances and theosophy were all the rage; even Pound, Idaho cowboy that he partly was, was not immune to talk of 'vibrations' and mysterious visitations.[5] Much of the complexity of modernism thus stems from its location at a crossroads between old and new science, and between orthodox religious belief and something which began to take its place, a primarily aesthetic 'religion' in which imagination and sensibility silently usurped dogma and belief. 'Art for Art's Sake', we call this, thinking, for example, of Walter Pater's appeal to 'a quickened, multiplied consciousness' in face of an otherwise irredeemable mortality, or of Arthur Symons's reworking of these ideas in his influential *The Symbolist Movement in Literature* (1899), where poetry is seen as 'before all things, an escape', an escape from mortality's 'sterile, annihilating reality in many dreams, in religion, passion, art; each a forgetfulness, each a symbol of creation'.[6] The motif of 'escape' was, of course, one which an emergent modernism would strongly challenge, but the idea of art as a kind of compensation for lost religious values would never quite disappear; indeed, as late as 1951, Wallace Stevens wrote that 'in an age in which disbelief is so profoundly prevalent, or, if not disbelief, indifference to questions of belief, poetry and painting, and the arts in general, are, in their measure, a compensation for what has been lost'.[7]

In the absence of clear transcendental sanctions, the matter of poetry's origin became even harder to define. Almost inevitably, the emphasis shifted to the forms of reverie and association through which the Paterian self, otherwise 'dwarfed into the narrow chamber of the individual mind', might recover a 'lifted horizon' in which the 'multiplied consciousness' could find its place in relation to other times and other worlds. Pater's famous evocation of the Mona Lisa (later lineated as verse in Yeats's *Oxford Book of Modern Verse*) thus discovered in Leonardo's painting an instance of a 'brief and wholly concrete moment – into which, however, all the motives, all the interests and effects of a long history, have condensed themselves, and which seem to absorb past and future in an intense consciousness of the present'. Pater's evocation of the painting suavely reports the woman's different imagined attributes as if they were simply self-evident – 'Hers is the head upon which all "the ends of the world are come", and the eyelids are a little weary' – the descriptive tone almost making us forget that to accept this synoptic account we have had to surrender to a trance-like reverie in which 'The presence that rose thus so strangely beside the waters' is at once the mother of Helen of Troy and of Mary (the image is said at the outset to be 'expressive of what in the way of a thousand years men had come to desire', thus licensing our willing and collective capitulation).[8]

Pater's emphasis on the image as an exemplification of concreteness and compression exerted a strong, if often unacknowledged, influence on the new poetics, though its modernist proponents would also be concerned to find ways of avoiding the tendency to solipsism stimulated by these richly interiorised cadences and narcotic atmospheres. In Yeats's early poems, though, the Paterian influence is unalloyed, with poetic reverie offering a heightened emotional state in which the poet willingly surrenders to some external power. Nowhere is this clearer, perhaps, than in Yeats's essay 'The Symbolism of Poetry' (1900):

> The purpose of rhythm, it has always seemed to me, is to prolong the moment of contemplation, the moment when we are both asleep and awake, which is the one moment of creation, by hushing us with an alluring monotony, while it holds us waking by variety, to keep us in that state of perhaps real trance, in which the mind liberated from the pressure of the will is unfolded in symbols.[9]

Yeats's talk of 'prolong[ing] the moment of contemplation' nods deliberately to Pater's fantasy of 'expanding that interval, in getting as many pulsations as possible into the given time'.[10] In curbing 'the pressure of the will', the mind is able to grasp itself in symbolic forms of which it had previously had no knowledge. In 'The Symbolism of Poetry', Yeats also proposes that 'All sounds, all colours, all forms, either because of their preordained energies or because of long association, evoke indefinable and yet precise emotions, or, as I prefer to think, call down among us certain disembodied powers, whose footsteps over our hearts we call emotions.'[11] We notice that Yeats unembarrassedly 'prefers' to attribute these patterns of association to external 'disembodied powers' rather than to more mundane operations of the mind.

The hazy borderline between sleeping and waking is a recurring motif of these early poems, with the poet 'hushed' like a baby into a state of imaginative receptivity. The figure appears too in the poems by Pound that bear the strong imprint of Yeats's 1899 collection, *Wind Among the Reeds*. In 'Histrion', for example, Pound conjures with the idea that 'the souls of all great men pass through us, / And we are melted into them, and are not / Save reflexions of their souls'.[12] Here the romantic aesthetic of the arrested moment allows the past to return, but at the expense of the poet's sensibility, which is invaded or possessed in the act of imitation: 'So cease we from all being for the time, / And these, the Masters of the Soul, live on'. Here the poet is literally inspired, the very breath he takes barely his own. In this fantasy of metempsychosis or transmigration of the soul lies a concept of the mask or persona, something Pound drew partly from Yeats, who in turn drew it partly from Nietzsche's description of the 'great man': 'When not speaking to himself, he wears a mask. He rather lies than tells the truth: it requires more spirit and *will*.'[13] Pound's early collections – *Personae* (1909), *Canzoni* (1911), *Ripostes* (1912) and *Lustra* (1916) – show him developing the use of masks so as to abandon the passive 'inspirational' mode and replace its ventriloquism with a medium that weaves together another's voice with the one the poet temporarily adopts as his own. It is perhaps not surprising that these early writings were closely associated with Pound's evolving practice of translation, for poetry by this account is seen to originate not in self-expression but in the division or tension between the subject and its other.[14] For while the persona or mask might seem to suggest merely a concealment of the self, it actually exposes poetic identity as a complex weave of different times and different voices. To speak of the *poetics* of modernism rather than of specific modernist poems is, then, to acknowledge this particular relation of poet to medium, for poetics, from the Greek *poesis*, denotes 'making', a definition which, while it prizes craft above 'mere' inspiration, also ultimately requires us to attend less to the poet as maker than to the poem as the event of making. Such an event is akin to what J. Hillis Miller has termed the 'linguistic moment' in which 'the poetic medium, reflexively taking itself as its object, renders itself or its referentiality opaque and problematic'.[15]

Modernist poets seem in this sense to have found myriad ways of taking up the challenge of Symbolist poet Stéphane Mallarmé: 'If the poem is to be pure the poet's voice must be stilled and the initiative taken by the words themselves, which will be set in motion as they meet unequally in collision.'[16] The particular question of 'purity' would become less important for Mallarmé's successors, but the idea of ceding authority to 'the words themselves', which would then meet not in purposeful sequence but in some kind of unexpected 'collision', would constitute one of the deepest unifying strands of modernist poetics. The stilling of the poet's voice is there, for example, in T. S. Eliot's hugely influential concept of poetic impersonality: 'Poetry is not a turning loose of emotion, but an escape from emotion; it is not the expression of personality, but an escape from personality. . . . The emotion of art is impersonal.'[17] For this reason, as Eliot observes elsewhere of Pound's early work, 'The poem which is absolutely original is absolutely bad; it is, in the bad sense, "subjective" with no relation to the world to which it appeals.' By way of contrast, he concludes, 'Pound is often most "original" in the right sense, when he is most "archaeological" in the ordinary sense.'[18] Eliot thus gives an historical dimension to Mallarmé's idea of a handing over to 'the words themselves', locating the origin of the poem in the writer's dialogue with literary tradition.

Here we begin to approach a paradox which lies at the heart of one type of modernism, for Eliot's formulation assumes that the otherness that shadows poetic expression is at once the force of the new, of something that has not been thought or said before, *and* the voice of tradition itself which is heard again in the poet's words. Indeed, for Eliot and Pound, the definitively modern tone is actually characterised by its literariness: 'The ordinary life of ordinary cultivated people is a mush of literature and life', Eliot tells us, and Pound, going directly to the source, observes that master ironist Jules Laforgue 'writes not the popular language of any country but an international tongue common to the excessively cultivated, and to those more or less familiar with French literature of the first three-fourths of the nineteenth century'.[19] The reference to the 'excessively cultivated' acknowledges the decadent aspect of Laforgue's fascination with neologism and with a language more artificial than social, and also implies that Pound's own sense of an 'international tongue' is more robustly public in its assumption that an authentically modern poetry will be both polyglot and allusive. His remarks are made in a short piece celebrating the work of Marianne Moore and Mina Loy, poets who, in Pound's view, display the art of 'logopoeia' or 'poetry that is akin to nothing but language, which is a dance of the intelligence among words and ideas and modification of ideas and characters'.[20] The dance is the dance of irony which offers the necessary escape from sentimentality and romantic expressivism, providing a strategic means by which to affirm the self as strong and authoritative, as 'modern' rather than 'decadent'.

When Pound remarked admiringly of Eliot that 'He has actually trained himself *and* modernized himself *on his own*',[21] it was with the tacit recognition that the training had been greatly aided by Eliot's discovery of Laforgue in the pages of Arthur Symons's *The Symbolist Movement in Literature*. Irony and modernism thus cohabit from the start, not only because irony delights in linguistic nuance and allusion but also because in doing so it becomes the very medium of 'cultivated' social intercourse, as Eliot's 'The Love Song of J. Alfred Prufrock' and Pound's 'Portrait d'une Femme' variously attest. The ostentatiously cosmopolitan idiom of the literary salon or café has its reflex not only in the multilingualism of *The Waste Land* and *The Cantos*, but also in the conception they share of contemporary language as hybrid and constantly changing. Here the American language seems to offer a particularly dynamic resource: Pound notes that the internationalism of Loy and Moore is 'a distinctly national product', and Loy herself writes of this 'English enriched and variegated with the grammatical structure and voice-inflection of many races', concluding that 'it was inevitable that the renaissance of poetry should proceed out of America, where latterly a thousand languages have been born'.[22]

This cacophony of languages runs deep in the modernist sense of experience as being, in Eliot's words, 'chaotic, irregular, fragmentary'. Amidst this chaos, however, 'in the mind of the poet these experiences are always forming new wholes', a process Wallace Stevens aptly terms 'hybridisation' ('Mr. Eliot's *Prelude* with the smell of steaks in passageways, is an instance, in the sense that the smell of steaks in the Parnassian air is a thing perfectly fulfilling').[23] The hybridity of the modern idiom and its mobility between different vocabularies and registers thus underwrite the principal structuring devices adopted by modernist poets. If their work seems difficult it is because it is paratactic and elliptical in its deepest impulse, responding to the speed and discontinuity of contemporary experience: 'The life of a village is a narrative', writes Pound; 'In the city the visual impressions succeed each other, overlap, overcross, they are "cinematographic".'[24] The new poetics must meet the challenge of this urban dynamism, though in contrast to Impressionism (which Pound associates negatively with Futurism) the theory of the image ('Imagism(e)') which he developed around 1912 with H.D. (Hilda Doolittle), Richard Aldington and F. S. Flint regards the poet not as passive receptor but as 'directing a certain fluid force against circumstance, as *conceiving* instead of merely reflecting and observing'.[25] In contrast to the partial self-effacement of the 'personae' poems, what is proposed here is a poetics which seems to assume a much stronger sense of agency. Clarity and concision are now the order of the day, as Pound and his colleagues agree three basic principles:

1. Direct treatment of the 'thing' whether subjective or objective.
2. To use absolutely no word that does not contribute to the presentation.

3. As regarding rhythm: to compose in the sequence of the musical phrase, not in sequence of a metronome.[26]

These are the 'rules', then, by which one might produce that 'intellectual and emotional complex' which constitutes the image, though Pound's businesslike manner is elsewhere belied by his more intuitionist view that 'Poetry is a centaur' whose movements are sudden and unpredictable when 'the mind is upborne upon the emotional surge'. Indeed, it is, for Pound, one difference between poetry and prose that 'In the verse something has come upon the intelligence. In the prose the intelligence has found a subject for its observations. The poetic fact pre-exists.' [27]

An otherwise straightforward piece of technical advice is thus complicated by yet another claim for the exteriority of the poem's origin. Indeed, even when Pound speaks in his first proposition of 'direct treatment of the "thing"', his scare quotes (a warning so far ignored by all commentators) indicate that he is thinking not of a material object to be visually represented but of the 'poetic fact' in which the poem is deemed to originate: 'I think one should write vers libre only when one "must", that is to say, only when the "thing" builds up a rhythm more beautiful than that of set metres'.[28] Far from being an object, this 'thing' is actually the 'complex' itself which constitutes the image, a verbal and affective assemblage whose syntax incorporates a literal spacing. Pound describes his most famous imagist poem, the two-line 'In a Station of the Metro' ('The apparition of these faces in the crowd; / Petals on a wet, black bough.')[29] in precisely these terms: 'In a poem of this sort one is trying to record the precise instant when a thing outward and objective transforms itself, or darts into a thing inward and subjective.'[30] Again, these 'things' are not single objects, but arrangements in social and psychic space which the poem delicately conjoins, while leaving the semicolon at the end of the first line to gesture toward relationship rather than bluntly to assert it. This element of reserve or reticence is in part a reflection of the convention of Japanese haiku on which Pound loosely draws for the image, but it also underlines the openness and provisionality of a modernist poetics understood as the event of making rather than as its completed act. And, while the objects in the poem are easily recognised, the 'thing' which results from their combination has a singularity that makes it difficult to insert the poem's perception into any larger explanatory context (hence, perhaps, Pound's deliberately unspecific designation of it as simply a 'thing').[31]

The Imagist poems may be limited achievements in themselves, constrained by a too refined and fragile decorum, but their partial disembodiment and their resistance to conceptualisation are features which would govern modernist poetics henceforth. There is a curious tension between the emphatic clarity and precision of such poems, on the one hand, and the kind of indeterminacy they simultaneously cultivate, on the other. In 'Liu Ch'e', for example, we read:

> The rustling of the silk is discontinued,
> Dust drifts over the court-yard,
> There is no sound of footfall . . .[32]

The rustling has apparently ended, though it is in fact perpetuated in the drawn-out syllables of 'discontinued' and still heard in the sibilant sounds of the line, just as the woman's steps echo on in the marked spondee of her 'footfall'. Effects of this kind which make the poem resistant to paraphrase are fundamental to the poetics of modernism, from these early Imagist poems through to Eliot's *Burnt Norton* (1935), where, rather similarly, 'Footfalls echo in the memory / Down the passage we did not take.'[33]

Mystical indeterminacies such as these propel us toward the larger matter of discontinuity as a founding principle of modernist poetics, for it is in this that the new decisively announces itself. Pound's *Cantos* are perhaps the most extreme development in this direction, with their elaboration of the image and the Chinese ideogram as models for an elliptical organisation of 'luminous details'.[34] Here most clearly the force of the new is to be felt not just in the content of the poem's materials but in the form itself, as a dislocation and disordering of syntax. This is what Eliot has in mind when he says that 'poets in our civilization . . . must be *difficult*', that 'The poet must become more and more comprehensive, more allusive, more indirect, in order to force, to dislocate if necessary, language into his meaning.'[35] For his part, Pound parodied the debilitating effects of modern cliché and political rhetoric in *Hugh Selwyn Mauberley* (1920), and in his work on the first of the *Cantos* he also quickly decided that the dramatic monologue he had adapted from Browning would not provide a sufficiently radical 'dislocation' of the norms of public speech. In revised versions of the first three *Cantos*, the verse accordingly became more 'indirect' as Pound cut rapidly between different items, leaving the reader to reckon with the resulting 'thing' without overt authorial guidance:

> So-shu churned in the sea.
> Seal sports in the spray-whited circles of cliff-wash,
> Sleek head, daughter of Lir,
>     eyes of Picasso
> Under black fur-hood, lithe daughter of Ocean;
> And the wave runs in the beach-groove . . .[36]

The definite articles here ('*the* sea', '*the* beach-groove') are cunningly self-reflexive, seeming to gesture toward a known landscape but in fact referring only to that brought into being by the poem. At the same time, the items named in the text are drawn into apposition not by any overarching argument, but by a pattern of rhythmic phrasing, syncopated once again by Pound's signature spondees.

Compare these lines from Eliot's *The Waste Land*:

> But at my back from time to time I hear
> The sound of horns and motors, which shall bring
> Sweeney to Mrs. Porter in the spring.
> O the moon shone bright on Mrs. Porter
> And on her daughter
> They wash their feet in soda water
> *Et O ces voix d'enfants, chantant dans la coupole!*[37]

Eliot's lines work in larger prosodic units, and, while they are clearly determined by the ironic tension between modernity and the past which structures the whole poem, the elliptical handling of literary allusions (from Andrew Marvell, John Day and Paul Verlaine) gives them a rich depth and variousness of tone. It is this sinuous mobility that, in keeping elements hovering in some kind of suspension, allows both poems to nudge history toward the condition of myth, though they do so to rather different ends. In *The Waste Land*, myth is invoked as something external to a chaotic modernity and capable of bringing order to it for that reason (this is the 'mythical method' Eliot discerned in Joyce's *Ulysses*);[38] in *The Cantos*, it testifies to what Pound calls 'a sort of permanent basis in humanity',[39] and can provide both a vehicle for 'extraordinary' experience and a paradigm of the poem's own metamorphic handling of its materials. In each case, though, myth is valued at once for its antiquity and for its alterity – 'The first myths arose when a man walked sheer into "nonsense"',[40] Pound writes – and it thus provides a perfect expression of that tricky interface between the alien 'new' and the known tradition which underlies this modernism's attempt to 'Make it New'.[41]

That paradoxical relation is pushed – deliberately – almost to breaking point in the early poems of H.D. where the otherness attaching to myth provides figures for a drama of self-division and engulfment. In the poems of *Sea Garden* (1916), the 'I' is repeatedly 'shattered' and 'scattered', with writing projected as an act of cutting or incision which reveals the otherness within the self. H.D.'s synthetic Greek landscapes may superficially resemble Pound's, but they are unremittingly hard and inhospitable, an austere backdrop for a psychic drama more violent than anything in *The Cantos* or *The*

*Waste Land*. And the idea that the 'new' is a form at once alien and destructive appears in other versions of modernist poetics which more deliberately
divest themselves of any dependence on the traditional and the canonical. In
William Carlos Williams's *Kora in Hell: Improvisations* (1920) and *Spring
and All* (1923), for example, both poetry and prose are used to produce a
modernism defiantly at odds with that of Pound and Eliot. In his 1918 'Prologue' to the first of these volumes, Williams railed against the tendency to
'rehash' and 'repetition' in the work of his two famous contemporaries,[42]
and with *Spring and All* he had Eliot's recently published *The Waste Land*
in his sights:

> If I could say what is in my mind in Sanscrit or even Latin I would do so. But
> I cannot. I speak for the integrity of the soul and the greatness of life's inanity;
> the formality of its boredom; the orthodoxy of its stupidity. Kill! kill! Let there
> be fresh meat. . . .[43]

Alluding ironically to the close of Eliot's poem and its hopeful invocation of
voices from outside the Western tradition ('Shantih shantih shantih', 'The
Peace which passeth understanding'),[44] Williams offers a Dadaist account
of the stupidity of 'life' and celebrates the hyperbolic act of destruction that
will finally free us from it.[45] The imperative is not now to 'Make it New', for
the act of invention is one which tacitly obliterates the 'it' of Pound's formulation. Instead, Williams banks everything on poetry's capacity to become
a violent yet objectless expression of the new – 'Yes, the imagination drunk
with prohibitions, has destroyed everything afresh in the likeness of that
which it was. Now indeed men look about in amazement at each other with
a full realization of the meaning of "art".'[46] Poetics here assumes the force
of an *un*making and it is this that Williams opposes to the reverential *hom-
mages* of Pound and Eliot, preferring instead Picasso's association of creation
with destruction, and the transformative energy which had so impressed him
when he saw Marcel Duchamp's *Nude Descending a Staircase* at the 1913
Armory Show: 'I burst out laughing from the relief it brought me! I felt as if
an enormous weight had been lifted from my spirit for which I was infinitely
grateful.'[47] That mixture of laughter and relief that Williams felt on first
encountering the *Nude* echoes in his poems of the 1920s, their mixed registers and frequently outlandish gestures trumpeting poetry's power to make
the world new and different ('There is no thing that with a twist of the imagination cannot be something else').[48] Williams's use of scientific metaphor
to define the imagination (which is 'an actual force comparable to electricity
or steam')[49] may recall some of Pound's formulations, but the emphasis here
is not on a force producing models of order (the magnet creating pattern

in the iron filings), but rather on 'expulsive' energies which are disorderly and unpredictable.[50] 'The imagination goes from one thing to another', for which reason, says Williams, referring to *Kora in Hell*, 'I let the imagination have its own way to see if it could save itself. Something very definite came of it.'[51]

The exuberance of Williams's work can also be felt in Wallace Stevens's *Harmonium* (1923). Stevens shared Williams's immediate reaction to *The Waste Land* – 'Eliot's poem is, of course, the rage. As poetry it is surely negligible. . . . Personally, I think it's a bore'[52] – and his early poems are ostentatiously playful, vividly coloured and full of a bohemian exoticism. Stevens once said of his poem 'The Emperor of Ice-Cream' that it has 'something of the essential gaudiness of poetry', and the word 'gaudiness', associated as it is with feasting and entertainment, aptly conveys the jubilant tones in which Stevens celebrates the liberation of poetry from belief and from 'the gaunt world of reason'. 'The final belief', he would later conclude, 'is to believe in a fiction which you know to be a fiction, there being nothing else'. For Stevens, as for Williams, the imagination is conceived as 'a violence from within . . . pressing back against the pressure of reality', and he, too, often compares it with the abstracting modes of modern painting.[53] But where Williams in *Spring and All* is mistrustful of metaphor, preferring to seek out instead 'those inimitable particles of dissimilarity to all other things which are the peculiar perfections of the thing in question', for Stevens 'Reality is a cliché / From which we escape by metaphor'.[54] In 'the *mundo* of the imagination' where, as the use of the Spanish word implies, a familiar world becomes unfamiliar, 'all things resemble each other'. This is not to say, of course, that all things are the same (indeed, 'identity is the vanishing-point of resemblance') but that 'the structure of reality' 'binds together' its constituent elements. Since the imagination 'must adhere to what is real', the poem also seeks out 'a partial similarity between two dissimilar things', death and ice-cream, for example, and in doing so establishes its own world, a 'living singularity'.[55]

In this sense, 'the interest of the poem is not in its meaning but in this, that it illustrates the achieving of an individual reality'. Stevens makes this observation in a reading of a poem by Marianne Moore which is constructed, characteristically, from a series of recondite sources. The poem, which is about folkloric depictions of the ostrich ('He "Digesteth Harde Yron"'), is especially admired by Stevens because it shows how the writer can begin with mere 'facts' and proceed to attain a new level of abstraction. Several aspects of his account are striking. First, we note that yet again the origin of the poem lies elsewhere (Moore, says Stevens, 'finds only allusion tolerable' and, like Eliot, she helpfully provides endnotes to signal this); and second, that the poetic activity of 'making' is a matter of 'thought and not sense', 'thought', that is, not as personalised reflection but as composition, in a sense similar, perhaps, to what Gertrude Stein had in mind when she spoke of 'Composition as Explanation'. To achieve this, the writer has had to effect 'the substitution for the idea of inspiration of the idea of an effort of the mind not dependent on the vicissitudes of the sensibility'.[56] What Stevens calls the 'living singularity' of the poem is thus to be discovered not in some identification with the poet's feeling but in the *syntax* of the work, in the particular arrangement of words that, like the conjunction of planes in a painting, allows 'contact with reality as it impinges on us *from outside*, the sense that we can touch and feel a solid reality which does not wholly dissolve itself into the conceptions of our own minds'.[57] Stevens quotes the following as an example:

> jewel-
> gorgeous ugly egg-shell
> goblet.

The deliberate placing of the words as single items and the elaborate phonetic patterning that contains them and weighs their respective valencies produces what Williams calls a 'condition of imaginative suspense' in which nothing can be presupposed or known in advance.[58] In his reading, Stevens clearly grasps Moore's text as a poem in the making, a disclosure of a new and 'particular reality' within the texture of a language not easily susceptible to interpretation.[59]

Pound in some advice to Williams pitches upon the best word for this effect – 'opacity':

> You thank your bloomin gawd you've got enough Spanish blood to muddy up your mind, and prevent the current American ideation from going through it like a blighted colander.
>
> The thing that saves your work is opacity, and don't forget it. Opacity is NOT an American quality. Fizz, swish, gabble, and verbiage, these are *echt americanisch*.[60]

Rather similarly, Williams, while criticising 'empty symbolism', notes in appropriately opaque manner that 'Marianne Moore escapes. The incomprehensibility of her poems is witness to at what cost (she cleaves herself away) as it is also to the distance which the most are from a comprehension of the purpose of composition.'[61] Stevens's own view of the matter is perhaps best summed up in his aphorism, 'Poetry must resist the intelligence almost successfully.'[62]

Such resistance to the 'blighted colander' of easy comprehension extends beyond surface features such as the recondite vocabularies employed by writers like Stevens and Moore, and is grounded in a syntax which often seems to become more opaque and compacted as modernism unfolds. Take, for example, the opening lines from a 1927 poem of W. H. Auden:

> Who stands, the crux left of the watershed,
> On the wet road behind the chafing grass
> Below him sees dismantled washing-floors,
> Snatches of tramline running to the wood,
> An industry already comatose,
> Yet sparsely living.[63]

The deliberate awkwardness of the writing and its way of disorienting the reader in its very opening word (should we construe this as he 'Who stands' or 'Who[ever] stands'?) powerfully convey the stranger's perplexity in the face of a landscape at once 'comatose, / Yet sparsely living'. The bits of machinery that litter the place speak for themselves, but the writing gives us little help in determining any larger sense of relationship; indeed, it is as if the stranger's failure to understand what has happened here is enacted in the constant undermining of what seem at first sight to be appositional phrases but turn out to be uncertainly located: what is the relation of the 'crux' to the one who stands, for example, and is it the 'chafing grass' that is below him or the 'washing-floors'? Where, in fact, *is* the stranger standing? The opacity here is not something commonly associated with Auden's work and indeed the second stanza of the poem moves abruptly into the kind of direct address that would become one of the hallmarks of his later style: 'Go home, now, stranger, proud of your young stock, / Stranger, turn back again, frustrate and vexed.'

Other writers, though, would mine more systematically the possibilities of syntactical difficulty as the mark of the definitively new. 'Objectivist' poet George Oppen, for example, included in his first volume *Discrete Series* (1934) an untitled poem that opens thus:

> Who comes is occupied
> Toward the chest (in the crowd moving
>           opposite
> Grasp of me).[64]

Like Auden's lines, Oppen's leave us groping for reference points as the scene unfolds, the contorted syntax insisting that we are confronting (in Stevens's words) 'a solid reality which does not wholly dissolve itself into the conceptions of our own minds'. Oppen continues:

In firm overalls
The middle-aged man sliding
Levers in the steam-shovel cab, –
Lift (running cable) and swung, back
Remotely respond to the gesture before last
Of his arms fingers continually –
Turned with the cab.

A series of mechanical shifts and gestures produces a syntax at once indeterminate in its parsing of items and at the same time emphatic in its subordination of the poem's movement to the paradoxical motions of the man and the cab (each moving differently, but at the same time, in a systematic confusion of the linear and circular). In one sense, Oppen's poem might be read as a sort of summation of the modernist poetics reviewed in this chapter, being at once about literal construction – in this case the laying of cable and the complex interaction of physical sinew and mechanical motion – and about poetics as an event of making, an event whose syntax carries everywhere the imprint of some kind of resistant otherness. 'I was', Oppen would later recall, 'even in 1929 (discrete series) consciously attempting to trace, to reproduce, the act of the world upon consciousness',[65] and it is this 'act', the perennial harbinger of the new, that literally in-forms the poem. The poetries of modernism may be various, then, but as this text by Oppen shows, they have at least one consistent strand in their use of the verbal medium to figure an 'outside' to poetic invention, an otherness which might 'resist the intelligence almost successfully' and in so doing bear authoritative witness to the new.

## NOTES

1. Ezra Pound, *The Cantos*, 4th edn (London: Faber and Faber, 1987), p. 755.
2. Pound, *The Cantos*, p. 471; Jacques Derrida, 'Che cos'è la poesia?', in Peggy Kamuf (ed.), *A Derrida Reader: Between the Blinds* (Hemel Hempstead: Harvester Wheatsheaf, 1991), pp. 229, 231. For a helpful reading of this difficult essay, see Timothy Clark, *The Theory of Inspiration: Composition as a Crisis of Subjectivity in Romantic and Post-Romantic Writing* (Manchester University Press, 1997), pp. 259–79.
3. Ezra Pound, *Literary Essays of Ezra Pound*, ed. T. S. Eliot (London: Faber and Faber, 1954), p. 154; T. S. Eliot, *Selected Essays*, 3rd edn (London: Faber and Faber, 1951) pp. 281–91; Wallace Stevens, *Collected Poetry and Prose* ed. Frank Kermode and Joan Richardson (New York: The Library of America, 1997), p. 671.
4. This characterisation of the 'new' is indebted to Derek Attridge, *The Singularity of Literature* (London: Routledge, 2004), and Timothy Clark, *The Poetics of Singularity: The Counter-Culturalist Turn in Heidegger, Derrida, Blanchot and*

*Later Gadamer* (Edinburgh University Press, 2005), though the terms used here are not always identical with theirs.

5. See, for example, Helen Sword, *Ghostwriting Modernism* (Ithaca: Cornell University Press, 2002). On the hermeticism informing modernism generally, see also Anthony Mellors, *Late Modernist Poetics: From Pound to Prynne* (Manchester University Press, 2005).

6. Walter Pater, *The Renaissance: Studies in Art and Poetry*, ed. Donald L. Hill (1873; Berkeley: University of California Press, 1980), p. 190; Arthur Symons, *The Symbolist Movement in Literature* (1899; New York: E. P. Dutton and Co, 1958), p. 94.

7. Wallace Stevens, *Collected Poetry and Prose*, p. 748.

8. Pater, *The Renaissance*, pp. 187, 198, 118, 98.

9. W. B. Yeats, *Essays and Introductions* (London: Macmillan, 1961), p. 159.

10. Pater, *The Renaissance*, p. 190.

11. Yeats, *Essays and Introductions*, pp. 15, 67.

12. Ezra Pound, *Collected Early Poems of Ezra Pound*, ed. Michael King (London: Faber and Faber, 1976), p. 71.

13. Friedrich Nietzsche, *The Will to Power: In Science, Nature, Society and Art*, trans. Walter Kaufmann and R. J. Hollingdale (New York: Random House, 1968), p. 505.

14. See Ezra Pound, 'Vorticism' (1914), reprinted in Ezra Pound, *Gaudier-Brzeska: A Memoir* (1916; New York: New Directions, 1970), p. 85: 'I began this search for the real in a book called *Personae*, casting off, as it were, complete masks of the self in each poem. I continued in a long series of translations, which were but more elaborate masks.'

15. J. Hillis Miller, *The Linguistic Moment: From Wordsworth to Stevens* (Princeton University Press, 1985); quoted in Timothy Clark, *The Theory of Inspiration*, p. 48.

16. Stéphane Mallarmé, *Selected Prose Poems, Essays and Letters*, trans. Bradford Cook (Baltimore: Johns Hopkins University Press, 1956), p. 40.

17. Eliot, *Selected Essays*, p. 21.

18. T. S. Eliot, 'Introduction: 1928', in Ezra Pound, *Selected Poems* (London: Faber and Gwyer, 1928), pp. 10–11.

19. Eliot, 'Introduction: 1928', p. 10; Pound, *Literary Essays*, p. 283.

20. Ezra Pound, *Selected Prose 1909–1965*, ed. William Cookson (New York: New Directions, 1973), p. 424.

21. Ezra Pound, *Selected Letters 1907–1941*, ed. D. D. Paige (New York: New Directions, 1971), p. 40.

22. Mina Loy, *The Lost Lunar Baedeker*, ed. Roger L. Conover (New York: Farrar, Straus and Giroux, 1996), p. 158. A suggestive comparison is Randolph S. Bourne, 'Trans-National America' (1916), in Carl Resek (ed.), *War and the Intellectuals: Collected Essays 1915–1919* (New York: Harper and Row, 1964), p. 120, which sees American internationalism as a counter to 'the indistinguishable dough of Anglo-Saxonism'.

23. Eliot, *Selected Essays*, p. 287; Stevens, *Collected Poetry and Prose*, p. 779.

24. Ezra Pound, [Review of] *Poésies 1917–1920*, by Jean Cocteau, *Dial* 70.1 (January 1921), 110.

25. Pound, 'Vorticism', p. 89. For a fuller account of relations between Futurism, Impressionism and Imagism, see my *Modernisms: A Literary Guide* (Basingstoke: Palgrave Macmillan, 1995), pp. 170–3.

26. Pound, *Literary Essays*, p. 3.

27. Pound, *Literary Essays*, pp. 4, 52, 53–4.

28. Pound, *Literary Essays*, p. 12.

29. Ezra Pound, *Personae: The Shorter Poems*, ed. Lea Baechler and A. Walton Litz (New York: New Directions, 1990), p. 111. In its first version, in *Poetry* (April 1913), the lines had extended spacing: 'The apparition   of these faces   in the crowd   : / Petals   on a wet, black   bough.' The poem was reprinted with the colon ending the first line in Pound's 1914 essay 'Vorticism' but subsequent reprintings change this to a semicolon. The *Poetry* version is reproduced in Pound, *Personae*, p. 251. For a textual history of the poem, see Randolph Chilton and Carol Gilbertson, 'Pound's "Metro" Hokku: The Evolution of an Image', *Twentieth Century Literature* 36.2 (1990), 225–36.

30. Pound, 'Vorticism', p. 89.

31. See Timothy Clark, *The Poetics of Singularity*, p. 84: 'The "*Da*" or the mere "there" to which lyric poetry gives access is necessarily very hard to describe or pin down, for it is not a matter of the perception of particular things, nor of states of mind, but something "prior", the inexplicability of what is both obvious and singular.'

32. Pound, *Personae*, pp. 110–11.

33. T. S. Eliot, *The Complete Poems and Plays* (London: Faber and Faber, 1969), p. 171.

34. Pound, *Selected Prose*, p. 21.

35. Eliot, *Selected Essays*, p. 289.

36. Pound, *The Cantos*, p. 6.

37. Eliot, *Complete Poems and Plays*, p. 67.

38. T. S. Eliot, '*Ulysses*, Order and Myth' (1923), in Frank Kermode (ed.), *Selected Prose* (London: Faber and Faber, 1975), p. 177. Eliot famously finds in myth 'a way of controlling, of ordering, of giving a shape and a significance to the immense panorama of futility and anarchy which is contemporary history'.

39. Ezra Pound, *The Spirit of Romance* (1910; New York: New Directions, 1968), p. 92.

40. Pound, *Literary Essays*, p. 431.

41. Pound's talismanic phrase first appears in his work in the 1930s, but nonetheless has a strong and clear connection to the work before this.

42. William Carlos Williams, *Imaginations*, ed. Webster Schott (New York: New Directions, 1971), p. 24.

43. Williams, *Imaginations*, p. 90; ellipsis in the original.

44. Eliot's gloss of the final line, *Complete Poems and Plays*, p. 80.

45. See William Carlos Williams, *I Wanted to Write a Poem: The Autobiography of the Works of a Poet*, ed. Edith Heal (London: Jonathan Cape, 1967), p. 60: 'I didn't originate Dadaism but I had it in my soul to write it. *Spring and All* shows that.'

46. Williams, *Imaginations*, p. 93.

47. Quoted in Bram Dijkstra, *The Hieroglyphics of a New Speech: Cubism, Stieglitz, and the Early Poetry of William Carlos Williams* (Princeton University Press,

1969), p. 9; see Stevens, *Collected Poetry and Prose*, p. 741: 'does not the saying of Picasso that a picture is a horde of destructions also say that a poem is a horde of destructions?'

48. Williams, *Imaginations*, p. 81.
49. Williams, *Imaginations*, p. 120.
50. See Pound, *Literary Essays*, p. 154; Williams, *Imaginations*, p. 111.
51. Williams, *Imaginations*, pp. 14, 116.
52. Stevens, *Collected Poetry and Prose*, p. 940.
53. Stevens, *Collected Poetry and Prose*, pp. 768, 679, 903, 665, 657.
54. Williams, *Imaginations*, p. 18; Stevens, *Collected Poetry and Prose*, p. 920.
55. Stevens, *Collected Poetry and Prose*, pp. 679, 686, 687, 686, 645, 690, 778.
56. Stevens, *Collected Poetry and Prose*, pp. 703, 701, 744.
57. Stevens, *Collected Poetry and Prose*, p. 701; my emphasis.
58. Williams, *Imaginations*, p. 120. He continues: 'Not to attempt, at that time, to set values on the words being used, according to presupposed measures, but to write down that which happens at that time.' Compare Jacques Derrida, *Dissemination*, trans. Barbara Johnson (University of Chicago Press, 1981), p. 220, on Mallarmé: 'the suspense is due only to the placement and not to the content of the words'.
59. Stevens, *Collected Poetry and Prose*, p. 701.
60. Quoted in Williams, *Imaginations*, p. 11.
61. Williams, *Imaginations*, p. 101.
62. Stevens, *Collected Poetry and Prose*, p. 910.
63. W. H. Auden, *The English Auden: Poems and Dramatic Writings, 1927–1939*, ed. Edward Mendelson (London: Faber and Faber, 1977), p. 22.
64. George Oppen, *New Collected Poems*, ed. Michael Davidson (New York: New Directions, 2002), p. 14.
65. Michael Davidson (ed.), 'An Adequate Vision: A George Oppen Daybook', *Ironwood* 26 (Fall 1985), 30.

# 4

CRISTANNE MILLER

# Gender, sexuality and the modernist poem

Debates concerning the topics of gender and sexuality were ubiquitous in the West around the turn of the century. Active women's movements throughout Europe, the British Isles and the United States brought women's legal rights and social positioning to political consciousness, and the study of sexuality fuelled the new fields of psychology and sociology, as well as being a favourite topic of the popular press. This period coined the words 'homosexuality' (first used in the USA in 1892) and 'feminism' (around 1910), and there was enormous interest in both defining and blurring boundaries between 'masculine' and 'feminine' behaviours. In the late nineteenth century, normative categories had primarily to do with gendered, not sexual, behaviour and experience – whether one manifested appropriate characteristics for a man or woman. Heterosexuality was assumed, but masculinity or femininity were the salient markers for the cultural norm, and initially also for the new sexually directed vocabulary. Sexual object choice became linked to categories of sexuality only later in the century and after a period of definitional murkiness, when individuals perceived as manifesting the general mental characteristics of the opposite sex were considered to be sexually 'inverted', 'homosexual' or belonging to a 'third-sex'.[1] Moreover, this mental state was judged according to appearance (clothes, haircut), professional choices and manner. Hence, during these decades, there was opportunity for a fluidity of personal performance or definition among categories of sexual being, even as there was increasing pressure for stricter normative and more sexually focused categorisation. The scholarship on these evolving gender and sexual normative definitions is now vast, and no aspect of modernist poetry remains untouched by them – from an understanding of individual poets' anxieties and desires in relation to their changing times, to the readings of particular poems, to analysis of the new aesthetic as it was practised and theorised by this generation of writers.

By the mid-twentieth century, however, the process of canonisation had decoupled the formal study of modernism from cultural politics and narrowed it almost entirely to literature by men. Those women marginally included were presented without reference to their extensive writing on gender, and the work of male poets dealing with gender crisis and sexuality either dropped out of favour or was read in ways ignoring gender. The study of modernist literature was hence understood only in relation to what were deemed public or intellectual (gender-neutral) historical phenomena – the First World War, the waning of Western imperialism, crises in theology and hermeneutics, urbanisation and technological innovation. Apart from noting the era's increased representation of sexual behaviour, most scholars saw gender and sexual norms as largely irrelevant to modernist poetics and took male leadership and pre-eminence for granted.

Such erasure prevented decades of readers from perceiving one of the most revolutionary aspects of modernism; namely, it was the first literary and artistic movement in which women played major roles both nationally and internationally, not just in writing modernist prose and poetry but in developing its foundational ideas and in shaping literary production through editing, publishing and financial assistance. 'Little magazines' (non-commercial, usually short-lived ventures open to experimentalism in the arts) were key to the circulation of poetry in the period, and some of the most influential such magazines were founded and edited by women.[2] Among white Americans, Harriet Monroe founded *Poetry* in 1912; Margaret Anderson and Jane Heap founded the *Little Review* in 1914; and Marianne Moore edited the *Dial* from 1925 to 1929. In a different form of editing, Amy Lowell published three anthologies of Imagist poetry between 1915 and 1917. Among African Americans, Jessie Fauset was literary editor of *Crisis* (1919 to 1926); Gwendolyn Bennett guest-edited one of the three issues of *Black Opals* and wrote a weekly literary column for *Opportunity* from 1926 to 1928; and Pauline E. Hopkins founded the *New Era* in 1916.

In England, Dora Marsden founded and edited *The Freewoman* (1911), later retitled *The Egoist* in 1914, when Harriet Weaver became editor. Literary editors for *The Egoist* included Hilda Doolittle, known as H.D. (1914–17). Also in England, Virginia Woolf founded the Hogarth Press with her husband Leonard; and H.D. and Bryher founded and, with Kenneth MacPherson, edited the first film journal in English, *Close-Up* (1927–33). In Ireland, Evelyn Gleeson founded the Dun Emer Industries and Press in 1902, renamed the Cuala Press in 1903 by Elizabeth Yeats, and managed and run entirely by women. Irish-born and New Zealand-raised Lola Ridge moved to New York and founded the Ferrer School's *Modern School* magazine in 1912, was associate editor of *Others* until 1919 and American editor of *Broom*. Taken together with presses run by American women living in Paris, these women published work by every major Anglo-American writer of the period, and they were responsible for some of the most groundbreaking early modernist publications.

Nineteenth-century ideologies of gender had defined 'separate spheres' for women's and men's work, roughly based on a private/public dichotomy and identifying motherhood and married domestic life as the realms suited to women's 'natural' talents and abilities. In contrast, early twentieth-century feminism assumed that men and women shared human characteristics and that one needed only to be competent and 'professional' to succeed in any field, although in practice many professions remained difficult for women to enter. Such thinking encouraged men and women to collaborate closely in founding and editing yet other magazines and presses, as well as founding and running theatre and arts organisations. Explorations of gender and sexual identity were among the topics shared by male and female writers, often in explicit connection with other conceptual categories undergoing thorough scrutiny during the period, especially race and class.

Predictably, the pressure of these changes in women's lives also led men to fear a loss of power and prestige. Among male writers, this preoccupation generally took the ambivalent form of simultaneous admiration for an empowered female presence or ideal and scorn for values socially defined as feminine, sometimes extending to women themselves – as in Austrian Otto Weininger's internationally popular *Sex and Character* (1903) and to a lesser extent in the theories of his compatriot Sigmund Freud.

Distinguishing masculine and feminine properties under the categories 'Man' and 'Woman' (and thereby typically blurring the line he claims to draw between gendered characteristics and actual men and women), Weininger argues that Man consists of mind and spirit whereas Woman's 'whole being, bodily and mental, is nothing but sexuality itself'.[3] In countries with strong professional arts organisations and philosophically oriented avant gardes, such as France and Germany, anxiety about loss of male privilege manifested itself in philosophical celebration of the feminine in men and intense, albeit inconsistent, misogyny, like Weininger's. In Italy, Filippo Tommaso Marinetti's 1909 'Manifesto of Futurism' declares '*We will glorify war . . . and scorn for woman*' and asserts that Futurists 'will fight moralism, feminism, every opportunistic or utilitarian cowardice'.[4] In the USA and British Isles, misogyny was typically more restrained and most male writers supported feminism in a general form. Ezra Pound and Wyndham Lewis, for example, used their 1914 *Blast* to 'BLESS' 'FEMALE QUALITIES, FEMALES' and to praise Suffragettes for their 'energy'.[5] Perhaps both for this reason and because modernist Anglo-American poetry does not begin to appear until the 1910s, female modernist poets do not exhibit the 'fear of punishment' for desiring radical gender change exhibited by turn-of-the-century prose writers like Charlotte Perkins Gilman, Kate Chopin and Edith Wharton, whose heroines commit suicide or go mad when they see the narrowness of the life choices open to them.[6] The women of 1914 – the year of Gertrude Stein's *Tender Buttons*, Mina Loy's first published poems, Anderson and Heap's founding of the *Little Review*, Marianne Moore's first serious submission of poems to little magazines and H.D.'s becoming literary editor of *The Egoist* – did not experience their choices as narrow.

Even those men most known for supporting their female peers, however, revealed misogynistic attitudes in some of their writing. Pound, for example, promoted the work of H.D. and Marianne Moore, among other women, and acted as literary advisor to a number of little magazines, but often gave female form in his poems to that which he condemned: Europe is 'an old bitch, gone in the teeth' in *Hugh Selwyn Mauberley* and female figures represent the 'aenaemic' bourgeoisie in 'The Garden' and 'Les Millwins'.[7] In 'Portrait d'une Femme', the speaker states, 'Your mind and you are our Sargasso Sea' – that is, the sea that causes shipwrecks because of its cross-currents. 'Bright ships' (presumably captained by men through these treacherous waters of relationship) have 'left you this or that in fee' but 'there is nothing! In the whole and all / Nothing that's quite your own. / Yet this is you'.[8] Woman, in short, accumulates the 'Ideas, old gossip, oddments of all things' stranded by men, defining herself wholly in relation to second-hand experience, knowledge and thought. Eliot's 'Portrait of a Lady' presents its subject as hysterically needy, with a voice like 'the insistent out-of-tune / Of a broken violin' and hands twisting the stalk of a (Whitmanian, hence sexual and phallic?) lilac. While Eliot's speaker seems somewhat embarrassed at his own role in the non-relationship, he at least escapes (like the expatriate Eliot himself) 'abroad', while the woman is 'buried' amid her 'bric-à-brac'.[9] In a private letter to Moore, Pound refers to her 'Nathaniel Hawthorne frigidities' and his own 'exquisite cockleshell' that 'calls at so many ports . . . behold me // even upon the threshold of your Presbyterian stair-turn // my lechery / capable of all altitudes'.[10] Moore's response to this letter was mild, but in a review of his *A Draft of XXX Cantos* she pointedly questions, 'is not the view of woman expressed by the Cantos older-fashioned than that of Siam and Abyssinia?'[11]

William Carlos Williams, who of all the great male modernist poets was perhaps most supportive of his female peers and respectful generally of women, wrote intensely sympathetic portraits of women, like that in 'To A Poor Old Woman // munching a plum on / the street', or the 'big young bareheaded woman' who 'pulls the paper insole' out of her shoe 'to find the nail // That has been hurting her'. In 'The Raper from Passenack', Williams may be the first poet – male or female – to present sympathetically the distress and anger of a raped woman: 'Only a man who is sick . . . would do a thing like that', she says; 'it's the foulness of it can't / be cured. And hatred, hatred of all men / – and disgust'.[12] On the other hand, Williams also participates in traditional patterns of male voyeurism and aggressive heterosexual desire. In 'The Ogre', a male speaker sends his lascivious 'thoughts . . . over and under and around' a 'sweet child, / little girl with well-shaped legs', and there is much scholarly debate about whether 'The Young Housewife' relates a scene analogous to sexual abuse. There, Williams's speaker compares the 'uncorseted' housewife he apparently sees with some frequency while driving down her street to 'a fallen leaf', after he has fantasised about her inside her house 'in negligee'; the poem ends: 'The noiseless wheels of my car / rush with a crackling sound over / dried leaves', perhaps suggesting indifference verging on violence toward the 'fallen leaf' he has just admired.[13] More explicitly, the 'Beautiful Thing' passage in Book III of *Paterson* (1949) suggests a sadistic attraction to the concept of the whored virgin, in spite of the symbolic association of this 'every-woman' with life force and poetry.

Jean Toomer's *Cane* is similarly ambivalent in its representation of black women: Toomer is sympathetic to women's sexual and economic oppression, but the women themselves tend to merge in their surreally beautiful, almost mythic function as a link for the male speaker to what he sees as a dying African-American culture. Although tenderly drawn, his women function largely in a way that would be recognisable to German Expressionists as a nostalgic return to the romantic 'eternal feminine'. In short, many aspects of traditional gender ideologies remained entrenched for this era's male poets, despite active personal and professional support for women and ambivalent celebrations of the feminine. For most male writers of the period, Pound's 'Make it New' did not apply to gender roles.

While women were also susceptible to the power of tradition, they typically battled it more self-consciously and with less ambivalence in their lives and poetry, in part because they had more to gain from a change in the status quo. H.D. reveals the greatest attraction to masculine, or phallic, power in her poetry but also insistently redefines roles for women in her retheorising of aesthetic values. In 'Eurydice', the speaker initially sees herself as passive, 'broken at last' because Orpheus has failed to free her from hell, but she proclaims defiantly at the end of the poem that turning inward for inspiration has given her 'more fervour / than you [Orpheus] . . . I have more light'. 'Sheltered Garden' declares that 'beauty without strength, / chokes out life' and instead calls for the wind to 'break, / scatter these pink-stalks, / snap off their spiced heads,' seeking 'to find a new beauty / in some terrible / wind-tortured place'.[14] The 'sheltered' woman-on-a-pedestal can produce only 'beauty without strength'; new beauty, in contrast, will come with women's experience of all aspects of life, and the new poem, she implies, should reveal women's shared experience of these forceful winds – formally in its broken sparseness as well as topically. H.D. frequently revised Greek mythology to construct narratives of psychological affiliation and liberation for women. Her *Helen in Egypt* (1961) rewrites traditional and modernist epic (like that of Pound's *Cantos*) by shifting epic focus from male-centred military and public history to spiritual/psychological exploration celebrating female power. Here H.D. defines the feminine as a crucial psychological resource for all people interested in cultural change.

Marianne Moore similarly revises aesthetic values in relation to gender. In 'Roses Only', she uses the long-standing association of women with flowers to criticise traditional female expectation. Your form, she tells women/roses, indicates that 'you must have brains'; moreover, 'if you are brilliant, it / is not because your petals are the without-which-nothing of pre-eminence'. Instead, she concludes, 'your thorns are the best part of you'. Through the connection with 'brilliance' and 'brains,' 'thorns' are revealed as those aspects of being that demonstrate intelligent independence, that protect a creative woman from 'the predatory hand' of masculine need or of her own internalised cultural expectation. 'Beauty is a liability', she states in the first line of the poem, but the combination of petals and thorns can lead to 'brilliance'.[15] In poetry as well, the highest goal should be coordination of the sharply realistic with what is imagined or felt, not the mere loveliness of petal-like lyricism. As she puts it in 'Poetry', 'genuine' poems present 'imaginary gardens with real toads in them'.[16] In her own syllabic-metred, syntactically complex verse, often brimming with traditionally unpoetic fact and allusion, Moore models the thorny and brilliant poem.

H.D.'s and Moore's calls to women to define their own capacities rather than following (male) cultural expectation resonated with the platforms of popular women's movements, and Moore even campaigned for women's suffrage. Many of her early poems, written between 1914 and 1921, in the heyday of early feminism, criticise traditional gender categories or express in a variety of ways that 'men have power / and sometimes one is made to feel it' ('Marriage').[17] At the same time, Moore's verse is optimistic in asserting that women and other economically and politically marginalised people will resist their oppression. It is equivalent to 'The Labors of Hercules', as she titles one poem, to eradicate gender, racial and social prejudice from the world but she asserts the possibility and desirability of such change. While such assertions are consonant with the manifestoes of their male contemporaries, Moore and H.D. relate the need for a new aesthetics explicitly to a transformation in women's lives. Moreover, their equation of aesthetics with social change implies the inadequacy of any poetic that isolates itself from the pressing issues of the period, similarly implying that problems of nationalism, xenophobia and world war are not wholly differentiable from acts of gender performance.

While female poets of the Harlem Renaissance produced only a small corpus of poetry, they helped shape the aesthetics of the new African-American avant garde. All black poets of this era felt that their personal success had public significance in contributing to racial uplift, but women especially struggled with the contradiction of embracing both the anti-bourgeois aesthetic of the new arts and full respect for middle-class black women, countering the grotesque 'mammy' and 'Jezebel' stereotypes.[18] Gwendolyn Bennett and Helene Johnson wrote several poems redefining and extolling a new black womanhood. Bennett's 'To a Dark Girl' places its central figure between the past of 'old forgotten queens' and slavery, calling for women self-consciously to ally themselves with their past and potential 'queenliness' and let their 'full lips laugh at Fate' despite the inevitable sorrows it will bring them.[19] Both write of female sexual desire – a particularly complex topic because of centuries of black female exploitation by white men and white imagination of them as hyper-sexualised. Their poems also refute misogynistic Harlem Renaissance representations of black women by associating natural and urban beauty with the feminine and asserting women's importance to race pride.

Gertrude Stein's *Tender Buttons* provides nothing as specific as Moore's and H.D.'s formulations of 'new beauty', but critics have read this series of highly disjunctive prose-poems as performing a feminised aesthetics. This interpretive reading relies on French psychoanalytic theory, developed by Jacques Lacan (working from Freud) and later by Luce Irigaray and Hélène Cixous, among other feminist theorists. Such theory understands language as a system developed in relation to phallic authority, the law of the father, and hence regards the 'logos' (language in its philosophical essence) as the profoundest tool of patriarchy, since it manifests the cultural order – especially as scripture and law. Language use that is 'phallogocentric' asserts its authority through set meanings, definitions and rules determining correctness. In contrast, language use that disrupts phallogocentrism may be understood as an '*écriture feminine*', a radical dissent from language-as-law. In the first poem of her collection, 'A Carafe, That Is a Blind Glass', Stein refers to 'a system to pointing. All this and not ordinary, not unordered in not resembling. The difference is spreading.'[20] Perhaps Stein indicates here that meaning is not bound – it spreads; it is reached by indirect association ('pointing'). By disposing of the usual crutches to understanding (grammar, a logical progression of ideas, pursuing one line of thought at a time), she demands newly associative cognitive processes. 'A single image is not splendor', she writes in 'A Piece of Coffee'; images in her poems come in floods, intermingled, and they are often suggestively sexual in their juxtapositions and sound-play.[21] The fact that this volume's sections are titled 'Objects', 'Food' and 'Rooms', and that all the poems work in some manner from domestic spaces and relationship, also suggests Stein's assertion that women's, and more specifically her and Alice B. Toklas's joined lesbian, lives are as much the stuff of serious poetry as any traditional epic or elegiac subject. In *Tender Buttons*, Stein divorces women's domesticity from the realm of the sentimental or private, and asserts its significance for the avant garde.

Next to Stein, British-born Mina Loy was the most formally radical English-language writer of the early 1910s, and most of her early poems constitute biting satires of gender relationship. In 'Virgins Plus Curtains Minus Dots', Loy condemns the patriarchal system of economic exchange (*dot* is French for 'dowry') that keeps women behind chained doors until their fathers marry them off: 'Nobody shouts / Virgins for sale / Yet where are our coins / For buying a purchase'.[22] In 'At the Door of the House', 'A thousand women's eyes' look at Tarot cards, 'Looking for the little love-tale / That never came true' and cannot come true as long as women are regarded as men's possessions. 'The Effectual Marriage or the Insipid Narrative of Gina and Miovanni' depicts a scholar who 'kindly kept' his wife in the kitchen: 'Of what their peace consisted', Loy comments acerbically, 'We cannot say / Only that he was magnificently man / She insignificantly a woman'.[23] At the poem's end we learn that Gina is mad, as any woman must be in a culture that so entirely subordinates her to a husband. Loy associated briefly with the Italian Futurists and even published a 'Futurist Manifesto' in 1914. During the same year, however, she also wrote a 'Feminist Manifesto' (first published in 1982), in which she commands women to 'Leave off looking to men to find out what you are **not** – seek within yourselves to find out what you **are**'; 'For the harmony of the race, each individual should be the expression of an easy & ample interpenetration of the male & female temperaments.'[24]

Ideas about gender development and blending, currently associated with a few thinkers such as Freud or Carl Jung, were pervasive during the 1910s and 1920s, and poets showed strong interest in both the thinkers and the ideas. H.D. and Bryher were friends of British sexologist Havelock Ellis, and H.D. underwent therapy with Freud. German Jewish poet Else Lasker-Schüler also knew Freud and was a friend of Magnus Hirschfeld, the most important advocate for homosexual rights of the era. Like those of many poets, however, Lasker-Schüler's ideas of an ideal mingling of masculine and feminine characteristics within the individual stemmed from the *zeitgeist*, not the work of a particular psychologist. Lasker-Schüler devoted a lifetime to attempts to break down identity categories: Jewish and German, male and female, straight and gay, spiritual and material. For several years she took the name 'Prince Yussuf (Joseph) of Thebes' and used this persona to collapse gender categories, insisting that she was simultaneously of both genders and polymorphously sexual. Several female artists and writers of this generation in Europe and the USA similarly elided gender divisions through masculine attire, using male pseudonyms, or taking masculine names or roles in their private lives. Some openly proclaimed their homosexuality. A particularly flamboyant example in the USA was blues singer and song writer Ma Rainey, whose 'Prove It on Me Blues' asserts: 'Went out last night with a crowd of my friends / They must have been women, cause I don't like no men.'

Much early feminist criticism on female poets argued for the consideration of a separate women's tradition of poetry, constructed either in parallel or in opposition to men's. Later forms of this argument refer to women's counter-strains, or oppositional discourse, within a single poetic tradition. Current studies in modernism see the aesthetic practices dominating formal experimentation in this period as including multiple overlapping strains, sometimes even within the work of a single poet. Looking at the patterns of support and cooperation among male and female poets in their various roles as editors, publishers, advisors, lovers and friends, it is clear that they saw themselves as deeply allied in the cultural work of creating new forms and concepts of art and shared aesthetic principles. Nonetheless, men's and women's particular articulation and shaping of these principles took gendered and sometimes sharply oppositional form.

While women were retheorising art in relation to changing expectations for women's lives, male poets for the most part continued to theorise in terms associated with masculinity. On the one hand, this suggests a resistance to re-examining expectations for their gender in the ways that women were reimagining theirs; on the other, their articulations did reflect changing conceptions of cultural authority and masculinity. More than any other poet of this era, Eliot makes anxieties about masculinity central to his poetry. In his notes to *The Waste Land*, he calls the hermaphroditic Tiresias 'the most important personage in the poem, uniting all the rest. . . . What Tiresias *sees*, in fact, is the substance of the poem'.[25] In the poem itself, however, the meeting of the sexes in Tiresias suggests their profound failure to (re)produce anything of value. Tiresias is 'old' and has both 'foretold' and 'foresuffered' the mechanical lovemaking between the 'young man carbuncular' and 'typist' that he witnesses, helpless to infuse meaning or affection into their encounter.[26] Elizabeth Bishop famously remarked that *The Waste Land* is 'about impotence', not symbolic, but Eliot's own: the poem both topicalises failed communication between men and women as representative of cultural sterility and expresses Eliot's anxieties about his capacity for relationship. European political instability and an increasingly consumerist popular culture are, for Eliot, of one piece with a world in which hetero-sexual men are impotent or engage in meaningless intercourse with women and cosmopolitan decadence prevails: an American man in London may be propositioned by a 'Smyrna merchant' 'in demotic French'.[27] What Tiresias witnesses is the failure of fertile intercourse at any level.

Masculine authority was imagined in various relations to male sexual-ity, just as it led to the various perceptions of women reviewed previously. According to Renée Riese Hubert, the European avant garde tended to be more heterosexual in its ideologies than were the looser groupings of Anglo-American modernism. There was a 'scarcity of gay and lesbian partnerships' in French Surrealism, and a 'similar absence of homosexuals' characterised Dada.[28] Yet, while Breton and most Surrealists condemned (especially male) homosexuality, German and Austrian Expressionists celebrated the spiritual joining of men in intense erotic friendship in an outpouring of homoerotic, and some homosexual, expression. Poet Stefan George was famous for his circle of male followers, and Kurt Hiller (who edited the first anthology of Expressionist poetry) campaigned actively for homosexual rights. Here, the bolstering of male authority was as apt to occur through recovered Greek traditions of idealised masculine beauty and love (or at least homosocial bonding) between men as within heterosexually based roles of masculine prominence.

Anxiety about masculinity was not peculiar to poets. During the last decades of the nineteenth and the first decade of the twentieth century, a discourse of aggressive masculinity pervaded many spheres. Zionists in Austria and Germany promoted a muscular Judaism, refuting stereotypes of the Jew as culturally 'feminine'. In the USA several popular books simi-larly masculinised Christianity, constructing an activist Jesus in opposition to Victorian sentimental representations of a gentle 'saviour'. Theodore Roosevelt's presidency made public an association of political leadership with rough-and-ready virility. Organisations like the Boy Scouts (founded in 1907 in Britain) encouraged the tough independence of boys. A similar masculinisation occurred in intellectual spheres. Throughout the nineteenth century, the medical profession and other branches of science distanced them-selves from both religion and folk- or communally based practices like herb-ology and midwifery, dominated by women. By the end of the century, the most authoritative cultural discourse of the West was that of technology and the 'hard' sciences, in direct contrast to the 'soft' discourses of sentiment and the body.

In this context, it is hardly surprising that male poets throughout Europe and the USA tended to theorise the principles of their verse in the language of science, mathematics and abstraction or impersonality.[29] As previously mentioned, Italian Futurists glorified technology and excoriated femininity and feeling. In his 'Dada Manifesto' of 1918, Tristan Tzara writes that 'DADA is the mark of abstraction'; 'we aren't sentimental . . . we are preparing . . . to replace tears by sirens'.[30] In the 'First Manifesto of Surrealism' (1924), André Breton defines Surrealism multiply as 'psychic automatism in its pure state', 'a war in which I am proud to be participating', and 'the "invisible ray" which will one day enable us to win out over our opponents'.[31] Eliot declares in 'Hamlet' (1919) that 'the only way of expressing emotion in the form of art is by finding an "objective correlative"; in other words, a set of objects, a situation, a chain of events which shall be the formula of that *particular* emotion.'[32] Similarly, in 'Tradition and the Individual Talent' (1919), Eliot stresses the need for 'depersonalization', a process that enables art 'to approach the condition of science' and that stems from 'a continual extinction of personality'. 'Great poetry', Eliot states, 'may be . . . composed out of feelings solely'; it is 'the intensity of the artistic process . . . that counts' in creating great art; yet the burden of his argument evokes the authority of 'formula[s]', 'the condition of science'.[33] Similarly, Pound defines Vorticism first through reference to physics and machines: a vortex 'is the point of maximum energy, / It represents, in mechanics, the greatest efficiency'. Later, he turns to mathematical language: the 'primary pigment' of a poem is an image, and the poet's 'images have a variable significance, like the signs $a$, $b$, and $x$ in algebra' not the 'fixed value' of numbers or symbols.[34] In 1919, he calls for a new poetry that is 'harder and saner . . . free from emotional slither'.[35]

In 'The Noble Rider and the Sound of Words' (1942), Wallace Stevens similarly writes that the poet's 'measure . . . is the measure of his power to abstract himself'. Later, he makes this same point borrowing language from recent discoveries in physics: 'as a wave is a force and not the water of which it is composed, which is never the same, so nobility is a force . . . . It is the imagination pressing back against the pressure of reality'.[36] In praising Moore's poetry, Stevens turns to Plato's insight that 'the only reality that mattered is exemplified best for us in the principles of mathematics'; Moore, he finds, shares Plato's asceticism. In 'The Figure of the Youth as Virile Poet' (1943), Stevens quotes William James, who writes that metaphysicians 'can't make a decision, can't buy a horse, can't do anything that befits a man'; 'For all the reasons stated by William James', he then concludes, 'we do not want to be metaphysicians.' The poet has a 'masculine nature', is 'master of our lives', hence cannot 'dwell . . . apart in his imagination, as the philosopher dwells in his reason, and as the priest dwells in his belief', but instead exercises his power in the realm of fact.[37] If poetry is like mathematics, science, fact, then it indeed has cultural status as 'virile' or masculine.

While women writing modernist poetry would have agreed with Eliot that it is 'the intensity of the artistic process, the pressure, so to speak under which the fusion takes place', that counts in poetry, and while many were personally interested in science, in theorising the new aesthetics they tended to use a language more expressive of the body, feeling and their own immediate cultural positioning.[38] Moore, for example, was an avid reader of natural history and promoted an 'X-ray-like inquisitive intensity' as the basis for poetry, calling her own poems 'Observations', but her most important essays were titled 'Humility, Concentration, and Gusto' and 'Feeling and Precision' – a combination of characteristics revealing what she felt was the necessary balance in art. Great poetry must proceed from, and in its rhythms embody, 'gusto', an intensity stemming from personal pleasure and enthusiasm. In direct discursive opposition to Pound's and Eliot's statements, Moore writes that 'art is but an expression of our needs; is feeling, modified by the writer's moral and technical insights'.[39] Similarly, in 'Notes on Thought and Vision', H.D. argues that the 'highest development' of any man or woman must result from the 'equilibrium, balance, growth of [body, mind, over-mind] at once'; physical relationships and feeling ('the love-mind') are as necessary as 'the brain' or 'over-mind' in producing art, or bringing 'the world of vision into consciousness'.[40]

Stein, whose interest in science is evident in her having attended medical school, is even more specific in opposing what she calls 'Patriarchal Poetry' in a 1927 poem-essay. Patriarchy, Stein implies, repeatedly attempts to renew 'an intermediate rectification of the initial boundary between cows and fishes. Both are admittedly not inferior in which case they may be obtained as the result of organization industry concentration assistance and matter of fact and by this this is their chance and to appear and to reunite.' Like cows and fish, men and women are different but 'both are admittedly not inferior' and the characteristics of one may be obtained by the other through 'concentration' and common sense. Much of the essay concerns itself with 'To be we' or the chance to 'reunite'. Like many of her female peers, Stein was committed to the idea of gender neutrality and women determining their own paths of development: 'Let her try. / Never to be what he said'. Later she calls for 'Patriarchal Poetry reclaimed renamed replaced and gathered together as they went in and left it more . . . letting it be a chance for them to lead to lead to lead not only by left but by leaves', and finally that 'Patriarchal Poetry might be finished to-morrow'. While Stein's grammar and word choice are often abstract, there is a distinct materiality in the way she uses words themselves, especially through her extreme repetition.[41] In her collaged phrases and repetitions, Stein points toward a moment when a new kind of poetry 'leaves' the 'Patriarchal' behind and allows those doing the 'replac[ing]' 'to lead'.

Writers like Stein, Loy, H.D. and Moore were engaged directly both with mainstream literary culture and with their male peers in dialogue about ways to understand their mutual invention of new poetic forms. While they emphasised different aspects of concern in theorising their endeavours, they found stronger points of resonance than contrast in their thinking. These women opposed themselves not primarily to their fellow poets but to a culture of masculinist authority, which they (individually and variously) linked with patriarchy, militarism, hierarchies based on gender and racial assumptions, phallogocentricism and egocentricity. While men tended to associate outmoded ideas and forms with the (feminine) bourgeoisie and women associated the out-of-date with patriarchy, they in practice regarded each other as allies in constructing new forms of expression and understanding.

Sexuality was not as explicitly theorised as gender roles in relation to aesthetics, and was less frequently the focus of poetic narrative, but sexual pleasure and desire pervade the work of this period. Heterosexual love appears in countless poems. Edna St Vincent Millay famously wrote in 'First Fig', 'My candle burns at both ends', implying the pleasures of unrestricted passion, even though it is short-lived. In 'Thursday', she acerbically comments to an apparently complaining jilted lover: 'I loved you Wednesday, – yes – but what / Is that to me?'[42] Dorothy Parker gives an equally cynical view of fidelity in heterosexual relationships in a number of acerbic verses: 'Unfortunate Coincidence' reads in its entirety: 'By the time you swear you're his / Shivering and sighing; / And he vows his passion is / Infinite, undying – / Lady, make a note of this: / One of you is lying.'[43] Much of Pound's early verse uses troubadour models to explore the role of the (male) poet as lover and political leader, and many of his Chinese and Provençal translations are poems of heterosexual longing, most spoken by men but some – like the lovely 'The River-Merchant's Wife: A Letter' – by a woman. Stevens and Williams often figure the poet/speaker/thinker as male and the world of physical beauty, sensuality and natural being as female – for example, the female park to Williams's man/city in *Paterson*, and the 'Fat girl' 'my green, my fluent mundo' in Stevens's 'Notes Toward a Supreme Fiction'.[44]

Hart Crane gives a different spin to this traditional association of woman with the physical. Although not openly homosexual in his poetry, Crane centres the energy of several poems around male bonding, as implied in 'Voyages'. There, Crane describes the sensual movement of a female sea before addressing his lover. In a section of *The Bridge* called 'The Dance', Crane represents the American continent as Pocahontas, 'thy bride immortal . . . virgin to the last of men' and, in italicised marginalia, asserts that '*your blood / remember*[s] */ its first / invasion of her / secrecy*'.[45] The most erotically charged moment of 'The Dance', however, presents the speaker's encounter with her '*chieftain / lover*'. In this fantasy of merger, the speaker partakes in Native male activity and ritual, concluding 'We danced, O Brave, we danced beyond their farms'. Such energy of bonding reaches its peak in *The Bridge* in 'Cape Hatteras', an elegy to Whitman, where Crane's speaker imagines the older gay poet with one hand 'upon my heart' and concludes 'My hand / in yours, / Walt Whitman – / so – '.[46]

Langston Hughes was considerably more guarded about his sexuality, and scholars still argue variously that he was asexual, bisexual and gay. In poems like 'When Sue Wears Red', Hughes celebrates heterosexual passion: when 'Susanna Jones' wears red, her beauty 'Burns in my heart a love-fire sharp like pain'. Like Williams, Hughes writes of women or in female voices with deep sympathy and, like Toomer, with open recognition of their economic and social oppression. In 'Cora', a woman speaks of her newly broken heart, without hope that her life will change, because 'The ones I love. / They always treat me mean'. Other poems, however, have homoerotic overtones: in 'Water-Front Streets', 'lads put out to sea / Who carry beauties in their hearts / And dreams, like me'; in 'Joy', the speaker 'went to look for Joy . . . / And I found her / Driving the butcher's cart / In the arms of the butcher boy!'[47]

Amy Lowell published poetry more openly lesbian in focus than any of her contemporaries. 'Venus Transiens', 'Vicarious' and 'A Decade' are among several poems that express Lowell's devotion to Ada Russell; in the latter, Lowell states when they first met 'the taste of you burnt my mouth with its sweetness', but 'Now you are like morning bread . . . [and] I am completely nourished.'[48] Gertrude Stein did not publish the equally celebratory 'Lifting Belly' (written around 1916) until 1957; there she writes, 'Kiss my lips. She did. / Kiss my lips again she did. / Kiss my lips over and over and over again she did. . . . Lifting belly is so kind. / Lifting belly fattily. / Doesn't that astonish you. / You did want me. / Say it again'.[49] *Tender Buttons* also centres itself in the physicality of living and women's bodies – presumably the primary point of reference for those 'Buttons'. In contrast, the bisexual H.D. published no poetry about her relationships with women, but wrote explicitly about lesbianism in prose, especially *HERmione* (1927). Lasker-Schüler so thoroughly fuses any intense relationship with physical bonding that her love poems approach the surreal: 'your diamond dreams / Cut my veins open'; 'I dig without tiring in your breast / For the golden joys of Pharaoh', she writes in 'To the Barbarian', speaking in her persona as Yussuf. As female poet writing in a male persona to a man in a love scene in which each penetrates the other, Lasker-Schüler makes traditional gender and sexual distinction impossible.

Acknowledging the centrality of gender and sexual concerns to the poetry of this period transforms an understanding of the poets, poetry and aesthetics of modernism. Poems and essays not typically collected or anthologised become central to discussion of the period, as is the case with Moore's 'Roses Only', Stein's 'Patriarchal Poetry' and Loy's 'Feminist Manifesto'. Canonical poems by men like *The Waste Land* and *The Cantos* enjoy increasingly complex readings when understood in relation to contemporary gender pressures on men and women, and in relation to the poetry and theories of their female peers. Similarly, the (sexual and homosocial) relationships of male and female poets are understood in new and more nuanced ways in relation to their verse. Finally, modernist poetry itself is more clearly seen as resulting from the radical changes of gender expectation and sexual definition transforming men's and women's lives during the early twentieth century as well as from the social changes produced by new technologies, the rise of the metropolis and from the horrors of world war. For the male and female writers of this period, issues of gender and sexuality were not isolated from other aspects of their worlds and thought. Study of modernist poetry now increasingly recognises that crucial integration.

## NOTES

1. On the history of gender and sexuality, see Nancy Cott, *The Grounding of Modern Feminism* (New Haven: Yale University Press, 1987); George Chauncey, *Gay New York: Gender, Urban Culture, and the Making of the Gay Male World 1890–1940* (New York: Basic Books, 1994), pp. 13, 47–9; Laura L. Behling, *The Masculine Woman in America, 1890–1935* (Urbana: University of Illinois Press, 2001); and James W. Jones, *'We of the Third Sex': Literary Representations of Homosexuality in Wilhelmine Germany* (Frankfurt: Peter Lang, 1990).
2. The best single source on female editorial work is Jayne E. Marek's *Women Editing Modernism: 'Little' Magazines and Literary History* (Lexington: University Press of Kentucky, 1995). On American women's modernist activities across the spectrum of the arts, see Cristanne Miller, 'Marianne Moore and the Women Modernizing New York', *Modern Philology* 98.2 (2000), 339–62.
3. *Geschlecht und Charakter* (1903; Munich: Matthes and Seitz, 1980), p. 217.
4. F. T. Marinetti, 'The Founding and Manifesto of Futurism', in Vassiliki Kolocotroni et al. (eds), *Modernism: An Anthology of Sources and Documents* (University of Chicago Press, 1998), p. 251.
5. Wyndham Lewis (ed.), *Blast 1: Review of the Great English Vortex* (1914; Santa Barbara: Black Sparrow, 1981), pp. 27, 151.
6. This is a primary theme of Marianne DeKoven's essay 'Modernism and Gender' in Michael Levenson (ed.), *The Cambridge Companion to Modernism* (Cambridge University Press, 1999), pp. 174–93.

7. Ezra Pound, *Personae: The Shorter Poems*, ed. Lea Baechler and A. Walton Litz (New York: New Directions, 1990), pp. 188, 85, 94.

8. Pound, *Personae*, pp. 57–8.

9. T. S. Eliot, *Complete Poems and Plays* (London: Faber and Faber, 1969), pp. 19, 20.

10. Quoted in Bonnie Kime Scott, *The Gender of Modernism: A Critical Anthology* (Urbana: Indiana University Press, 1990), p. 364.

11. Marianne Moore, *Complete Prose*, ed. Patricia C. Willis (New York: Viking, 1986), p. 272.

12. William Carlos Williams, *Collected Poems*, vol. I, *1909–1939*, ed. A. Walton Litz and Christopher MacGowan (New York: New Directions, 1986), pp. 383, 384, 385, 386.

13. Williams, *Collected Poems*, vol. I, pp. 95, 57. Marjorie Perloff reviews the argument on both sides of this debate in *The Dance of the Intellect: Studies on Poetry in the Pound Tradition* (Cambridge University Press, 1985). See also Linda Kinnahan, *Poetics of the Feminine: Literary Tradition and Authority in William Carlos Williams, Mina Loy, Denise Levertov, and Kathleen Fraser* (Cambridge University Press, 1994).

14. H.D., *Collected Poems 1912–1944*, ed. Louis Martz (New York: New Directions, 1983), pp. 54, 55, 20, 21.

15. Marianne Moore, *Becoming Marianne Moore: The Early Poems, 1907–1924*, ed. Robin G. Schulze (University of California Press, 2002), p. 83.

16. Moore, *Becoming Marianne Moore*, p. 73.

17. Moore, *Becoming Marianne Moore*, p. 120.

18. On Harlem Renaissance female poets, see Nina Miller, *Making Love Modern: The Intimate Public Worlds of New York's Literary Women* (Oxford University Press, 1998), and Gloria T. Hull, *Color, Sex, and Poetry: Three Women Writers of the Harlem Renaissance* (Bloomington: Indiana University Press, 1987). The best collection of their work remains Maureen Honey (ed.), *Shadowed Dreams: Women's Poetry of the Harlem Renaissance* (Brunswick: Rutgers University Press, 1989).

19. Cary Nelson et al. (eds), *Anthology of Modern American Poetry* (New York: Oxford University Press, 2000), p. 528.

20. Gertrude Stein, *Writings 1903–1932*, ed. Catharine R. Stimpson and Harriet Chessman (New York: The Library of America, 1998), p. 313.

21. Stein, *Writings 1903–1932*, p. 315.

22. Loy, *The Lost Lunar Baedeker*, ed. Roger L. Conover (New York: Farrar, Straus and Giroux, 1996), p. 22.

23. Loy, *Lost Lunar Baedeker*, pp. 33, 35, 36, 37.

24. Loy, *Lost Lunar Baedeker*, pp. 154, 155.

25. Eliot, *The Complete Poems and Plays*, p. 78.

26. Eliot, *The Complete Poems and Plays*, pp. 68–9.

27. Eliot, *The Complete Poems and Plays*, p. 68.

28. Renée Riese Hubert, *Magnifying Mirrors: Women, Surrealism, and Partnership* (Lincoln: University of Nebraska Press, 1994), p. 1. On the male bias of early Surrealism, see Susan Suleiman, *Subversive Intent: Gender, Politics, and the Avant-Garde* (Cambridge, Mass.: Harvard University Press, 1990).

29. Lisa Steinman, *Made in America: Science, Technology, and American Modernist Poets* (New Haven: Yale University Press, 1987) is the best work on this subject.

30. Tristan Tzara, 'Dada Manifesto', in Kolocotroni et al. (eds), *Modernism*, p. 277.

31. André Breton, 'First Manifesto of Surrealism', in Kolocotroni et al. (eds), *Modernism*, pp. 307, 311.

32. T. S. Eliot, *Selected Essays*, 3rd edn (London: Faber and Faber, 1951), p. 145.

33. Eliot, *Selected Essays*, pp. 17, 18, 17.

34. Lewis (ed.), *Blast*, p. 153; Ezra Pound, 'Vorticism' (1914), reprinted in Ezra Pound, *Gaudier-Brzeska; A Memoir* (1916; New York: New Directions, 1970), pp. 84, 88.

35. Ezra Pound, 'A Retrospect', in Kolocotroni et al. (eds), *Modernism*, p. 378.

36. Wallace Stevens, *Collected Poetry and Prose*, ed. Frank Kermode and Joan Richardson (New York: The Library of America, 1997), pp. 657, 665.

37. Stevens, *Collected Poetry and Prose*, pp. 700, 679, 685.

38. Eliot, *Selected Essays*, p. 19.

39. Moore, *Collected Prose*, p. 402.

40. H.D., 'Notes on Thought and Vision', in Kolocotroni et al. (eds), *Modernism*, pp. 383, 385.

41. Stein, *Writings 1903–1932*, pp. 571–2, 575, 582, 601.

42. Edna St Vincent Millay, *Collected Poems* (New York: Harper & Row, 1956), pp. 127, 129.

43. Nelson et al. (eds), *Anthology of Modern American Poetry*, p. 333.

44. Stevens, *Collected Poetry and Prose*, p. 351.

45. Hart Crane, *The Complete Poems and Selected Letters and Prose of Hart Crane*, ed. Brom Weber (New York: Doubleday & Company, 1966), pp. 74, 71.

46. Crane, *The Complete Poems*, pp. 93, 95.

47. Langston Hughes, *The Collected Poems of Langston Hughes*, ed. Arnold Rampersad (New York: Vintage, Random House, 1994), pp. 30, 119, 96, 63.

48. Amy Lowell, *Selected Poems*, ed. Melissa Bradshaw and Adrienne Munich (Brunswick: Rutgers University Press, 2002), p. 62.

49. Stein, *Writings 1903–1932*, p. 425.

# PART II

# Authors and alliances

# 5

## LAWRENCE RAINEY

# Pound or Eliot: whose era?

'Our age beyond any doubt has been, and will continue to be, the Age of Eliot', wrote the novelist and critic Conrad Aiken in a commemorative essay which appeared shortly after T. S. Eliot's death in 1965.[1] Opinion on the other side of the Atlantic concurred: the headline over Eliot's obituary in the London *Times* declared him 'The Most Influential English Poet of His Time'.[2] Consensus so uniform inevitably invites dissent, and it was only six years later that the distinguished critic Hugh Kenner published a provocative and influential book, one still essential for anyone striving to assess Anglo-American modernism. Its title, *The Pound Era*, implicitly repudiated the widespread belief that Eliot had dominated his age.[3] It was Ezra Pound, instead, who had reshaped the poetic and literary sensibility of a generation.

Four decades later, a reader may legitimately wonder which of these arresting figures was truly the major poet of his time. Yet to pose that question in that way may also obscure more than it illuminates. For what does it mean to declare that one poet or another was 'the poet of his age'? Would it be a strictly historical statement, a question of how many readers preferred or even purchased the works of either? Would it be a matter, say, of counting up the number of book reviews and news items that featured one or the other? Or a matter, say, of somehow measuring influence, totalling the number of imitators that later gathered around either? There are countless ways that we might reformulate that question, but one good starting point might be to reconsider the decade that was most plainly the era of neither, or perhaps of both – the decade when Pound and Eliot collaborated to achieve a profound transformation in the conventions of modern poetry, the years 1914 to 1923.

Ezra Pound moved to London in the autumn of 1908. T. S. Eliot arrived there six years later, in the autumn of 1914. As it so happened, Conrad Aiken, Eliot's friend from his student days at Harvard, was also in London. Still captivated by the unpublished poems that Eliot had completed back in 1911, Aiken had recently offered two of them ('Prufrock' and 'La Figlia Che Piange') to Harold Monro, editor of *Poetry and Drama*, then the principal journal for new poetry in England. Monro had dismissed both as 'absolutely insane'.[4] Undaunted, Aiken now urged Eliot to visit someone else whom he had met over the summer, the American poet Ezra Pound: 'You go to Pound. Show him your poems.'[5] On 22 September, Eliot called on Pound and introduced himself, and a few days later sent him a selection of poems. 'Then in 1914 . . . my meeting with Ezra Pound changed my life. He was enthusiastic about my poems, and gave me such praise and encouragement as I had long since ceased to hope for. Pound urged me to stay . . . and encouraged me to write verse again.'[6] By the end of the month Pound was promising Eliot that he would get 'Prufrock' published in *Poetry*, the Chicago magazine started in 1912 by Harriet Monroe and already the most prominent journal for new poetry in the United States. 'He wants me to bring out a Vol. after the War', Eliot enthused to Aiken in late September.[7]

The Ezra Pound whom Eliot met in 1914 was not only a poet, but a cultural impresario whose skills had been honed in the cultural debates that shook London during the period 1912–14. The catalyst of those debates had been Filippo Tommaso Marinetti, the founder of Futurism.[8] With the opening of the first exhibition of Futurist paintings in London in March 1912, accompanied by a sensational media campaign which included Marinetti's manifestoes and dramatic lectures, the question of what it might mean for art to be modern had acquired new urgency. Marinetti had turned a systematic assessment of contemporary change into the theoretical basis for a coherent aesthetics that could represent the modern world across a range of arts and media, promulgating both aesthetics and paradigmatic works through the medium of a novel intellectual formation, a collectivity buttressed by publicity and theatricality.[9]

Pound's initial response had been the formation of a literary 'school' called Imagism, launched in late 1912 and early 1913, one that welcomed brevity and 'precision' while damning 'interminable effusions'.[10] Imagism turned out to be a hesitant and uncertain project. It rejected the notion of 'a revolutionary school' or any suggestion 'that one writes poetry to a theory', echoing contemporary reviewers who had condemned the Futurist paintings as 'rather a theoretic extension than a spontaneous development'.[11] Not only was Imagism anti-programmatic; it also shunned the collective identity cultivated by Futurism. Instead it represented a more informal, more casual gathering that occurred when 'two or three young men agree, more or less, to call certain things good'. Viewed as a blueprint for cultural activism, its scope was narrow, anti-theoretical, and devoid of the sociohistorical sweep that characterised Futurism. Who, after all, would want to defend 'interminable effusions'? And because the 'school' lacked a journal or other forum in which to develop, it lacked institutional focus. The result was predictable.

In September 1913 the journal *Poetry and Drama* devoted an entire issue to Futurism, one that included the translation of a new manifesto by Marinetti, thirty pages of poems by himself and his colleagues, and a reflective editorial that assayed his significance for the contemporary cultural scene. Tellingly, the previous issue had devoted only two paragraphs to Imagism.

By March 1914, when the first anthology of Imagist poetry (*Des Imagistes*) was at last published in New York, Imagism was limping towards its demise. By now plans were well advanced for a new magazine that would be called *Blast* and edited by the artist Wyndham Lewis (with financing from a young woman named Kate Lechmere). The first number, published on 1 July 1914 (some twelve weeks before Eliot and Pound's first encounter), trumpeted the creation of a new movement, Vorticism – an announcement that tacitly implied an end to Pound's involvement with Imagism. It did so with truculent manifestoes that owed much to Marinetti's example, and for contemporary reviewers the similarities were many and obvious, despite the pains that both Lewis and Pound had taken to criticise Marinetti and distinguish their movement from his.[12]

Perversely, Imagism, far from withering away, was suddenly propelled in a totally unforeseen direction. Amy Lowell, the wealthy heiress of a prominent New England family and the contributor of a single poem to *Des Imagistes*, now turned up in London at just the moment when *Blast* was an object of controversy. Invited to a dinner on 15 July to celebrate *Blast*'s publication, she bridled at several perceived slights by Pound's associates. She resolved to set up a rival faction of Imagism which would publish its own anthology, to be called *Some Imagist Poets*, and allow contributors to select their own poems rather than submit them to anyone's editorial judgement (such as that which Pound had exercised over the volume *Des Imagistes*).[13] Buttressed by Lowell's considerable talents as a publicist, the later Imagism proved so successful that it became the Koīne of modern poetry during the period 1915–20, free verse tied to direct treatment and sincerity.

This complex play of competing forces – Futurism, early Imagism, Vorticism, and later Imagism (or 'Amygism', as Pound disparaged it) – was rendered still more complex by Pound's overlapping editorial roles. In 1914 he was still serving as 'Foreign Editor' of *Poetry* (Chicago). He was also acting as an informal advisor to *The Egoist*, a London bimonthly publication devoted to advancing an uneasy melange of extreme individualist, feminist and libertarian thought, and in that role he had brought about the serial publication of James Joyce's first novel, *A Portrait of the Artist as a Young Man*. (The first instalment had appeared on 2 February 1914; the last would appear on September 1915.) When his role as Foreign Editor of *Poetry* ended in 1915, Pound began to search for another journal that could provide an outlet for new materials. With funds ($2,350 per year) provided by a committee of donors organised by New York lawyer and cultural patron John Quinn, Pound reached an agreement with the *Little Review* that would allow him to edit an independent section within that journal, pay contributors' fees and even give himself a modest salary of £60 per year.[14] Here, from 1917 to 1919, Pound would publish poems by Eliot, the novel *Tarr* by Wyndham Lewis and the first thirteen episodes (of eighteen) of Joyce's *Ulysses*.

Pound and Eliot were very different personalities. Pound was outgoing and ebullient, and his self-confident judgements could slip into obiter dicta that seemed tactless, arrogant or simply offensive. In worldly affairs he was reckless, perennially trusting that something would turn up to keep him going. Some four months before Eliot's arrival, he had married Dorothy Shakespear on the understanding that she would receive an annual income from her family that would suffice for her needs, while Pound would have to earn his own income. He was not, in other words, obliged to earn a steady income, but could survive in a bohemian fashion by patching together occasional royalties, payments for essays, gifts from his parents, or revenues earned for editorial services of one sort or another. Eliot, instead, was reserved and diffident; he was also prudent and cautious, and was deeply instilled with a work ethic which made it impossible for him to accept the uncertainties of journalism and patronage that attended Pound. When Eliot married Vivien Haigh Wood in June 1915, some nine months after his arrival in England, he promptly set about finding a regular job, though it would take another twenty months before he found a satisfactory position with Lloyds Bank in early 1917.

As writers, too, Pound and Eliot were also quite different, at least when they first met in 1914. Their differences can be described in many ways, but as a first step we can compare two poems written at roughly the same time, the period 1911–12, assaying their different uses of those fundamental components of poetry: rhythm, diction and syntax. Consider Pound's poem 'The Return', first published in 1912 (all italics are mine, for emphasis). It begins with a visionary moment in which ancient gods and heroes, not further identified, are returning to the present:

> *See, they return*; ah, *see the tentative*
> Movement, and the slow feet,
> The trouble in the pace and the uncertain
> Wavering!
>
> *See, they return*, one, and by one,          5
> With fear, as half-awakened;

At line 10 the poem abruptly shifts from their returning in the present tense to a meditation on their vanished glory in the past tense, concluding:

> Haie!   Haie!                                        15
>     *These were the* swift to harry;
> *These the* keen-scented;
> *These were the* souls of blood.
>
> Slow on the leash,
>     pallid the leash-men.[15]        20

At the beginning of the poem, a speaker who is fascinated by the unfolding spectacle addresses himself and unidentified companions with repeated injunctions ('See, they return' (1, 5) and 'see the tentative / Movement' (1–2)), while the gods and heroes themselves seem bewildered at their own return to the world of the present. As if still drowsy with the sleep of centuries, their movements are all 'tentative' (1), 'uncertain' (3), 'wavering' (4), advancing 'with fear' (6). At line 10 the poem shifts from the present tense to the past, and with that shift comes a change in diction, which now bristles with phrasing that recalls Homeric epic ('the "Wing'd-with-Awe"' (10), or 'Gods of the wingèd shoe' (12)) or echoes the ecstatic note of ancient Greek ('Haie! Haie!' (15)), establishing a firm contrast between the pallid state of these beings in the present and their vitality in the past. Counterpointing this contrast in diction is another change in syntax: the speaker's fascinated injunctions give way to the repetition of a demonstrative pronoun ('these') that is connected by a copula to the epithets that follow: 'These were the . . .' (lines 10, 16, 18). Yet the verb 'to be' is often deemed the weakest and least vivid in the English language, and one might argue that the three instances of 'These were the . . .' inadvertently undermine the contrast between pallid present and vital past which the poem otherwise strives to establish. Still, it could be argued instead that the understated character of 'were' only acts as a foil to the epithets that follow, so enhancing the larger antithesis of present and past. In either case, syntax is being sacrificed in favour of rhythm: in the second half of the poem all but two of its eleven lines begin with an accented syllable, so that rhythm now becomes the primary vehicle for the contrast being drawn by the poem. Rhythm, to be sure, is acting in concert with other rhetorical devices, in this case the use of anaphora (or the repetition of the same word or words at the beginning of successive sentences: 'These were the . . .' and 'These the . . .'). But, since the repeated words no longer perform a strictly communicative or semantic function, that having been exhausted in their first utterance, they assume a rhythmic function, so much so that rhythm itself can seem to be the poem's theme, the vital rhythms that throbbed in the past set off against the uncertain pulse that appears in the visionary moment of the present. To achieve that, syntax is assigned a much smaller role within the poem's rhetoric than either diction or rhythm, while the role of rhythm is enhanced at its expense. In the poem's closing lines, syntax vanishes in favour of pure juxtaposition: 'Slow on the leash, / Pallid the leash-men'.

If we compare 'The Return' with a portion of 'The Love Song of J. Alfred Prufrock', completed a year earlier in the summer of 1911, we discern some critical differences. Consider two verse-paragraphs from the poem's third part, as Prufrock reaches a crisis in his deliberations:

> And would it have been worth it, after all,
> After the cups, the marmalade, the tea,
> Among the porcelain, among some talk of you and me,
> Would it have been worth while,
> To have bitten off the matter with a smile,                   5
> To have squeezed the universe into a ball
> To roll it toward some overwhelming question,
> To say: 'I am Lazarus, come from the dead,
> Come back to tell you all, I shall tell you all'–
> If one, settling a pillow by her head,                        10
>     Should say: 'That is not what I meant at all.
>     That is not it, at all.'
>
> And would it have been worth it, after all,
> Would it have been worth while,
> After the sunsets and the dooryards and the
>                        sprinkled streets,                      15
> After the novels, after the teacups, after the
>                        skirts that trail along the floor–
> And this, and so much more?–
> It is impossible to say just what I mean!
> But as if a magic lantern threw the nerves in
>                        patterns on a screen:
> Would it have been worth while                                20
> If one, settling a pillow or throwing off a shawl,
> And turning toward the window, should say:
>     'That is not it at all,
>     That is not what I meant, at all.'[16]                     24

Though we could reduce the complexity of these verse-paragraphs by fore-grounding their grammatical skeleton ('Would it have been worth while . . . If one . . . should say: "That is not what I meant, at all."'), doing so would strip away the dreamy and compulsive repetitions, substitutions and displacements. What are lines 1 and 4 in the first verse-paragraph reappear in the second as lines 1–2. What in the first paragraph is a prepositional phrase that takes up the entire second line ('After the cups, the marmalade, the tea') is reformulated in the next verse-paragraph into something swollen over two lines: 'After the sunsets and the dooryards and the sprinkled streets, / After the novels, after the teacups, after the skirts that trail along the floor'. And, as if to betray the compulsive gaze that focuses on those 'skirts that trail along the floor', the syntax then breaks away into an independent clause ('It is impossible to say just what I mean!') followed by an adversative clause that is both a non sequitur and a painfully lucid self-assessment ('But as if a magic lantern threw the nerves in patterns on a screen') before using repetition to resume the original train of thought ('Would it have been worth while . . .'). Syntax, here, complements rhythm and diction to create textured and contradictory effects that defy easy summary: complex hypotheticals and conditionals signal an engagement with the world that Prufrock has never had and will never truly have, while digressive prepositional phrases skirt with compulsive avoidance before fixating on a metonym for the source of Prufrock's terror ('after the skirts that trail along the floor'). Viewed in terms of how the two poets deploy poetry's fundamental components, Pound tends to foreground the elements of diction and rhythm and to minimise that of syntax, whereas Eliot uses keeps all three in a complex and constantly shifting interaction.

During the first stage of their collaboration, from 1914 to 1917, emphasis fell on Pound's efforts to draw attention to Eliot's work and get his early poems published in an independent volume, a stage that effectively ended when *Prufrock and Other Observations* (1917) was published by the Egoist Press in London, its costs underwritten by a secret subsidy, which Pound himself furnished. The second stage, which lasted from 1917 to 1920, was marked by a more direct collaboration, as Pound recalled in 1932:

> That is to say, at a particular date in a particular room, two authors, neither engaged in picking the other's pocket, decided that the dilutation of *vers libre*, Amygism, Lee Masterism, general floppiness had gone too far and that some counter-current must be set going. . . . Remedy prescribed, *Émaux et Camées* (or the Bay State Hymn Book). Rhyme and regular strophes.
>
> Results: Poems in Mr. Eliot's *second volume*, not contained in his first . . . also 'H. S. Mauberley.'[17]

Pound's recollection cites 'Amygism' and 'Lee Masterism' (the latter being the vogue for Edgar Lee Masters that followed the extraordinary success of his *Spoon River Anthology*, first published 1915)[18] as indices of popular taste, juxtaposing both against *Émaux et Camées* (Enamels and Cameos), the title of a collection of poems first published in 1852 by the French poet Théophile Gautier (1811–72). Gautier's carefully chiselled poems, his detachment from subjective emotions, and his cultivation of external appearances rather than individual psychology had represented a protest against the combination of careless verse and indulgent self-pity that typified Romantic followers of Alfred de Musset (1810–57) – counterparts to the contemporary practitioners of 'Amygism, Lee Masterism'. Gautier's octosyllabic lines in quatrains offered a form that could prove a testing ground for something different, and, for Eliot, always devoted to Baudelaire, it was high praise that Gautier had later received the dedication of his *Fleurs du mal* (1857). But Eliot himself later recalled this moment in terms less polemical than Pound's: 'We studied Gautier's poems and then we thought, "Have I anything to say in which this form will be useful?" And we experimented. The form gave the impetus to the content.' Writing in 1918, Eliot also commented:

> Technique . . . can only be learned, the more difficult part of it, by absorption. Try to put into a sequence of simple quatrains the continuous syntactic variety of Gautier or Blake, or compare these two with A. E. Housman. Surely professionalism in art is hard work on style with singleness of purpose.[19]

For Eliot, this 'hard work' resulted in seven poems, sometimes called 'the quatrain poems', that were published between the summer of 1917 and that of 1919.[20] For Pound, instead, it led to motifs discernible in 'Moeurs Contemporaines', an unsuccessful attempt at social satire, and *Hugh Selwyn Mauberley* (1920), for many critics Pound's finest poem. The quatrain poems, for Eliot, became an experiment in a new poetics of extremism. Consider the opening of 'Whispers of Immortality', a poem structured by ironic juxtaposition into two parts:

> Webster was much possessed by death
> And saw the skull beneath the skin;
> And breastless creatures under ground
> Leaned backward with a lipless grin.
>
> Daffodil bulbs instead of balls           5
> Stared from the sockets of the eyes!
> He knew that thought clings round dead limbs
> Tightening its lusts and luxuries.

Then there is the beginning of the second part:

Grishkin is nice; her Russian eye
Is underlined for emphasis;
Uncorseted, her friendly bust
Gives promise of pneumatic bliss.                    20

The couched Brazilian jaguar
Compels the scampering marmoset
With subtle effluence of cat;
Grishkin has a maisonette.[21]

This is poetry that is being structured by violent contrasts, both at macro- and micro-levels. The disjuncture between the moral extremism of Webster and the ethical flaccidity of Grishkin divides the poem into its two main parts. But within the section devoted to Grishkin there is another antithesis between Grishkin and the jaguar, or on a still smaller level between the learned 'pneumatic' and the plebeian 'bliss'. While traces of a speaker appear in the poem, it would be difficult or impossible to give a psychological portrait of him. The tone is arch, cold, impersonal, and the point of view is resolutely focused on the external, with a relishing of the macabre – a deliberate assault on the conventions that cherished direct treatment and sincerity as the touchstones of genuine poetry, protocols of the period's free verse. The movement of thought is rapid, while the unlikely rhymes call attention to themselves as artefacts that are made, not found. Ironies become so expansive that they engulf the entire poem, and here too are the techniques that will later structure *The Waste Land*: 'abrupt juxtapositions, the reliance on temporal oppositions, the rapid shifts in point of view, the impersonal voice and the more tightly controlled rhythms'.[22] The poem's grim machinery devours its prey without pity.

Compare Pound's use of the quatrain in a section from his long poem *Hugh Selwyn Mauberley*:

The tea-rose tea-gown, etc.
Supplants the mousseline of Cos,
The pianola 'replaces'
Sappho's barbitos.

Christ follows Dionysus,
Phallic and ambrosial
Made way for macerations;
Caliban casts out Ariel.

All things are a flowing,
Sage Heracleitus says;
But a tawdry cheapness
Shall outlast our days.

> Even the Christian beauty
> Defects – after Samothrace;
> We see τὸ καλόν
> Decreed in the market place.

The section ends with biting irony:

> O bright Apollo,
> τίν' ἄνδρα, τίν' ἥρωα, τινα θεόν,
> What god, man, or hero
> Shall I place a tin wreath upon![23]

Pound's use of the quatrain in this sample is not governed by an overarching antithesis that gives the section a comprehensive structure. Instead the quatrains unfold as autonomous units in a list of denunciations, one that draws a stark, even static contrast between the sexual and aesthetic vitality of the pagan past ('Phallic and ambrosial') and a present still subject to the life-denying ethos of Christianity. But, as if uncertain whether this contrast can bear the explanatory weight which is being put on it, one quatrain growls about 'tawdry cheapness' while still another damns 'the market place', as if conflating Christianity and capitalism. And confusion is compounded when one asks how Caliban, the pre-Christian and earthy 'native' who inhabits an island in Shakespeare's *Tempest*, can serve as a figure for Christianity. Of course the extreme constraints of such short lines (only five to seven syllables) require a simplified syntax; but the succession of short clauses in the indicative mood creates a tone oscillating between disciplined denunciation and tiresome repetition. Rhythm and diction, as earlier in 'The Return', take precedence, but a precedence that seems to be being achieved at the cost both of syntactic and intellectual complexity.

By the time that *Hugh Selwyn Mauberley* was published in June 1920, Pound had already moved away from London and settled in Paris. The third and most dramatic stage of the collaboration transpired with him and Eliot living in different cities – and under the shadow of looming change. As Eliot wrote to John Quinn at the beginning of 1920, describing Pound:

> The fact is that there is now no organ of any importance in which he can express himself, and he is becoming forgotten. It is not enough for him to publish a volume of verse once a year – or no matter how often – for it will not be reviewed and will be killed by silence. . . . I know that Pound's lack of tact has done him great harm. But I am worried as to what is to become of him.[24]

Though Pound soon found employment as a talent scout working for the *Dial* out of Paris, with his salary secretly furnished by John Quinn, his growing isolation and financial insecurities would worsen in the years ahead.

Eliot, instead, completed his first book of criticism, *The Sacred Wood*, in June 1920, and then, after a hiatus of six months consumed by personal matters, entered into a period of extraordinary creative activity. Late in January 1921, he wrote the first in a series of 'London Letters', intended to furnish the American readers of the *Dial* with news about the London literary scene. Over the next year, while also writing *The Waste Land*, Eliot would write ten essays: four were 'London Letters'; three treated poets of the seventeenth century (Andrew Marvell, John Dryden and the Metaphysical poets), published in the *Times Literary Supplement*; and three covered caricature, the heritage of Baudelaire and the difference between prose and poetry.[25] Together these essays present the discontinuous yet coherent outline of an aesthetics of the histrionic, a hyperbolic idiom of wildness and ferocity. One key term in Eliot's critical vocabulary is 'surprise', a term he stresses again and again. Praising Marvell's 'high speed' and 'succession of concentrated images', he observes how these are then exploited: 'When this process has been carried to the end and summed up, the poem turns suddenly with that surprise which has been one of the most important means of poetic effect since Homer.' Citing another passage by Marvell, Eliot remarks: 'There is here the element of *surprise* . . . the surprise which Poe considered of the highest importance, and also the restraint and quietness of tone which makes the surprise possible.' Writing when well into work on Part II of *The Waste Land*, he lauds Dryden for offering 'the most sustained display of surprise after surprise of wit from line to line . . . something very near to parody', while in the same essay he dismisses a passage by another poet for lacking 'the element of *surprise* so essential to poetry'. Writing in mid-June, while working on the first half of Part III, Eliot reformulates his view: 'The strange, the surprising, is of course essential to art . . . The craving for the fantastic, for the strange, is legitimate and perpetual; everyone with a sense of beauty has it.' The strange, the surprising, the fantastic, something very near to parody . . . in a word, histrionics. Other terms, cognate in meaning, also preoccupy Eliot – among them 'ferocity'. Praising Marie Lloyd, the music-hall star, he commends her possession of 'wit' that is 'mordant, ferocious'. Citing another music-hall star whom he admired, Eliot writes: 'The fierce talent of Nellie Wallace . . . holds the most boisterous music hall in complete subjection.' He finds some contemporary caricatures compelling because 'They have some of the old English ferocity', and relishes Baudelaire's dictum concerning caricature: 'Pour trouver du comique féroce et très-féroce, il faut passer la Manche' ('To find comedy that is ferocious and very ferocious, one has to cross the English Channel').[26] A related if more muted term is 'intensity' and the cognate words 'intense' and 'intensify', which appear twenty-one times in Eliot's essays from the first half of 1921.[27] But Eliot also deploys another term far more extreme than 'intensity'. He celebrates the Metaphysical poets because in their works 'the most heterogeneous ideas are yoked by violence together'. He rates Baudelaire above Dryden because he 'could see profounder possibilities in wit, and in violently joined images'. And he enthusiastically adopts Baudelaire's view on what distinguishes English comedy: 'le signe distinctif de ce genre de comique était la violence' ('The distinctive sign of this kind of comedy was violence').[28] Ferocity, intensity, violence – companions to the strange, the surprising, the fantastic, something very near to parody. Little wonder that Eliot's essays of the time also show him so responsive to caricature and music hall, modes of cultural production which thrive on wild exaggeration, a *bizarrerie* of likeness and illusion, a grotesque machinery of extremism. Here was the aesthetics that informed his writing of *The Waste Land* over the course of 1921.

On 2 January 1922, Eliot turned up in Paris, bringing the sheaf of typescripts, drafts and autograph fair copies which he had assembled over the last year for a long poem. When he submitted these to Ezra Pound for advice and suggestions, what transpired is widely recognised as one of the greatest acts of editorial intervention on record. With uncanny insight, Pound urged Eliot to remove the large tracts of narrative that then furnished the beginning to Parts I, III and IV of the poem: a 54-line sequence which depicted a rowdy night on the town in Boston; an 89-line sequence, written in couplets imitating those of Pope, that described the activities of Fresca, a wealthy London socialite; an 83-line account of the final voyage of Phlebas. He pruned another 27 lines from the central scene in Part III, which recounts the tryst of the unnamed typist and 'the young man carbuncular', and also made another 200 minor editorial changes, typically altering isolated words and phrases.[29]

Pound's editorial interventions helped shape the poem into the work of wild, irredeemable fury that we know today. His deletion of the three narratives meant that the poem lacked the kind of spatio-temporal and logical-causal connectedness that are properties of realistic storytelling. Instead characters, or more accurately mere voices, were now heard within a sonic landscape that was deeply enigmatic and fraught with hints of apocalyptic menace. Identity in *The Waste Land* is shrouded in mystery. Characters rarely have names: the middle-class woman who speaks at the beginning of Part II remains as nameless as the working-class neighbour of Lil and Albert at the end. They also lack any of the features that typically signal individual identity: eyes or hair of a certain colour, bodies of a certain height or build. (Only the young man carbuncular is . . . well, carbuncular, and has 'one bold stare'; the ghoulish woman in Part IV has 'long black hair', but it makes 'whisper music'; and, more weirdly, only the 'bats with baby faces' have human features.) They may be agents, but they seldom act. Instead, action is either delegated to dissevered body parts via synecdoche or inanimate things via personification, or else it mysteriously transpires through the passive voice: footsteps shuffle, hair spreads and glows in fiery points, the eyes and back turn upward, exploring hands encounter no defence, faces sneer and snarl; there are months that breed and mix and stir, seasons that cover, feed and surprise, snow that is forgetful, shadows that stride behind you or rise to meet you, the evening hour that strives homeward, the human engine that waits like a taxi throbbing waiting, the currents that pick bones in whispers, dry grass that sings, towers that toll, a door that swings, limp leaves that wait for rain, a jungle that crouches; vanity requires no response, while death undoes so many; sighs are exhaled, while stockings, slippers, camisoles and stays are piled. This is oneiric syntax, wild and Gothic, eerie and menacing because it severs that basic connection between agent and action, eerier still when punctuated by oracular mumbles uttered by uncertain voices ('Twit twit twit' or 'Jug jug jug jug jug jug') or sinister sounds that issue from hollow places ('And voices singing out of empty cisterns and exhausted wells').[30]

Late in January 1922, after he had returned to London, Eliot informed Pound that he was now thinking of omitting Part IV in its entirety. Pound insisted that the brief section of ten lines be retained, explaining his view in terms that border on tautology: 'Phlebas is an integral part of the poem; the card pack introduces him, the drowned phoen. sailor, and he is needed ABSoloootly where he is.'[31] Yet his appeal to the cards dealt out by Madame Sosostris in Part I is suggestive, for it implies that he assigned her and the card pack a certain degree of authority – threadbare authority, perhaps, yet enough for the needs of the poem. 'She must', one critic has observed, 'provide the dots that the rest of the poem must connect into a semblance of plot.'[32] The key word in that comment is 'semblance', to be taken in the strong sense as 'an assumed or unreal appearance of something; mere show'. What *The Waste Land* needed wasn't plot or narrative coherence, but the likeness of a plot, a likeness that would swiftly dissolve into illusion. For it requires only a moment to recall that Madame Sosostris is a charlatan, that the drowned Phoenician sailor isn't even a card in the traditional Tarot pack, or that the text, when she discloses the drowned Phoenician card, swiftly divorces itself from narrative, intruding cruelly: 'Those are pearls that were his eyes. Look!'[33] Phlebas the Phoenician, whose reappearance in Part IV seemingly promises narrative connectedness between the first and later parts of the poem, turns out to be another figure in the poem's grim histrionics of non-relationship. *The Waste Land* doesn't have a narrative; instead, it has the scent of a narrative, hovering in the air like a perfume after someone has left the room.

Pound's second major intervention in the poem's evolution concerned its publication. While Eliot was still visiting Pound in Paris in January 1922, Pound also received a visit from the American publisher Horace Liveright, who was then engaged in acquiring new authors for the firm of Boni and Liveright. Swayed by Pound's enthusiasm for the poem, Liveright offered $150 advance against 15 per cent royalties and promised publication in the autumn list. But when he received a preliminary reading copy of the poem, Liveright expressed a concern that would have huge reverberations: 'I'm disappointed that Eliot's material is as short. Can't he add anything?'[34] It was to address this concern that Eliot reached his decision to add notes to the poem, notes that would take up just enough space to make the poem seem viable as an independent book. But when he actually came to writing the notes several months later, Eliot grew anxious that a mere scent of narrative might not furnish enough connectedness of the sort that readers would expect of a long poem. Just as Joyce, when nearing the completion of *Ulysses*, had grown nervous that his work would appear too incoherent and had responded by devising several schemata or charts which suggested that the entire project was governed by arcane correspondences of colours, technics and various symbols, so Eliot decided to forestall a similar charge by hinting at an obscure but discernible 'plan' that was governing the poem: 'Not only the title', he wrote in his very first note, 'but the plan and a good deal of the incidental symbolism of the poem were suggested by Miss Jessie L. Weston's book on the Grail legend: *From Ritual to Romance* (Cambridge).'[35] It was a bogus statement not borne out by what we now know about his actual composition of the poem, but it would lead to several generations of critics who earnestly accepted the assertion that Weston and the Grail legend were central to the poem, and with it the implication that the poem was not a work of hyperbolic and lacerating opacity, but one operating comfortably within the confines of conventional symbolism.

With the poem's publication as a book secured, the question of its appearance in a periodical still remained. Though Eliot was offered $150 (£35) for the poem by Scofield Thayer, a co-editor of the *Dial*, he turned it down: he thought it a poor sum for a year's labour and he had recently learned that another author was receiving considerably larger sums for short stories that Eliot deemed very poor. Discussions stalled for months until Pound suggested a solution to the impasse: Eliot could be given the annual Dial Award with its prize of $2,000 (£450) as an unofficial price for the poem, so allowing Thayer to still pay him only his original offer of $150 and preserve the pretence that he had not capitulated to Eliot. By mid-August all the parties agreed on this solution, though two further provisions were added at the request of Horace Liveright. The *Dial* publication of the poem would include only the text of the poem, not the accompanying notes, which instead would appear exclusively in the book version. Further, the *Dial* would purchase 350 copies of the book in advance, enough to guarantee that the book publication would at least break even.[36] The outcome proved highly successful. The media attention that came with the Dial Award generated intense discussion about the merits of a poem that was difficult or even unintelligible: at least fifty reviews of the poem were published during the next year. In the United Kingdom, instead, there were only twelve reviews, nine of which were hostile.[37] Media attention, in turn, translated into sales. In the USA, its sales totalled 5,000 copies. The book version of *The Waste Land* that appeared in Britain, issued in 443 copies by the Hogarth Press on 12 September 1923, did not sell out until 11 February 1925.

Pound was fully aware of *The Waste Land*'s importance and registered his praise abundantly in contemporary correspondence. Yet its achievement in no way deterred him from pursuing his own work, which now responded to *The Waste Land* in a startlingly original way. During the summer of 1922, while negotiations over *The Waste Land* were stalled, Pound toured several towns in northern Italy he had never seen before. In May he saw for the first time the Tempio malatestiano or church of San Francesco, in Rimini, an unfinished building constructed around 1450 by Sigismondo Malatesta (1417–64), the town's ruler. Deeply impressed, Pound soon found himself fascinated by the circumstances behind its construction. He returned to Paris and began an extensive programme of historical research into Sigismondo's life and times. In early 1923 he returned to Italy and toured cities associated with Sigismondo and libraries that contained documents pertaining to him, a journey that took in Rome, Bologna, Rimini, San Marino, Pennabilli, Fano, Pesaro, Urbino, Cesena and Ravenna. After gathering more than 700 pages of notes, he finally completed four cantos now known as the Malatesta Cantos (Cantos 8–11) in early April 1923. They begin with a combative quotation from *The Waste Land*:

> These fragments you have shelved (shored).
> 'Slut!' 'Bitch!' Truth and Calliope
> Slanging each other sous les lauriers:
> *That* Alessandro was negroid. And Malatesta
> > Sigismund:
>
> *'Frater tamquam et compater carissime:*     5
> > *tergo*
> > > (. . . *hanni de*
> > > > *. . dicis*
> > > > > *. . . entia*

Equivalent to: Giohanni of the Medici, Florence)   10
Letter received, and in the matter of our Messire
Gianozio
One from him also, sent on in form and with all due
dispatch[38]

The first line of this passage quotes from the conclusion to *The Waste Land*, line 430 ('These fragments I have shored against my ruins') and tacitly quarrels with its bleakness. To shore fragments against the ruins of modernity is merely to shelve them or consign them to a form of academic oblivion. This work, instead, will transform them into new and living structures, and with line 5 it begins to do just that through a practice of intransigent quotation. For here the poem starts citing a letter written by Sigismondo Malatesta on 7 April 1449, one addressed to Giovanni de' Medici (1421–63), the youngest son of the legendary Cosimo de' Medici (head of the family that guided Florence during its golden age). Yet the passage does more than just quote and translate the text; it conspicuously mimics the graphics of the original document that is still housed in the state archive in Florence, where the address on the back (or in the scholarly Latin term for it, *tergo*) of the envelope has become worn away through the course of the centuries, so that the name 'Giohanni de Medicis, Florentia' ('Florentia' is the Latin name for Florence) has been reduced to mere scraps, '. . . *hanni de l. . dicis l . . . entia*', scraps which the poem now restores to intelligibility: 'Equivalent to: Giohanni of the Medici, Florence'. The Malatesta Cantos, then, will gather fragments from the past in order to restore identities, truths effaced by the passage of time and history.

That restoration entails a practice of quotation that is taken to still further extremes by the time we reach Canto 9, the second of the four Malatesta Cantos:

'*Magnifice ac potens domine, mi singularissime*
I advise yr. Lordship how I have been with master Alwidge who has shown me the design of the nave that goes in the middle of the church and the design for the roof and . . .'                        (9:125–7; ellipsis in the original)

By this point, even the ragged-right margin characteristic of poetry has vanished, and with it the venerable distinction between poetry and prose. For Michael André Bernstein, this 'represents one of the decisive turning-points in modern poetics, opening for verse the capacity to include domains of experience long since considered alien territory'.[39] But incorporating texts taken from historical documents entails consequences that are more complicated than simply the acquisition of new subject matter (history). Historical texts, when incorporated into poetry, assume a curious doubleness. On the one hand, within the poetry they take on a new function, becoming metaphors for not having metaphors, ciphers of the real and actual, or even fictions (if you will) of not having fictions; on the other hand, they never wholly relinquish their referential and historical status, for that very status is the precondition for their being able to function as metaphors for not having metaphors.

The various writers of the many source documents became counterparts to the multiple voices that Eliot had used in *The Waste Land*, all but allowing the poem to dispense with a presiding consciousness. One says 'all but' because of course only a presiding consciousness can inform us that a fragmentary address is found *tergo*, or 'on the back' of a document, or can translate that address: 'Equivalent to: Giovanni de' Medici, Florence.' Doing so, moreover, raises questions about the historical accuracy or knowledge of that consciousness. Pound himself knew this, and during an interview that he gave in early 1923 to the *New York Herald*, he addressed it when discussing the recently completed Malatesta Cantos: 'I want my work . . . to withstand all historical criticism.'

The problem of historical accuracy is vexing. Consider one critic who infers that 'the personality of Sigismundo is shown by juxtaposing his prose instruction concerning a painter he wishes to engage with a lyric he writes for Isotta degli Atti'; the brief lyric appears at lines 70–83 in Canto 8, coming after two businesslike letters:

> 'Ye spirits who of olde were in this land
> Each under Love, and shaken,
> Go with your lutes, awaken
> The summer within her mind . . .'

Alas, the view that this lyric is one that Sigismondo 'writes for Isotta degli Atti', while undoubtedly echoing Pound's understanding, is mistaken. For the lyric in question was actually written by Simone Serdini, a minor poet from the city of Siena who had enjoyed close relations with Rimini and its ruling house. As sometimes happened in the Renaissance when anthologies of poetry were assembled, poems by minor poets were later ascribed not to them, but to more famous persons with whom they were associated, in this case the house of Malatesta and specifically Sigismondo Malatesta. The mistake occurred in a manuscript that is found in the Vatican Library, where the attribution was encountered and accepted without hesitation by Charles Yriarte (1832–98), a French journalist-historian who reported the poem and its attribution in his 1882 biography of Sigismondo, *Un Condottiere au XVe siècle*. Yriarte claimed that this poem was 'the most characteristic of all his [Sigismondo's] works', that it was addressed to Isotta degli Atti, and that it had a 'capital importance . . . for the history of art in Rimini' because it furnished 'the key to the enigma' of the many bas-reliefs that decorate the interior of Tempio malatestiano.[40] But already in 1911 an Italian scholar named Aldo Francesco Massèra had re-examined this and other poems allegedly concerning Isotta degli Atti in an essay that was published in the foremost journal for the study of Italian literature. Yriarte had never bothered to check other manuscript collections; against the single testimony of the Vatican manuscript stood eleven others that assigned the poem to Serdini.[41] Pound, despite his wide reading in materials concerning Sigismondo and the Tempio, never came across the essay by Massèra. By 1922–3, when he was writing the Malatesta Cantos, he was drawing on scholarship that was both mistaken and out of date. Worse still, Simone Serdini had died by 1420 at the latest, making it unlikely that his poem referred to Sigismondo (then three years old), to Isotta degli Atti (then not yet born) or the Tempio malatestiano (then not yet constructed).

Pound faced several difficulties. For one, he lacked training in the discipline of palaeography, the study of ancient, medieval and Renaissance writing systems (they differed sharply from our own, using radically different styles of writing, complex systems of abbreviation, and so on) that is indispensable to anyone who wishes to work, as Pound did, with primary documents and sources. As a result, he sometimes produced perplexing problems, as in the lines that begin the fourth Malatesta Canto:

> E grādment li antichi cavaler romanj
> davano fed a quisti annutii.
> (11.1–2)

Even a learned reader will be puzzled by terms such as *grādment*, *fed* or *annutii*, since they form part of no language known to man. Pound, in these lines, was trying to transcribe a passage from a fifteenth-century chronicle that he had located in Rimini. But his lack of palaeographical training meant that he couldn't recognise a device called fusion, by which writers of the period would fuse or meld together the strokes of adjacent letters with commensurate shapes in order to save both space and time. He was, therefore, troubled by a word such as '*grandemente*' (where fusion occurs between '*d*' and '*e*' and between '*t*' and '*e*') or '*fede*' (again between '*d*' and '*e*'). Again, because he did not know that a common contraction in this period was a horizontal stroke above a letter, which signalled the omission of a liquid (typically '*m*' or '*n*'), he couldn't recognise that the word that he transcribed as *grādment* was in fact *grandemente*, or 'greatly'. Though Pound set out to restore identities effaced by history, he sometimes produced not restored, but mistaken identities.

For another, Pound was the victim of his own interpretative biases. In the course of the nineteenth century a grand romantic myth had grown up around the figure of Sigismondo Malatesta. He had been turned into an almost Byronic figure who had committed monstrous crimes, including the murder of his first two wives, yet who had somehow fallen in love with Isotta degli Atti to such an extent that his reconstruction of the church of San Francesco effectively became a temple of love that was dedicated to her. The first part of this myth, that Sigismondo was a monster, was demolished by the work of Giovanni Soranzo, an Italian historian who showed that the principal charges against Sigismondo emanated from the papal court of Pius II, were advanced for identifiable political reasons, and were contradicted by numerous and more reliable documents.[42] The second part of this myth, that the Tempio was a monument to Isotta, was also demolished by the work of Giovanni Soranzo.[43] But this dimension of Soranzo's work Pound elected to ignore. He was too eager to assimilate the court of Sigismondo to the culture of courtly love in Provence, too eager to see it as an index of neopagan rebellion or of a sexual vitalism mysteriously transmitted from antiquity to Provence, and from Provence to Rimini. But the view that the Tempio was a monument to Isotta was already dying by 1923, when Pound published the Malatesta Cantos, and since the Second World War it has never been seriously revived. Scholars today view the church as one that expresses conventional piety and the aspirations to dynastic self-aggrandisement typical of the ruling houses of such Italian city-states.

The Malatesta Cantos were an immense but also a deeply flawed achievement. In creating an unprecedented poetics of the document, Pound opened up possibilities that were further explored by a number of major poets, including William Carlos Williams in *Paterson* and Charles Olson in *The Maximus Poems*. He also anticipated many of the concerns that sprang up around the notion of documentary poetics in the 1930s, including some dimensions of the work undertaken by dissident Surrealists who assembled the journal *Documents*. But his assertion of sexual vitalism and his eagerness to view the Tempio as a monument to Isotta are insights that scarcely sustain the strains of the text's surface complexity. A bravura innovation in poetic technique and subject matter, spellbinding glimpses of turbulent life in the Italian quattrocento – these will suffice for some readers. Not for all.

The publication of the Malatesta Cantos turned into a fiasco. Pound at first planned to publish them simultaneously in the *Dial* in the USA and the *Criterion* in the UK, replicating the publication of *The Waste Land*. But already on 31 March 1923, Scofield Thayer, the co-editor of the *Dial* then residing in Vienna, wrote to his co-editor residing in New York: 'Your desire to publish further cantos of Pound emphasizes to me the very real and wide divergence in our tastes and indeed judgements. . . . I absolutely cannot forego my privilege of vetoing almost everything from Ezra Pound, as from pretty much all his circle.'[44] When the journal's general manager wrote to Pound around 19 May, asking that he give the *Dial* more time to reach a decision on the Malatesta Cantos, Pound sensed trouble and withdrew his offer of publication. 'I must ask you to return me my manuscript', he replied.[45] Meanwhile, however, Eliot had already written to him confirming that he wished to publish the new cantos in the *Criterion*, but also proposing a lower price that presupposed simultaneous publication in the *Dial*: 'I wired to say we will print poem in July and it will come to about £20. That is the best we can do, especially *as* it is appearing in the *Dial*.' Eliot, of course, knew nothing about the collapse of the plans for publication in the *Dial*. Much worse, he also reacted sharply to Pound's opening citation of *The Waste Land*, 'These fragments you have shelved (shored)':

> I object sharply on tactical grounds to your 1st line. People are inclined to think that we write our verses in collaboration as it is, or that you write mine and I write yours. With your permission we will begin with line 2. No time to write more.

In a hasty postscript he added: 'I like Cantos immensely, except for details of personal fancy. Certainly a great pioneer invention in method.'[46]

Pound, with no other publisher on the horizon, acceded wearily to Eliot's request: 'All right, delete first line, if it worries you.'[47] Nothing could have more clearly marked how fundamentally their roles had changed since their first encounter only nine years earlier in 1914. Then it was Eliot who found himself without an outlet in which he could publish his poetry. Now it was Pound whose only outlet remained a journal edited by Eliot. Then it had been Pound who could bestow a favour by using his editorial contacts on Eliot's behalf. Now the roles were reversed – with the coda that Pound now had to accept Eliot's censorship or court the risk of his poems not being published at all. When Pound wrote in September to complain that his payment for the poem had been too low, Eliot replied: 'I remember writing to you that it would be 'about "20". It was £18. I can go the extra £2, but I don't think that we can go beyond. As you did not demur at the time I presumed that you were satisfied.'[48] It was an inglorious ending to a glorious collaboration.

Pound and Eliot, of course, did not drift apart solely because of their misunderstandings about the Malatesta Cantos; those misunderstandings, instead, were merely the index of increasingly different lifestyles, ideologies and career trajectories. Pound was all but disappearing from the literary scene, as Eliot had foreseen in 1920. His next book, *A Draft of XVI. Cantos* (1925), may well have been a superb experiment in modern verse; but its appearance in a deluxe edition that was limited to ninety copies meant that it had virtually no audience. The same was true of his next major publication as well, *A Draft of Cantos 17–27* (1927). Eliot, meanwhile, published *Poems 1909–1925*, the work that finally brought him critical success with reviewers and a substantially larger public. By January 1926, Eliot was giving the prestigious Clark Lectures at Cambridge University, already a controversial figure with an important following.[49]

Other changes, too, were pulling them in different directions. In January 1923, while travelling in Italy to research materials for the Malatesta Cantos, Pound had his first experience with militant Fascists in the town of Rimini, and by late 1923 and early 1924 he was lobbying with a well-connected friend for a personal interview with Mussolini.[50] His adherence to Italian Fascism, or to the mythical figure of Benito Mussolini, was complete by the end of the year. 'I bet on Italian fascism years ago and came here to live in the middle of it', Pound later recalled.[51] Pound had left Paris for Italy in late 1924.

The other major change in Pound's life was personal. In the summer of 1923 he met Olga Rudge, who would become his lifelong companion. But, since Pound was still married to Dorothy Shakespear, he felt obliged to conceal an arrangement that many would frown upon. Moving to Italy was also a way to do that. In July 1925, his daughter by Olga Rudge was born. Eliot, instead, underwent his own, very different crisis. In 1927 he became a Christian convert, and in 1928 he announced his new faith within the preface to his new book, *For Lancelot Andrewes*, a collection of eight recent essays. In his preface, Eliot announced that he was now a 'classicist in literature, a royalist in politics, and anglo-catholic in religion'.[52] It was a deliberately provocative statement, often quoted since then as if it sufficed to characterise the whole of Eliot's work and life, an impression that Eliot himself would later help to foster.

If the period 1914–23 could be plausibly described as the age of Pound and Eliot, the period after 1923 became the age of Eliot alone. His waspish and elegant prose became the benchmark of critical fashion, and under the single word 'classicism' he summarised the end-point of a critical and aesthetic evolution that had been far richer and more complex than that term could ever suggest. But journalists and critics sometimes need slogans or phrases which can seem to summarise a larger, more complex change; the term 'classicism' sufficed to give Eliot an easily identifiable position, one that both distinguished him from his contemporaries and seemingly marked a new era in literary taste. Eliot, in effect, became the personification of that era, and, with his receipt of the Nobel prize in 1948, the identification of man and era became complete. By then Ezra Pound, under indictment for wartime broadcasts that he had made through Radio Rome, was in St Elizabeths Hospital for the Criminally Insane. He had been adjudged mentally incompetent to stand trial.

Strangely, then, the Pound era began shortly after Eliot's death in 1965. In part it was Hugh Kenner's hugely influential volume that began the process in 1971. But what gave it a new and sudden power was yet another change in taste seemingly epitomised in the term 'postmodernism', one that now assigned new urgency to Pound's poetics, set over and against Eliot's. Pound could now viewed as a precursor to the postmodern, while Eliot was consigned to an earlier but now exhausted age of Symbolist aesthetics. The critic who most forcefully articulated this view was Marjorie Perloff, in an influential book called *The Poetics of Indeterminacy: From Rimbaud to Cage* (1981), one that is still in print today.

For Perloff, modernism consisted of 'two separate though often interwoven strands'. One was 'the Symbolist mode', represented by Baudelaire and Eliot; the other was 'the anti-Symbolist mode of indeterminacy or "undecidability", of literalness and free play', represented by Pound and others (Gertrude Stein, William Carlos Williams, Samuel Beckett and John Ashbery).[53] In this schematic account of literary history, *The Waste Land* became an exemplary work: 'its temporal and spatial dislocations' were a facade that only briefly concealed 'a perfectly coherent symbolic structure'. Consider the character of Mr Eugenides, the merchant from Smyrna (the italics are mine):

> Mr. Eugenides the Smyrna merchant is a figure of multiple *symbolic associations*. He has already been introduced in 'The Burial of the Dead' as 'the one-eyed merchant' of Madame Sosostris' Tarot pack; he reappears, moreover, in 'Death by Water' as Phlebas the Phoenician. In ancient times, Phoenician and Syrian merchants were among those who spread the mystery cults throughout the Roman Empire; these mystery cults were, *as Jessie Weston tells us*, later associated with the Holy Grail. The sacred mystery of which Mr. Eugenides is the bearer, however, is only the shrivelled grape in the form of 'currants,' and his proposition to the narrator is thus a travesty of the Fisher King's invitation to the quester outside the Grail Castle. As the one-eyed man of the Tarot card, the merchant also *symbolizes death or winter* . . . The one-eyedness of the merchant on the Tarot card also *symbolizes blindness*, and most of the inhabitants of the Waste Land are, of course, blind in one form or another.[54]

Here Eliot's careless note, which had urged that 'the plan and a good deal of the incidental symbolism of the poem were suggested by Miss Jessie L. Weston's book', was being taken literally. A work of hyperbolic and lacerating opacity, one peopled by uncertain voices and enigmatic identities, now became a tidy narrative with solid characters who furnished the poem's symbolic key (a 'Fisher King' and a 'quester', for example, even though neither term appears anywhere in the poem itself). Troublesome details went unmentioned (the one-eyed merchant is not even a real card in the Tarot pack, while Madame Sosostris is a charlatan). The poem was being crushed into the Procrustean pattern furnished by Jessie Weston; the 'perfectly coherent symbolic structure' that Weston discerned in medieval legend was reassigned to Eliot's more unruly masterpiece.

In opposition to *The Waste Land* stood the Malatesta Cantos. Consider Canto 8, lines 5–10, a passage we have already seen:

> The lines, in short, do not convey information; rather, they take certain facts and present them from different linguistic perspectives (formal, florid Italian; broken Italian words; English translation) as if to undercut their history. Fact, in other words, is being transformed into fiction.[55]

But, as an attentive reader will have already noticed, there are no words of Italian in the passage that has been quoted here; the words 'Magnifice vir . . .' and *'tergo'* are in Latin. It may be true that 'fact . . . is being transformed into fiction' somewhere in this account, but if so it is not a result of the poem's activity.

At one point the same critic catalogues the techniques deployed in the Malatesta Cantos:

> Closely related to such artful mistranslation is the purposely incorrect rendering of the Italian itself. In the letter to Giovanni di [*sic*] Medici which opens Canto 8, for example, Pound has Sigismundo say:
>
>> And tell the *Maestro di pentore*
>> That there can be no question of
>> His painting the walls for the moment,
>> As the mortar is not yet dry
>> And it wd. be merely work chucked away
>> (*buttato via*)
>
> In the original, the Italian phrase is *gettata via*, which means 'thrown away'. Pound substitutes the harsh '*buttato via*', partly to suit his own meaning – 'chucked away' – and partly, no doubt, for comic sound effect.[56]

To support her claim about 'the Italian phrase' found 'in the original', the critic urges the reader to 'See Yriarte, p. 381', so referring to a book by Charles Yriarte, *Un Condottiere au XVe siècle*, one of many sources used by Pound when writing the Malatesta Cantos. However, it is obviously a mistake to confuse the published transcription by Yriarte with 'the original', a document that is still preserved in the *Archivio di stato*, or state archive, of

Florence. Pound himself understood this distinction, for in March 1923, he went to the *Archivio* and examined the original letter, correctly noting that it reads '*buttato via*', not '*gettata via*' as reported by Yriarte. Pound, here, is correcting Yriarte and restoring an accurate reading of the letter's original phrasing, and if there is a 'comic sound effect' to be discerned here, it may stem less from Pound than from his critic.

Such mistakes, small yet telling, were marshalled to turn Pound into the founding figure of what was called 'the other tradition', or the 'anti-Symbolist mode of indeterminacy or "undecidability", of literalness and free play'. He became the consummate poet of the age – not the age when he was actually alive and practising his craft, but the decades between roughly 1970 and 2000, decades when the shadows cast by Eliot's reputation, or by the classicism and symbolism that he was thought to represent, left little scope for assaying poetic modes and styles not easily assimilable to those cultural phantasms. To the extent that such accounts opened up space for appreciating a wider range of poetic possibilities, we should be grateful to them, even as we acknowledge that the Eliot of *The Waste Land* or the Pound of the Malatesta Cantos which they depicted were critical fictions that obscured as much as they illuminated. For even such fictions can be useful – for a while. The critical fiction that once conflated Eliot with classicism, the 'age of Eliot', was useful – for a while. It enabled critics and others to traverse the transition from late romantic assumptions about poetry to more modern and elastic ways of conceiving poetic possibility. The critical fiction of a 'Pound era', if we can so designate the period when Pound was turned into an anti-Eliot whose poetics were deemed more prescient and forward-looking, offered a way to negotiate the transition from post-Eliotic assumptions about poetry to modes of understanding that could accommodate very different ways of conceiving poetry's potential. But more recent work on both Pound and Eliot has shown that both poets were more complex and compelling than such fictions have allowed. They were useful fictions – for a while. But the time now demands appraisals with more nuance and subtlety. The age of 'the Age of . . .' has ended.

## NOTES

1. Conrad Aiken, 'T. S. Eliot', *Life* (15 January 1965), 93.
2. *The Times* (London), 5 January 1965.
3. Hugh Kenner, *The Pound Era* (Berkeley: University of California Press, 1971).
4. Conrad Aiken to Joy Grant, 31 August 1962, quoted in Joy Grant, *Harold Monro and the Poetry Bookshop* (London: Routledge & Kegan Paul, 1967), p. 101.
5. T. S. Eliot, 'The Art of Poetry, I: T. S. Eliot', *Paris Review* 21 (Spring–Summer 1959), reprinted in George Plimpton (ed.), *Writers at Work: The Paris Review Interviews, Second Series* (Harmondsworth: Penguin, 1977), p. 95.

6. T. S. Eliot, *Letters of T. S. Eliot*, vol. I, *1898–1922* (New York: Houghton Mifflin, 1988), p. xvii.

7. Eliot, *Letters*, p. 58.

8. Marinetti's arrival on the scene in March 1912 reignited a debate which had started earlier with the post-Impressionism exhibition of 1910. For contemporary reviews of that exhibition, see J. B. Bullen (ed.), *Post-Impressionists in England* (London: Routledge, 1988).

9. For a more extensive discussion, see Lawrence Rainey, *Institutions of Modernism* (New Haven: Yale University Press, 1998), pp. 10–41.

10. Ezra Pound, 'Editorial Comment: Status Rerum', dated 10 December 1912, *Poetry* 1.4 (January 1913), 123–7; reprinted in Lea Baechler et al. (eds), *Ezra Pound's Poetry and Prose Contributions to Periodicals* (New York: Garland, 1991), vol. I, p. 112.

11. Anon, 'Fine Art Gossip', *Athenaeum* 4402 (9 March 1912), 290.

12. See Solomon Eagle (i.e. John Collins Squire), 'Current Literature: Books in General', *New Statesman* 3.65 (4 July 1914), 406: 'Almost all the pictures reproduced are (like the typesetting of the first pages), Futurist in origin, and nothing else. And as for the productions of the literary Vortices, these are not even so fresh as that . . . *Blast* is a flat affair. We haven't a movement here, not even a mistaken one.' See also Anonymous, 'The Futurists', *New Statesman* 3.66 (11 July 1914), 426: 'One can forgive a new movement for anything except being tedious: *Blast* is as tedious as an imitation of [music-hall comedian] George Robey by a curate without a sense of humour. . . . [T]o make up of the pages of *Blast* a winding-sheet in which to wrap up Futurism for burial is to do an indignity to a genuine and living artistic movement. But, after all, what is Vorticism but Futurism in an English disguise – Futurism, we might call it, bottled in England, and bottled badly? . . . [T]he two groups differ from each other not in their aims, but in their degrees of competence.'

13. For a fuller account, see Humphrey Carpenter, *A Serious Character: The Life of Ezra Pound* (Boston: Houghton Mifflin, 1988), pp. 252–4.

14. See B. L. Reid, *The Man from New York: John Quinn and His Friends* (New York: Oxford University Press, 1968), p. 343.

15. Ezra Pound, *Personae: The Shorter Poems*, ed. Lea Baechler and A. Walton Litz (New York: New Directions, 1990), pp. 69–70.

16. T. S. Eliot, *The Complete Poems and Plays* (New York: Harcourt Brace, 1969), p. 6.

17. Ezra Pound, 'Harold Monro', *Criterion* 11.45 (July 1932), 581–92; reprinted in Baechler et al. (eds), *Ezra Pound's Poetry and Prose*, vol. V, p. 363.

18. Pound reviewed Masters's *Spoon River Anthology* twice, expressing approval with qualifications. See 'Webster Ford', *The Egoist* 2.1 (1 January 1915), 11–12; reprinted in Baechler et al. (eds), *Ezra Pound's Poetry and Prose*, vol. II, pp. 1–2; and 'Affirmations: Edgar Lee Masters', *Reedy's Mirror* 24.13 (21 May 1915), 10–12; reprinted in Baechler et al. (eds), *Ezra Pound's Poetry and Prose*, vol. II, pp. 86–9.

19. Eliot, 'The Art of Poetry', in Plimpton (ed.), *Writers at Work*, p. 95; T. S. Eliot, 'Professional, or . . .', *The Egoist* 5.4 (April 1918), 61.

20. The seven were: 'The Hippopotamus' (1917), 'Mr. Eliot's Sunday Morning Service' (1918), 'Sweeney Among the Nightingales' (1918), 'Whispers of

Immortality' (1918), 'Burbank with a Baedeker; Bleistein with a Cigar' (1919), 'Sweeney Erect' (1919) and 'A Cooking Egg' (1919).

21. Eliot, *The Complete Poems and Plays*, p. 32.

22. Michael Levenson, *A Genealogy of Modernism: A Study of English Literary Doctrine, 1908–1922* (Cambridge University Press, 1984), p. 163.

23. Pound, *Personae*, p. 187.

24. Eliot, *Letters*, p. 358.

25. The ten essays have only recently been republished. See Lawrence Rainey (ed.), *The Annotated 'Waste Land' with Eliot's Contemporary Prose* (New Haven: Yale University Press, 2005), pp. 135–201.

26. Rainey (ed.), *The Annotated 'Waste Land'*, pp. 149, 152, 174, 175, 186, 168, 169.

27. The essays are 'The Romantic Englishman', 'The Lesson of Baudelaire', 'Andrew Marvell' and 'Prose and Verse', all in Rainey (ed.), *The Annotated 'Waste Land'*, pp. 141–65.

28. Rainey (ed.), *The Annotated 'Waste Land'*, pp. 194, 180, 169.

29. For Pound's interventions, see Valerie Eliot (ed.), *The Waste Land: a Facsimile and Transcription of the Original Drafts* (New York: Harcourt Brace, 1971).

30. Eliot, *The Complete Poems and Plays*, p. 48.

31. Eliot, *Letters*, p. 505.

32. Calvin Bedient, *He Do the Police in Different Voices: 'The Waste Land' and Its Protagonist* (University of Chicago Press, 1986), p. 36.

33. Eliot, *The Complete Poems and Plays*, p. 38.

34. Horace Liveright to Ezra Pound, 11 January 1922, Yale, Beinecke Library, Bird Papers, Folder 23.

35. Eliot, *The Complete Poems and Plays*, p. 50.

36. This account somewhat simplifies a very complicated story; see Lawrence Rainey, *Revisiting 'The Waste Land'* (New Haven: Yale University Press, 2005), pp. 71–101.

37. For a list of the reviews, see Rainey (ed.), *The Annotated 'Waste Land'*, pp. 256–9.

38. The only text of the Malatesta Cantos which gives line numbers and furnishes annotations is that in Lawrence Rainey (ed.), *Modernism: An Anthology* (Oxford: Blackwell, 2005), pp. 64–89, which is followed here. The canto number and line numbers are cited within the text. See also Ezra Pound, *The Cantos*, 4th edn (London: Faber and Faber), pp. 28–52.

39. Michael André Bernstein, *The Tale of the Tribe: Ezra Pound and the Modern Verse Epic* (Princeton University Press, 1980), p. 40.

40. Charles Yriarte, *Un Condottiere au XVe siècle: Rimini: études sur les lettres et les arts à la cour des Malatesta* (Paris: Jules Rothschild, 1882), pp. 139, 141 n.1, 218.

41. Aldo Francesca Massèra, 'I poeti isottei', *Giornale storico della letteratura italiana* 57 (1911), 5–7, 15–21.

42. See Giovanni Soranzo, *Pio II e la politica italiana nella lotta contra i Malatesti (1457–1463)* (Padua: Fratelli Drucker, 1911). See also his studies leading up to the book: Giovanni Soranzo, 'Un' invettiva della Curia Romana contro Sigismondo Malatesta': [part 1] *La Romagna* 7 (1910), 462–89; [part 2] *La Romagna* 8 (1911), 15–175; and [part 3] *La Romagna* 8 (1911), 241–88.

43. Giovanni Soranzo, 'La Sigla SI di Sigismondo Pandolfo Malatesta', *La Romagna* 6 (1909), 303–24. Soranzo examined the entwined letters 'S' and 'I' that are carved throughout the church of San Francesco, a sign which the romantic myth viewed as a composite cipher for both Sigismondo and Isotta, evidence that the church was dedicated to her. Soranzo demonstrated that it referred only to Sigismondo. For Pound's response to this debate, see Lawrence Rainey, *Ezra Pound and the Monument of Culture: Text, History and the Malatesta Cantos* (University of Chicago Press, 1991), pp. 186–98.
44. Unpublished letter from Scofield Thayer to James Sibley Watson, Jr, 31 March 1923; New York Public Library, *Dial* Papers.
45. Unpublished letter from Ezra Pound to James Sibley Watson, Jr, 29 May 1923; New York Public Library, *Dial* Papers.
46. Unpublished letter from T. S. Eliot to Ezra Pound, 'Sunday' [27 May or 3 June 1923], University of Indiana, Lilly Library, Bird Papers.
47. Unpublished letter from Ezra Pound to T. S. Eliot, 12 June [1923]; London, collection of Mrs Valerie Eliot.
48. Unpublished letter from T. S. Eliot to Ezra Pound, 14 September 1923; University of Indiana, Lilly Library, Bird Papers.
49. The lectures are reported in T. S. Eliot, *The Varieties of Metaphysical Poetry*, ed. Ronald Schuchard (New York: Harcourt Brace, 1993).
50. On these events see Lawrence Rainey, *Institutions of Modernism* (New Haven: Yale University Press, 2001), pp. 107–46.
51. Ezra Pound, revised version of unpublished essay, 'Fascism or the Direction of the Will'; Yale, Beinecke Library, Pound Papers, Folder 3360, ts. 2.
52. T. S. Eliot, *For Lancelot Andrewes* (London: Faber & Gwyer, 1928), p. ix.
53. Marjorie Perloff, *The Poetics of Indeterminacy: From Rimbaud to Cage* (1981; Northwestern University Press, 1983), p. vii.
54. Perloff, *The Poetics of Indeterminacy*, pp. 13, 12–13.
55. Perloff, *The Poetics of Indeterminacy*, p. 183.
56. Perloff, *The Poetics of Indeterminacy*, p. 186.

# 6

RACHEL BLAU DuPLESSIS

# H.D. and revisionary myth-making

H.D. (Hilda Doolittle [Aldington], 1886–1961), with these initials as her authorial signet, had a literary career as an author of lyric poetry, long poems, essay/memoirs and novels and, briefly, as a film-maker and actress. Born in the United States from a well-to-do, intellectual family, adherents of Moravian Protestantism, H.D. became an expatriate writer and British citizen, living in London and later in Switzerland. She had a complex relational life as a bisexual woman, was married with one daughter (from an affair), enjoyed a number of erotic relationships with men and women, and lived in a companionate, lesbian relationship with Bryher (Winifred Ellerman, 1894–1983) for the majority of her life. She was theoretically and personally invested in psychoanalysis, archaeological discoveries, classical culture, cinema, the occult and comparative religious study; she also meditated the array and meanings of her erotic and relational ties in richly layered prose and poetry, including memoirs of her brief but important analysis with Freud. Both world wars profoundly affected her writing. Indeed, many of modernism's most distinctive long poems were written in large measure to confront these wars, to give accounts of their damage and to construct alternative meanings.

H.D.'s critical reputation, like that of many other modernist women, was quite uneven until the advent of feminist scholarship. Despite her full writing career and panoply of fascinating texts, she was seen as Imagist (or short-poem writer) only, localised to some work in the 1910s as fully representative, with her total oeuvre sometimes marginalised and discredited. Some poets and fewer academics (like Robert Duncan, Denise Levertov and L. S. Dembo) always insisted on her pertinence; H.D.'s own careful archive at Beinecke Library, Yale University, set up by H.D. and Norman Holmes Pearson, assisted the recovery of her importance by a growing number of scholars. The feminist criticism of the 1970s constructed a dynamic counter-public sphere of enquiry. This re-reading and reassessment of many women writers, sometimes under the particularist rubric of 'female modernism', articulated their gender-inflected concerns, including literary, ideological and material conditions, as well as textual strategies. This scholarship also mapped scintillating networks (both women only and all genders) that repositioned the literary, editorial and publicising work of female modernists at all points along the continuum of production, dissemination, reception. The oeuvre of H.D., with its interests in representing sexuality and understanding the erotic meanings of personal and cultural structures, was also available for studies that occurred in the 1990s under the rubric of sexuality (gay, lesbian, queer) studies. This picture of modernism was enhanced throughout this period of reception by an insistence on modernist cultural studies, on putting literary networks and artworks into the historical, social and political contexts of debates, events, issues and practices. This has been further inflected with a reaffirmation of the importance of explicitly textual, material, bibliographic studies and – of particular concern for poetry – of close reading, for a moment of critical reception that combines rich contextual and textual study (often under rubrics like social formalism, cultural poetics, social philology and socio-poiesis). The bibliographic, textual and contextual efforts of scholars and students of new modernist studies have had implications for other central writers whose writing of long poems also marked that era – notably T. S. Eliot and Ezra Pound. The very fact of this Companion chapter, charged explicitly with comparing H.D.'s work in the mythopoetic long poem to theirs, is a measure of her increasingly canonical status.

In a 1923 review of *Ulysses*, T. S. Eliot introduced the term 'mythical method' to describe the intensely wrought, witty, saturating 'continuous parallel' between Homer's *Odyssey* and James Joyce's epic novel, parallels functioning on all scales, from narrative event and allegorised detail to character, and in every tonality, for multiple purposes, from contrasting to universalising. Never mind Joyce's humane comedy and parodic subversions; his 'mythical method' was described as a way 'of controlling' and 'of ordering' what Eliot saw as modernity's 'immense panorama of futility and anarchy'.[1] Despite his pessimistic ideological investments, Eliot here announced a concern for ancient myth, ethnography and religion that characterises much notable writing of the modern period, including his own just-published poem. Eliot simultaneously raised the question whether the modern was a sordid, inadequate fragment of a (postulated) prior wholeness, ennobled by the paralleling motifs, and/or whether it was possible to claim cultural fullness for modernism because such a method reanimated and recast fundamental mythic events, acts, rituals, narratives within modernity. Eliot's *The Waste Land* (1922) did not use its mythic framework with the allegorical assiduity of Joyce; there is still significant debate over the degrees to which 'vegetation myths' of dying and reborn gods, along with the Parcival quest for sexual-spiritual healing, and the purported Tiresian overview, fully saturate the poem, but there is no doubt Eliot was correlating modern manifestations of squalor, sexual predation and impotence with the death stage of the vegetation myth. Because *The Waste Land*'s many citations, languages, voices and narrative vectors place readers into a disordered world filled with avatars of loss, the poem has long been seen as a symptom of the disease of alienation and despair that it diagnoses. The formal question as to whether or not the poem's 'fragments' cohere is also an ideological question as to whether there is rebirth, hope or plausible order in the modern world. The ambiguities of *The Waste Land*'s mythopoetic intervention thereupon became a cultural situation in itself. Responses to *The Waste Land* were many (e.g. by Hart Crane, William Carlos Williams, Louis Zukofsky), including by Eliot himself, Pound and H.D. Even if the later mythopoetic poems do not address *The Waste Land* directly, it is clearly a lurking, vital presence.

It is first important to note that H.D. did far more mythopoetic writing than can be discussed here, including plays (*Hippolytus Temporizes*), many lyric poems ('Pygmalion', 'Helen', 'Circe'), interpretative translations (*Ion* by Euripides) and novels (*Palimpsest*). Here we can examine the specific 'mythical methods' (in the plural) of H.D. (*Trilogy*, *Helen in Egypt*) and her socio-religious cultural interventions in comparison with the different long poems of Eliot (*Four Quartets*) and Pound (*The Cantos*). These works (and more – by W. B. Yeats and Williams) were produced with an intense attention to mythology and religion that began, for modernism, with the critique of literal Christianity, with the interpretations of mythic and folkloric stories after James Frazer's *The Golden Bough* (third edition, 1906–15), a masterpiece of modern comparative religious scholarship, and with the 'Cambridge anthropologists' like Jane Ellen Harrison, who linked the origin of drama to religious ritual and did ancient Greek cultural studies.

The word 'revisionary', applied to mythopoetic writing and operating as a particular 'mythical method', gained its currency from a feminist scholarship animated by a 1971/1979 essay by Adrienne Rich that named a cultural imperative for women as writers and critics – to investigate, undermine, critique and destabilise 'myths'. 'Not to pass on a tradition but to break its hold over us' were Rich's words, quite pertinent to H.D.'s mythopoetic projects.[2] 'Myth' was a capacious term by which was meant culturally important stories (like fairy-tales and folklore), conventional narratives and their teleology (like the marriage/death plots of nineteenth-century novels), mythological/religious materials (Greco-Roman, Christian, Norse, sometimes Jewish and more), and ideologies (as in Roland Barthes's *Mythologies*).

Mythopoetic work confronts stories and structures of feeling that are culturally hegemonic, and discovers the conflicts and debates that myths codify and synthesise. Thus mythopoetic writing is a mode in which one pursues serious cultural ambitions via maximum cultural scope, both across places and down into time. Certain writers construct affirmative myth (as the male–female relations loosely mythologised in Williams's *Paterson*); some writers reassert hegemonic belief systems, claiming their essential validity (Eliot's *Four Quartets*); some writers invent their own mythic systems (as Yeats did); and some, like H.D., revamp and realign specific myths. H.D.'s simultaneous assumption of mythological responsibility and her rupture and critique raised cultural stakes considerably, even grandly. The retelling of mythological stories, the application of such stories to contemporaneous life is hardly a new impulse in literature, but the torquing of myth had particular value as a mark of critique, not affirmation, during an era in which discussion of gender institutions was lively and in which social location and its nuanced insights made serious claims on literary and cultural study. Propelled by the questions raised by gender analysis, the mythopoetic long poems *Trilogy* and *Helen in Egypt* were 'rediscovered' and analysed with scholarly rigour, poetic empathy and cultural fortitude.

H.D. was invested in alternative mythopoesis from the beginning of her poetic career. Her early lyric writing drew on Greek mythology, with poems on Greek figures and eloquent transformations of lyrics from the *Greek Anthology* and Theocritus. These poems explored a sublime emotional space that was both gendered and ungendered, erotic, febrile and austere. Her focus upon the moments of 'akra' or high intensity in these lyrics drew upon the emotional/erotic essence of an Alexandrine, heterodox (not classicising) Hellenism.[3] The depiction of arousal, heightened feeling, desire, yearning and judgement often took as subjects the figures in mythology, such as 'Helen'. These works combine exposure and fragility with a sense of defiance and assertion, as in the serial poem that tells the Eurydice 'story' as resistance to and anger at Orpheus for his failed quest to redeem her from death. H.D. wrote not only the passionate outcry of a subjective voice but constructed, from Greek drama, choral lyrics with collective voices. The focused intensities of her earliest works struck Ezra Pound so forcefully that he claimed H.D. as the exemplary 'Imagist', both exemplar of and inspiration for the movement he had, in 1912, under construction. This characterisation of H.D. reverberated through her career: it helped limit her reception to the works of her youth.

What did H.D. accomplish in her two central long poems? Certainly a rejection of the limitations of rationalist, materialist approaches to the real, the mythopoetic force of *Trilogy* lies also in its critique of a purely, rigidly patriarchal religion and of an orthodox, immobile religion.⁴ This is accomplished by a poem structured as poetic prophecy and entrance to a reality beyond the empirically verifiable – what H.D. calls 'spiritual realism'. She explores 'symbols of the past / in to-day's imagery', but also boldly extends such symbols by her tactics of visionary reading.⁵ In *Trilogy*, she rewrites the Bible (stated in Revelation as canonically closed, a claim she pointedly disputes) by adding linkages and new narratives to that Book, makes a syncretic fusion of Great Mother religions and Christianity (something that continues Christianity's own capacious syncretisms). She fuses and braids Christian, Jewish and Arab characters and allusions in her animation of the happy surprise of a matriarchal 'girl' or female power appearing (as a recurrent epiphany) at the core of patriarchal religion to alter it from within. At the same time the poem is meditative in tone and intimate in mode, ruminating over civilisation's shards, for the speaker/character 'I' is living through and thinking about war, destruction, survival, from the ruins of the Second World War, constructing and reading 'runes' to understand recurrent historical patterns of violence and consider how to change them. Indeed, survival under the bombing of London seems to have left H.D. with a fevered, noble hope for a postwar spiritual-political transformation, and with a sense of a world-historical test she had passed. *Trilogy* could be profitably read in relation to a linked intervention, the full text of *The Gift*, a memoir of her family's and her nation's spiritual intensities and arousals. In H.D., self-analysis and reflection are often integrated with cultural and historical analysis; she insisted upon a spiritual politics in this memoir and in her long poems.

*Trilogy* (written in 1942–4, published in 1944–6) is built in lyric sections of argument; it is thoroughly syntactic, not (as in Pound's *Cantos*) fragmented, and is a major serial poem of meditation and cultural assessment. *Trilogy* is doubly syncretic (of Christianity and ancient religions; then of the three religions of Abraham) as well as boldly claiming analytic, critical power over canonical texts (like Revelation), adjusting and qualifying the Bible by means of the narrator's own visionary practices. The work is structured architecturally, in various arcs of 'three' that are pleasurable, didactic and dialectical in their force as they fold into one another in ways quite interesting to interpret. Analogies for the form given in the poem's text are the Delphic priestess's prophetic seat (tripod) whose three legs signify art, religion, healing (a trinity that is one); another mythic object is the caduceus (shell or bud; rod; snakes), equally able to imply art, religious power and medicine. While each of these key images seems to settle into one of the three sections, they also infuse each into all, in a mobile dramatising of post-Christian trinitarian thinking that replaces the male and/or gender-'neutral' Trinity with a 'trilogy' or triple-logos infused with female, maternal, messianic baby, and mother-father powers. In the second two sections of *Trilogy* are odd, unexpected, illuminating epiphanies of goddess figures: a breast-like jewel formed by alchemy; a May-apple tree triumphantly flowering, although charred by bombs; and Bona Dea herself, carrying a sheaf of flowers, wheat or the Holy Infant. The first section glistens with avatars of goddesses, notably Isis, and suggests the narrative solution, an equalising of mother with father gods, although it at first appears to be dominated by a patriarchal (though somewhat maternal) 'Amen'.

The defence of art (*The Walls Do Not Fall*) immediately evokes its frightening and stunning setting – destroyed London after the Nazi Blitz, and comprises a quotidian honouring of domestic artefacts, for a revaluing of 'goods' whose deeper meaning is 'gods' that must be reclaimed and examined. *The Walls Do Not Fall* offers an ironically self-critical discussion of her own poetry, answering its detractors ('obscure', 'escapist'), along with a stunning display of that which had been disparaged: puns, word associations, subtle rhymes and half-rhymes, networks of sound echoes, ease of allusion, cross-cultural range, and overt moments of anagram-based phonemic play and metonymic chains, revealing why Freud's tactics of free association became important to her work. At the same time, *Trilogy* is lucid, even expository, with each section pulsing the argument forward, or taking eccentric detours that turn out, with narrative glee, to become central to the quest for a gender-balanced spiritual realism, among other braided quests. The second section (*Tribute to the Angels*) describes the church bells tolling the advent of a number of angelic presences whose various hermetic names draw on Muslim, Hebrew and Christian traditions. This section features a triple epiphany of Mary, each affirming one of the three root images (healing, religion and art). The third epiphany, a resurrection image of 'Psyche the butterfly' and of the revisionary Lady carrying the unwritten Book (rather than a sacred Baby) has been much, and duly, cited. This breakthrough moment of vision of a totally new 'madonna' – Our Lady of the Blank Book – enables a new religious synthesis by this Lady's implied blessing of the opening of the canon (and of the writing of this poetry) by female investigation, inspiration, authority and critique. This central epiphany reveals the goddess of revisionary mythopoesis with H.D. as her prophet.

The final section (*The Flowering of the Rod*) tells a complicated tale of one of the three Magi bringing myrrh to the baby Jesus, a tale filled with the prefigurations, foreshadowings and narrative loops quite dear to H.D. (and close in narrative impact to *Helen in Egypt*). The force of the woven narratives – the honouring of Mary Magdalene as a gnostic figure of power, her articulate defiance of male knowledge and power in the figure of Kaspar, and the boldly depicted conversion of Kaspar away from patriarchal thought – have all been much cited as examples of H.D.'s proto-feminist, or at least revisionary, thinking. *Trilogy* is an artful, cunning and noble example of mythopoetic revision, and this transgressive critique of culture was undoubtedly H.D.'s purpose. It is not (only) that H.D. prefigures a certain kind of feminist critique of myth, but rather that her concerns to have culture, religion and society honour and reclaim the buried matrisexual and matriarchal roots offer a cultural diagnosis taking on world-historical issues – like the origins of war and the devaluing of women in culture. To accomplish *Trilogy*'s mythopoetic synthesis, H.D. did serious reading about religious heterodoxy, whether gnostic forms of Christianity, kabbalistic (mystical) aspects of Judaism, ancient Egyptian religious myths, or other spiritual and cultic materials.

Another of H.D.'s mythopoetic long poems, *Helen in Egypt* (1961), is formally and intellectually fascinating but less immediately accessible in argument and 'findings' than *Trilogy*, though it is similarly a serial work. It rests on a simple, if duplicitous proposition elaborated in certain ancient sources: that Helen was never at Troy; her apparent presence there was an illusion and a delusion. *Pace* Homer, Helen was 'really' in Egypt for the whole Trojan War, having been magically 'translated' there; that word, implying textual practices, cultural interchange, transformation of one story into another and sublime wafting is resonant.[6] The canard of Helen's fault (like Eve's) needs to be challenged and withdrawn; thus the term 'Palinode', which means 'retraction', is the title of the first 'book', while etymologically it means 'song sung again' – certainly also true to the repetitive, dreamy texture.

A number of formal observations can be made about this novel-length work. First, in genre it is synthetic, for it seems to mix epic ambition and narrative allusions to the Trojan War with dramatic materials and dialogue (including a dynamic use of the plays of Euripides as source), and, as well, with lyrical meditative panache, it deploys textual versions of dissolves, overlays, flashbacks, flash-forwards, cross-cutting and other tactics influenced by cinema. Second, while it was originally written in short poem sections only, a (perhaps gently baffled) query from her friend Norman Holmes Pearson happily led H.D. to add italicised prose abstracts at the beginning of each poem unit, for an evocative doubling of the complex narrative, and some clarification of it, although throughout the work narratives are suspended, discontinuous, deferred, made deliberately mysterious. Third, H.D. herself focused on the epigraphical term 'palimpsest', originally referring to a writing partially erased on a parchment that is then reused, a layering of texts, susceptible to doubled and shadow readings. The term is pertinent to this work with its endless interpretative process of working over and working through narratives, thus altering and linking them differently as they are retold and reinterpreted. The impression is thus a ghost story in cultural consciousness with an elusive, dreamlike, metamorphic feeling, and all the characters remaining in historical-spiritual suspension. Fourth, specific symbolic images – the hieroglyphic 'sign', the nenuphar or water lily, as well as Helen's 'veil', offer several more analogies for the practice of this poem. The hieroglyph with its visual/alphabetic doubleness thereby condensed questions of presence, representation and interpretation. The nenuphar suggests a lotus meditation, exfoliating petals until the core is found – or disappears into multiplicity. The veil evokes disclosure, hiding, evanescence and as well the structure of folding, wherein all parts of the poem seem to touch all other parts. Hence this work is 'linear' only because all writing is; the various parts of the work double and triple over each other, offering alternative tales and interpretations. Other very striking images are of weaving and (with parallels to *Trilogy*) the moment of hatching a butterfly, Psyche, or the soul. The indeterminacy between core story or solution (recognise Thetis; honour the Mother) and a work of folds (without single story) is just one of many reading effects. The work sets out the stark binary – female/male, or Helen as adulteress, reviled cause of the Trojan War and its disasters, her 'fall' propelled by sexual desire, faced with Achilles as soldier, even proto-fascist, filled with rage, prone to sexual assault, and complicit in the human sacrifice of Iphigenia. The poem rejects female fault totally and manages male metamorphosis. The work's depiction of Helen as ruminative reader of her own mythography, not as narcissistic wanton, revises aeons of cultural blame, by equalising fault so that male figures are equally complicit in bringing on the war (this treatment of Helen parallels H.D.'s scrutiny and rehabilitation of Venus in *Trilogy*). However, the poem pushes this cultural task of revaluation by entering a deconstructive zone of gender revisions to make fusions and crossovers between Helen and Achilles that query and undermine the rigid conventions of sheer maleness, sheer femaleness in favour of 'New Mortals' who have emerged from polarised genders ready for renewals based on the synthesis of apparent opposites. Similarly, Egypt and Greece are reconciled, which seems to mean that interminable interpretative reading practices, mystical in import (under the aegis of Thoth) are connected with the decisive, but devastating, actions characteristic of Greek myth and culture, often involving rape, aggression and passionate familial discord with political implications. The poem proposes that Eros (love) and Eris (strife), in the characters of Paris and Achilles and also in the twin pairs born from the egg out of which Helen was hatched, are set in dialectical motion, sometimes reconciled, sometimes not. Similarly La Mort (death) and L'Amour (love) intertwine and change each in relation to the other. All the characters, like revenants from a shadow world, are formed by a depth-charge of erotic/passionate feeling – heterosexual, homosocial, incestuous, matrisexual. The second of three books ('Leuké', or the white island), introducing the character Theseus (and drawing upon Freud and the psychoanalytic practices in which H.D. participated), allows Helen to 're-weave' familial and erotic relationships in a number of transformative ways, further multiplying narrative strands. The third of the three books, 'Eidolon', or idol/image, centring on Thetis, the mother of Achilles, offers the serious proposition that two gigantic failures – the cultural failure to acknowledge the mother or to acknowledge pre-oedipal or matrisexual desires, and the personal failure to honour erotic desire – create social, political, psychic ruptures and deep wounds at enormous social and historical cost. The labyrinthine mythological metamorphoses characteristic of this work are nothing less than a re-reading and critical retelling of much of Greek mythology and literature with the purpose of generating a major intervention into contemporary post-Second World War devastation and hope, and of proposing a major world-historical healing for a problematic issue (female fault) that is aeons old. The grandeur of H.D.'s ambition is patent; it is explored in the grandiose richness of this text.

The 'mythical method' that H.D. seemed to use is critique by torquing familiar texts via a psychoanalysis of culture as a whole. Stories that seem familiar are gradually pushed in critical directions; unlike affirmative uses of myth, hers construct a realm of critical negativity (this is a positive term). Trilogy's sense of a substratum of spiritual presence has analogues with Pound's work, although H.D.'s access moments are narratively more sustained. However, H.D.'s Trilogy has most in common with Eliot's Four Quartets; indeed, there is some evidence of their mutual attention as each completed their respective poems. Yet their mythopoetic purposes differ markedly.

The 'mythical method' in later Eliot also occurs with structural finesse, four poems with five parallel sections layer over each other. The work is repetitive, symmetrical, semantically and rhetorically patterned, with many fourfold allusions; form is disciplinary and even penitential in its regularity. This poem also addresses the bombing of London in a somewhat chilling Pentecostal image – the fire dropped by a Nazi bomber is parallel to the miraculous fire settled on the heads of early Christian disciples because of its import, recalling us to fundamental truths, even by difficult paths. Eliot's yearning to argue for orthodox Anglicanism as a shapely and historically appropriate cultural bulwark (in his terms, a faith) for our wounded time is the central task of his poem. Eliot assesses and draws upon Christian sources, including Dante in the purgatorial mode, though mostly British (that is, non-heteroclite, non-cosmopolite, non-Waste Land) sources, but the myth as used by him is not revisionary but devotional. (My use of 'myth', meaning culturally important story, as applied to the beliefs of Christianity, is secularly motivated.) The poet does not question the assumptions of Christianity nor critique its stories (this of course by choice and on principle) but finds in universalised Christianity an appropriate consolation and a world-historical necessity. This is marked by the discovery and repeated evocation of fundamental tenets (or miracles) of Christian faith as the solution to modern anomie, fear and spiritual grief; these tenets are Annunication, Incarnation, Pentecostal epiphany and Redemption. The pun on 'still' in this work points both to an attentive humility as spiritual position and to an affirmation of Christianity's perpetual relevance. Not revision but arousal to adhesion is the desired goal in Eliot's late long poem; hence the purposes and structures of feeling differ markedly from H.D.'s critical-mythic interventions, although both poems are notably architectonic.

Pound's mythographic methods in *The Cantos* are much more dispersed, as moments of magical presence where the ancient gods and goddesses or their imagistic avatars appear occur as epiphanic visionary bursts amid a field organisation of vectored, intersecting and dispersing materials. On one level Pound treats 'myth' as simply one part of the brilliant gists he is salvaging, not better than any nugget of insight: multilingual citations, documents, quotidian observations, historical figures and incidents, dialectal dialogue, sharply delineated images, and numerous acontextual details. Yet, because they have a solemn and sometimes erotic intensity, his poetry seems to invest greatly in these heightened moments drawing on myth. What is distinctive about *The Cantos* from a mythopoetic point of view is Pound's disdainful disinterest in Christianity (except as latently polytheistic) and his virulent (anti-Semitic) contempt not so much for Judaism (about which he knew little, except for the practice of male circumcision) as for (heavily stereotyped) Jews. Both western polytheism and eastern Confucian ethics are valued for their organic and hierarchical relation to natural and political power. The supplanting of an 'organic' relation to land, and to cultic ritual of cycles of sowing and harvesting, the undercutting of 'sacredness' of place and the spirits of place are, for Pound, the fault of the Judaeo-Christian tradition, especially of its monotheism. Throughout his career, Pound continually offered idealised evidence of a repressed 'secretum' of pagan fertility and mystery religions and rituals underneath monotheistic culture. Some of the intermittent mythic bursts in *The Cantos* may be mimetic of this 'secretum' triumphantly emerging through the shards, shames and disorders of contemporary culture and politics.

Because *The Cantos* were a life-work, they underwent many changes of concept absorbed into, marking and sometimes fissuring the work. At one point, Pound seems to have projected using Dante's *Commedia* as his master text, much as Joyce had used Homer. The Hell Cantos, responding to the First World War and to political-social symptoms and crises occasioning Pound's bitter disgust, occur early in the work; yet from that point on, hell, purgatory and paradise are dispersed, circulating, intermittent. His paradisial moments are civic, not theological, but they fuse the secular and the mysteries. Pound foregrounded a multiplicity of sociocultural forces; thus a field or ideogrammic splay of intersecting materials characterises *The Cantos* formally. Pound maintained an organicist sense of culture's varied elements, yet these elements needed a unitarian, phallic principle of active will to organise scattered, directionless materials; for Pound, the enemies of such unification were also virulently powerful. The poem fought by making a strained simulacrum of a transformed culture organised by central, affirmative concepts and offering recurrent evidence of political and economic malfeasance treated as absolutes. In his poem, Pound idealised historical figures whom he saw as embodying transformative, masculine will: Malatesta, Confucius, Mussolini. There is much debate whether Pound, too, can be seen as organising poetic dispersal by active will or whether *The Cantos* are a problematic monument.

Can one fairly state that Eliot's and Pound's revisionary mythopoetic tactics or their 'mythical methods' are masculine and H.D.'s are female/feminine? No, that proposition oversimplifies things. Poetic method is a neutral (but never uninvested) tool, and no formal or structural tactics of writing long poems can possibly be intrinsically gendered, but only gendered by cultural ascription, convention, ideology or agreement. However, all writers implicitly or explicitly take up relationships to the gender materials of culture and society in their work, and these can be studied even if the writers did not comment directly upon such issues. There are many gender-laden arguments and attitudes in Eliot, H.D. and Pound, and their various cultural myths and mythopoetic acts may be productively studied from that perspective and in relation to other social locations.

Further, poems may interrogate, resist, affirm or reproduce cultural myths and values. Thematically, H.D.'s mythopoetic works made self-consciously critical interpretations of major cultural myths involving gender. She offered the bold argument that matrisexual yearnings ('Egypt'), incest, erotic desire and the mother need fundamental acknowledgement; otherwise we are left with the historical-mythic legacy of militarism ('Greece'/'Rome'), the Command, violence, rape and the (non-maternal) patriarch. Similarly, she argued that religion (notably Christianity) must honour the powerful mother-goddess at its root and affirm its own occulted syncretic polytheism. H.D.'s gender critique was a cultural intervention concerning ideological patterns of patriarchy, including gender polarisation, misogyny, female 'fault' and 'Fall'.

H.D. saw her mythopoetic poems as acts of cultural resistance, heterodoxy and critique; Eliot saw his *Quartets* as spiritual affirmation; Pound used mythopoesis to evoke a utopian space of hierarchic organic order beyond satire and social rage.

## NOTES

1. T. S. Eliot, *Selected Prose*, ed. Frank Kermode (London: Faber and Faber, 1975), p. 177.
2. Adrienne Rich, 'When We Dead Awaken: Writing as Re-vision', in *On Lies, Secrets, and Silence: Selected Prose 1966–1978* (1971; New York: W. W. Norton, 1979), p. 35.
3. Eileen Gregory, *H.D. and Hellenism: Classic Lines* (Cambridge University Press, 1997), pp. 129–39.
4. Susan Stanford Friedman, *Psyche Reborn: The Emergence of H.D.* (Bloomington: Indiana University Press, 1981), pp. 87–120.
5. H.D., *Trilogy* (New York: New Directions, 1973), pp. 48, 29.
6. H.D., *Helen in Egypt* (1961; New York: New Directions, 1974), p. 1.

# 7

ANNE FOGARTY

# Yeats, Ireland and modernism

In his introduction to *The Oxford Book of Modern Verse*, W. B. Yeats (1865–1939) pronounced with careful qualification: 'I too have tried to be modern.'[1] This statement, simultaneously tentative and emphatic, sums up the difficulties both of considering Yeats as a modernist *tout court* and of taking the measure of the undoubted modernism of his work from 1900 onwards. Not least of the factors seemingly setting him at a remove from this literary revolution is the fact that he was a member of an earlier generation than Ezra Pound (1885–1972) and T. S. Eliot (1888–1965), who were a couple of decades younger than him. Yeats, in fact, is at once inside and outside this movement. On one level, he may be viewed as an instigator and central practitioner of modernist poetry but, on another level, he is of note because he deviates from, or implicitly unsettles, any historiographical or conceptual map of modernism that we might want to adopt. Yeats, unlike Pound or Eliot, the poets with whom he is most closely connected in the early decades of the twentieth century, awkwardly occupies the roles of eminent precursor, revolutionary pioneer, sceptical antagonist and belated exponent of modernism. Multiplying such complications, in his later work, he appears in part to renege on some of the political radicalism of high modernism while never abandoning its creative potential and its anarchic promotion of change and social renewal. Paradoxically, Yeats is both a proleptic modernist and a late arrival in a movement that he helped to shape but never fully embraced.

In 'How To Read', Pound triumphantly proclaimed the demise of English dominance of literature and declared that 'the language is now in the keeping of the Irish (Yeats and Joyce)'. However, he immediately retracted this plaudit when he added that 'since the death of Hardy, poetry is being written by Americans'.[2] In this muddled schema, Yeats is simultaneously the apogee and the vanishing point of modern poetry; his Irishness seems to mark him out for, and yet instantly disqualify him from, consideration. Indeed, in most subsequent histories of modernism he continues to occupy a similarly shadowy position. Yeats is often either an absent presence or simply a foil to the more central figures of Pound and Eliot. Hugh Kenner, for example, who sees Pound as the key practitioner of modernist poetry, alludes to Yeats merely tangentially in his influential study, *The Pound Era* (1971). It is only when Kenner, in *A Colder Eye: The Modern Irish Writers*, evolved the theory that international modernism rejected Anglocentrism and Leavisite notions of a great tradition in favour of provincialism that Yeats, too, is admitted to the select company of twentieth-century avant-garde artistry.[3] Even then, the radicalism that is attributed to him is outflanked by the innovations of James Joyce, who more readily conforms to Kenner's criteria for the politically untrammelled, cosmopolitan modern writer. Similarly, Graham Hough, in his analysis of the modernist lyric, routinely takes stock of Yeats but ultimately gives priority to the work and precepts of T. S. Eliot.[4] C. K. Stead, likewise, reclaims Yeats by accommodating him in his analysis of the intractable aesthetic problems bequeathed by romanticism to modernity, primarily the question of the distance between life and art.[5] Yet, despite this recasting of the lines of literary influence, Eliot still takes precedence as the prototype of the modernist poet. Lawrence Rainey's recent anthology of modernism, however, counters this long-standing ambivalence about the status of Yeats by definitively rescuing him from the margins of this literary movement.[6] The inclusion of an ample selection of his poems from 1914 to 1939 positions him at the forefront of twentieth-century experimentation. Nonetheless, Rainey still retains vestiges of the map of modernism propounded by Kenner since texts by Pound inaugurate the initial section, preceding – but overlapping chronologically with – those of Yeats. In this realigned view, Pound remains in place as the self-appointed originator and impresario of modernism, but his counterpositioning with the Irish poet deftly suggests the tensions underlying any overly neat account of the evolution of twentieth-century poetry.

The problem of locating Yeats within modernism is, to some degree, symptomatic of the notorious slipperiness and imprecision of this term and the complexity of the historical phenomena and upheavals that it describes. Most critics now question unitary accounts of this literary period that view it as the product of an Anglo-American hegemony or the single-minded creation of lone artists. Instead, a plurality of competing and geographically diverse alternative modernisms is mooted that encompasses peripheries such as Scotland and Ireland and European and American departures such as Futurism, Surrealism and the Harlem Renaissance. In like manner, the history of modernism is now envisaged less as a sudden rupture or as a linear progression climaxing in the achievements of the 1920s but as a series of traces, false starts, successive waves and the joint output of a multinational cast of collectives and coteries.[7] The late nineteenth-century antecedents of modernism, it is pointed out, need to be acknowledged as much as the later aftershocks of the movement in the writing of the 1930s. Indeed, Marjorie Perloff extends the ambit of modernism even further by arguing for its continuing existence into the twenty-first century; she holds that the aesthetic debates of the modernist revolution remain unresolved and persistently resurface in current poetic practices.[8] Furthermore, studies of individual authors have revealed that modernism is not a matter of an undeviating espousal of a radical aesthetic or credo but rather a spectrum of fluctuating styles, stances and modulating ideological allegiances. As Michael Levenson observes, the narrative of this literary movement is in itself unstable as its principals keep changing and the work of its main exponents often only fulfil the brief of its key tenets for short periods.[9] Modernism is less an unyielding and invariable disposition than a constantly altering but interconnected series of negotiations and debates.

This chapter argues that W. B. Yeats fits such newly tooled, revisionist accounts of literary modernity precisely because of the unwieldy, multifaceted nature of his artistic and political career, his involvement in several different cultural spheres in Ireland, Britain and the USA and the successive phases of his poetic oeuvre. Moreover, his modernism, as this investigation intends to demonstrate, is the outcome of his engagement with the Irish literary revival, on the one hand, and with aspects of international and regional poetic communities, on the other hand, as mediated by his relationship with Pound in particular but also with the Rhymers' Club and the Symbolists. The example of Yeats, hence, complicates the trajectory of early twentieth-century poetry and illustrates the interaction between the apparent provincial backwaters of Galway, Sligo and Dublin and more metropolitan zones of contact such as London, Paris and Rapallo. His recuperation and construction of an Irish literary tradition and his discovery of the importance of folklore and oral verse undergird his experimentation with poetic form. In addition, I want to show that Yeats's poetry and aesthetics are of pressing relevance to a history of modernism because of their exacting self-reflexivity. They reflect upon key preoccupations of modern verse, such as the nature of subjectivism, the links between tradition and modernity, the necessity for form, the desire for transcendence, the question of artistic autonomy and the intersection between politics and literature. In what follows, I shall track the peculiar aspects of Irish modernism as they are shaped by the different phases of Yeats's poetic career. Particular attention will be devoted to the ways in which the Irish literary revival moulded his poetic vision and themes. His collections, *The Tower* (1928) and *The Winding Stair and Other Poems* (1933), will then be examined as instances of his signal contribution to modernist achievement and will be juxtaposed with Eliot's *The Waste Land* and Pound's *The Cantos*. Finally, the political extremism, self-revision and renewed experimentation of Yeats's later poetry in his *New Poems* (1938) and *Last Poems and Two Plays* (1939) will be briefly considered as further manifestations of his ongoing engagement with modernist concerns.

The Irish literary revival was a protean phenomenon. It united numerous different cultural, political and economic initiatives, all of which shared the aim of reawakening national self-interest and spearheading the quest for independence from British rule. For example, such diverse groups as the Gaelic Athletic Association, launched in 1884 to sponsor native Irish games, the cooperative movement, set up by Sir Horace Plunkett in 1889 to foster rural development, and the Gaelic League, founded by Douglas Hyde in 1893 to promote the Irish language, were expressions of a broad-based search for political autonomy and for the retrieval and reformulation of a collective ethnic identity.[10] The historical circumstances inducing this social and political ferment in late nineteenth-century Ireland are intricately multi-layered. The rupture caused by the Great Famine (1845–9) led to a society that hovered between the traditional and the modern and that was imprinted by a profound trauma that lastingly altered its social and cultural structures. In the aftermath of the huge losses – reckoned at over two million – through death and emigration caused by the cataclysmic mid-century failure of the potato crop, a shift took place from a tillage economy centring on smallholdings to more streamlined modern practices of large-scale livestock production. The development of the railway and commercialisation abetted this process. In addition, a centrally imposed national education system ensured high levels of literacy. Successive nationalist campaigns under Daniel O'Connell and, later, Charles Stewart Parnell turned the Irish parliamentary party into a highly effective force for change and also mobilised and enhanced the efficacy of nationalist organisations in the country. Yet, simultaneously, under English colonial rule other forms of progress were impeded. A pre-capitalist peasant economy persisted, especially in the west of Ireland, as well as an outmoded, neo-feudal landlordism. However, as many commentators have pointed out, modernism thrives precisely in such uneven and intractable social conditions. The temporal discontinuities, political upheavals, the ever-present quest for national self-authentication and repeated clashes between the traditional and the new that predominated in Ireland at the end of the nineteenth century provided an ideal forcing ground for this literary revolution.

Yeats's involvement in revivalism was as variegated, far-reaching and vexed as his contribution to modernism. But, crucially, his engagement with Irish cultural and political disputes shaped his evolving sense of his role as a poet and fuelled his ruminations and pronouncements about the requisite aesthetic for a burgeoning nation. These debates, hence, are not simply an inert backdrop to his work since they precipitate his many reformulations of his poetic philosophy and persona. Moreover, although his early lyrics with their predilection for ethereal imagery, effete sentimentalism and dreamlike settings are commonly viewed as belonging to the manner of the so-called Celtic Twilight, they contain nascent aspects of his mature style and act as a prelude to his own peculiarly devised forms of modernism. Memorably, in 'To Ireland in the Coming Times', a poem that closes *The Rose* (1893), Yeats aspires to be a spokesperson for the Irish people and a conduit for the visionary utopianism that he aligns with the credo of nationalism:

> *Know, that I would accounted be*
> *True brother of a company*
> *That sang, to sweeten Ireland's wrong,*
> *Ballad and story, rann and song . . .*[11]

Even though he would programmatically abandon salient aspects of his youthful aesthetic and style and modify many of his political beliefs, his assumptions that the lyric voice is not simply a vehicle for privatised self-expression but has a communal sweep and that poetry gives access to deep-seated, arcane truths remain unaltered in his later work. His commitment to Irish politics both goads him into modernism in a manner that differs significantly from Pound and Eliot and also lastingly imprints it.

Fredric Jameson has argued that, for all its endeavour to break loose from tradition and to inaugurate a new cultural order beginning in the present, modernism is peculiarly concerned with the rewriting of narratives of the past.[12] As Yeats's essays and journalism from the 1890s vividly illustrate, the ways in which the past might be renegotiated and commandeered were a matter of fierce debate in the Irish literary revival. A burning question for all engaged in this movement was how to salvage and retrieve what might be deemed the authentic core of Irish national identity and to make it manifest both culturally and politically. Above all, the means by which a downtrodden Gaelic tradition could be revivified in the realms of language and literature were hotly disputed. Contentiously, Douglas Hyde in 1892 advocated the ousting of Anglophone influence and its replacement by a resolutely self-contained and isolationist native culture.[13] Even though Yeats subscribed to many of the ideals of nativism, he objected to Hyde's exclusionary vision and countered that a national literature would be 'none the less Irish in spirit from being English in language'.[14] He cited American authors such as Walt Whitman and Henry David Thoreau – whose work he admired and emulated – to lend weight to his contention that the English language could be renovated and radicalised from within. Belonging by birth to Protestant Anglo-Ireland, and hence situated at a remove from the native

Irish inheritance that he championed, Yeats made a virtue of his ambivalent position and his lack of knowledge of the Irish language. Instead, he set himself the task of intermarrying the dual traditions of the country. Partisanship and class allegiance may have dictated his stance, in part. But, ultimately, the paradoxical account of tradition that he propounded – at once open and yet historically anchored, timeless and yet insistently local – was an outcome of his quarrels with more narrowly defined forms of Irish nationalism and of Celtic antiquarianism. In addition, his belief in the promise of nationalist renewal coloured his view of the self-constituted literary history that he invoked. In 'Nationality and Literature' (1893), he posited that writing moves through three successive cycles, progressing from the epic and ballad through the dramatic to the lyric. In accordance with this evolutionary model, he diagnosed that late nineteenth-century Irish literature was retarded because it was still lodged in the heroic or epic phase; however, it was also imbued with immeasurable possibility due to the 'unexhausted material lying within us in our still unexpressed national character'.[15] By contradistinction with English literature, which had advanced to the lyric cycle but also entered a period of decadence and decline, the Irish literary tradition that Yeats marshalled up, even though still embryonic, was implicitly endowed with revolutionary potential. Tellingly, it was the domain of the lyric which would most aptly reveal this capacity for innovation and change.

Inspired by the writings of Douglas Hyde, Lady Gregory and George Sigerson amongst many others, Yeats's discovery of the rich seams of Irish folklore and his work as an amateur but pioneering anthropologist in the 1890s reinforced his political beliefs and helped to crystallise facets of the utopian aesthetic that underpinned his poetry. If the thrust of Poundian modernism was to 'Make it New', then the impetus of Yeats's equally innovatory vision was to recover the old and the immemorial. Through connecting with and harnessing the energies of ancient Ireland, a revolutionary art would be born. Investigation of the oral culture of the Irish countryside and of a lively collective repository of supernatural legends about the Sídhe, or fairy folk, acted as a preliminary to this process of change. In *The Celtic Twilight*, a folklore compilation first published in 1893, for example, Yeats described Irish rural belief systems with the distantiating scrutiny of an ethnographer and the empathetic insight of a storyteller.[16] The tales and sayings that he assembled during his travels in the West of Ireland and recalled from his childhood in Sligo and Dublin provided evidence of the innate mysticism of the local peasantry, opened up the possibility of an organically cohesive social world and demonstrated the ancient roots of Celtic culture. It was not just that the esoteric lore of Irish country people provided Yeats with enabling metaphors for his verse; it also allowed him to gain access to a substratum of timeless, mystical knowledge that provided a counterweight to the fragmentation and divisions of modernity. In such a context, the writer functioned as a cultural translator who salvaged vestiges of a premodern era which, in turn, had a transformative effect on his work. Above all, the orality, unmediated links with the material world, metaphysical speculativeness and communal embeddedness of this earlier culture became part of the complex apparatus of the modernist poet.

The rivalry between the Gaelic and English languages was but one aspect of the language question during the Irish literary revival. An equally intense debate revolved around the issue of style and its function in a political literature. Yeats's membership of several different artistic and nationalist communities in Ireland and England at the end of the nineteenth century influenced his emphatic but shifting pronouncements about these topics. His lifelong quest for a unique style owed much to his desire to break free from the unsatisfactory literary models and aesthetic philosophies proffered to him in his youth. Although the mid nineteenth-century verse of the Young Irelanders, such as Thomas Davis and Charles Gavan Duffy, enjoyed a new vogue during the 1890s, it was ultimately rejected by Yeats on account of its rhetoric and patently ideological designs. Likewise, as he made clear in *Autobiographies*, he felt an aversion to the cold abstraction of much of contemporary English Pre-Raphaelite and Victorian verse.[17] His experimental association with the short-lived confraternity, the Rhymers' Club, also foundered. In 'The Tragic Generation', he attributed the abortive lives of its members, including Lionel Johnson and Ernest Dowson, to the shortcomings of Aestheticism which forced poetry to become privatised and fatally self-referential.[18] Even though Symbolism, introduced from Europe by Arthur Symons, exerted an undoubted influence, it too was deemed by Yeats, at least retrospectively, to be flawed because of its rootlessness and eclecticism. In his essays, he denominated numerous literary antecedents, including William Blake, James Clarence Mangan, William Morris and Walter Pater, but ultimately his restless and far-flung search for literary role models that ranged from Geoffrey Chaucer to Rabindranath Tagore betokened a modernist urge to break with tradition while reconfiguring it completely.[19] A poet's style was no longer an automatic inheritance nor even a matter of ruthless self-invention. From the 1890s onwards, Yeats saw himself as in quest of a fresh aesthetic that would allow him to intermarry his desire for a poetry that served a public role while eschewing rhetoric, permitted expression of the private dramas of the inner self while having a universal dimension and captured the disjunctions and dissonance of the modern world while not renouncing a unity of structure.

Due to their diffusiveness, the precise moments of origin of modernism are difficult to pinpoint. By the same token, Yeats's self-induction into a more avant-garde aesthetic and his dismantling of the idealising premises and sentimental mannerisms of his youthful verse were gradual rather than instantaneous. However, his quarrels with many of the tenets and goals of the Irish literary revival ushered in a phase of proleptic modernism that is evident in the work that he produced from the early twentieth century onwards. This transition is one that Yeats himself acknowledged: when outlining the stages of development of modern poetry, he observed with acerbic nicety that 'in 1900 everybody got down off his stilts; henceforth nobody drank absinthe with his black coffee'.[20] This alteration in sensibility is already palpable in his 1904 collection, *In the Seven Woods*. In 'Adam's Curse' in this volume, for example, he abandoned the apocalyptic mood of his earlier lyrics and adopted a new casual style and muted mood in order to sketch an affecting account of the joint travails of love and art. The conflicts between beauty, the desire for transcendence and the quotidian are thus reframed in this meditation; they remain metaphysical issues but are now resituated as part of a human drama. Maud Gonne and her sister, 'that beautiful mild woman', while still acting as ciphers of the ineluctable nature of female beauty, are also endowed with more commonplace roles as friends and interlocutors:

> We sat together at one summer's end,
> That beautiful mild woman, your close friend,
> And you and I and talked of poetry.
> I said, 'A line will take us hours maybe;
> Yet if it does not seem a moment's thought,
> Our stitching and unstitching has been naught.'

Poet and beloved are no longer caught in a predetermined pattern of opposition. Rather, they function as unwitting foils to each other; both must 'labour to be beautiful' and both are at the mercy of the onslaughts of time. The final lines reinvoke the symbolist cosmography of Yeats's earlier work, but immediately dislocate it by infusing it with the bathos of a resigned self-knowledge:

> I had a thought for no one's but your ears:
> That you were beautiful, and that I strove
> To love you in the old high way of love;
> That it had all seemed happy, and yet we'd grown
> As weary-hearted as that hollow moon.[21]

The deliberate simplicity of the concrete imagery, the ironising self-reflexivity, the satirical nuances and the oblique delineation of the everyday were to become an integral part of the armature of Yeats's poetry in the following decade.

It is in *Responsibilities: Poems and a Play*, a volume published in 1914, that his espousal of a modernist aesthetic made itself most fully apparent. The political upheavals he experienced as a playwright and as founder and director of the Irish National Theatre Society with Lady Gregory, J. M. Synge and AE (George Russell) acted as further catalysts for his poetic reinvention of himself. An additional spur for his realigned literary manner was his friendship with Ezra Pound that rapidly ensued from their first meeting in London in May 1909.[22] Their complex relationship, while founded on mutual influence, was also typified by alternating bouts of admiration and dissension. Compounding this intricate liaison, during the three winters, 1913–16, that Yeats and Pound spent together as intellectual *confrères* and artistic collaborators in Stone Cottage, Sussex, each poet in turn played the role of mentor of, and apprentice to, the other. Even though several of his initial publications had been modelled on the ethereal style of the early Yeats, especially *A Lume Spento*, Pound also famously corrected and tightened drafts of texts that eventually appeared in *Responsibilities*, thereby aiding and abetting – but not originating, as he was wont to claim – the emergence of a transformed Yeatsian poetic.[23] In his two admiring reviews of the volume, he contrived unreservedly to endorse the 'change of manner' in Yeats's style while yet firmly distinguishing it from the radicalism of Imagism, the rules of which he had recently formulated.[24] Despite his innovations, Yeats, in his eyes, remained associated with nineteenth-century Symbolism and the aesthetics of the 1890s. Both poets ultimately generated their versions of modernism by drawing upon and often strategically misreading their overlapping aesthetic precepts to legitimate seemingly divergent principles and aims.

The economic directness that Yeats assumed as the hallmark of a modern mode of artistry informed the subject matter as well as the style and imagery of *Responsibilities*. Overtly topical, satirical verse, such as 'To a Wealthy Man who promised a Second Subscription to the Dublin Municipal Gallery if it were proved the People wanted Pictures', 'On those that hated *The Playboy of the Western World*, 1907' and 'September 1913', were interleaved with poignant love poems, such as 'Fallen Majesty', and bacchanalian meditations on the afterlife, such as 'Running to Paradise' and 'The Mountain Tomb'. The stridency of the satirical denunciations, in particular, evinces a new sense of alienation from, and disaffection with, contemporary reality. A heroic Ireland of dead immortals – such as the idealism associated with John O'Leary in 'September 1913' or with Parnell in 'To a Shade' – is counterposed with an anti-heroic present. Several of these frenetic, jarring and often foreshortened lyrics deploy concrete images to give voice to esoteric truths or fragmentary insights: 'The Dolls' and 'A Coat' unfurl pointed but cryptic allegories about art, while 'The Magi' reflects on the recursive cycles of history by reimagining the return of the biblical kings in a renewed search for the 'uncontrollable mystery on the bestial floor'.[25] Above all, the formal variety and miscellaneous moods of the collection suggest that Ireland is now splintered into numerous conflicting zones, a crassly conservative nation of clerics and shopkeepers, an untamed rural domain of beggars, hermits and visionaries, and a liminal sphere that permits a transit to moments of transcendence.

The most enduring of Yeats's compositions in this first phase of his experimentation with modernist technique may be found in *Michael Robartes and the Dancer*, published in 1921. Unlike the jolting juxtapositions and dissonances of *Responsibilities*, this collection fruitfully interweaves satire and lyric exploration, history and mythology, image and idea. It is framed by major alterations in the poet's life in the personal and political spheres: his recent marriage to George Hyde-Lees and the birth of his daughter, on the one hand, and the trauma and bitter aftermath of the 1916 Rising, on the other. In 'Easter 1916', published belatedly in this collection, a resonant assessment of the Rising is achieved through the use of theatrical metaphors to describe the cataclysmic change that it wrought. The 'casual comedy' and satirical charges of the first half of the poem cede to the heroic tragedy and declamatory insistence of the second half. In restaging the events of 1916 in symbolic terms, Yeats succeeds in transmuting the events of politics into art. Even though the redounding refrain, 'All changed, changed utterly / A terrible beauty is born', seems emphatic, it is hedged with images that underscore the divided response to this violent event.[26] Change in the poem is ambiguously rendered as both idealism and fanaticism, yet it is a process in which the poet includes himself as he invents and adopts a symbolic language capable of providing its measure. 'The Second Coming' is, similarly, a crisis lyric that conjures up the dramatic scenario of a perverted replay of the original Nativity to capture the impact of the major calamities of twentieth-century history, including the First World War, the Bolshevik Revolution and the War of Independence in Ireland. The poem, however, leaves undetermined whether the apocalyptic rebirth presaged is a welcome portent or a vision of horror. In inventing metaphoric vehicles to describe change, modernism paradoxically both submits itself to modernity but also resists its advances.

The pendant volumes, *The Tower* (1928) and *The Winding Stair and Other Poems* (1933), may be seen as Yeats's key contribution to the annals of modernist poetry. Although their themes had been anticipated by his preceding work, they enunciated a more searching, subtly imagined and differentiated vision of world affairs and of Irish politics. They constitute Yeats's searing philosophical summation of modernity and metacritique of the strategies and possibilities of modernism. As will be seen, it is particularly in their assessment of history, their treatment of the themes of alienation and fragmentation and the conceptualisation of the modern subject, whether as the ageing poet-surveyor or as the unruly outcast, Crazy Jane, that they provide a telling and uniquely configured counterweight to *The Waste Land* and *The Cantos*.

The composite image of the tower which operates simultaneously as the informing metaphor, theme and location of his book of poems permitted Yeats to fuse a universal topos with a private archive of associations and an arcane symbol with a material object. Further, this redolent cipher bridged several temporal domains through uniting personal biography with public history. The tower in question was Thoor Ballylee, a ruined Anglo-Norman keep that Yeats purchased in County Galway in 1916 and converted the following year. It had originally been built by the members of the de Burgo dynasty as they expanded their power-base in the west of Ireland during the late medieval period. Hence, it encapsulated the beginnings of the colonial conquest of the country. The sale of the property arose due to changes in legislation introduced by the late nineteenth-century land acts which facilitated the gradual handover of property from Anglo-Irish landowners to the native Irish. Thoor Ballylee had once been part of the estate of Lady Gregory, Yeats's friend and literary collaborator, who lived close by. Accordingly, the change in ownership of the tower and the surrounding land – which was purchased by local shareholders – symbolised a significant shift in civic governance and the advent of political independence. Yeats's occupancy of the tower, however, complicated this process as socially he belonged to the very class, the Anglo-Irish, now under siege in the newly emerging Ireland. Symbolically in his poetic invention, he situated himself at a flashpoint between several intersecting histories that converged on the tower and awkwardly straddled several clashing roles as visionary and victim, custodian and dispossessed, oppressor and outcast. Tellingly, after the publication of *The Tower*, Yeats ceased living in Thoor Ballylee for practical and personal reasons, thus fulfilling the thematic insights of his work, the precariousness of ownership and tenancy and the tenuousness even of imaginative and spiritual dominion.

The publication history of *The Tower* also illustrates its elusive hybridity, the complex positioning of a cultural artefact in a colonial culture and the variable sociopolitical contexts of the modernist book. Issued by Macmillan in 1928, it was assembled from three prior short collections that appeared under the auspices of Cuala Press, the cottage publishing industry run by

Yeats's sisters. The poems were reordered in the final collection and several texts were also omitted. Consequently, as George Bornstein has argued, it is impossible to pinpoint the essence or final form of this volume, which was subsequently reorganised once again for the posthumous publication of Yeats's *Collected Poems*.[27] *The Tower*, in effect, is a phantom made up of several shifting sequences and modulating patterns. Further, Yeats's practice of dual publication, through a metropolitan London-based imprint and his sisters' artisan press, created several competing identities, destinations and audiences for his work. The Cuala Press, originally called Dun Emer Press, was founded as part of the nationalist endeavour to establish local industry and specifically to give employment to women.[28] Its radical socialist and feminist underpinnings are evident in its carefully crafted productions, which regularly included a colophon denominating the place of publication and the names of the printing staff. Although the print runs were small and sales were achieved via subscription lists, the Cuala Press did not merely target a local coterie audience as it was heavily dependent on overseas sales, especially in the United States. Conversely, the Macmillan edition of *The Tower*, even though designed for wider dissemination in the marketplace, is given the appearance of an ornate, handmade work of art through the inclusion on the cover and dust jacket of T. Sturge Moore's engraving of a tower mirrored by its reflection in water.[29] Thus, Yeats's work traffics ambiguously between spheres: it is at once an item of international commerce, a by-product of nationalist principles of democracy and self-determination, an example of shape-shifting modernist textuality and a mutable but high-minded work of art.

In its current structure, *The Tower* opens with 'Sailing to Byzantium' and concludes with 'All Souls' Night'. Hence, the volume progresses from a text expressing the desire to escape into a perfect, transcendent world to a poem of conjuration that summons the spirits of the dead and commands them down to earth. A trajectory out into the other world is offset by an encounter with spirits on the earthly plain. Such a dialectical balancing of counterforces also typifies the patterns of temporal change discerned by Yeats in *A Vision*, the idiosyncratic study of esoteric philosophy that he published in 1925. In this text, he contended that history was organised like a series of inverted cones or spiralling gyres and consisted of alternating cycles of primary and antithetical phases. The primary dispensation was associated with feminine principles such as order, democracy, abstraction and unity, while the antithetical was linked with masculine attributes such as evil, war, power, aristocracy and art. Moreover, even though these opposing eras occurred consecutively, they also interpenetrated and overlapped.

The overriding themes of *The Tower*, as announced by the opening poem, are old age, loss, disorder, the chaos of the modern world and, as Terence Brown has observed, the necessity for power.[30] The final line of 'Sailing to Byzantium', in alluding to 'what is past, or passing, or to come', redirects attention from the golden sphere of art to the transience of earthly existence but does so as proof of the ordering capacity of poetry.[31] In all of the succeeding texts, the retrospection of old age provides a disturbing vantage point upon Irish history, casting into relief its violence and destructiveness. However, despite this emphasis on the recurrence of loss and cruelty and the perennial registering of the futility of existence – since as the poem, 'Nineteen Hundred and Nineteen', bleakly declares, 'Man is in love and loves what vanishes'[32] – the antinomial vision underpinning the collection still succeeds in locating temporary moments of consolation or at least stoic acceptance. But, equally, history is depicted as a thwarted dialectic; its antitheses continue to be unleashed and never lead to stasis.

Not least amongst the innovations of this volume is that Yeats designed flexible poetic forms to give contour to the unwieldy subject matter of modernity and to encapsulate his apprehension of the spiralling and recursive revolutions of historical change. The sequence poems that predominate at the opening and ending of *The Tower*, including the title poem, 'Meditations in Time of Civil War', 'Nineteen Hundred and Nineteen' and 'All Souls' Night', concretise the cyclical nature of temporality while also mirroring its randomness. Unlike the allusiveness and fragmentation that characterise *The Waste Land* and *The Cantos* and run the risk of unravelling the processes of signification entirely, Yeatsian formalism establishes unity and coherence even as it also articulates the splintered nature of experience. The broken but still intact linearity of the sequence poems, which is adhered to even by the shorter texts in the collection, permits an intermeshing of perceptions while never suppressing the counter-forces that lie in wait to sabotage existence and pervert order. Even as each poetic meditation opens out to encompass widening aspects of historical memory, it braids and intermarries them into a continuum. Moreover, due to his investment in what Jefferson Holdridge terms 'the terrible sublime' – that is, moments of dissolution and violence that threaten to undermine the very basis of the self – Yeats problematically conceives of enlightenment as emanating even from disruption and bloodshed.[33] Hence, the brutality of history and its moments of breakdown, while being laid bare, also become part of a continuous design.

An analysis of the title poem illustrates such patterns. The initial section of 'The Tower' homes in on the isolated subject and emotively depicts the plight of the ageing self and artist:

> What shall I do with this absurdity–
> O heart, O troubled heart – this caricature,
> Decrepit age that has been tied to me
> As to a dog's tail?[34]

The second longer segment counters this narrowness of focus and broadens into a protracted and expansive survey of the former denizens of the tower and of the surrounding district throughout the ages, including members of the eighteenth-century elite, the 'rough men-at-arms' that were involved in local skirmishes and outcasts such as Raftery, the Gaelic poet. The historical panorama of selves and counter-selves conjures up the figure of Red Hanrahan, a half-crazed, visionary poet who featured in Yeats's *The Secret Rose* (1897). He furnishes a further mask or anti-self for the poet and in so doing enables a simultaneous enlargement of sympathy to subsume all of human decrepitude and an intensified submersion in personal and collective memory, both phantasmagoric and historical:

> Did all old men and women, rich and poor,
> Who trod upon these rocks or passed this door,
> Whether in public or in secret rage
> As I do now against old age?
> But I have found an answer in those eyes
> That are impatient to be gone;
> Go therefore; but leave Hanrahan,
> For I need all his mighty memories.[35]

The altering stress patterns, despite the regular eight-line stanza, and the erratic use of rhyme and off-rhyme further enhance the antitheses of desire and fulfilment, empathy and self-obsession. The third and final instalment of the poem shifts from the contemplation of bodily decline and the accumulating losses of history to an examination of the soul and the recuperative function of art. Here the mood also modulates from despair to acceptance and even exhilaration. The declamatory tone of the ending, however, cedes to a trailing vision that painfully tracks physical diminishment, a mounting litany of deaths and the bittersweet lure of the natural world. While soul-making and 'a bird's sleepy cry' are held in unresolved apposition, it is implied that the power of the artist still wins through due to its facility for juxtaposing, if not fully harmonising, such untenable antinomies:

> Now shall I make my soul,
> Compelling it to study
> In a learned school
> Till the wreck of body,
> Slow decay of blood,

Testy delirium
Or dull decrepitude,
Or what worse evil come–
The death of friends, or death
Of every brilliant eye
That made a catch in the breath–
Seem but the clouds of the sky
When the horizon fades;
Or a bird's sleepy cry
Among the deepening shades.[36]

Another wide-ranging sequence poem, 'Meditations in Time of Civil War', marries the pervasive modernist theme of the disintegration of the self with an investigation of the processes of historical change and privation. The subject, while under threat in Yeats's oeuvre, is never faced with ultimate dissolution because of its implication in cycles of personal, historical and social renewal. 'Meditations in Time of Civil War' is centrally concerned with the uncomfortable divisions of Irish history that – at the time of its composition – were still being played out during the bloody interlude of the civil war which pitted rival political factions against each other. The successive subdivisions of the poem choreograph an even starker staging of the clashes between civilisation and violence and between art and destruction than in 'The Tower'. Further, the house, whether the gracious ancestral demesne of the Anglo-Irish landlord or Yeats's ancient tower, is discovered to be grounded on the actions of 'bitter and violent men'. Yet, this abiding contradiction culminates in the first section of the poem in a lament for the passing of Anglo-Ireland which uneasily balances the recognition of the need for social redress with an overwhelming nostalgia for a culture in recession:

What if the glory of escutcheoned doors,
And buildings that a haughtier age designed,
The pacing to and fro on polished floors
Amid great chambers and long galleries, lined
With famous portraits of our ancestors;
What if these things the greatest of mankind
Consider most to magnify, or to bless,
But take our greatness with our bitterness?[37]

The intermeddling of stylistic registers typical of modernism further underlines the historical and ideological divides that Yeats is at pains to elucidate. An offhand banality allied with a suggestive invocation of natural imagery, for example, is used to pattern the encounter between the poet and 'an affable

Irregular', a member of the Irish Republican Army who is fighting in local hostilities. The prayerful intercession that ends the penultimate section of the poem seems – at least implicitly – to open up the possibility of renewal and unity in the image of bees, signs of plenitude and industry, returning to build a hive in the crumbling tower:

> We had fed the heart on fantasies,
> The heart's grown brutal from the fare;
> More substance in our enmities
> Than in our love; O honey-bees,
> Come build in the empty house of the stare.

But consolation is refused as the final part of this poetic dissection of the fluctuations of history resurrects all of the bitter conflicts that it had seemingly suppressed. The visionary artist climbs to the top of the tower and is visited by 'monstrous familiar images' in which the eternal opposition of order and murderous destruction is renewed.[38] Art is imbricated with the violence of historical processes and cannot extricate itself from their self-perpetuating repetitions.

Similar preoccupations are also evident in 'Leda and the Swan'. In retelling this mythical story, Yeats is revisiting a classical tale much favoured by poets and sculptors through the ages who tended, however, to see it as an untroubled tale of divine encounter. By contrast, Yeats firmly modernises and radicalises the legend by restoring attention to its physicality and the brutality of the rape of Leda. Disjunction and division are registered both thematically and formally. The use of a caesura in the opening line ('A sudden blow: the great wings beating still') and of a line division in line 11 underscores the atmosphere of crisis and irregularity. In addition, Yeats deliberately overlays the structures of the European and the English sonnet to magnify the sense of breakdown; the poem may be variously read as dividing into an octave and sestet, in the Petrarchan manner, or as conforming to the Shakespearean mode and splitting into three quatrains and a couplet. Traditional forms are decomposed by the modernist artist to achieve the dissonant effects that he requires. Despite its foregrounding of violation, ambivalence and epistemological uncertainty, however, still predominate in the text. Although the rape of Leda resulted in the birth of Helen of Troy and the deadly conflicts with which she was associated, allegorically, the visitation of a human by a god also suggests the possibility of an inrush of divine afflatus. The terrible sublime of history, it is intimated in the final lines, may still permit the acquisition of wisdom and provide the pathway to artistic inspiration:

Being so caught up,
So mastered by the brute blood of the air,
Did she put on his knowledge with his power
Before the indifferent beak could let her drop?[39]

The ambiguous positioning of the modernist artist is likewise placed under
scrutiny in 'Among School Children' and 'All Souls' Night'. In the former
text, irony is used to puncture the putative authority of the poet who is
unmasked as simply 'a sixty-year-old smiling public man' while on a visit to
the Sisters of Mercy school in Waterford. The extended reverie that follows
from this dislocating recognition depicts art neither as a Platonic quest nor
as a search for mastery. The memory of the 'Ledean body' of his beloved,
Maud Gonne, leads to a redefined modern aesthetic that is captured by the
culminating metaphors of the blossoming chestnut tree and of the performing dancer.[40] In this light, art is reconceived as process and embodiment.
This new formulation of a corporeal but mystical artistry dissociates it from
damaging myths of potency and from outdated illusions of order while refusing to relinquish, in typical Yeatsian manner, a belief in the necessity for
form and for transcendent authority. 'All Souls' Night', following its eerie
mustering of the ghosts of dead friends, also concludes with a complex,
self-conscious peroration about the role of the poet and the processes of
creativity:

Such thought – such thought have I that hold it tight
Till meditation master all its parts,
Nothing can stay my glance
Until that glance run in the world's despite
To where the damned have howled away their hearts,
And where the blessed dance;
Such thought, that in it bound
I need no other thing,
Wound in mind's wandering
As mummies in the mummy-cloth are wound.[41]

The poet here remains a visionary or adept who is committed to a perpetual
apprenticeship and to an unremitting quest for elusive wisdom. Negation
and death may now be the grounds of modern art but, nonetheless, The
Tower, Yeats's grandiloquent and monumental probing of the conditions of
modernity and of the nature of contemporary Ireland, ends fittingly with an
image of self-sufficiency and resolve.

Such patriarchal pretensions, however, are dislodged by his next volume
of verse, The Winding Stair and Other Poems. The phallic imagery of his
previous work is called into question by the feminine image of the spiral

staircase, with its suggestion of sinuousness, domesticity and inwardness. Yeats's invention in this collection of a female mask or persona, Crazy Jane, in the sequence entitled 'Words for Music Perhaps', may be examined as a final instance of his experimental endeavour to forge a new, self-reflexive poetic aesthetic by redefining aspects of gender and voice and by continuing to scrutinise the ontological foundations of the lyric. Like many of his projected selves, Crazy Jane is a composite figure: she unites traits of the renegade beggars and outcasts in the many ballads about Ireland that he had composed, while also drawing on various literary stereotypes of the madwoman and witch. Cast as a social rebel, who excoriates convention, she is associated with an unapologetic eroticism and a desublimated physicality. Above all, Yeats uses her as a mouthpiece to decry the Catholic morality that he saw as having gained a further stranglehold on Irish society since the setting up of the Free State in 1922. Her unfettered pronouncements are designed as a challenge to the encroaching censorship of the newly founded Irish polity. Thus, in 'Crazy Jane and the Bishop', she openly declares her love for Jack the journeyman and attacks the bishop as a 'coxcomb',[42] while in 'Crazy Jane Talks with the Bishop' she enunciates a profanely pagan philosophy:

> A woman can be proud and stiff
> When on love intent;
> But love has pitched his mansion in
> The place of excrement;
> For nothing can be sole or whole
> That has not been rent.

Ultimately, through the nihilism, uncontainable libidinal energies and insubordination of Crazy Jane, Yeats attempts not just to invert bourgeois morality but to assert a new philosophy of difference where 'fair and foul are near of kin'.[43] Yet, the masculine privilege of the modernist poetic voice still remains intact as, ultimately, Crazy Jane ventriloquises the author's thoughts and does not speak in her own demotic but affects an educated register that has been imposed on her. Yeats's modernist redefinition of gender opens up the question of difference but cannot fully accommodate the voice of the Other.

The poetry of Yeats's final years, 1935–9, is haunted by a sense of belatedness and elegy but may still be seen as stamped by the modernist strategies that he had evolved at the beginning of the twentieth century. Indeed, *New Poems* published in 1938 builds into its title an ironic commentary on his age as well as a tongue-in-cheek reference to the modernist desire for innovation that he distrusted but with which he was indissolubly associated, both artistically and politically. Some of the extremism and political utopianism of his proleptic adoption of a new poetic is dissipated in his later work as he periodically adopted conservative, anti-democratic and even fascist views. 'The Curse of Cromwell', for example, is a harsh, nihilistic lament for the passage of time and the loss of civilised values which dismisses and denounces the modern world. However, 'The Black Tower', the final poem that Yeats composed, in January 1939, gathers together the anarchic energies of his later writing and reprises the image that acted as the locus for many of his modernist explorations and inventions. The tower now has been abandoned to a motley group of soldiers and servants in a premodern era who seem to be spent after some prolonged battle. However, the poem ends with an expectation of an imminent but unspecified revolutionary change or apocalypse ('the king's great horn'); the anticipation of renewal still charges even this parting reworking of a modernist trope:

> There in the tomb the dark grows blacker,
> But winds come up from the shore,
> They shake when the winds roar,
> Old bones on the mountain shake.[44]

Perversely, Yeats's anthology of modern verse for Oxford University Press bypasses most modernist poetry; the preface is dismissive of Eliot because of his plainness and banality, and of Pound because of his obsession with flux and his predilection for style over form. However, these omissions and misprisions are symptomatic and not merely wilful and accidental. Yeats's own modernism does not fully synchronise or mesh with the practice of his fellow poets. It had its roots in the politics of the Irish literary revival and in the ideals of cultural nationalism which he espoused, but against which he also rebelled. The transformations in Irish society that he sought involved the preservation of a richly endowed oral tradition that was in danger of being lost and the defence of social and cultural ideals that he increasingly linked with the world and achievements of the Anglo-Irish. His belief in unity of being and his lifelong, heterodox research into esoteric philosophy and mysticism, in addition, gave his poetry a visionary force that separated him from his peers. Because of his unique heritage and disposition and his wary rejection of many of its goals, Yeats's pioneering adoption of modernism has often been overlooked. However, in its radical juncture of the traditional and the new, its promotion of a materialist aesthetic with spiritualist underpinnings, its reinvention of formalism to encompass flux, fragmentation and change and its intermarriage of symbolist and political themes, his poetry is an indispensable chapter in the history of twentieth-century avant-garde writing.

## NOTES

1. W. B. Yeats (ed.), *The Oxford Book of Modern Verse, 1892–1935* (Oxford: Clarendon Press, 1936), p. xxxvi.
2. Ezra Pound, *Literary Essays of Ezra Pound*, ed. T. S. Eliot (London: Faber and Faber, 1954), p. 34.
3. See Hugh Kenner, *A Colder Eye: The Modern Irish Writers* (New York: Alfred A. Knopf, 1983).
4. See Graham Hough, 'The Modernist Lyric', in *Modernism: A Guide to European Literature 1890–1930*, ed. Malcolm Bradbury and James McFarlane (Harmondsworth: Penguin, 1976), pp. 312–22.
5. See C. K. Stead, *The New Poetic: Yeats to Eliot*, revised edition (1964; London: Continuum, 2005).
6. See Lawrence Rainey (ed.), *Modernism: An Anthology* (Oxford: Blackwell, 2005). The selections from Yeats's poetry and essays are on pp. 301–74; they are preceded by the poetry and prose of Pound on pp. 39–113.
7. See Tim Armstrong, *Modernism: A Cultural History* (London: Polity, 2005); Alex Davis and Lee M. Jenkins (eds), *Locations of Literary Modernism: Region and Nation in British and American Modernist Poetry* (Cambridge University Press, 2000); Astradur Eysteinsson, *The Concept of Modernism* (Ithaca: Cornell University Press, 1990).
8. See Marjorie Perloff, *21st-Century Modernism: The 'New' Poetics* (Oxford: Blackwell, 2002).
9. See Michael Levenson, *A Genealogy of Modernism: A Study of English Literary Doctrine 1908–1922* (Cambridge University Press, 1984), pp. vii–xi.
10. For histories of the revival, see Margaret Kelleher (ed.), *New Perspectives on the Irish Literary Revival, Irish University Review* 33.1 (Spring/Summer 2003); P. J. Mathews, *Revival: The Abbey Theatre, Sinn Féin, The Gaelic League and the Co-operative Movement* (Cork University Press in Association with Field Day, 2003); and Betsey Taylor FitzSimon and James H. Murphy (eds), *The Irish Revival Reappraised* (Dublin: Four Courts Press, 2004).
11. W. B. Yeats, *The Poems*, ed. Daniel Albright (London: Everyman, 1990), p. 70.
12. See Fredric Jameson, *A Singular Modernity: Essay on the Ontology of the Present* (London: Verso, 2002), pp. 40–1.
13. See Douglas Hyde, 'The Necessity for De-Anglicising Ireland', in *Language, Lore and Lyrics: Essays and Lectures*, ed. Brendán Ó Conaire (Dublin: Irish Academic Press, 1986), pp. 153–70. The lecture was first delivered to The National Literary Society, Dublin, 25 November 1892.
14. W. B. Yeats, 'The De-Anglicizing of Ireland', *Uncollected Prose by W. B. Yeats*, vol. I, *First Reviews and Articles 1886–1896*, ed. John P. Frayne (London: Macmillan, 1970), p. 255.
15. W. B. Yeats, 'Nationality and Literature', *Uncollected Prose*, vol. I, p. 273.
16. See W. B. Yeats, *Mythologies* (London: Macmillan, 1959), pp. 5–140.
17. W. B. Yeats, *Autobiographies: Memories and Reflections* (1955; London: Bracken Books, 1995), p. 181.
18. See Yeats, *Autobiographies*, pp. 279–349.
19. See W. B. Yeats, *Essays and Introductions* (London: Macmillan, 1961), for his accounts of the writers that inspired him.

20. Yeats, *The Oxford Book of Modern Verse*, p. xi.

21. Yeats, *The Poems*, pp. 106, 107.

22. On the friendship between Ezra Pound and Yeats, see Richard Ellmann, *Eminent Domain: Yeats Among Wilde, Joyce, Pound, Eliot and Auden* (New York: Oxford University Press, 1967), pp. 57–87, and James Longenbach, *Stone Cottage: Pound, Yeats and Modernism* (Oxford University Press, 1988).

23. For discussion of Pound's corrections to the early drafts of these poems, see William H. O'Donnell (ed.), *Responsibilities: Manuscript Material by W. B. Yeats* (Ithaca: Cornell University Press, 2003), pp. xxxiv–xxxix.

24. Pound, *Literary Essays*, p. 379. This review of *Responsibilities* originally appeared in *Poetry* (Chicago) 4.2 (May 1914), 64–9.

25. Yeats, *The Poems*, p. 177.

26. Yeats, *The Poems*, pp. 229, 228.

27. See George Bornstein, *Material Modernism: The Politics of the Page* (Cambridge University Press, 2001), pp. 65–81.

28. For a history of the press, see Liam Miller, *The Dun Emer Press, Later The Cuala Press* (Dublin: Dolmen, 1973).

29. For a reproduction of T. Sturge Moore's cover design, see Bornstein, *Material Modernism*, p. 75.

30. See Terence Brown, *The Life of W. B. Yeats* (Dublin: Gill and Macmillan, 1999), p. 315.

31. Yeats, *The Poems*, p. 240.

32. Yeats, *The Poems*, p. 254.

33. Jefferson Holdridge, *Those Mingled Seas: The Poetry of W. B. Yeats, The Beautiful and the Sublime* (University College Dublin Press, 2000), pp. 40–53.

34. Yeats, *The Poems*, p. 240.

35. Yeats, *The Poems*, pp. 242, 243.

36. Yeats, *The Poems*, p. 245.

37. Yeats, *The Poems*, pp. 246, 247.

38. Yeats, *The Poems*, pp. 250, 251.

39. Yeats, *The Poems*, p. 260.

40. Yeats, *The Poems*, p. 261.

41. Yeats, *The Poems*, p. 282.

42. Yeats, *The Poems*, p. 306.

43. Yeats, *The Poems*, p. 310.

44. Yeats, *The Poems*, p. 379.

# 8

DREW MILNE

# Modernist poetry in the British Isles

Mina Loy's poem 'Brancusi's Golden Bird' was first published, next to a photograph of Brancusi's sculpture, in the same 1922 issue of the *Dial* as T. S. Eliot's *The Waste Land*. If *The Waste Land* has become familiar as a pivotal text in the institutionalisation of Eliot,[1] Loy's poem remains unassimilated, still suggestive for what might become of twenty-first-century neo-modernism.[2] 'Brancusi's Golden Bird' is one among several poems in which Loy finds analogues and affiliations in the persons and works of her contemporaries. Elliptical and witty, these poems carve out transfers of energy from language used as an imagistic mode of description to a more synthetic, aesthetic compound. Combining free-verse forms, vowel over consonant patterns, with a sense of the play of concretion on the page, her poems have a sculptural and musical palpability. 'Brancusi's Golden Bird' moves from what might seem like a representation of another medium towards a poetics whose delight in Latinate concretion sits deftly across line breaks and intimations of a new silence in writing:

> an incandescent curve
> licked by chromatic flames
> in labyrinths of reflections
>
> This gong
> of polished hyperaesthesia
> shrills with brass
> as the aggressive light
> strikes
> its significance
>
> The immaculate
> conception
> of the inaudible bird
> occurs
> in gorgeous reticence[3]

Such textures could be read as a compound of currents in Futurism, Cubism and Vorticism. There are features akin to elements in the poetry and poetics of Apollinaire, Gertrude Stein and Wyndham Lewis, and in ways that look forward to the wit and artifice of Frank O'Hara. Exercises in comparison nevertheless miss the extent to which Loy's poetry, although informed by an astute and critical relation to contemporary avant gardes, proposes something different, a modernist poetics of social wit, artifice and aesthetic sensibility that is engaging and original. The orientation of Loy's modernism can be gleaned from her critical remarks in 'Gertrude Stein' (1924):

> Modernism has democratized the subject matter and *la belle matière* of art; through cubism the newspaper has assumed an aesthetic quality, through Cezanne a plate has become more than something to put an apple upon, Brancusi has given an evangelistic import to eggs, and Gertrude Stein has given us the Word, in and for itself.[4]

As her own paintings and lampshades confirm, Loy's democratic modernism was concerned with modernism across the arts as well as with avant-garde conceptions of design. While her poems could be read as exemplary negotiations of problems familiar from critical accounts of Ezra Pound and T. S. Eliot, her work satirises the more monumental and heroic postures of her modernist male contemporaries. Moreover, as Peter Nicholls suggests,

> in *Love Songs* (1915–1917) and her long poem *Anglo-Mongrels and the Rose* (1923–5), modernist irony is fundamentally reformulated, as the reflexivity of her style turns the force of critique back upon the self instead of directing it outwards, against other people. . . . [T]he frame of what we normally think of as Anglo-American modernism is turned inside out, as style is grasped not as the privileged vehicle of avant-garde authority but rather as witness to its metaphysical pretensions.[5]

The continuing vitality of her poetry suggests very different modes of reading from those institutionalised as Anglo-American modernism.

Loy was very well connected to avant-garde circles and at the centre of social networks in London, Paris, Florence and New York, counting among her acquaintances and admirers such luminary figures as Filippo Tommaso Marinetti, Marcel Duchamp, Stein, Pound, Edward Gordon Craig, Djuna Barnes and William Carlos Williams. It is all the more surprising, then, that a British poet so well connected should appear only in the margins of so many accounts of modernist poetry. In 1922, she could be seen as a figure on the cusp of achieving critical recognition as significant as Eliot, and yet, despite the sustained brilliance of her 1923 collection, *Lunar Baedeker*, Loy remains the lesser-known poet. Many different stories could be told to account for this. Loy wrote fascinating aphorisms, manifestoes, pamphlets and critical essays, but her poetry is not easily positioned through her criticism. While modernism was evidently a movement in which women writers were central, critical models have often excluded women writers from any but social or biographical accounts.[6] Writers of the centrality of Stein are often not even recognised as poets. The texture of Loy's work, with its controversial sexual and social politics, resists philological commentary or any easy location within the academic study of poetry. Her Futurist feminism also resists feminist critical paradigms developed in the second half of the twentieth century. Perhaps the most paradoxical barrier to recognition of Loy's work, however, is the extent to which her work resists nationalist or regional categories. This helps to illustrate difficulties central to any account of modernist poetry in the British Isles.

Born in London in 1882 of English and Hungarian parents, Loy lived and worked in Munich, Paris, Florence and New York, spending most of the 1920s and 1930s in Paris, before returning to America in 1936. Although she became a naturalised American citizen in 1946, her earlier career is that of a London Englishwoman at the cosmopolitan heart of European modernism. Attempts have been made to claim Loy as an 'American' modernist,[7] but her intellectual trajectories and geographical displacements are also characteristic of British modernism. Loy's work dismantles and satirises what it might mean to be an English or British woman. This is perhaps best exemplified by her own long auto-mythological poem *Anglo-Mongrels and the Rose*.[8] It remains paradoxical, then, that Irish and American writers – notably W. B. Yeats, Pound and Eliot – should remain so central to critical accounts of modernist poetry in the British Isles, while poets of British origin, such as Loy, should have come to seem un-English or un-British. As well as providing a striking but by no means unique example of democratic, modernist poetic practices developed out of Britain, her career also illustrates the way national categories have marginalised British modernist poets. Comparable patterns of geopolitical marginality can be seen in the reception of poets such as David Jones, Hugh MacDiarmid and Basil Bunting. The preoccupation of many British modernists with the development of internationally self-reflexive poetry in English has left British modernists at odds with European and American accounts of modernism. Along with the shrinking global power of British imperialism, the reduction of horizons from international poetics of writing in English to specifically English or British geographical contexts has been particularly damaging for British modernist poets working through internationalist, metropolitan or cosmopolitan concerns. Samuel Beckett, for example, is hardly an Irish, English, British, French or even a

German modernist, but his work cuts across such categories while also being central to English- and French-language modernist poetics. Beyond nationalist narratives and the fallibility of merely geopolitical identity categories, the critical interest is in the continuing vitality of modernist modes which offer alternatives to the now exhausted modernism of the Yeats–Eliot–Pound paradigm.

In their 1927 book, *A Survey of Modernist Poetry*, Laura Riding and Robert Graves seek to placate the 'plain reader'. This fictional character's supposed resistances to modernist poetry are to be confronted and overcome. They begin with a close reading of a poem by E. E. Cummings. Despite apparent 'technical oddities', absence of capitals, lack of punctuation and so forth, his poem is shown not to be 'a mere assemblage of words, a literary trick', but something 'capable of yielding the kind of experiences customarily expected from poetry'.[9] In short, beneath the apparently newfangled surface, there lies a deeper continuity with traditional poetry. The suggestion is not that Cummings is a superficial modernist who harbours a premodernist conception of poetry, though this could be argued. Rather, the reading offers the more general reassurance that modernist poetry is readable and continuous with poetic tradition. Sketching tendencies in French poetry associated with Mallarmé, Rimbaud and Valéry, they suggest the importance of French modes imitated by modernist English poetry. Overall, they provide a provocative overview of modernist poetry in English, but an overview primarily concerned to legitimate and defend modernist poetry against imagined scepticisms. Symptomatically, even such an early characterisation of a specifically 'English' modernist poetry begins with the need to address the kind of opposition dramatised by the critical fiction of the 'plain' reader.

The strategy of *A Survey of Modernist Poetry*, then, is not to trumpet a manifesto or make pronouncements on the overthrow of established values which might make modernist poetry exciting. Rather, the book seeks to reassure readers that the modernism in question is not fashionable or modishly contemporary but thoroughly traditional, and amenable to close reading. This might be taken as a template for the curiously apologetic, defensive, often conservative or tradition-bound approaches put forward by many avowed modernists in Britain. In trying to make modernism more intelligible and sympathetic, British modernists have often sought to domesticate the quality of those determined affronts to bourgeois tastes and values associated with Futurism, Vorticism, Constructivism, Dada and Surrealism.[10] Defensive domestication of modernism has been more significant, however, at the level of publicity and critical discussion, while the more substantive engagements of British modernist poetry have often been diverted by internalising resistances to modernism within poetic theory and practice. This in part explains why the fate of modernist poetry in Britain bears so little resemblance to the more Eurocentric history of the avant garde implied by Peter Bürger.[11] Mina Loy's exemplary engagement with avant-garde art and poetics could be traced through Dada and Surrealism to later modernist poets working in Britain, such as Kurt Schwitters, Bob Cobbing, Edwin Morgan and Ian Hamilton Finlay. Discussion of explicit avant-garde groupings and strategies is largely absent from the account given by Riding and Graves, and this is echoed by their preference for the looser umbrella of 'modernism'. Suggesting the seriousness of a modernism distinct from avant gardism, Riding and Graves present themselves as determined to resist false accommodations with plain readers, both in this book and in their poetry: 'The real discomfort to the reader in modernist poetry is the absence of the poet as his protector from the imaginative terrors lurking in it.'[12] The terrors may be merely imaginary, and the reality merely uncomfortable, but there is something rather bland about the prospect of a modernism that is only mildly uncomfortable, bracing perhaps, rather than revolutionary. Their defence of the impersonality of 'genuinely' modernist poetry remains torn between assertions of the necessary difficulty of impersonal modernism and special pleading for the ease with which such difficulties might be accommodated.

Poetry in Britain has long struggled with diffuse hostilities to anything resembling modernism, but perhaps the more disabling tendency is the internalisation of such hostilities by poets otherwise sympathetic to modernism. Self-imposed restrictions on the potential radicalism of modernist poetics have cramped many a British modernist poem, burdening intimations of modern freedoms with romanticist shades. Modernists have also wasted valuable energy finding critical strategies to overcome indifference to their work, especially perhaps in Britain, but often in a self-defeating focus on the sensibilities of nonexistent, indifferent or fictional readers. Conscious and unconscious hostilities to modernism have nevertheless been active and widespread. Anti-modernists of various kinds have queued up to suggest that modernism has never taken root in Britain, or is marginal to what are presented as more central or more mainstream currents.

Resistances to modernism have defined many tendentious anthologies which have simply ignored the variety of poetry produced in the British Isles. Some resistances reflect considered preferences for earlier eighteenth- and nineteenth-century modes of poetry, while others are shaped by anti-metropolitan, anti-intellectual or Anglo-Saxon attitudes. Keith Tuma's recent *Anthology of Twentieth-Century British and Irish Poetry* is unusual in the way it positions modernism, seeking to redress a bias which, in his preface, Tuma describes as follows:

[I]t is the contemporary poetry that is most obviously indebted to an inter-national modernism that has fared worst in many of the anthologies of British and Irish poetry published over the last thirty years, especially by major pub-lishers in England, which until recently have seemed interested in perpetuating the influence of the Movement's anti-modernism as it emerged in the 1950s. I find the logic that declared a British (or Irish) poetry engaged with modernist traditions somehow 'foreign' to traditions purportedly more native or indige-nous altogether suspect. As a number of poets included here from earlier in the century demonstrate, it is simply no longer possible to pretend that modernism never happened in English poetry.[13]

As so often, there is evident strain here in the categories of British, Irish or English poetry. Despite the prominence of such boundaries in the title of his anthology, Tuma gives greater prominence to work informed by the more international horizons of modernism. There are still, however, literary his-torians concerned to sideline the importance of modernism in Britain. Chris Baldick's revisionist literary history argues that modernism was marginal in British poetry, writing dismissively of the 'flamboyant irrationalism'[14] of poets variously associated with Surrealism such as Dylan Thomas, Gascoyne and Charles Madge.[15] Baldick mentions David Jones in the context of dis-cussing representations of the First World War, but finds no room for figures as important as Hugh MacDiarmid, Loy or Basil Bunting. MacDiarmid, Jones and Bunting are also absent from the more sympathetic account of modernism suggested by Peter Nicholls's *Modernisms*. The battle between modernists and anti-modernists is continuously reworked while remaining within surprising levels of mutual indifference and ignorance. Despite being the metropolitan centre of an English-speaking 'commonwealth', the eco-nomic capital of the nineteenth century and a home of sorts for modernists such as Karl Marx, London appears never quite to have generated the avant-garde cultures associated with Berlin, Paris or New York. Malcolm Bradbury notes that 'The belief that Paris was the true capital of the Modernist arts, and London an anti-capital, was familiar enough from the 1880s onward.'[16] There are nevertheless historical moments, social clusters and international mediations that make up the discontinuous history of London modernism, from, say, William Blake to Allen Fisher.

Hostility to modernist poetry often reflects forms of provincialism or local-ism which prefer not to address the realities of a shrinking British empire, and the emergent metropolitanism of international capitalism. Many radi-cal writers and critics who might in other contexts be understood as mod-ernists have themselves attacked modernism as an elitist and reactionary cultural formation. Intriguing examples of such political resistances to mod-ernism are provided by British socialists from George Orwell to Raymond

Williams.[17] Within academic literary accommodations, the critical focus on the European and Anglo-American modernisms of Yeats, Joyce, Pound and Eliot have overshadowed the range of alternative modernist poetic practices developed in Britain. In one sense, modernist poetry in the British Isles has never quite overcome such resistances, real or imaginary, to become a settled critical orthodoxy or dominant position. But in another sense this peculiar domestication of embattled but defensively marginalised modes of modernist poetics defines what is distinctive about the fate and development of British modernism. The critical task, however, is to read British modernist poetry through some recognition of such difficulties but not by focusing on what might make such work 'British' – or indeed, Scottish, Welsh, Irish or part of some non-English but English-speaking diaspora – but by engaging with the substantive concern of different poetries in the light of possible cosmopolitan solidarities.

The domestication of modernism within a reconstruction of English poetic 'tradition' remains one key strategy, both within modernist poems, notably in *The Waste Land*, but also in the selective modernism institutionalised within critical representations. Different traditions have been offered to off-set the seemingly un-English or un-British dynamics of Anglo-American and European modernism, but the need to read British modernism through the history of English poetry cuts against the very possibility of what might make it 'modern'.[18] Along lines pioneered by Riding and Graves, moreover, critics have often preferred to discuss works amenable to close reading practices and explications rather than arguing for poetic practices less amenable to such critical scrutiny. Less evident or widely recognised, however, is the fragile solidarity forged by poets of American and English origins – such as Riding and Graves – across their transatlantic differences.

There is much that remains interesting in the critical reflections offered by Riding and Graves – for example, the way they disparage a modernism that is no longer modern, describing Georgianism and Imagism as 'dead movements'.[19] They criticise Imagism and its manifestoes as a 'stunt of commercial advertisers'; dismiss the 'insipidity' of H.D. (Hilda Doolittle);[20] and offer a sympathetic discussion of Stein. Some of their conceptual formulations are also highly suggestive for thinking about the politics of modernist poetic form: 'Modern poetry, that is, is groping for some principle of self-determination to be applied to the making of the poem – not lack of government, but government from within.'[21] Note the elasticity of *groping* in this formulation, undercutting any impression that authoritative autonomy has been achieved or declared. The radical attempt to develop poetry as a practice governed from within is indeed a key feature of what distinguishes self-consciously modernist poetic theory and practice from, say, types of poetry that happily regurgitate received categories and conventions without questioning what governs the processes of poetry.

Willingness to theorise poetic practice and to offer arguments that account for the formal and technical considerations elaborated in new work marks out an awareness of modernism more concerned with critical legitimacy than with reproducing historical traditions or inherited conventions. Especially revealing for the fate of modernism in the Britain Isles, however, is the way that the English modernism of Riding and Graves is so self-consciously defensive and articulated as an alliance of traditionalism and close reading. They read Hart Crane and Eliot, for example, through comparisons with Shakespeare, Milton and Tennyson. Further evidence of an emerging critical formation within British modernism is their apparently anachronistic account of Gerard Manley Hopkins as a modernist poet, a critical position echoed by F. R. Leavis.[22] Their chapter on punctuation and spelling in Shakespeare and Cummings is a striking example of modernist practical criticism, an example which predates protocols of close reading associated with I. A. Richards, William Empson and the New Criticism. The close readings offered in *A Survey of Modernist Poetry* were a direct spur to Empson, influencing the work that led to *Seven Types of Ambiguity* (1930). Indeed, it could be argued that Riding and Graves are part of a process in which modernist poetry in Britain became as influential for the development of criticism as for the development of poetry.

Eliot is the key figure in this peculiarly English domestication of modernism as criticism, in part through the centrality felt and ascribed to *The Waste Land*, but also through the power he exercised as an editor for the *Criterion* and for Faber and Faber. Eliot's criticism, notably his formulations of literary tradition and metaphysical poetry, provide the influential model by which the energies of enthusiastic readers of modernist poetry in Britain were diverted into critical readings of the history of English poetry. Eliot's 1926 Clark lectures on metaphysical poetry, although only published in 1993,[23] are an important symptom of the emergence of modernist criticism in Cambridge.[24] Eliot and his followers controlled many of the cultural institutions which have mediated modernism in the British Isles, obscuring or marginalising the range of alternatives within modernism. Attempts have been made to renew Eliot's avant-garde affinities.[25] Eliot's influence has nevertheless helped lock British modernism within a peculiar double bind whereby the forms of modernism which have seemed most viable, successful or popular are not those of the self-conscious avant garde, but forms which can be read as inheritors of premodernist English poetry, notably in retrospective conceptions of the modernism of seventeenth-century poetry.

The ideological emphasis on a singular 'tradition' of 'English' poetry, aside from offering a highly restrictive simplification of many different tendencies, obscures poets whose work is less evidently 'English' in its sense of geographical, linguistic, literary or historical context. MacDiarmid's poetry often engages critically with Eliot.[26] The decisive breakthrough in MacDiarmid's synthetic language of written poetry, however, is his use of the resources provided by dictionaries, beginning with the resemblances he found between Jamieson's *Etymological Dictionary of the Scottish Language* and James Joyce's *Ulysses*.[27] While indebted to the work and example of Pound, MacDiarmid was undoubtedly a Scottish nationalist concerned to reinvent and rework the resources of Scottish language and history, writing against what he perceived as the English ascendancy.[28] His role in developing a Scottish Renaissance[29] also has a socialist conception of international solidarities, interested in German and Russian modernisms as well as in Joycean poetics. After his early work in synthetic Scots, MacDiarmid's synthetic English is more consistently international and determined to stretch the otherwise restricted lexical range associated with 'English' poetry. The results are perhaps most sustained and explicit in poems such as 'On a Raised Beach' and *In Memoriam James Joyce*, the poems where any reader nervous of literary Scots diction might best begin an engagement with MacDiarmid's poetry.[30] As the poet Tom Leonard has argued:

> Seen as a whole, MacDiarmid's work – whether in 'Synthetic Scots', 'Synthetic English', or in the large chunks of untranslated French . . . – all of it stands for a life-long advocacy of, and concentration on, lexis itself: anti-existential in its insistence on the validity of the naming process, and through this process deliberately and constantly ignoring the boundaries of what would be considered 'correct' lexis for poetry.[31]

MacDiarmid's explorations in Joycean poetics and into the limits of language as the lexis of poetry remain important. Despite honourable mentions, the difficulty of assimilating MacDiarmid to Anglo-American modernism is such that some have even been tempted to position him as an early postmodernist. Nancy Gish writes, for example, that: 'It now seems increasingly clear that MacDiarmid wrote post-modern works in the early 1930s, works that seemed simply unpoetic or aesthetically unsuccessful by accepted critical standards of their time.'[32] Rather than engaging with the awkward periodicities associated with postmodernism, it is perhaps more important to recognise how MacDiarmid's radical rethinking of language in poetry breaks with restricted conceptions of poetry and with the critical standards which have been imposed upon British modernism both then and now.

More generally, the work of modernist poets in the British Isles rarely fits the categories pioneered by Eliot's Anglo-American modernism. Subsequent constructions of national traditions which have sought to separate American and Irish poetry from English poetry have left the critical contexts for reading English and British poetry in some confusion. Even the work of those closely associated with Eliot's critical models, such as Empson, is obscured when European or Anglo-American frames are applied. Empson's criticism remains significant in shaping approaches to the reading of poetry, not least in fostering a taste for ambiguity and structural complexity in poetic language, and could be understood as a major development of modernist poetics within criticism. As relevant to reading John Donne or Hopkins, his criticism reconstitutes earlier poetries in the light of modernism. Powerful strategies of formalist reading rewrite earlier texts, effectively generating a way of writing modernist poetry by other means, while implying a more passive preservation of literary history. Insofar as such criticism finds modernist potential in the history of English poetic tradition, there is as much urgency in discerning the modern qualities of Donne as in reading twentieth-century poetry. Symptomatically, moreover, the modernism of Empson's own poetry turns in on an acute reflexivity of form which seems to offer highly traditional poetic qualities. His formalism maintains the appearance of traditional literary forms, while his more modernist concerns with deeper questions of language, form and process are less easily recognised. His poems appear to ask for readings akin to Empson's own readings of Donne. Empson could be read, accordingly, as a modernist working through a dialogue between different levels of criticism, poetics and practice. It has been more common, however, for the very formal concentration and containment of Empson's poetry to seem conservative in its relation to tradition, even anti-modernist. Empson's criticism, moreover, has often appeared more helpful for reading earlier traditions than for understanding avant-garde formations resistant to protocols of close reading. Veronica Forrest-Thomson's *Poetic Artifice* takes issue with both Empson's criticism and his poetry, but, although her theory, poetics and poetic practice work out and away from Empson, her book is unusual in making explicit the importance of Empson for any account of modernist poetry in the British Isles.[33]

Despite such exceptions, the modernism of Empson's poetry and its development through modernist critical reflexivity remains largely unrecognised and unaccounted for. Perhaps the simplest explanation for this is that his poems do not immediately strike readers as being untraditional in the ways often found characteristic of modernism. Read against the work of American modernist poets, Empson's poetry might seem old-fashioned, too 'English', too bound up with the traditions of English poetic history or too lacking in formal radicalism. Given the importance for many American modernists of rejecting the shared heritage of poetry in English, it is perhaps unsurprising that such complaints have been levelled against British modernists by many American readers, and indeed by British readers whose approach to modernist poetry is through American or Anglo-American models. There is an important sense in which the reception of modernism in Britain is often historically out of step with, say, French or American developments, producing compounds of modern and premodern forms, and suggesting different models of literary progress and innovation.

Discussing the neglected work of John Rodker, Andrew Crozier suggests a process of reorientation needed to read writers whose modernism might unsettle received ideas and tastes: 'But if we are to read Rodker fully we need to renegotiate the canons of modernist decorum which condition our taste, and recognize that Rodker was able to make of modernism something more than we expect.'[34] Rodker's importance as a publisher and translator in the London–Paris modernist nexus – he published important work by Eliot, Pound and Wyndham Lewis – has long been recognised by scholars of literary modernism. More difficult, however, is the process of learning to read Rodker's poetry and poetic novel *Adolphe 1920* as more than merely secondary examples of familiar modernist paradigms. A similar willingness to reconsider overlooked poets working in Britain has seen renewed interest in poems such as Nancy Cunard's *Parallax* (1925).[35] Early critics, such as Leavis, dismissed *Parallax* as a 'simple imitation' of *The Waste Land*.[36] More recent discussions have emphasised critical differences which would decentre the importance of Eliot.[37] Empson's very English modernism, although informed by Eliot's Anglo-American modernism, exemplifies the way in which modernist British poetry might not even be recognised as modernist in more international contexts. Empson himself, moreover, was effectively exiled from Britain, living and working in Japan and China through the 1930s and 1940s, and his work can only with difficulty be contextualised geographically as that of an English or British poet.

The assimilation of modernism within English or British poetry remains awkward. Some writers explicitly question the validity of such 'national' categories in their poetry, but the loose pertinence of geopolitical identities is also a feature of poets such as Empson, Loy or Bunting, who lived and worked outside Britain for important parts of their lives. Lynette Roberts, for example, whose neglected poetry, most notably the long poem *Gods with Stainless Ears* (1951), is sometimes offered as an example of Welsh modernism, was born in Buenos Aires, Argentina, and spent most of her teenage years being educated in England.[38] Published under the auspices of Eliot's editorial role at Faber and Faber, *Gods with Stainless Ears* is also dedicated to

Edith Sitwell, herself a writer associated, somewhat superficially, with modernist poetic artifice. Although Laura Riding, notably in the period of her relationship with Robert Graves, owed much to British and English contexts, her work is scarcely assimilated within accounts of British or American modernism. Regionalists and nationalists have often preferred to cultivate their own back gardens, but the intranational and imperial history of British identities tends to unravel romantic and premodern fictions of national identity. To borrow an expression from Loy, modernist poets in Britain are perhaps better understood as 'Anglo-Mongrels'. British modernists have often been as concerned to rethink the status of English as the language of their work, as with using English as the language of England. Given the global reach of English as a language, modern English poetry need not always be read back through the history of English poetry.

Little is gained, then, by squeezing the work of linguistically and geographically nomadic writers back within the various regional or national identities competing within the British 'Isles'. Such categories have nevertheless worked to obscure the distinctive concerns of writers working in the British Isles, sometimes through the tendency to perceive such work as *less* modernist, or, conversely, through the tendency to see modernist poetry as somehow un-English or un-British. Writing more than half a century after the pioneering account of modernist poetry offered by Riding and Graves, Edward Lucie-Smith offers a symptomatic and historically acute hesitation. His 'Introduction to the Revised Edition' of *British Poetry Since 1945* notes how his earlier introduction had made the following claim:

> Poets in Britain are still coming to terms, not only with Britain's changed position in the world and the sudden upsurge of American literature, but with the fact of modernism itself. The past quarter of a century, with its pattern of action and reaction, has seen a painful adjustment to the fact that the modern sensibility is here to stay.[39]

Lucie-Smith's anthology included MacDiarmid, David Jones, Bunting and Gascoyne as relevant 'sources' for recent developments. By 1985, his confidence in the centrality of modernism has diminished:

> I now wonder if that adjustment really took place, at least in the sense which I described, and if it did, whether it wasn't ephemeral.... [T]he full reconciliation between the modernist spirit and British poetry which I looked forward to in 1970 has yet to take place.[40]

A sense of the unfinished assimilation of modernism within British poetry is provided by Lucie-Smith's note on how the influence of Graves 'formed a middle ground between modernism and old-fashioned Georgianism'.[41]

Graves, as his collaboration with Riding in writing *A Survey of Modernist Poetry* suggests, was interested in modernism. It nevertheless remains hard to discern modernist affinities in his poetry. Lucie-Smith's notes to other poets also reveal the awkwardness of insisting on models from English literary history while acknowledging non-English categories. Of David Jones he writes, 'A poet-artist, Jones was the Celtic and twentieth-century equivalent of William Blake. At the same time, he stands in the modernist tradition.'[42] Of Bunting, he writes: '*Briggflatts* does in fact, bring something distinctively English to the Pound tradition, a highly-wrought, deliberately musical quality which has both Marvell and Milton behind it.'[43] Such helpful characterisations nevertheless lean rather too heavily on the legitimation of an English literary 'tradition'. The sketch of Bunting's work begs questions as to whether Pound's poetic practice is not also 'distinctively English', and, if not, how far a Poundian poetics might imply a less English musical quality.

Some of these terms are reworked more fully by Donald Davie, a critic and poet partly influenced by Empson, whose arguments for neo-Augustan poetics suggest an anti-modernist orientation, but who nevertheless took some interest in modernists such as Pound. Of Bunting, Davie writes that:

> Bunting is undoubtedly a modernist, in the sense in which Pound is a modernist, though T. S. Eliot also. Historically this is Bunting's unique importance; for in the present century there is no British-English poet of whom as much can be said. And so Bunting's existence is an embarrassment to the numerous English historians who would have it that modernism in poetry was a temporary American-inspired distraction from a native tradition which persisted, undeterred though for a time invisible, behind the marches and counter-marches of modernist polemics. Still, Bunting wore his modernism with a difference, an English or British difference.[44]

The 'or' here reflects an important political equivocation between English and British political identities. While Davie acknowledges Bunting's importance, he assimilates his work to presumed modernist paradigms, with only a modest qualification of the perceived singularity of Bunting's position. Elsewhere, the qualified isolation of British modernism by conceding marginal exceptions is evident in Davie's observation that:

> For the rather few people nowadays who still believe that modernism was something that really happened to or in our poetry, something of which the energies are not yet spent, three names are commonly brought up to show that the modernist impetus survived in the generation after Pound: David Jones, Anglo-Welshman; Basil Bunting, Northumbrian Englishman; and Hugh MacDiarmid, Lowland Scot.[45]

Who belongs in 'our' poetry? Regionalisation works here as much to side-line 'local' writers as to divert recognition of the complexity of modernist affiliations. The list of figures whose work has energies not yet spent can be extended to include Loy, Rodker, Riding, Lynette Roberts and Charles Madge. The awkwardly 'British' range of modernist poetry produced out of the British Isles involves the work of many more poets and critics, not least poets such as Empson or even Graves, whose engagement with modernism is more than superficial but less than explicit. Given that the term 'modernism' is itself so vague and capacious as to seem empty, it is tempting simply to abandon such attempts at critical contextualisation, and focus on some individual poems and poets. Much can indeed be learned from ignoring the received critical paradigms and beginning with a sustained investigation into the work of poets such as Loy or Bunting. But, even if the dynamics of modernism generate critical paradigms which now need to be abandoned, there is more to be gained from engaging with the full range of international modernist poetics with which British poets have long been in dialogue and to which they have made so many distinctive contributions.

## NOTES

1. See Lawrence Rainey, *Institutions of Modernism: Literary Elites and Public Culture* (New Haven: Yale University Press, 1998).
2. See the collection of anonymous tributes to Mina Loy in Drew Milne (ed.), *Pig Cupid: A Homage to Mina Loy* (Cambridge: Parataxis Editions, 2000).
3. Mina Loy, *The Last Lunar Baedeker*, ed. Roger L. Conover (Manchester: Carcanet, 1985). pp. 18–19.
4. Mina Loy, *The Last Lunar Baedeker*, p. 298.
5. Peter Nicholls, *Modernisms: A Literary Guide* (London: Macmillan, 1995), p. 222.
6. See, however, Bonnie Kime Scott (ed.), *The Gender of Modernism: A Critical Anthology* (Bloomington: Indiana University Press, 1990).
7. Virginia Kouidis, *Mina Loy: American Modernist Poet* (Baton Rouge: Louisiana State University Press, 1980).
8. See Loy, *The Last Lunar Baedeker*, pp. 109–75.
9. Laura Riding and Robert Graves, *A Survey of Modernist Poetry* (London: Heinemann, 1927), p. 24.
10. See David Gascoyne, *A Short Survey of Surrealism* (London: Cobden-Sanderson, 1935); Alan Young, *Dada and After: Extremist Modernism and English Literature* (Manchester University Press, 1981); and Nicholls, *Modernisms*.
11. Peter Bürger, *Theory of the Avant-Garde*, trans. Michael Shaw (Manchester University Press, 1984); and see the no-less-Eurocentric orientation in Richard Murphy, *Theorizing the Avant-Garde* (Cambridge University Press, 1999).
12. Riding and Graves, *A Survey*, p. 136.
13. Keith Tuma (ed.), *Anthology of Twentieth-Century British and Irish Poetry* (New York: Oxford University Press, 2001), pp. xxi–xxii. See also Keith Tuma,

*Fishing by Obstinate Isles: Modern and Postmodern British Poetry and American Readers* (Evanston: Northwestern University Press, 1998).

14. Chris Baldick, *The Oxford English Literary History*, vol. X, *1910–1940*, *The Modern Movement* (Oxford University Press, 2004), p. 108.

15. On Madge, see Drew Milne, 'Charles Madge: Political Perception and the Persistence of Poetry', *New Formations* 44 (Autumn 2001), 63–75.

16. Malcolm Bradbury, 'London 1890–1920', in *Modernism: A Guide to European Literature 1890–1930*, ed. Malcolm Bradbury and James McFarlane (Harmondsworth: Penguin, 1976), p. 174.

17. See, for example, Raymond Williams, *The Politics of Modernism: Against the New Conformists*, ed. Tony Pinkney (London: Verso, 1989), pp. 49–63.

18. For some pertinent antidotes to the 'modern', see Frank Kermode, 'The Modern' (1965–6), *Modern Essays*, 2nd edn (London: Fontana, 1990), pp. 39–70.

19. Riding and Graves, *A Survey of Modernist Poetry*, p. 12. For Imagism, see the invaluable anthology, Peter Jones (ed.), *Imagist Poetry* (Harmondsworth: Penguin, 1972).

20. Riding and Graves, *A Survey of Modernist Poetry*, p. 122.

21. Riding and Graves, *A Survey of Modernist Poetry*, p. 47.

22. See F. R. Leavis, *New Bearings in English Poetry: A Study of the Contemporary Situation* (London: Chatto & Windus, 1930).

23. T. S. Eliot, *The Varieties of Metaphysical Poetry*, ed. Ronald Schuchard (London: Faber and Faber, 1993).

24. See Francis Mulhern, *The Moment of 'Scrutiny'* (London: New Left Books, 1979).

25. Marjorie Perloff, *21st-Century Modernism: The 'New' Poetics* (Oxford: Blackwell, 2002), pp. 7–43.

26. See, for example, Nancy Gish, 'MacDiarmid Reading *The Waste Land*: The Politics of Quotation', in Nancy K. Gish (ed.), *Hugh MacDiarmid: Man and Poet* (Orono, Maine: The National Poetry Foundation, University of Maine/Edinburgh University Press, 1992), pp. 207–29.

27. See Hugh MacDiarmid, 'A Theory of Scots Letters' (1923), in *Selected Prose*, ed. Alan Riach (Manchester: Carcanet, 1992), pp. 16–33.

28. See MacDiarmid, 'English Ascendancy in British Literature' (1931), in *Selected Prose*, pp. 61–80. This essay was first published in Eliot's journal, *The Criterion*.

29. For the term 'Renaissance', see, for example, Maurice Lindsay (ed.), *Modern Scottish Poetry: An Anthology of the Scottish Renaissance, 1920–1945* (London: Faber and Faber, 1946), an anthology which includes poetry by Hugh MacDiarmid, Adam Drinan (a.k.a. Joseph MacLeod) and W. S. Graham. See also Douglas Dunn (ed.), *The Faber Book of Twentieth-Century Scottish Poetry* (London: Faber and Faber, 1992).

30. Both poems are included in Hugh MacDiarmid, *Complete Poems, 1920–1976*, 2 vols, ed. Michael Grieve and W. R. Aitken (London: Martin Brian & O'Keeffe, 1978).

31. Tom Leonard, *Intimate Voices: Selected Work 1965–1983* (Newcastle upon Tyne: Galloping Dog, 1984), p. 97.

32. Nancy Gish, 'Introduction', in *Hugh MacDiarmid: Man and Poet*, p. 15.

33. See Veronica Forrest-Thomson, *Poetic Artifice: A Theory of Twentieth-Century Poetry* (Manchester University Press, 1978).
34. Andrew Crozier, 'Introduction' to John Rodker, *Poems and Adolphe 1920*, ed. Andrew Crozier (Manchester: Carcanet, 1996), p. viii.
35. See Nancy Cunard, *Parallax* (Cambridge: Parataxis Editions, 2001).
36. Leavis, *New Bearings*, p. 197.
37. See David Ayers, *Modernism: A Short Introduction* (Oxford: Blackwell, 2004), pp. 12–23, 24–38.
38. See Lynette Roberts, *Collected Poems*, ed. Patrick McGuinness (Manchester: Carcanet, 2005), pp. 41–78.
39. Edward Lucie-Smith (ed.), *British Poetry Since 1945*, revised edn (Harmondsworth: Penguin, 1985), p. 23.
40. Lucie-Smith (ed.), *British Poetry*, pp. 23–4.
41. Lucie-Smith (ed.), *British Poetry*, p. 40.
42. Lucie-Smith (ed.), *British Poetry*, p. 43. See also Drew Milne, 'David Jones: A Charter for Philistines', in Iain Sinclair (ed.), *Conductors of Chaos: A Poetry Anthology* (London: Picador, 1996), pp. 260–3.
43. Lucie-Smith (ed.), *British Poetry*, p. 49.
44. Donald Davie, *Under Briggflatts: A History of Poetry in Great Britain 1960–1988* (Manchester: Carcanet, 1989), pp. 41–2.
45. Davie, *Under Briggflatts*, p. 217.

# 9

BONNIE COSTELLO

# US modernism I: Moore, Stevens and the modernist lyric

'Wallace Stevens is beyond fathoming, he is so strange; it is as if he had a morbid secret he would rather perish than disclose and just as he tells it out in his sleep, he changes into an uncontradictable judiciary with a gown and a gavel and you are embarrassed to have heard anything.'[1] Was there ever such an instance of the pot calling the kettle black? Moore's poems too seem to harbour a secret behind their complicated surfaces, and in her work as well one feels the brisk, moral conclusions are a bit too abrupt, and not completely transparent as summaries of the prismatic turns that precede them. Despite her intense 'capacity for fact'[2] which won the admiration of Objectivists such as William Carlos Williams and Louis Zukofsky, Moore's sensibility, and even her idea of what poetry is, brings her closer to the abstract, philosophical Stevens. 'No fact is a bare fact, no individual fact is a universe in itself', wrote Stevens, celebrating Moore's creation of 'an individual reality' out of the diversity of idiom and image that is the record of the world imagined. The task of the poet is to bring 'the thing' into an aesthetic integration where it takes on the character of an artist's world, created or discovered. Moore recognised early that Stevens too was creating such an 'individual reality'.[3] She was one of the first to appreciate *Harmonium* in her review 'Well Moused, Lion', in which she admires the 'riot of gorgeousness' in his imagination. 'One is excited by the sense of proximity to Java peacocks, golden pheasants, South American macaw feather capes, Chilcat blankets, hair seal needlework, Singalese masks, and Rousseau's paintings of banana leaves and alligators. We have the hydrangeas and dogwood, the "blue, gold, pink and green" of the temperate zone, the hibiscus, "red as red" of the tropics.'[4] Of course this exhilarating list sounds a lot like a Marianne Moore poem, recalling particularly the exotica of 'The Plumet Basilisk' which she was writing just when *Harmonium* was reissued, and at a time when many readers, feeling the urgency of social problems, had little patience for a 'riot of gorgeousness'. No wonder Stevens, reviewing Moore's *Selected Poems* in 1935, could speak of this poet of scientific precision and moral intensity as a 'romantic' fond of 'frangipani' and 'moon-vines'.[5] Moore recognised in herself the same danger she recognised in Stevens: the danger of baroque excess and romantic solipsism which would turn on itself to produce an equally inadequate bareness, a craving for the primitive or the reductive. Behind this mutual admiration was a common project, to forge each his or her own 'individual reality' but one 'adequate to the profound necessities of life' and thus cleaving to the real.[6] Both were attempting to become, in their distinct ways, what Moore called 'literalists of the imagination' who sought to create 'imaginary gardens with real toads in them'.[7]

While reading these poets together we should begin by acknowledging their significant differences. While Stevens may conceive 'the romantic' as the central urge of all poetry, he clearly belongs more directly than many other modernists to the romantic tradition. He recognises the quest for permanence and longs for ideal beauty, while sceptical of successful metaphysical transport. Moore's work is classical by comparison, and more Aristotelian than Platonic, in its enthusiasm for observation, its passion for (if also suspicion of) classification, and in its ethical thrust. Yet each poetic project implies the other: Stevens's 'pure poetry' becomes, as he explores it, a matter of cultural survival, and Moore's ethical values find example in aesthetic behaviour. Moore's 'particulars' arise from a world of words and Stevens's abstractions are prompted in physical reality. For each their innovations came less from a feeling of belonging to a movement or collective compulsion to 'Make it New' as a self-justifying dictum than as a 'byproduct of sincerity', an idiosyncrasy (Moore) or eccentricity (Stevens) that marked the individual artist's dynamic relation to a centre.

### Inventing the American modern lyric

While Eliot and Pound abandoned America in their pursuit of culture, Moore and Stevens were among those who chose to stay at home, finding in their native soil enough substance to satisfy their intelligence and taste. There was certainly an emergent American avant garde, at least in New York, which found its social and literary outlet in magazines such as *Others* (which published many works by Stevens and Moore) and gathering places such as Alfred Stieglitz's 291 Fifth Avenue Gallery. As Moore wrote, excellence 'has never been confined to one locality'.[8] Like Aaron Copland and Charles Ives in music and Arthur Dove and Marsden Hartley in painting, Stevens and Moore looked to the American landscape for unclaimed subject matter and sought an idiom appropriate to it. America had its literary past, of course, but it needed rediscovery as a site for modernism; there was even the sense that America, with its robust, entrepreneurial spirit and its unclaimed spaces, might be uniquely suited to artistic innovation. Williams is more often credited with developing an art 'in the American grain', but Stevens and Moore shared his ambition without accepting his essentialism. Modernism could not remain a European import; 'John Constable they could never quite transplant / And our streams rejected the dim Academy'.[9] For Moore and Stevens a 'characteristic American' was, before anything else, an individual. He or she might absorb old world influences, past and present. Moore from Missouri remained an Anglophile, Stevens from Pennsylvania a Francophile, but neither would be satisfied with a derivative art.

'What Columbus discovered is nothing to what Williams is looking for', wrote Stevens to Moore (rather dismayed, if we read further on, at having to relinquish the adventure because 'there's a baby in the house').[10] Stevens expressed his anxiety in the fate of Crispin, of 'The Comedian as the Letter C', who, after an allegorical journey across the seas, in search of the primitive and a New World aesthetic, finds himself settled into a 'nice shady home' in Carolina, a domestic style rather reduced from the sublime ambitions that launched him from 'Bordeaux to Yucatan'. Crispin concludes, with resignation, 'So may the relation of each man be clipped.' In Stevens's Columbian narrative the poet-hero abandons the overcultivated European past where 'man is the intelligence of his soil' and passes through 'the world without imagination' where, in a kind of sensory overload, he is 'washed away by magnitude'. Crispin is 'at sea' and remains overwhelmed in the lush landscape of the Americas, but he makes his way towards a new principle, the reverse of his older view. Now 'the soil is man's intelligence'. From 'lutanist of fleas', he becomes 'poetic hero . . . without regalia, a searcher for the fecund minimum'.[11] In the movement from quest to settlement Stevens shows himself restless amidst the forms he has 'conceived' (his poems, in the words of the title of his final section, his 'Daughters with Curls'). Stevens's solution to this disappointment was to abandon narrative, indeed all teleology, after 'The Comedian as the Letter C' and to write the quest for a satisfactory stance as an endless dialectic, a movement back and forth between north (social, austere, male) and south (romantic, lush, female), between the directives of reality and imagination. His business travel, which took him from his home in Hartford, Connecticut to sites in Georgia and Florida, became a prompt to this visionary shuttle. We tend to think of Stevens as a poet of the mind, but the American landscape, its features, its place names, its diversity, would remain important to him throughout his career, from the pastoral of 'Sunday Morning' to the sublime of 'The Auroras of Autumn'.

Marianne Moore bristled at the genteel-age notion that one must go abroad for culture, and the frequent corollary that everything foreign is superior. Born near St Louis (at the 'conjunction of the Monongahela and the Allegheny'), but living in New York City ('the center of the wholesale fur trade') after 1918, she addressed the question of national style and character in many of her poems, especially 'England'.[12] As she often does, Moore begins with the title as the first word of the poem, undercutting its salience. Here she offers a wry Cook's tour of the world's idealised places, parodying the tendencies to associate geographic fact with cultural essence. England, 'With its baby rivers and little towns . . . the / criterion of suitability and convenience', Italy 'with its equal / shores – contriving an epicureanism from which the grossness has been / extracted', and similarly France, Greece, 'the East', have been celebrated as possessing superior qualities unobtainable in the cruder, newer America. But Moore interrupts this meandering list mid-sentence and mid-stanza, turning to 'America' in the second half of the poem, exploring its paradoxes, its diversity, and making implicit links between landscape and language, to present a national identity that is both distinctive and uncontainable, flawed and dynamic; a rich resource for poetry:

> America where there
> is the little old ramshackle victoria in the south, where cigars are smoked on the
> street in the north; where there are no proof readers, no silkworms, no
> digressions.[13]

Her negatives echo the assumption of America's 'lack' – it is a 'languageless / country in which letters are written / not in Spanish, not in Greek, not in Latin' – but also redirect it. Moore's own language can hardly be called 'plain', and she was herself a fastidious proofreader. On the other hand, there is something 'linksless' about her associative leaps, something omnivorous about her taste for diverse images. Her poetry seems far from the 'plain American' of William Carlos Williams (known for his simple images and declarative sentences); but Moore's language is nevertheless alive with the texture of American idiom, including the far-from-plain phrase 'raining cats and dogs' which she incorporates and transforms here. The delightful expression proves the opposite of what the sentence seems to be saying: America does indeed have its own language, inclusive and dynamic, and the poet will harness it. Moore had been reading H. L. Mencken's *The American Language* and shares his complaint against both American primitiveness and European exclusivity. The poem takes on a defensive position:

> The letter *a* in psalm and calm, when
> pronounced with the sound of *a* in candle, is very noticeable, but

> why should continents of misapprehension have to be accounted for by the
> fact? Does it follow that because there are poisonous toadstools
> which resemble mushrooms, both are dangerous?[14]

In America, Moore concludes, one is as likely as anywhere to find 'excellence'; she will be a selective advocate, not a chauvinist. Flawed as it is, America might be an exceptional place in which to discover the diverse textures of excellence, rather than a narrow menu. The end of the poem offers a catalogue (an anti-hierarchical form favoured in American literature) in which she presents a selection of excellences. Her long lines and elusive syntax, inspired more by Henry James than by Walt Whitman, carry a tonal and phenomenological range which seems suited to the celebration of such diversity.

## Language and prosody

Moore's attitude toward language mirrors this American openness to finding excellence anywhere. She declares that poetry must not 'discriminate against "business documents and / school-books"'.[15] Both forms of discourse enter the texture of her verse, along with the language of advertising, of natural history, of speeches to congress and conversations on the street. Baxter's *Saints Everlasting* takes its place beside *Scientific American*. They are not left as raw chunks of the world outside the poem, but rather enter her lyric flow. Moore was wary of 'a high sounding interpretation' but she was not afraid to employ a multisyllabic word if the occasion called for it. In 'To a Snail' she admires compression, but also calls it by its technical name: 'Contractility'. The snail's 'occipital horn' contains 'the principle that is hid'.[16] In what other poetry of the period can we find a word like 'pseudopodia' or 'dikdik' or 'icosphere' next to 'the unforced passion of the Hebrew language'? Typically her elongated syntax and specialised diction is reined in with pauses for simple phrases and monosyllabic words, giving the impression of sharp conclusion. 'Truth is no Apollo / Belvedere'; it will 'be there when the wave has gone by'.[17] But such epigrammatic conclusions do not master the diversity of the poem; they enter the crucible of its language. While Moore's poetry includes a striking range of linguistic textures, not all her quotations are meant as models of 'excellence'.

Stevens used variant speech acts and registers of diction the way some poets use imagery. He is best known for employing the language of philosophy: syllogistic, abstract, analytical. But he experimented with a great many other discourses as well – biblical and liturgical language; courtship rhetoric; Shakespearean flourishes; folk idiom, foreign words and phrases. To read a Stevens poem (perhaps any poem), it is as important to attend to these variant textures as to their semantic meaning. Language is never a transparent medium for Stevens. Like Moore, he was fond of place names. If she heard history revealing itself in the syllables of 'the Mononegahela and the Allegheny', he heard the wilderness in Oklahoma and Tennessee and the exotic in Tehuantepec and even Florida.[18] Always alert to the pun, his native 'Reading' declared itself a world of words. Like Moore's 'plain American' Stevens's 'plain sense of things' is more complex than it appears to be. We know we have not in fact reached 'the end of the imagination' when it is described as 'inanimate in an inert savoir'.[19] To be an American poet is not to reject foreign influences or to specialise in the plain style alone, but to open one's writing to the full range of the 'voice that is great within us'.[20]

Free verse as we know it is an American invention, at least that's how American poets have seen it, Pound and Williams both tracing their freedoms to Walt Whitman. But, while Stevens and Moore can be admired for their considerable formal inventiveness, neither poet wrote free verse regularly. Stevens's preferred form was blank verse, a flexible meditative line that followed in the tradition of Milton and Wordsworth. In 'The Idea of Order at Key West', Stevens made the form his own by inventing a pivotal syntax and structure of repeating sounds ('But it was she and not the sea we heard. // For she was the maker of the song she sang').[21] Blank verse is iambic pentameter, but Stevens experimented as well with shorter lines, as in the tetrameters of 'The Man with the Blue Guitar' or 'A Postcard from the Volcano'. Stevens varied his stanza lengths but had a particular fondness for the three-line stanza in his longer poems. In 'The Man with the Blue Guitar', the two-line stanza has a thematic purpose: it mirrors the theme of chord and discord, the dialectic of real and represented. Because Stevens rhymes only rarely, those moments of rhyming tend to have a special 'rightness'. Moore is the more innovative of the two poets at the level of form, introducing syllabics into the American idiom, perhaps another influence from her study of Greek and Latin poetry. But she makes syllabic verse entirely modern and American. Stevens's Comedian had declared that 'prose shall wear the poem's guise at last',[22] but it is Moore who in fact accomplished this feat, far more even than Williams, who included prose chunks in *Paterson* and who worked with everyday idioms. Disliking the insistence of metrical lines (the tiddly-winks of the syllables) she worked with a patterned lineation independent of the semantic and syntactic orders of the poem, but establishing a clear visual design. Where the line breaks of free verse tend to involve local emphases or ruptures, Moore's line breaks obeyed a shape established in the first stanza and then operating chromosome-like throughout. Competing aural and visual systems allow a poem such as 'Poetry', for instance, to sound like argumentative prose but to establish a poetic environment that will then cue the imagination to the enigmas of poetry. While Moore's stanzas often have a visual or numerical basis, she was by no means indifferent to the sounds of poetry. The work of assonance and alliteration, as well as the play of word length, create an exciting texture. And occasionally she turned to rhyme. 'The Fish', also in syllabics, employs a couplet pattern, but because the line breaks are not aurally determined the rhymes become more subtle until the surprising rupture of 'ac- / cident – lack / of cornice' brings the latent violence of the poem to the sonic surface.[23] In later work Moore would be inspired by the contrapuntal effects of Mozart and Scarlatti to create a fresh music for poetry. In a poem such as 'The Jerboa' we can see how Moore, within a uniform syllabic stanza form, creates a contrast between the decadent, overly manipulated world of Romans and Egyptians, on the one hand, and the modest, nature-based aesthetic on the other, through a clarification of this contrapuntal style. The Egyptians, whose tombs were being uncovered in this period,

> had their men tie
> hippopotami
>     and bring out dappled dog–
>     cats to course antelopes, dikdik and ibex.

Moore's language implicitly contrasts the jerboa:

> a small desert rat,
> and not famous, that
>     lives without water, has
>     happiness.

The poem, like the jerboa, 'honors the sand by assuming its color'. So we hear a certain amount of celebrative mimicry in her writing:

> By fifths and sevenths,
> in leaps of two lengths,
>     like the uneven notes
>     of the Bedouin flute.[24]

Moore and Stevens were confirmed in their sense that a high standard of modernist art could be achieved in America, and that it might even have its own distinct American character. But they were ultimately more interested in the collective, international, effort of modernity that would help them in finding an aesthetic that could 'suffice' for their time.

## Study of images

The most significant project of modernist poetry was the renovation of the image, for behind it moved a profound philosophical quest: in the image poets could treat the central question of the relation between imagination and reality. How can poetry convey a sense of experience without merely gesturing to reality or copying appearances? How can the image become a vital sign of the poet's vision, uniting mind and world, and not merely a transmitter of conventional illusions or ideas? The romantic tradition, British and American, fixed the correspondence between image and idea to a transcendental metaphysics. Symbolism was an extension of this idea, a mode that, in the words of W. B. Yeats, could 'call down among us certain disembodied powers' and link the laws of art to the laws of the universe.[25] The modernist image continues many of the drives of romanticism and Symbolism, but the dominant sense of the world as a place of change and metamorphosis, and of the mind as a creator of relative truths rather than a perceiver of absolutes, called for aesthetic adjustments. The image must at once convey the poet's imaginative presence, the force of his or her experience and 'personality', as Stevens called it, and at the same time acknowledge itself as only a part of a boundless, perspectiveless, unfixable real which would include the visible and the invisible.

In America this very negotiation of scepticism and belief had fostered a new epistemology, called 'pragmatism', that privileged cognitive process over precept; its influence, through Emerson to William James, John Dewey and others, can be seen throughout American poetry. In Moore's poetry this tension found expression in poems that enfold multiple perspectives, examples that dodge their own generalisations, in metaphors and symbols that take on a particularity in excess of their semantic function, or simply a shifting priority of image and idea. In Stevens, the fecundity of nature, its 'immense dew', brings forth a responsive fecundity of the imagination, not images to fix the real like a gemstone, but 'flinging / Forms, flames, and the flakes of flames'.[26] Poetry is not a representation of 'things as they are'; it changes them to things of the imagination which in turn plays a chord with reality. In 'The Man on the Dump' Stevens responds, as mid-century approaches, to the seemingly endless quest of modernism for fresh images. He begins with an example of how hackneyed these images have become: 'the sun is a corbeil of flowers the moon Blanche / Places there, a bouquet. Ho-ho . . . the dump is full / Of images'. The clamour to 'Make it New' has itself grown tiresome: 'the freshness of night has been fresh a long time . . . One grows to hate these things except on the dump.' The dump is privileged as a place of transition 'between things that are on the dump (azaleas and so on) / And those that will be (azaleas and so on)', yet the overall feeling is of weariness and disgust.[27] Earlier Stevens had experimented with an array of such images as he now finds on the dump. *Harmonium*, perhaps under the influence of the fashion for Imagism, abounds in short, image-centred poems. But even in these we can see Stevens's drive to abstraction. 'Thirteen Ways of Looking at a Blackbird' never really allows us to see a blackbird except as a figure in a mental puzzle, whereas Williams's white chickens beside the red wheelbarrow are presented to us as objects ontologically prior to any ideas we may have about them. 'The Snow Man' may evoke an ideal of direct apprehension, 'nothing that is not there and the nothing that is', but this has an abstract rather than a phenomenal presence in the poem.[28]

There are many sensuous pleasures, even for the visual imagination, in Stevens's compositions. 'Thirteen Ways' is a composition in black and white exploring a range of problems in space and perspective. The same is true of 'Six Significant Landscapes', with its exploration of relational scale and its play of shadow and substance. But the images are neither scenic (like Frost's), presentational (like Williams's) or symbolist (like Yeats's). They are, Stevens insisted, metaphors: changes wrought on reality in order to engage with it. Lacking this confidence in the image as access to a metaphysical realm, Stevens feared that images merely 'add', and that they have no real dynamic relation to reality or to our experience of reality. Poetry then is just a superfluous place apart, an imaginary garden. Is metaphor a turning-away or a turning-toward? Is it a move from one relative position to another or a transport to something supreme? Sometimes 'all of appearance is a toy' and the metaphors are exuberant and flamboyant. At other times Stevens seems quite severe in critiquing 'the motive for metaphor'. It is a 'shrinking from / The weight of primary noon'. But it is only by metaphor that we can name reality, 'the ABC of being . . . The vital, arrogant, fatal, dominant X'.[29]

While Moore's poetry seldom discusses the image in such an abstract, philosophical manner, her approach to it remains for her an epistemological, even an ethical, and not merely a technical problem. Unlike Stevens, Moore cleaves to the particular. Even in her earliest poetry, which follows the structure of the emblem tradition, she never leaves the object far behind. 'To a Steam Roller' may represent a force of personality more than of physics, but the physical world is integrated into the poem at every turn, pressing back on the abstract statements as if to demonstrate that percept cannot be steamrolled by precept. Concrete particulars and abstractions are juxtaposed in the poem without assimilating transitions, so that the physical world can never be reduced to mere example, never become 'steamrolled' by generalisation:

> Sparkling chips of rock
> are crushed down to the level of the parent block.
>> Were not 'impersonal judgment in aesthetic
>> matters, a metaphysical impossibility,' you
> might fairly achieve
> it.[30]

'The Fish' (which Louis Zukofsky included in his 'Objectivist' issue of *Poetry*) is image-dominant until the end, when a thematic connection (implicit all the time in the treatment of the images) emerges more directly. In many poems, such as 'Peter', about a cat and its movements, Moore employs a collage effect, not fixing a single image but creating a dynamic, prismatic idea of the object through the assembly of other images and metaphors. To an extent unmatched by any other poet of her time (or any time), these poems reveal their 'capacity for fact' while at the same time pursuing formal and thematic purposes independent of a representational function. 'An Octopus', Moore's longest poem, offers an extreme case of how her radical metonymies accommodate an ultimately metaphoric, even allegorical, function. The opening words of the poem, 'An Octopus / of ice', present us with a challenge as a creature from the deeps of the sea, the lowest point of the earth, serves as the image of Mount Rainier, the highest point in America, and as a fluent becomes a frozen reality.[31] By making the title the first line Moore marks this radical disjunction, and other ruptures follow. Moore's purpose is less to present us with a pictorial description of Mount Rainier than to create a reading experience, a poem of the mind, as exhilarating and challenging as these geological heights. This is an American sublime, both natural and rhetorical, to equal Percy Shelley's Mont Blanc. But these snowy heights do not open for her Emerson's 'transparent eyeball', any more than Stevens claims to be the snow man that can see 'nothing that is not there'. We do not have what Emerson called 'an original relation to reality'. Rather, Moore's Mount Rainier is a figure for that elusive reality – the American wilderness, and by extension the world itself – that calls to us through our endless attempts to encompass it in images and words.

Moore's poetry shows great respect for the independence of the physical world as it is brought into the technologies of human scrutiny and exploitation: writing, museum exhibition, art and commerce. In mid-career Moore would move even further in the direction of the object, populating her poems with such exotic creatures as the ostrich, the pangolin, the elephant, the buffalo. The poet, it would seem, has become a natural historian. And indeed Moore spent much of her time in these years researching her menagerie in the Brooklyn Museum and elsewhere, although throughout she pays tribute to the life beyond the sphere of human touch. But the impulse of the fable remains strong even as the accuracy of the natural historian fuels the imagination. Moore's animals, while they are respected as unique beings, also display features and behaviours to be found, or sought, in the human world. 'To a Snail' declares that 'contractility is a virtue / as modesty is a virtue'; like the snail, the poem is marked by 'the absence of feet' and Moore's own artistic intuition is surely at work in 'the principle that is hid'.[32]

The Jerboa, similarly, enacts the very values Moore wishes to embody in her poetry: 'Part celestial and part terrestrial', this kangaroo rat unites spirit and matter. Moore's Plumet Basilisk and Frigate Pelican resemble Stevens himself, who, like 'the unconfiding frigate-bird hides / in the height and in the majestic / display of his art' and, like Moore, is able to

> foil the tired
> moment of danger that lays on heart and lungs the
> weight of the python that crushes to powder.[33]

## Lyric subject

'I celebrate myself, and sing myself', writes Walt Whitman, inventing a new, expansive and inclusive lyric subject for American poetry. American poetry would speak not only for the self, but for the other as a part of the self and both as capable of encompassing the cosmos. Later American poets, Moore and Stevens among them, would scrutinise this expansive, romantic self and gauge its limits. Stevens's imperial 'Hoon' of 'Tea at the Palaz of Hoon' certainly sounds Whitmanian as he declares:

> I was the world in which I walked, and what I saw
> Or heard or felt came not but from myself;
> And there I found myself more truly and more strange.[34]

And the figure striding alone on the beach in 'The Idea of Order at Key West' seems a feminine descendant of Whitman who 'ebbed with the ocean of life'. But Stevens does not present these figures as himself; rather, they are stances in dialogue with other stances and perspectives, such as the speaker in 'Bantams in Pine-Woods' who damns the afflatus of the romantic-poet-as-strutting-cock and recalls him to a different measure of reality – that of the 'inchling', who takes the measure of reality and 'fears not portly Azcan nor his hoos'.[35] Marianne Moore's Presbyterian roots taught her to know the 'I' as a centre of moral danger; her 'armored animal[s]' defend as much against the ego as against outside aggressors. Standing on a beach in Maine, her view obstructed by another visitor, she reflects: 'it is human nature to stand in the middle of a thing, / but you cannot stand in the middle of this'. In the guise of an elephant in 'Melanchthon', she remarks, 'The I of each is to // the I of each / a kind of fretful speech / which sets a limit on itself', and much of her poetry would negotiate between this imposing, fretful 'I' and what the eye and other faculties bring to it from the observable world.[36] The autobiographical or confessional lyric of a later generation (Sylvia Plath, Allen Ginsberg, Robert Lowell) emerged as a refusal of modernist constraints. But when an

'I' announces itself in Moore or Stevens, it is often a mask (like Hoon), an agent ('I placed a jar in Tennessee') or a commentator or respondent ('I, too, dislike it' or 'I have something / that I like better').[37] Moore's 'The Steeple-Jack' was originally published as 'Part of a Novel, Part of a Poem, Part of a Play', and grouped with 'The Hero' and 'The Student'. '[E]ach in his way, / is at home', she tells us.[38] The poet's vision emerges in the prism of these perspectives. Anomalous and impersonal speakers dominate the work of these poets, for whom the lyric subject is no longer an empowered visionary, but the product of the mind's 'conscientious inconsistency'.

Moore's restraint with regard to the imperial or the narcissistic 'I' ('the only seller who buys, and holds on to the money') should not be confused with a lack of poetic authority, however.[39] A determining, discriminating agent emerges unmistakably from Moore's selective observations and quotations, though often in the form of irony and understatement. The voice that describes the seaside scene in 'The Steeple-Jack' reveals little but formal attention, yet the juxtaposition of 'eight stranded whales / to look at' and 'the sweet sea air coming into your house' suggests a dissonance undermining the surface pastoral ideal.[40] A similar irony informs the opening observations of 'The Jerboa' that 'an artist, a freedman' made a grotesquely enlarged image 'in front of the Prison at St. Angelo'.[41] In the early poetry Moore often employs a 'you', responding with praise or criticism to a statement or action of another and forming a lyric subject in address. The apostrophe may be to an inanimate or non-human object that emblematises a principle ('To a Prize Bird', 'Roses Only', 'To a Chameleon') or to a human figure ('To a Strategist' about Disraeli) or 'Those Various Scalpels' (about a woman dressed to kill). Moore exposes as many flaws as virtues of temperament in the disposition toward language. False airs and attitudes are undercut, naive stances exposed. In '"He Wrote the History Book"', for instance, Moore responds to a conceited remark with her own sardonic quip: 'Thank you for showing me / your father's autograph.'[42] Moore's reader must be alert not only to the luminous phrase, but to the position of a given expression in the prismatic whole.

This kind of indirection may be associated with Moore's position as a female writer in a modernist era defined by a male aesthetic. Stevens gives us a hint of this aesthetic assumption in 'The Figure of the Youth as Virile Poet', where he asserts that the impulse of poetry is largely what, following Aristotle, he calls 'personality', not ego or psychological identity but something more like the force of individual will, a Nietzschean principle involving the taking on of powerful masks.[43] But Stevens never entirely inhabits the persona of the 'virile youth'. A feminine, receptive and experiential side shows in his many poems such as 'Infanta Marina' and 'The Idea of Order at Key West' in which muse-figure and poet-figure intertwine. Conversely, even without an insistent 'I', Moore's descriptions are a form of 'personal impersonal expressions' where her sensibility, and even her moral vision, reveals itself through metaphor, simile and juxtaposition.[44] As Moore gives her account of Roman and Egyptian cultures in 'The Jerboa', she seems merely to itemise their artefacts, but cumulatively the effect of all these contorted objects is grotesque. We experience directly, in the very baroque sounds of the poem and its endless inventory of luxuries, the 'too much' that heads the section and leads us to appreciate the 'abundance' of the unassuming, economical, desert rat.

Any discussion of subjectivity in Moore must wrestle with her distinctive mode of quotation, different from either Eliot's allusiveness or Williams's realism of raw data. Nor would it be accurate to call Moore's work multivocal. From the plethora of sources one stance, albeit a complex, dynamic one, emerges. Williams called Moore's 'Marriage' 'an anthology in rapid transit'.[45] Moore herself explained it as 'a collection of flies in amber'. But there is more here than a modest wish to frame the well said, or a democratic wish to voice the multitude involved in this strategy. In her use of quotation Moore may be renewing our sense of what constitutes poetry. Her notes break down the boundary between poetry and other discourses even as the form of the poem asserts this boundary. In her inclusion of material from such disparate sources as Francis Bacon, a fashion advertisement, Adam Smith and an emerita president of Bryn Mawr, Moore not only reveals her alertness to pithy language outside the realm of poetry, but she also makes the poem a place where this multiplicity finds a formal and conceptual unity. One can also understand Moore's quotation as a critique of the transcendentalist ideal of 'contact, contact'. Reality is already profoundly mediated by language and the poet draws her own vision from a world of words. (That is 'the raw material of poetry in / all its rawness'.) If the modernist poet is to 'Make it New', she cannot just add her voice to the din. She must listen to the babble and clear a 'place for the genuine'.[46]

## Poetry and ideas

What is modern poetry *about*? 'There are things that are important beyond all this fiddle', writes Moore, echoing the common complaint about poetry. What she says of France, with considerable ambivalence, is often said about poetry: 'the "chrysalis of the nocturnal butterfly" in / whose products, mystery of construction diverts one from what was originally one's / object – substance at the core'.[47] Can we find the substance of poetry in statements? And what is the relationship between the apparent subject matter of poetry and its ultimate significance? These questions are particularly interesting as we pose them in reading the work of Stevens and Moore. Stevens's propositional style has often led readers to treat him as a philosopher. Moore's work has at times the character of a didactic moral essay or a work of natural history. These qualities may seem at odds with modernism's tenet of art for art's sake, its scepticism concerning both rational thought and religious belief, and its preference for images over discursive statements. But a closer look at the work of these two American modernists reveals that, while it may contain statements, it is not contained by them. As Stevens put it, the evil of thought in verse is not the same as the good of thinking in poetry. Moore suggests something similar in 'The Mind is an Enchanting Thing': 'Unconfusion submits / its confusion to proof'.[48] Statements become part of the 'raw material of poetry' rather than its end. But to say that the purpose of poetry is to promote the life of the imagination is not to reduce the poet's subject matter to self-reference. We might say, instead, that the poem enacts or exemplifies the life of the imagination, particularly in a time of crushing dogmas on the one hand, and terrifying doubts on the other. Stevens's 'never-resting mind' is deeply dialectical, but it does not move in the direction of ideological synthesis, even as it seems to arrive. 'The prologues are over', the poet announces in a prologue; 'It is a question, now, / Of final belief'. Yet the title of the poem that contains this exhortation is 'Asides on the Oboe'. The 'question' produces not a firm or final answer but a series of 'asides'. The poem enacts the idea that 'the central man' must remain an abstraction and cannot be embodied in 'the metal heroes that time granulates'.[49] We conceive a centre out of the aggregate of our partial efforts, participate in that ideal through our eccentric 'asides'.

The earlier Stevens of *Harmonium* came close to realising a 'pure poetry' of 'gorgeous nonsense' where wordplay, sonic surface and flamboyant metaphor seem to overwhelm subject matter. 'The Emperor of Ice-Cream', for instance, robes the subject of death in the language of pleasure. The poem begins with a party and the style itself seems dressed for celebration: 'Call the roller of big cigars, / The muscular one, and bid him whip / In kitchen cups concupiscent curds'. The opening stanza closes with a gnomic imperative, more striking in sound than in sense: 'Let be be finale of seem.' Only in the second stanza, with its stark contrast of life and death, with its exposed, dehumanised corpse, do we understand that the scene is a funeral and that the 'emperor of ice-cream' is a personification of mortality. 'Let the lamp affix its beam', commands the speaker, modifying his first imperative to shed light on a starker reality.[50] Between these two imperatives Stevens finds his constant theme: desire drives the creative imagination which must ultimately confront its limit and its base.

*Ideas of Order* differs from *Harmonium* in many ways, not least in its relationship to 'ideas'. The 1930s made the ludic side of aestheticism seem indulgent. 'Be gay / civilly?' asks Moore oxymoronically, as she watches the frigate pelican soar.[51] What is the social responsibility of the poet in times of public distress? Stevens defends his work as 'pure poetry'. 'The more realistic life may be, the more it needs the stimulus of the imagination.'[52] Yet Stevens's 'ideas of order', while they are not social and political ideas, nevertheless arise within a world stirred up by the changes in these spheres of experience. As Stevens 'turns toward the town' and looks beyond the self-delighting experiments of his earlier work, it becomes apparent that he 'heard . . . the hungry that cried', that he especially 'think[s] about war'.[53] But, rather than forego the life of the imagination and take up the language of social realism and protest, he 'presses back against the pressure of reality', helping us to live our lives by imagining what might be.[54] For Stevens, one does not change reality by denying the imagination. Like Don Quixote, Mrs Alfred Uruguay, climbing her visionary mountain (Montevideo is the capital of Uruguay), makes an awkward figure, an elegant romantic trying to live an objectivist ideal. Having 'wiped away moonlight', she has reached a kind of impasse: 'her no and no made yes impossible'. Yet, perhaps by virtue of her quest for the real, she has a glimpse of another figure, descending the mountain, another kind of romantic, 'no chevalere and poorly dressed', a figure of Nietzschean will who nevertheless 'created in his mind, / Eventual victor . . . / The ultimate elegance: the imagined land'.[55] Stevens's late style is indeed 'poorly dressed' at times as he explores a mode of imagination that adheres to its base in reality. But 'the absence of imagination had itself to be imagined', as he says in 'The Plain Sense of Things'.[56]

Moore seems to have approached poetry as a form of social and ethical commentary early on, never really embracing the principle of 'pure poetry'. Rapacity and vanity are exposed and mocked, modesty and restraint are praised. In steamrollers and snails, buffalo and elephants, she exhibits and analyses various modes of ethical behaviour. Yet for Moore these ethical principles determine not only the subject matter but also the aesthetic choices of her poems. The imagination is an ethical faculty and her poems are designed to enact their moral lessons in terms of style. Moore's poems often contain epigrammatic utterances and when they arise at the end of a poem it is tempting to take them as a summation of all that came before. After a long catalogue of predilections and criteria in 'When I Buy Pictures', Moore concludes: 'it must acknowledge the spiritual forces which have made it'.[57] But the rhetorical simplicity of the statement must bear the weight of a very digressive poem full of unexpected images and radical leaps of association through which these 'spiritual forces' are traced. Like Stevens, Moore moved toward a clearer rhetoric in her late work. Poems like 'What are Years' and 'In Distrust of Merits' seem to relinquish the modernist fragmentations, ellipses and ironic understatement in favour of a more direct, public poetry. But '[t]here never was a war that was / not inward', Moore writes.[58] In both Stevens and Moore, that inward war becomes a defence against complacency and rhetorical platitude that would turn poetry into a vehicle for dogma.

For Moore and Stevens, questions about the function of the imagination involved not only political and social ideas, but ultimately religious feelings as well. In a sceptical age these two poets stand out for their will to believe. Moore was confirmed in her inherited Presbyterian faith (her grandfather and her brother were ministers, her mother a devout worshipper) and remained a lifelong member of the congregation. In the 1940s and 1950s she was recommending the work of Rheinhold Niebuhr, a Christian existentialist, to her friends. Moore found in poetry a way of praising creation and renovating fallen human vision. 'An Octopus' describes 'Paradise Park' at Mount Rainier and recalls 'such power as Adam had and we are still devoid of', the power of seeing and naming.[59] Her poetry is rich with biblical references and allusions and with references to the devotional tradition in poetry and prose. In 'The Jerboa', for instance, the story of Jacob and his descendants forms a counter-narrative to Roman and Egyptian decadence and prepares us for the fable of the jumping rat that, like Jacob, survives in the desert, bounds between the 'terrestrial' and 'celestial', and uses illusion to carry forward a divine purpose. During the war years Moore is particularly interested in the problem of heroism and it is clear that Christian ethics, with its principles of humility, restraint and otherworldliness, inform her definition of 'the hero'. Moore's animal poems reveal her thorough knowledge of and respect for biology and even for the impulses of science when they are directed to knowledge rather than possession, but her minute particulars are ultimately referred to a higher power of creation. 'The power of the visible / is the invisible.' Poetry is not a place to theologise – 'to explain grace requires a curious hand' – but a place to bear witness and praise: '"Again the sun! / anew each day; and new and new and new, / that comes into and steadies my soul."'[60]

Stevens's relationship to the religious conventions of his culture is in some ways more complicated. He had no patience for the old-time religion in which he was brought up. In 'A High-Toned Old Christian Woman' he blasphemes: 'Poetry is the supreme fiction, madame'. He will be 'ploughing on Sunday', or at least staying home to protest, as in 'Sunday Morning': 'why should she give her bounty to the dead?' The speaker of the poem denies the resurrection: 'The tomb in Palestine / Is not the porch of spirits lingering. / It is the grave of Jesus, where he lay'. But if one voice in Stevens announces the death of god and death as the mother of beauty, another still feels 'the need of some imperishable bliss'.[61] With the philosopher Vico, Stevens understands the religions of the past as evidence of the power of the human imagination, but its failure to recognise that power causes mankind's spiritual suffering. Stevens saw the ultimate task of poetry as the pursuit of this 'supreme fiction' that could fill the space in the imagination and in culture left by the failure of established religions. From 'To the One of Fictive Music', with its 'sister and mother and diviner love', to 'Notes Toward a Supreme Fiction', with its triadic structure and grandeur of scale, we find Stevens employing the rhetoric of religion to speak of an alternative that could somehow encompass modernity's relentless scepticism and sense of change. The challenge for him would be to construct a humanism that had the force of the idea of the divine. The criteria of this 'supreme fiction' are those Moore herself would embrace: 'it must be abstract' – not so much full of abstractions as evoking, making a place for, 'a principle that is hid', or condition that can never be embodied; 'it must change' – enchanting us by consistent inconsistency, by creations and decreations of life itself; 'it must give pleasure' – make our eyes dilate, our hair stand on end, satisfy a need.[62]

## NOTES

1. Marianne Moore, *Selected Letters*, ed. Bonnie Costello et al. (New York: Penguin, 1997), pp. 453, 456.
2. Marianne Moore, *The Poems of Marianne Moore*, ed. Grace Schulman (New York: Penguin, 2003), p. 171.
3. Wallace Stevens, *Collected Poetry and Prose*, ed. Frank Kermode and Joan Richardson (New York: Library of America, 1997), p. 703.
4. Marianne Moore, *The Complete Prose of Marianne Moore*, ed. Patricia C. Willis (New York: Viking, 1986), p. 92.
5. Stevens, *Collected Poetry and Prose*, p. 777.
6. Stevens, *Collected Poetry and Prose*, p. 705.
7. Moore, *The Poems*, p. 135.
8. Moore, *The Poems*, p. 142.
9. Stevens, *Collected Poetry and Prose*, p. 125.
10. Wallace Stevens, *Letters of Wallace Stevens*, ed. Holly Stevens (New York: Knopf, 1966), p. 246.
11. Stevens, *Collected Poetry and Prose*, pp. 32, 23, 37, 22, 35.
12. Moore, *The Poems*, p. 146.
13. Moore, *The Poems*, p. 141.
14. Moore, *The Poems*, p. 141.
15. Moore, *The Poems*, p. 135.
16. Moore, *The Poems*, p. 174.
17. Moore, *The Poems*, p. 136.
18. Moore, *The Poems*, p. 146.
19. Stevens, *Collected Poetry and Prose*, p. 428.
20. Stevens, *Collected Poetry and Prose*, p. 112.

21. Stevens, *Collected Poetry and Prose*, p. 105.
22. Stevens, *Collected Poetry and Prose*, p. 29.
23. Moore, *The Poems*, p. 128.
24. Moore, *The Poems*, pp. 190, 192, 194.
25. W. B. Yeats, *Essays and Introductions* (London: Macmillan, 1961), p. 157.
26. Stevens, *Collected Poetry and Prose*, p. 77.
27. Stevens, *Collected Poetry and Prose*, p. 184.
28. Stevens, *Collected Poetry and Prose*, p. 8.
29. Stevens, *Collected Poetry and Prose*, pp. 318, 257.
30. Moore, *The Poems*, p. 92.
31. Moore, *The Poems*, p. 167.
32. Moore, *The Poems*, p. 174.
33. Moore, *The Poems*, pp. 204, 205.
34. Stevens, *Collected Poetry and Prose*, p. 51.
35. Stevens, *Collected Poetry and Prose*, p. 60.
36. Moore, *The Poems*, pp. 224, 145, 123.
37. Stevens, *Collected Poetry and Prose*, p. 60; Moore, *The Poems*, pp. 135, 106.
38. Moore, *The Poems*, p. 184.
39. Moore, *The Poems*, p. 152.
40. Moore, *The Poems*, p. 183.
41. Moore, *The Poems*, p. 190.
42. Moore, *The Poems*, p. 101.
43. Stevens, *Collected Poetry and Prose*, p. 671.
44. Moore, *The Poems*, p. 150.
45. William Carlos Williams, *Imaginations* (New York: New Directions, 1970), p. 313.
46. Moore, *The Poems*, p. 135.
47. Moore, *The Poems*, pp. 135, 141.
48. Moore, *The Poems*, p. 259.
49. Stevens, *Collected Poetry and Prose*, pp. 179, 226, 227.
50. Stevens, *Collected Poetry and Prose*, p. 50.
51. Moore, *The Poems*, p. 205.
52. Stevens, *Collected Poetry and Prose*, p. 997.
53. Stevens, *Collected Poetry and Prose*, pp. 105, 183, 219.
54. Stevens, *Collected Poetry and Prose*, p. 665.
55. Stevens, *Collected Poetry and Prose*, pp. 225, 226.
56. Stevens, *Collected Poetry and Prose*, pp. 665, 428.
57. Moore, *The Poems*, p. 144.
58. Moore, *The Poems*, p. 252.
59. Moore, *The Poems*, p. 171.
60. Moore, *The Poems*, pp. 246, 225, 226.
61. Stevens, *Collected Poetry and Prose*, pp. 47, 16, 56, 53.
62. Stevens, *Collected Poetry and Prose*, pp. 70, 344.

# 10

MARK SCROGGINS

# US modernism II: the other tradition – Williams, Zukofsky and Olson

According to some accounts, the path-breaking work in American modernist poetry was done by expatriates like Ezra Pound, T. S. Eliot and Gertrude Stein, Americans who abandoned their relentlessly materialist and artistically unformed homeland to root themselves in the rich cultural humus of Europe. Just as significant, however, are the achievements of the 'nativist' poets whose work reflects both the cosmopolitan 'tradition' that Pound and Eliot sought in Europe and the immediate realities of the American scene. From New Jersey, William Carlos Williams forged a recognisably modernist poetry which is also irreducibly local and American. In Williams's wake, Louis Zukofsky and Charles Olson continued the experiments of this 'home-grown' modernism, in the process pushing American poetry into a mode that Olson would name 'post-modern'.

William Carlos Williams (1883–1963) was born in Rutherford, New Jersey, a distant suburb of New York City. His father was English, his mother Puerto Rican: 'Of mixed ancestry', he wrote Horace Gregory in 1939, 'I felt from earliest childhood that America was the only home I could ever possibly call my own. I felt that it was expressly founded for me, personally, and that it must be my first business in life to possess it.'[1] Pound teased Williams about his immigrant forebears, even as he figured Williams's 'foreignness' as an advantage amid the derivative sentimentality of early twentieth-century American letters: 'And America. What the hell do you a blooming foreigner know about the place[?] . . . The thing that saves your work is *opacity*, and don't forget it. Opacity is NOT an American quality. Fizz, swish, gabble and verbiage, these are echt americanisch.'[2]

The two men began their lifelong friendship as students at the University of Pennsylvania, where Williams was amused and intimidated by Pound's literary knowledge and well-rehearsed bohemianism. Pound would leave the United States for good in 1908; though he visited Europe, Williams stayed in Rutherford all his adult life, where he worked as a physician in general practice. Pound kept in close correspondence, and would constantly remind

Williams that he, Pound, was now at the centre of the 'new', while his friend remained a country doctor in a backwater America. But Williams was by no means isolated; he would frequently visit New York, an hour's drive away, and actively associated with a wide range of avant-garde writers and painters there. He closely followed the productions of the European modernists, as well.

Williams's early poems, collected in *Poems* (1909) and *The Tempers* (1913), are largely in traditional forms and metres. The young Williams was especially intoxicated by Keats, though that influence was balanced by his enthusiasm for Walt Whitman. By his third collection, *Al Que Quiere!* (1917), Williams had turned to free verse, some of it in the vivid mode of Pound's Imagist movement. The first real breakthrough in Williams's poetry was 'The Wanderer – A Baroque Study', a narrative poem reworked from 'an early Keatsian *Endymion* imitation'.[3] There are still traces of Keats in 'The Wanderer' as published in *Al Que Quiere!*, but the poem's overall thrust is to place the young poet precisely in the midst of contemporary American reality. 'How shall I hold a mirror to this modernity?' the poem's speaker asks, and in reply a grotesque, aged muse figure hauls him through a succession of contemporary scenes, including the crowds of New York's Broadway and a violent strike in Paterson, New Jersey, culminating in a baptismal ceremony in 'The Passaic, that filthy river'. This baptism brings a shock of reality, and the recognition of his own vocation, to the young poet: 'I knew the novitiate was ended / The ecstasy was over, the life begun.'[4]

'The Wanderer' announces Williams's fundamental theme – American reality, in all its gritty specificity – and in the books that followed *Al Que Quiere!* he explored that reality in jagged, flexible free-verse poems. In *Kora in Hell: Improvisations* (1920) and *Spring and All* (1923), two generically indeterminate, radically experimental books, Williams established himself as a major modernist writer, one of the few poets in America who could prove a nativist counterweight to Pound's and Eliot's expatriate modernisms.

*Kora in Hell* consists of eighty-four brief, disjunctive prose 'improvisations', sifted out of a year's worth of writings snatched between the busy doctor's office appointments and house calls. In the book's long Prologue, Williams vents his frustration with the highly polished work of Eliot (a 'subtle conformist' and an 'archbishop of procurers to a lecherous antiquity'), and the antiquarian Pound, 'the best enemy United States verse has'.[5] But Williams is also anxious to present his own conception of what vital poetry should be, a conception which he will increasingly encapsulate in the word 'contact': 'the thing that stands eternally in the way of really good writing is always one: the virtual impossibility of lifting to the imagination those things which lie under the direct scrutiny of the senses'.[6]

*Kora in Hell*'s Prologue advances a fierce polemic on behalf of the imaginative treatment of the commonplace: the 'improvisations' themselves are wildly uneven, veering from stream-of-consciousness outpourings to something like literary Cubism. It is in *Spring and All* that Williams brings his theory of the imagination and its concomitant poetics to a sharpened focus. The book's twenty-seven poems, in Williams's fully realised mature style, treat a number of subjects, lingering especially on the immediate particulars of the poet's surroundings and the paradoxes of American society. 'To Elsie', for instance, in what might be a sly jab at the ethnic purity of such poets as Eliot and Pound, begins, 'The pure products of America / go crazy'. Elsie, Williams's mentally retarded housemaid, is the product of a deracinated society, of 'imaginations which have no // peasant traditions to give them / character', a society which lives 'as if the earth under our feet / were an excrement of some sky'.[7] In 'At the Ball Game', the poet contemplates how the spectators at a baseball game, 'moved uniformly // by a spirit of uselessness', comprise a unity that is both 'beautiful' and 'terrifying' in its potential for violence against those on its margins: 'The flashy female with her / mother, gets it – // The Jew gets it straight. . . . It is the Inquisition, the / Revolution'.[8]

The bulk of *Spring and All* consists of polemical, reflective and quasi-philosophical prose passages, among which the poems are interspersed as illustrations, proofs, or occasionally outright interruptions. The polemics are directed, predictably, against those whom Williams calls 'the traditionalists of plagiarism', those who 'ask us to return to the proven truths of tradition, even to the twice proven, the substantiality of which is known'.[9] Williams clearly has in mind Eliot, the 1922 publication of whose *Waste Land* he would later name 'the great catastrophe to our letters'.[10] *Spring and All* is a sustained attack on the sense of belatedness evident in Eliot's poetry and criticism, the sensibility producing the line 'April is the cruellest month'. Williams, in contrast, celebrates the power of the imagination to effect a spring-like resurrection, to bring the particulars of existence, like Demeter bringing Persephone (Kora) out of Hades, out of the hell of muteness. In the first poem of the collection, Williams finds signs of new life in a seemingly barren, man-altered landscape. The plants, who 'enter the new world naked' – 'rooted they / grip down and begin to awaken'[11] – are both naturalistically observed and emblematic of the 'new world' poet's awakening stance towards his surroundings: an ostensible wasteland that teems with vital potential which it is his task to 'lift to the imagination' and bring to life.

Poetry does not hold a mirror up to nature, Williams argues, but, by a process analogous to nature's own, transfigures nature into new, living form. The contemporary poet must strive to heave the most seemingly insignificant, 'unpoetic' materials into the transfigured light of the imagination ('So much depends / upon // A red wheel / barrow'), and he must also work to wrestle objects and emotions away from their traditional poetic associations, the 'crude symbolism' that associates 'anger with lightning, flowers with love'.[12] 'The rose', Williams writes, with both Robert Burns' 'My luve's like a red, red rose' and Shakespeare's 'A rose by any other name' in mind, 'is obsolete' as metaphor or symbol: the contemporary poet must face the physical rose in the full vigour of his imagination, in the process transforming it into something like one of Juan Gris's Cubist still lives.[13]

*Kora in Hell* and *Spring and All* were collections too radical to attract a wide readership, and Williams's work of the 1920s, which he rightly felt was his best, went largely unnoticed. Over the course of the 1930s, working hard at his medical practice under the Depression's economic constraints, he published only two slim volumes of poetry, concentrating instead on prose fiction. But, with many interruptions, he was writing a long poem contemplated since at least 1925, a work that would centre upon the nearby city of Paterson.[14] While he published a number of brief lyrics from this poem over the years, the first volume of *Paterson* would not appear until 1946.

Pound's *Cantos*, which by 1946 stretched over four separate volumes, were a central instigation to *Paterson*. Pound had begun *The Cantos* doubting whether a long poem was even possible in the twentieth century. He overcame those misgivings as he proceeded, forging a modular, juxtapositional idiom for the modernist epic and incidentally providing Williams with a warrant for his own project, freeing him from reservations about the long poem's *raison d'être*.[15] Williams recognised the excellence of Pound's line in *The Cantos*, the splendid music of the poem and its finely textured weave of vivid images and allusions. But he believed that the foundational principles of Pound's epic – the contemporaneity of all ages, the notion of human culture as a global continuum over which the poet roamed at will – were deeply unsuited for an American poet committed to the particulars of an irreducibly local reality. *Paterson* would be something of an anti-*Cantos*,[16] deploying Pound's techniques of collage and quotation to explore the historical and imaginative entanglements of a single American locale: in Williams's words, 'a reply to Greek and Latin with the bare hands'.[17]

Williams chose Paterson as his subject because it was large enough to be a city, unlike Rutherford, but not an overwhelming metropolis like New York.[18] Paterson had a rich two-hundred-year history, and the Passaic Falls had made the city a centre of industry. Williams draws upon a wide variety of historical and journalistic sources for *Paterson*, and centres his poem on a handful of resonant symbols: the Falls; the surrounding mountainous landscape, personified as a woman; and Paterson, who is both a city and a gigantic, recumbent man. As 'Dr. Paterson', this figure is also an active character, a clear stand-in for Williams himself.

These large personifications, however, are in the service of an inductive poetics, devoted to the local – 'To make a start, / out of particulars / and make them general' – and to the concrete: 'no ideas but in things' is Williams's mantra in the poem.[19] Indeed, at times *Paterson* seems about to collapse in a welter of data and particulars, streaming by the reader like the water over the Falls. Williams associates the noise of the Falls with the inarticulate voice of American contemporaneity: it 'seemed to me to be a language which we were and are seeking and my search, as I looked about, became to struggle to interpret and to use this language'.[20] Unfortunately, the language Williams seeks never achieves full articulation in *Paterson*, despite the poem's many brilliant verse passages and sections of vivid reportage. The poem's very emphasis on the local and the eccentric obscures a comprehensive sense of Paterson itself, either as a living city or as a symbolic centre. *Paterson*, it would seem, is founded on constantly shifting conceptual pilings, and never quite hangs together as the compact whole towards which it aspires.[21]

Williams originally planned *Paterson* as a four-book poem, but he began working at a fifth even before the publication of Book IV in 1951. *Paterson* Book V appeared in 1958, and, while it has clear continuities with the other movements, it is perhaps best placed among Williams's other late collections, *The Desert Music and Other Poems* (1954), *Journey to Love* (1955) and *Pictures from Brueghel* (1962).[22] The poetry of these four books is the work of a far different man from the aggressive experimentalist of *Kora in Hell* or *Spring and All*. By the 1950s, Williams – old, ill and tired – had little taste for controversy and literary polemics. He was no longer much interested in pushing the envelope of available poetic forms and styles, and his writing was largely a consolidation of earlier achievements, a backward glance rather than a pressing onward. Such retrospection is evident in the beautiful 'Asphodel, That Greeny Flower' (*Journey to Love*), a long poem addressed to his wife Floss and an apology for decades of extramarital exploration.

Many of the late poems are written in Williams's 'triadic line', a series of three progressively indented phrases first introduced in *Paterson* Book II (1948), and which Williams later formalised in the concept of the 'variable foot'. The variable foot is something of an embarrassment to Williams scholars, but by it Williams sought rather confusedly to imbue his really quite intuitive free verse with a sense of order appropriate to a physical universe governed by Einstein's relativity.[23] While Williams's autumnal poems have little of the antinomian energy that propels his early works, they project a sweet intelligence and lyric delicacy often overborne in his more experimental writings. By his death in 1963, Williams was widely recognised as a major American poet, and his influence was widespread among younger writers.

Louis Zukofsky (1904–78) was the child of Yiddish-speaking Russian Jews, a product of the eastern European immigration that swelled the population of New York at the turn of the century. His first notable work was 'Poem beginning "The"' (1926), a witty and moving response to Eliot's *The Waste Land* from the perspective of a Jew, an outsider to the 'tradition' Eliot so valued, and a Marxist who believed fervently in the grand social experiment under way in Soviet Russia and the possibility of a workers' revolution in the West. Zukofsky had pursued his interest in poetry at Columbia University, and in 1927 he instigated a correspondence with Pound, who published 'Poem beginning "The"' in his magazine, the *Exile*. Pound became a mentor to the younger poet, introducing Zukofsky to his friends – notably Williams – and persuading Harriet Monroe to invite Zukofsky to guest-edit the February 1931 issue of her magazine *Poetry*. At Monroe's insistence that he present his selections under the banner of a new 'movement', Zukofsky came up with the name 'Objectivists'.[24] The doctrine of 'Objectivist' poetry – Zukofsky steadfastly avoided the nominal 'Objectivism' – was partly an extension of Pound's Imagist strictures, but Zukofsky went beyond Pound by introducing the critical terms 'sincerity' – the poet's stance of utmost fidelity, both to the experiences, ideas or sensations traced in the writing, and to the denotations, connotations and sound-values of the words used – and 'objectification', the tangible, object-like form into which the poem as a whole is cast, the 'rested totality' it assumes in the mind of the reader.[25]

Zukofsky's prose manifestoes for the Objectivist 'movement' are dense and obliquely argued documents, and proved less than successful in advancing the collective careers of the poets Zukofsky collected in the *Poetry* issue and in *An 'Objectivists' Anthology*, published the following year. The poets most often associated with the Objectivist name – Zukofsky, George Oppen, Charles Reznikoff, Carl Rakosi and Lorine Niedecker – would only begin to achieve a wider audience in the 1960s, long after they had outgrown whatever commonalities they shared in 1931.

Zukofsky struck up a long-standing friendship with Williams, who gave him his work to edit and revise, and who came to trust Zukofsky as a critical sounding board. Zukofsky's short poems show the influence of Williams's short-lined, speech-based poems, particularly those of *Spring and All*, but the long poem Zukofsky began in 1928, "*A*", demonstrates the degree to which he took Pound's work as a model. The early movements of "*A*" can, not unfairly, be read as a nativist and Marxist adaptation of the techniques of *The Cantos*. Beginning with a 1928 New York performance of Bach's *St Matthew Passion* – 'A / Round of fiddles playing Bach'[26] – these movements juxtapose the yearning for timeless, transcendent aesthetic stasis Zukofsky found in the *Passion* with the contemporary social and economic turmoils of the United States.

Despite the Poundian cast of the first movements of "*A*", the poem's evolution demonstrates that Zukofsky was far more than an ephebe of Pound's. The middle and late sections of "*A*" reveal that Zukofsky is, first and foremost, a *formalist*, a poet for whom the essence of poetry lies not in its rhetorical, figurative or communicative aspects, but in its form, in the traditional or innovative shapes into which the poet casts his words. The whole corpus of Zukofsky's mature writing can be read as a series of formal experiments – though some of those experiments stretch conventional definitions of poetic form.

Zukofsky would hopefully describe several of the early, collagistic movements of "*A*" as motivated by a 'fugal' form (though the appropriateness of the musical analogy is questionable); others play variations on more traditional forms. "*A*"–7 (1930) is a series of seven sonnets recapitulating the themes and images of the first six movements of the poem, and repeating verbatim many of their key phrases. "*A*"–9 is a pair of *canzoni*, close imitations of the intensely complex rhyme scheme and metrical patterns of the medieval Italian poet Guido Cavalcanti's 'Donna mi priegha'. The first half of "*A*"–9 (1938–40) adapts Marx's definition of value from *Das Kapital* to Cavalcanti's form; the second half (1948–50) repeats the exercise, this time using phrases from Spinoza's *Ethics*. "*A*"–11 (1950) adapts another Cavalcanti poem, the *ballata* 'Perch'io non spero'.

Zukofsky was deeply involved in left-wing politics through the 1930s (thereby attracting Pound's scorn), but his writing found little favour in the eyes of the American Marxist literary establishment, which was unable to see beyond straightforward, hortatory models of 'political' poetry. By the 1940s, he had shifted his interests from the seemingly intractable problems of the class struggle to the more mundane world of familial happiness, and the mysteries of human perception and affection. *Bottom: on Shakespeare* (published 1963), the massive prose work that occupied Zukofsky through the 1950s, is an analysis of *love* and *seeing* in the whole of the Shakespearean corpus, as well as a vast collage of quotations tracing the relationship of the eyes, the reason and the affections in western writing from the pre-Socratics to Zukofsky's own day.

The poetry of Zukofsky's later years is radically *occasional*. This is most evident in his short poems, which more often than not are the records of particular events or moments of perception. The latter movements of "*A*" (which remained his principal labour through its completion in 1974) manifest a complex interplay between the occasional (the events of Zukofsky's life and the history through which he is living); the intertextual (the books which he has been reading or to which he habitually returns, and which he quotes and adapts incessantly); and the formal. These latter movements are cast in a number of clearly defined forms, most of them based on some permutation of counting. (Zukofsky was fond of quoting the Platonic dictum, 'If number, measure and weighing be taken away from any art, that which remains will not be much.'[27])

Most striking in this regard are the movements ("A"–14, –19, –21, –22 and –23), in which Zukofsky employs a word-count prosody, where line length is determined not by stress, quantity or syllable count, but by number of words. "A"–22 and –23, the last-composed movements of "A", each consists of one thousand five-word lines. Upon this form Zukofsky plots six thousand years' worth of materials – quoted, translated, transliterated – so that each movement is a comprehensive history of the human world (a world, according to Hebrew scripture, around six thousand years old).

The last movement of "A" (though not the last-composed) is "A"–24, a six-part 'masque' composed by Zukofsky's wife Celia, which counterpoints excerpts from Zukofsky's poetry, fiction, drama and critical writings to Handel's harpsichord pieces. As Zukofsky acknowledges in his epigraph – 'The gift–/ she hears/ the work/ in its recurrence'[28] – the 'L. Z. Masque' is a fitting conclusion to "A", showing in a particularly concrete manner the systems of recurrence and repetition that Zukofsky felt were central to his own art and to the whole body of western culture. In keeping with Zukofsky's increasing impulse towards condensation and miniaturisation, his last project was *80 Flowers*, a series of eight-line, five-words-per-line poems that aim to wind in as much historical, literary and botanical lore as possible about each flower addressed, while constituting a precis of his life's work.

In "A"–12 (1950–1), Zukofsky had bid farewell to conventional notions of the poet's originality, reconceiving the act of poiesis as a remaking of what has previously been made, a re-saying of what has always already been said. This is perhaps most evident in the degree to which his later work consists of quotations – almost every word of "A"–22 and –23 and *80 Flowers* can be 'sourced' – and in his reconception of poetic translation. In his version of the complete Catullus (in collaboration with Celia), Zukofsky sought to 'breathe the literal meaning' of the Roman poet; to translate him, that is, with an attention directed more closely to the *sounds* of the Latin words than to their lexical meanings. Catullus's 'Odi et amo' (I hate and I love) becomes 'O th'hate I move love', for instance.[29] Zukofsky applied this technique of 'transliteration' to a wide range of foreign texts in his later works, in the process redefining translation as a sort of *formal* principle, in which the source text becomes a template determining the sounds and rhythms of the final English poem. Such translation is but one aspect of Zukofsky's far-reaching explorations of the formal possibilities of poetry and of the musical possibilities of words in combination.

Zukofsky's work has proved immensely influential over the three decades since his death, particularly upon the avant-garde Language poets. In his own lifetime, however, he worked largely in obscurity; only in the last two decades of his long career was his poetry vigorously promoted by such younger poets as Robert Creeley and Robert Duncan. For much of his life, Zukofsky failed to find an aesthetic community within which his writing could be received. In contrast, Charles Olson (1910–70) was spectacularly successful in establishing a company of readers. During his time as instructor and rector at Black Mountain College (1951–6), Olson fostered a nexus of creative activity so intense that it would give the name 'Black Mountain poets' to a group of influential younger writers, among them Creeley, Duncan, Denise Levertov and Ed Dorn. The relentless energy of Olson's lectures, his prose writings and his poetry had by the time of his death attracted to him a formidable range of commentators and imitators.

From the beginning, Olson conceived of himself as a scholar, a researcher. As a graduate student at Wesleyan University he did groundbreaking research on Herman Melville, and in 1947 published a work of visionary Melville criticism, *Call Me Ishmael*. Olson came to poetry late: he did not begin writing poems until his thirties. From the beginning he worked in the modernist modes of Pound, Williams and Hart Crane, though his admiration for Pound was tempered by first-hand experience of Pound's anti-Semitism when Olson visited the poet at St Elizabeths mental hospital. Olson made himself known as a major presence on the postwar poetic landscape with the long poem 'The Kingfishers' (1949) and a polemical essay in poetics, 'Projective Verse' (1950).

'The Kingfishers' is a response both to Eliot's *Waste Land* and to his more formally conventional and explicitly Christian *Four Quartets* (1944). In *The Waste Land*, Eliot had diagnosed the malaise of the West as profoundly spiritual, a debasement of sexuality and culture brought to a pitch in the pervasive secularism and materialism of the early twentieth century; the cure for this malaise, *Four Quartets* implied, lay in a recovery of a Christian cultural tradition. In contrast, 'The Kingfishers' presents a vision of societies lapsing into ruins precisely because of their failure to change, to respond to cultural and historical shifts in the manner described in Norbert Wiener's theory of 'feedback'. 'What does not change / is the will to change', the poem begins, and Olson proceeds to juxtapose vanished cultural orders (the Aztec civilisation destroyed by the Conquistadors, the Cambodian ruins of Angkor Wat) with hopeful signs of cultural rebirth like the Chinese Communist revolution of

Mao Zedong.[30] For Olson, contemporary culture's plight is not a matter of estrangement from the deity (as with Eliot) or of an unfair economic system (as in Pound). Rather, it is the result of almost 2,500 years of classificatory reason, beginning with Plato, which has estranged the human being from the natural order of which he or she is a part. To re-establish this connection, to recover the 'human universe' (as Olson calls it), the poet-pedagogue must look for its traces before and beyond the cultural record of the West. 'I pose you your question', 'The Kingfishers' concludes: 'shall you uncover honey / where maggots are? // I hunt among stones'.[31]

'Projective Verse' is an energetic, untidy polemic, an attack on 'inherited line, stanza, over-all form' on behalf of what Olson names 'COMPOSITION BY FIELD'. The essay revolves around a number of poetic principles, prominent among them that 'FORM IS NEVER MORE THAN AN EXTENSION OF CONTENT' (a restatement of the romantic doctrine of 'organic form') and 'ONE PERCEPTION MUST IMMEDIATELY AND DIRECTLY LEAD TO A FURTHER PERCEPTION'. '[G]et on with it', Olson exhorts, 'keep moving, keep in, speed, the nerves, their speed, the perceptions, theirs, the acts, the split second acts, the whole business, keep it moving as fast as you can, citizen.' 'Projective Verse' dismisses traditional rhyme and metre; it insists that the poetic line must stem from a somatic base, 'the breath, from the breathing of the man who writes, at the moment that he writes'. The essay dismisses as well traditional guidelines of syntax, logic and thematic progression, all in the service of creating the poem as a 'high-energy construct': 'A poem is energy transferred from where the poet got it (he will have some several causations), by way of the poem itself to, all the way over to, the reader.'[32] The poetics described (and enacted) in 'Projective Verse' could produce poems of remarkable scope, energy and formal improvisation (as well as pieces of shapeless, flailing obscurity). Projectivist poetry is part and parcel of Olson's desire to reintegrate the human being into the natural world, a nature conceived not as static categories but (in terms borrowed from Alfred North Whitehead) as a congeries of *processes*.

In 1951 Olson spent half a year in the Yucatán, studying Mayan remains and formulating his own position as an 'archaeologist of morning'. The clue to a 'post-modern' renewal, he was convinced, was to be found in societies outside of the baleful classifying impulse of Greek thought; 'the substances of history now useful', he wrote Creeley, 'lie outside, under, right here, anywhere but in the direct continuum of society as we have had it'.[33] Pound, in the transhistorical poetics of *The Cantos*, had made an important beginning, but for Olson his work was vitiated by its emphasis on classical and renaissance Europe and by Pound's reliance upon the 'beak' of his own ego to turn 'time into what we must now have, space & its live air'. In *Paterson*,

Williams displayed 'an emotional system which is capable of extensions & comprehensions the ego-system (the Old Deal, Ez as Cento Man, here dates) is not', yet by focusing on a single city 'Bill completely licks himself, lets time roll him under as Ez does not'.[34]

Williams might have failed in *Paterson*, but Olson acknowledged the value of settling down and learning as much as possible about a single location. As he told Dorn, 'Best thing to do is *to dig one thing or place or man* until you yourself know more about that than is possible to any other man. It doesn't matter whether it's Barbed Wire or Pemmican or Paterson or Iowa. But *exhaust* it. Saturate it. Beat it. And then U KNOW everything else very fast: one saturation job (it might take 14 years). And you're in forever.'[35] The subject of Olson's own 'saturation job', and the centre of his long sequence *The Maximus Poems*, would be (as with *Paterson*) a single American community: Gloucester, Massachusetts, where Olson had lived as a child, and at one time the busiest port of the North Atlantic fisheries. In Gloucester Olson found centred themes that had long obsessed him: the westward movement of European man; the experience of the immigrant confronted by vast American *space*; the struggle of the human being with the forces of nature embodied in the New England winters, the movements of fish populations and the vagaries of the sea.

*The Maximus Poems* begin as 'letters' addressed to the citizens of Gloucester by 'Maximus', a figure whose name (though little else) Olson borrows from the second-century philosopher Maximus of Tyre. That name – Maximus, 'largest' – encapsulates the expansiveness and self-sufficiency of Olson's speaker: Maximus is not so much a persona of Olson as (in the words of Sherman Paul) 'an aspect of Olson . . . the naming of what by means of the poem he would become; Maximus is *homo maximus*, Jung's individuated man, the man who has realized the self, who, having reconciled the opposites of his nature, is whole'.[36] Maximus is gadfly to Gloucester, railing against the 'pejorocracy' rife in the community, the inane 'mu-sick' that clouds the minds of his fellow citizens. He is above all a pedagogue, one who seeks to establish a renewed sense of polis among the Gloucesterians (and by implication all Americans), who would teach his listeners that their political and spiritual renewal depends upon their ability rightly to *see*: 'polis is / eyes'; 'There are no hierarchies, no infinite, no such many as mass, there are only / eyes in all heads, / to be looked out of'.[37]

Though centred on Gloucester, *The Maximus Poems* open themselves up to an extraordinary range of historical and mythic material, from the most archaic legends of the Greeks, to the tales of the Native Americans, to the ancient cosmological myths of the Sumerians. As Olson worked further and further into his sequence, he found the history of Gloucester too constraining a canvas, and the later volumes of *Maximus*, while never entirely losing sight of Gloucester, play out against a far more universal stage, emblematised in the illustration on the cover of *The Maximus Poems IV, V, VI* (1968): a map of continental drift, 'the Earth (and Ocean) before Earth started to come apart at the seams, some 125 million years awhile back'.[38] The last two-thirds of *The Maximus Poems* range over an astonishing variety of historical, etymological and mythical lore, following the wandering but always intense and intelligent attentions of Olson himself, *homo maximus*. Throughout, we are made aware of the interpenetrating imperatives of *topos* (space), *typos* (stance) and *tropos* (fact),[39] the three aspects of the human's being-in-the-world, the states that classificatory, hierarchical reason has worked to obscure, and the states that the poet would have us rediscover in order to return to the at-homeness enjoyed by the ancient Sumerians (and which he sensed in flashes among the peasants of the Yucatán).

Olson died in early 1970, and *The Maximus Poems: Volume Three* (1975), the largest instalment of the work, was prepared by his editors from a huge and untidy collection of manuscripts.[40] Olson left few instructions regarding the book, specifying only the first and last poems to be included. The book as it stands, all readers agree, is a heterogeneous and uneven collection: it includes some beautifully assured poems, several dream transcriptions, and a number of what read like notes *towards* poems to be written. The latter, however, are in keeping with Olson's late poetics, in which the poet's acts of research, of hunting out and seeking to order the data at hand, have become the primary activity of the poem, displacing any conception of the poem as completed, shapely utterance. Where Zukofsky's *"A"* ends with a gesture of enfolding, of bringing the poet's far-ranging labours and sources into a single, focused moment of 'love',[41] *The Maximus Poems* end in gesture of dispersal, of renunciation, Olson enumerating the items he has lost: 'my wife my car my color and myself'.[42] In the context of the sequence as a whole, however, this seeming deathbed testament marks a series of signposts on the poet's ambitious journey outward – an Odyssey-voyage whose ultimate end was always to root the human being more firmly in a single *space*, in the processes of a human universe.

## NOTES

1. William Carlos Williams, *Selected Letters* (New York: McDowell, Oblensky, 1957), p. 185.
2. Hugh Witemeyer (ed.), *Pound/Williams: Selected Letters of Ezra Pound and William Carlos Williams* (New York: New Directions, 1996), pp. 30–1.
3. William Carlos Williams, *I Wanted to Write a Poem: The Autobiography of the Works of a Poet*, ed. Edith Heal (Boston: Beacon Press, 1967), p. 26.

4. William Carlos Williams, *Collected Poems*, ed. A. Walton Litz and Christopher MacGowan, 2 vols (New York: New Directions, 1986), vol. I, pp. 108, 115.
5. William Carlos Williams, *Imaginations*, ed. Webster Schott (New York: New Directions, 1970), pp. 24, 26.
6. Williams, *Imaginations*, p. 14.
7. Williams, *Collected Poems*, vol. I, pp. 217–18.
8. Williams, *Collected Poems*, vol. I, p. 233.
9. Williams, *Collected Poems*, vol. I, pp. 185, 186.
10. William Carlos Williams, *The Autobiography of William Carlos Williams* (1951; New York: New Directions, 1967), p. 146.
11. Williams, *Collected Poems*, vol. I, p. 188.
12. Williams, *Collected Poems*, vol. I, pp. 224, 188.
13. Williams, *Collected* Poems, vol. I, p. 195; see Williams's comment in *Collected Poems*, vol. I, p. 502.
14. William Carlos Williams, *Paterson*, ed. Christopher MacGowan (New York: New Directions, 1992), p. xiii.
15. See Michael André Bernstein, *The Tale of the Tribe: Ezra Pound and the Modern Verse Epic* (Princeton University Press, 1980), pp. 194–6.
16. The term is Bernstein's, *Tale of the Tribe*, p. 200.
17. Williams, *Paterson*, p. 2.
18. Williams, *I Wanted to Write a Poem*, p. 72.
19. Williams, *Paterson*, pp. 3, 6.
20. Williams, *Paterson*, p. xiv.
21. See Williams's own inconsistent statements on the poem's structure in *Paterson*, pp. xiii–xiv.
22. See James E. B. Breslin, *William Carlos Williams: An American Artist* (1970; University of Chicago Press, 1985), pp. 172, 203–10.
23. See Williams, *I Wanted to Write a Poem*, pp. 80–3, and William Carlos Williams, *Selected Essays* (New York: New Directions, 1954), pp. 337–40.
24. Louis Zukofsky, *Prepositions+: The Collected Critical Essays*, ed. Mark Scroggins (Hanover: Wesleyan University Press, 2000), pp. 229–30.
25. Zukofsky, *Prepositions+*, pp. 12–18.
26. Louis Zukofsky, *"A"* (1978; Baltimore: Johns Hopkins University Press, 1993), p. 1.
27. For instance, see Zukofsky, *Prepositions+*, p. 6.
28. Zukofsky, *"A"*, p. 806.
29. Louis Zukofsky, *Complete Short Poetry* (Baltimore: Johns Hopkins University Press, 1991), p. 310.
30. Charles Olson, *The Collected Poems of Charles Olson*, ed. George F. Butterick (Berkeley: University of California Press, 1987), p. 86.
31. Olson, *Collected Poems*, p. 93.
32. Charles Olson, *Collected Prose*, ed. Donald Allen and Benjamin Friedlander (Berkeley: University of California Press, 1997), pp. 239, 240, 242, 240.
33. Charles Olson, *Selected Writings*, ed. Robert Creeley (New York: New Directions, 1966), p. 84.
34. Olson, *Selected Writings*, pp. 82–3.
35. Olson, *Collected Prose*, pp. 306–7.

36. Sherman Paul, *Olson's Push: Origin, Black Mountain, and Recent American Poetry* (Baton Rouge: Louisiana State University Press, 1978), p. 117.

37. Charles Olson, *The Maximus Poems*, ed. George Butterick (Berkeley: University of California Press, 1983), pp. 30. 33. On Olson as pedagogue, see Robert von Hallberg, *Charles Olson: The Scholar's Art* (Cambridge, Mass.: Harvard University Press, 1978), pp. 21–8, 59–63.

38. Olson, *The Maximus Poems*, pp. 167–8.

39. See Don Byrd, *Charles Olson's Maximus* (Urbana: University of Illinois Press, 1980), pp. 8–26.

40. For a description of the manuscripts and their editing, see George Butterick, *A Guide to the Maximus Poems of Charles Olson* (Berkeley: University of California Press, 1978), pp. xliv–lv.

41. Zukofsky, *"A"*, p. 803.

42. Olson, *The Maximus Poems*, p. 635.

# 11

SHARON LYNETTE JONES

# The poetry of the Harlem Renaissance

As one of the most significant literary movements of the twentieth century, the Harlem Renaissance (1900–40) reflects the significance of African-American cultural expression during the modernist period. Nonetheless, critical discussions of African-American literature typically treat *modernism* as a movement separate and distinct from the Harlem Renaissance. As Houston Baker notes, 'Traditionally in discussions of Afro-American literature and culture, "modernism" implies the work of British, Irish, and Anglo-American writers and artists of the early twentieth century.'[1] While this may stem from a tendency among critics to view African-American literature as separate and distinct from Anglo-American, British and Irish literature, the Harlem Renaissance's relationship and connection with the modernist movement reflects the conceptualisation of racial identity and consciousness during the early to mid twentieth century. Consequently, poetry of the Harlem Renaissance attempts to capture the perspective of African-American writers within the context of the modern world. African-American poets of the Harlem Renaissance such as Langston Hughes, James Weldon Johnson, Countee Cullen, Claude McKay, Jean Toomer, Alice Dunbar-Nelson, Helene Johnson, Georgia Douglas Johnson and Angelina Weld Grimké explored central themes such as history, identity, community, race, class, gender and heritage, which continue to influence contemporary African-American poetry and its rendering of the human experience.

Like their Anglo-American, British and Irish counterparts during the early twentieth century, writers of the Harlem Renaissance created poems which featured modernist characteristics such as fragmentation, multiple narrative voices/speakers, stream of consciousness, non-linear narrative and highly experimental language. Nevertheless, the Harlem poets also transformed and challenged modernist themes, techniques and strategies to convey the African-American experience, creating poetry which also incorporated aspects of black heritage in the United States, including the black vernacular (African-American English or Black English), blues/jazz rhythms and the oral storytelling tradition.

For writers of the Harlem Renaissance, Harlem, a section of New York City with a large African-American community and population, served as a symbol of the modern city and African-American identity. As James de Jongh notes, 'In a century marked by the vicious dynamics of the color line, Harlem has remained modernity's preeminent popular image of black racial being and interracial contact.'[2] The urban landscape of Harlem functioned as an important setting in Harlem Renaissance poetry, alternately representing optimistic and pessimistic views about the potentiality for the acquisition of the American Dream of social and economic success in the modern world for peoples of African descent. Harlem proved to be a site where many African Americans who migrated from the rural South to the urban North in search of social and economic opportunity settled due to the availability of affordable housing and landlords willing to rent to African Americans. As de Jongh stresses, 'Life in New York may have been harsh, but the migrants themselves often came from backgrounds of such extreme poverty and oppression that Harlem, in contrast, seemed to be the Promised Land.'[3] Similarly, Cary D. Wintz emphasises the importance of Harlem as a site of migration for African Americans, stating, 'One effect of the black migration was the emergence of Harlem as the black metropolis and the social and cultural center of black America.'[4] Not surprisingly, Harlem emerged as a microcosm of the African diaspora, and the interchange of cultural traditions among blacks from different geographical regions of the United States as well as blacks from Africa and the Caribbean led to Harlem's ascendance as a cultural capital. Although labourers and professionals came to Harlem in search of social and economic opportunity, this area also proved to be a magnet for black writers, artists and intellectuals. Since New York City was the centre of the publishing and artistic world, poets flocked to Harlem. De Jongh points out, 'By 1925, the allure of Harlem was a compelling influence on the consciousness of a vanguard of young black painters and writers waiting in the wings to be proclaimed as the New Negroes of the Harlem Renaissance.'[5] Poets of the Harlem Renaissance constitute a community of writers with a common interest in exploring the African-American experience. Thus, Harlem functioned as the locus or site of African-American cultural expression and a microcosm of the black diaspora. Harlem emerged as a dynamic, evolving and significant location of black life.

African-American social and political activism during the modernist period proved to be an important force in shaping the poetry of the Harlem Renaissance. The founding of the NAACP (National Association for the Advancement of Colored People, established in 1909) and the Urban League (created in 1911) profoundly influenced Harlem Renaissance poetry. As inter-racial civil rights organisations, the NAACP and the Urban League sought to use arts and letters as a means of facilitating equality. The NAACP published *Crisis* and the Urban League published *Opportunity* – both magazines func-tioned as publishing outlets for aspiring Harlem poets. These publications assisted in spreading the popularity of African-American poetry in this period directly to blacks and whites committed to civil rights. These highly influ-ential magazines launched the careers of African-American poets during the Harlem Renaissance by giving exposure to aspiring authors on a national and international scale. Although African-American poets also published in mainstream American publications, *Opportunity* and *Crisis* provided a forum for poetry exploring African-American cultural expression and racial identity.

The publication of *The New Negro: An Interpretation* in 1925 also proved important in promoting the poetry of the Harlem Renaissance within the con-text of the modernist movement. As Baker states, 'If we turn to the Harlem Renaissance of the twenties, it is difficult in the presence of a seminal dis-cursive act like Alain Locke's *New Negro* to conceive of that modern, Afro-American, expressive moment as other than an intensely successful act of national self-definition working itself out in a field of possibilities constructed by turn-of-the-century spokespersons.'[6] *The New Negro* emerged from a March 1925 issue of *The Survey Graphic*, also edited by Locke, focusing on the Harlem or 'New Negro' Renaissance. *The New Negro* featured poetry, prose and drama that focused on African-American culture and heritage; contributors included the poets Langston Hughes, Claude McKay, James Weldon Johnson, Jean Toomer, Anne Spencer, Georgia Douglas Johnson, Lewis Alexander and Angelina Weld Grimké.

This poetry explores the theme of racial identity from an African-American cultural perspective and orientation. The poetry represents the embodiment of the New Negro, as fashioned by Locke, for whom the New Negro symbol-ised a new identity for African Americans in the twentieth century: dynamic, strong, assertive and prideful of his or her African-American heritage. In his introductory essay, Locke explores the significance of Harlem as a cul-tural capital in New York with its promise of social, economic and artistic advancement for the New Negro: 'The migrant masses, shifting from coun-tryside to city, hurdle several generations of experiences at a leap, but more important, the same thing happens spiritually in the life-attitudes and self-expression of the Young Negro, in his poetry, his art, his education and his new outlook, with the additional advantage, of course, of the poise and greater certainty of knowing what it is all about.'[7] In his essay, Locke uses poetry by African-American poets such as Langston Hughes, Claude McKay and James Weldon Johnson to support his argument that a new-found pride and racial consciousness among African Americans would transform American society and usher in a new era of change and social progress.

*The New Negro* represents an early attempt at the canonisation of African-American writers and illustrates Locke's belief that art and letters could be used to increase awareness about racial issues and transform society. African Americans would assert their humanity through artistic contributions, which, in turn, would lead to more equitable treatment in society. The book also illustrates the intersection of the modernist ethos and African-American culture in the exploration of the dual identity of African Americans – being both American and black, or being both American and of African descent. The text represents a national and international re-evaluation of black cultural aesthetics, albeit that black writers, artists and intellectuals associated with the movement represent a multiplicity of voices and aesthetic positions.

Aesthetic debates and discussions regarding race, authorship and representation in African-American literary expression contributed to the output of African-American poetry during the modernist and Harlem Renaissance period. As I have argued elsewhere, African-American literature of the Harlem Renaissance can be categorised into three aesthetics – folk, bourgeois and proletarian. Literature of the folk aesthetic features the black vernacular (African-American English), dialect, and an emphasis on the oral tradition and a working-class perspective. In contrast, literature reflecting the bourgeois aesthetic uses Standard English, and avoids the African-American English or black vernacular as a form of expression. This literature reflects assimilation into middle-class Anglo-American cultural traditions and ideas. Literature of the proletarian aesthetic critiques class, gender and racial oppression, suggesting bourgeois and/or folk perspectives; proletarian literature seeks to promote social justice and equality for African Americans in direct and overt manners. This combination of aesthetics, rooted in black cultural production, represents the African-American literary response to the modernist movement.[8]

Poetry of the Harlem Renaissance emerging within the context of modernism reflects this combination of aesthetics. Poets such as Hughes, McKay and Toomer often evoke a folk aesthetic in their poetry due to the adoption of black vernacular and/or blues/jazz as structural devices, while the poetry of Cullen, Douglas Johnson, Weld Grimké, Dunbar-Nelson and Helene Johnson frequently represents a bourgeois aesthetic in its reliance on European stanza forms and Standard English. At the same time, these authors blend both the bourgeois and the folk aesthetic, ultimately to illustrate a proletarian critique of race, class and/or gender oppression. In this sense, they articulate an African-American response to the modernist aesthetic which is grounded in the African-American cultural context. Like their Anglo-American counterparts, T. S. Eliot, Ezra Pound and William Carlos Williams, these poets deploy modernist themes, imagery and experimentation with point of view/person, irony, tone, stream of consciousness and structure. Modernist themes such as alienation, dislocation, a sense of loss and a divided self also inform their work. While for modernist writers such as Eliot the city is perceived as a moral and spiritual wasteland, in Harlem Renaissance poetry the city, in particular Harlem, figures alternately as a site of both alienation and community for the migrant or outsider. In this sense, Harlem Renaissance poetry articulates an African-American response to the modernist aesthetic in history, culture and experience. Additionally, jazz and blues prove to be prominent thematic and structural devices, while the use of black vernacular or African-American English constitutes experimentation with language.

An analysis of representative Harlem poems illustrates the nature of its relationship with modernism. The diversity of voices in the Harlem poetic tradition reveals both how some poets incorporated and other poets resisted modernist conventions. Langston Hughes represents the way in which African-American writers worked within and against the modernist movement in the exploration of the human condition from an African-American perspective. Hughes emerged as one of the most prominent of the Harlem Renaissance writers. As A. B. Christa Schwarz has pointed out, 'Publishing his first poems in the early years of the Harlem Renaissance, Hughes quickly rose to prominence among the younger Renaissance writers, his popularity being matched only by Countée Cullen.'[9] Hughes's poems reflect a modernist impulse, yet through the appropriation of blues, jazz and the black vernacular, he injects an Afrocentric perspective and folk aesthetic with a proletarian sensibility. Additionally, for Hughes, the city (Harlem) represents a sense of the promise of a better life and the reality of deferred dreams. His poems represent both the cohesion and fragmented nature of the black community.

A strong black racial consciousness and folk aesthetic infuses his poems, which often reflect a black perspective and point of view. For example, in 'Mother to Son' (1922), Hughes uses the black vernacular to connect to the African-American 'folk' experience.[10] The speaker, an African-American woman, delivers a dramatic monologue in dialect to her silent son. The theme of perseverance and struggle against adversity permeates the poem as the mother tries to teach her son to continue to strive for social and economic opportunity. The message, by extension, can be applied to the African-American struggle for equality as the older generation (mother) counsels the younger generation (son) to hold on to a dream for a better life.

The theme of dreams is also an important concern of Hughes's poetry. 'Dream Variation' functions as a meditation on nature and racial identity.[11] The speaker of this 1926 poem wants wholly to identify and become one with the natural world. Yet the poem is insistently social: the racially coded references to night and day symbolise the relationship between blacks and whites in America. As Nathan Huggins asserts, 'The poet, again the Negro, identifies himself with the night; doubtless white men and the white world are the day and the sun.'[12] This imagistic poem reflects the racial consciousness that infuses the work of Harlem Renaissance writers during the modernist period. 'Harlem [2]' (1959) exemplifies the treatment of Harlem as a symbol by writers who matured during the Renaissance.[13] The representation of Harlem as a site of dreams deferred serves as a microcosm for the African-American experience. The speaker asks a series of questions about dreams, and the images of deferred dreams that follow suggest diminution, decay, death or illness. The negative associations connect with the sense of loss which permeates the poem, suggesting Harlem as a place alternately of hope and of despair. Harlem functions as a microcosm for the rest of the United States in relationship to African Americans.

Like Hughes, Claude McKay also addressed the politics of racial identity in his poetry. A native of Jamaica who migrated to the United States, McKay represents the international and global perspective of the Harlem Renaissance. Nevertheless, McKay's relationship with modernism remains highly complex. As Lee M. Jenkins observes, 'Doubly expatriated from Jamaica and the United States, McKay stands in problematic relation to Anglo-American modernism, to the Lost Generation, to the Harlem Renaissance, and to the broader African-American literary canon to which his poetry, and his fiction, is habitually conscripted.'[14] Jenkins highlights the importance of viewing McKay's achievement in the context of Caribbean literature. McKay's poetic production during the Harlem Renaissance may suggest how his work functions within and against modernism. Many of his poems embody a folk and a proletarian aesthetic in their rendering of the African-American experience, yet his work as a whole displays the diversity in his poetic voice. Other poems such as 'The White House' feature a more overt and direct reference to racism.[15] In the 1922 poem of that title, the house serves as a metaphor for the oppression of blacks in the United States. In addition to writing social protest poetry, McKay also used Harlem and the urban landscape as a source of literary inspiration. In 'The Harlem Dancer' (1917), the speaker describes the performance of a black female cabaret performer.[16] As de Jongh notes, McKay's speaker also directs us to a vision of an inner reality.[17] According to the speaker, the smiling female dancer symbolises an object of desire, yet the poem ends with a sense of the dancer's disconnection from her environment. The poem suggests a divided or fragmented self, with the woman representing a tension between her exterior world, the smile, and the interior world, which conveys a different emotion. The speaker suggests that, while physically present, the woman is not mentally or spiritually present. Thus, Harlem becomes a place where appearance conflicts with reality. In 'The Desolate City', the unnamed city serves as a metaphor for the human condition.[18] The city represents loss, despair, disease, pollution and sterility, and so has an affinity with the urban landscapes of the poetry of Anglo-American writers such as Eliot.

The religious and spiritual heritage of African Americans also remains a concern in the poetics of the Harlem Renaissance. While some modernist writers suggest that the contemporary world consists of a spiritual wasteland devoid of God or a higher power in control of man and woman's fate, some writers of the Harlem Renaissance celebrated religious and folk traditions in African-American culture. In his poem 'The Creation: A Negro Sermon', James Weldon Johnson seeks to retell the Book of Genesis, humanising God as a lonely man who seeks to create a world and man to feel a sense of community.[19] This 1920 poem reflects a more Afrocentric conception of God, refuting Eurocentric conceptions. By subtitling the poem 'A Negro Sermon' Johnson shifts the conception of God to an African-American context, particularly in the language and vernacular of the God-figure in the poem. The poem represents the experimentation with structure and theme that characterises Harlem modernism. 'O Black and Unknown Bards' (1908), like many Harlem Renaissance texts, seeks to celebrate black culture, heritage and spirituals through the exhibition of a folk aesthetic and a proletarian message.[20] The poem celebrates the oral heritage of African Americans in its emphasis on the black singers and songwriters who created the spirituals, a type of African-American religious music. The poem suggests that the legacy of these songs represents the foundations of African-American heritage. The poem also suggests that this musical tradition remains superior to the European musical tradition. The poem articulates that these singers/songwriters were instrumental in transforming the African religious traditions into Judaeo-Christian traditions. These poems embody a folk and a proletarian aesthetic in their evocation of the oral tradition, and their emphasis on racial pride and dignity.

Jean Toomer is another major poet of the Harlem Renaissance whose work embraces modernist innovation while connecting with the issue of African-American culture and identity to reflect a folk aesthetic. Toomer's *Cane* (1923) is a mixed-generic work of prose and poetry about the black experience. The text has a circular structure, with each part set in a different region of the United States, ranging from south to north and then returning to the southern setting. The text, both poetry and prose, reflects the confluence of the Harlem trinity of folk, proletarian and bourgeois aesthetics in its representation of black life and culture. The poems represent highly imagistic and fragmented meditations on black life in the United States. Poems such as 'Portrait in Georgia' convey an image of a lynching to suggest the reality of racial violence in the South.[21] The fragmented nature of the poem reflects a modernist sensibility and deploys modernist aesthetics to convey the harsh reality of racial violence. The imagistic 'Reapers' also uses modernist technique to interrogate violence.[22] *Cane* reflects a highly experimental poetry emerging from the Harlem Renaissance, but one infused with a black cultural context.

Known as the 'Black Keats', Countee Cullen represents a departure from utilising jazz and blues rhythms in Harlem Renaissance poetry or focusing on the folk aesthetic or perspective. Instead, his poetry reflects a bourgeois aesthetic, in structure and in form. Cullen uses English romantics such as Keats and Shelley as role models for his poems in terms of structure, rhyme and metre. Nevertheless, his poems focus on the African and African-American experience; thus, he employs European models to focus on Afrocentric topics. At the same time, tropes of alienation, fragmentation and the city inform his poems, which often use Harlem as a source of inspiration. In 'Harlem Wine' (1925), Cullen explores the significance of this black urban locus, using the metaphor of wine to suggest the fluidity of Harlem as a site of life and experience for African Americans in the modern world.[23]

Although Cullen departs from Hughes, Johnson, McKay and Toomer in his use of form, he, too, addresses the issue of racial identity in his poetry. 'Heritage' (1925) meditates on the issue of racial identity, exploring the meaning and significance of Africa to the African American.[24] In the late nineteenth and early twentieth centuries, an interest in Africa manifested itself in art and poetry as people looked outside the western world for inspiration. The alternate identification and alienation the speaker feels about Africa permeates the poem, mirroring the plight of blacks during the Harlem Renaissance trying to resolve the duality of being both American and of African descent. 'Yet Do I Marvel' chronicles the struggle of the black poet to render the black experience.[25] Cullen appropriates, like Eliot, classical allusions, to highlight the tension between past and present. He compares the struggle of black poets for civil rights with the ordeals of mythological figures such as Tantalus and Sisyphus. Cullen uses classical allusion as a means of commenting on the African-American experience, thus blending Eurocentism and Afrocentrism in offering a commentary on the plight and struggle of the black poet amid social, economic and cultural discrimination. The poem is a meditation on the black poet during the Harlem

Renaissance, who struggles to assert himself despite social, political and economic disenfranchisement.

Although many of Cullen's poems focus on the African-American experience specifically, other poems such as 'To John Keats, Poet. At Spring Time' illustrate how Cullen and other Harlem poets did not always focus primarily on racial politics.[26] The 1925 poem, which was dedicated to Carl Van Vechten (a white writer, photographer and promoter of the Harlem Renaissance), serves as a meditation on the life and death of Keats in tandem with the seasonal cycles of the natural world, with which Cullen's speaker feels a sense of communion. Cullen's poetry thus reflects the diversity of poetry in the Harlem Renaissance, and the merging of influences in this movement. While Cullen may differ from other modernist poets due to his adherence to traditional form, his meditation on the duality of human experience and identity and the ambiguity that tempers his poems nonetheless reference a modernist ethos.

African-American women poets also contributed to the literary achievement of the Harlem Renaissance, particularly in their articulation of race, class and gender issues. Their poetry represents a blending of folk, bourgeois and proletarian aesthetics in their attempt to capture the complexities of African-American life. In her important anthology *Shadowed Dreams: Women's Poetry of the Harlem Renaissance*, Maureen Honey states, 'Poetry was the preferred form of most Afro-American women writers during the 1920s.'[27] Nevertheless, black women faced a number of obstacles due to ideas about acceptable roles for women and, in particular, black women. At this juncture, due to sexist notions about gender, race and authorship, some publishers and promoters of black literature favoured male writers over female writers. As Gloria T. Hull points out, 'In a world that values and caters more to males, they enjoyed the lion's share of all the available goods and, in the field of literature, were more apt to be seriously encouraged as professional writers.'[28] Black female poets such as Alice Dunbar-Nelson, Helene Johnson and Georgia Douglas Johnson contributed to the Harlem Renaissance in their representation of African-American womanhood. At the same time, they challenged prevailing notions about black womanhood by placing the black female experience at the centre rather than at the margins of their examinations of the human condition.

Dunbar-Nelson's poetry reflects a bourgeois and proletarian aesthetic in structure and theme. For example, 'I Sit and Sew' comments on the tension between domestic work and socially proscribed gender roles.[29] The speaker sews during wartime, while men fight for their lives. The poem serves as a commentary on the battlefield of masculine space and the feminine space represented by home and sewing. The speaker ultimately questions this socially proscribed role for women. Despite the modernity of her subject matter, Dunbar-Nelson's poetry, like that of Countee Cullen, illustrates the influence of the romantic movement on Harlem Renaissance poetry. 'Violets' serves as a meditation on the interconnection between nature, God and love.[30] The poem's structure and form belie a modernist aesthetic, yet her poem reveals the diversity of poetic technique during the Harlem Renaissance.

Like Dunbar-Nelson, Angelina Weld Grimké also contributed to Harlem poetry with an emphasis on both a bourgeois and a proletarian aesthetic. Her poems suggest a blending of romantic sensibility and modernist themes of loss. In 'Tenebris' (1927), Grimké uses nature as a metaphor for race relations; a tree represents African Americans and their struggle for equality.[31] 'A Winter Twilight' centres on the power and significance of nature in the environment without an emphasis on racial politics.[32] The emphasis on themes such as loss and a sense of diminishment imbues this 1923 poem with the preoccupations of modernism. Grimké deftly blends a romantic poetic sensibility with a modernist ethos.

Like their male counterparts, women writers of the Harlem Renaissance also explore issues of racial identity. Helene Johnson meditates on the notion of black identity by utilising a proletarian and bourgeois aesthetic. In 'My Race' (1925), the speaker comments on African Americans as a collective group.[33] The poem deals with the identity of African Americans in the collective context of the Harlem Renaissance, suggesting that African-American identity continues to evolve. Her 'Sonnet to a Negro in Harlem' illustrates the tendency of Harlem writers to employ traditional poetic forms, such as the sonnet, and to appropriate these forms to meditate on black life.[34] The poem reflects the relationship between the individual and the city, celebrating the pride and distinctiveness of the negro, unnamed, who walks through the city streets. Similarly, Georgia Douglas Johnson's poetry meditates on the issue of racial identity, as poems detail personal relationships and portraits of people through the use of a folk, bourgeois and proletarian aesthetic. In 'The Heart of a Woman' (1918) Johnson explores themes of love and loss within the gendered and subjective context of a woman's romantic life, displaying her desire to invoke the inner thoughts of women.[35]

Poetry of the Harlem Renaissance represents diversity in perspectives and aesthetics. The complex connection of social, political and economic forces that created this movement left a legacy of poetry that continues to influence contemporary African-American writers. The relationship between the Harlem Renaissance and modernism is complex, illustrating the attempt by African-American writers and intellectuals to reflect an African American cultural perspective through the use of the African-American vernacular (black English), jazz/blues, the oral storytelling tradition and/or Afrocentric themes. Consequently, the Harlem Renaissance symbolises the collective voice of African-Americans authors in the era of modernity.

## NOTES

1. Houston A. Baker, Jr, *Modernism and the Harlem Renaissance* (University of Chicago Press, 1987), p. xiii.
2. James de Jongh, *Vicious Modernism: Black Harlem and the Literary Imagination* (Cambridge University Press, 1990), pp. 1–2.
3. De Jongh, *Vicious Modernism*, p. 6.
4. Cary D. Wintz, *Black Culture and the Harlem Renaissance* (Houston: Rice University Press, 1988), p. 17.
5. De Jongh, *Vicious Modernism*, p. 12.
6. Baker, *Modernism and the Harlem Renaissance*, p. 72.
7. Alain Locke (ed.), *The New Negro: An Interpretation* (New York: Arno Press and the New York Times, 1968), pp. 4–5.
8. See Sharon L. Jones, *Rereading the Harlem Renaissance: Race, Class, and Gender in the Fiction of Jessie Fauset, Zora Neale Hurston, and Dorothy West* (Westport: Greenwood Press, 2002), pp. 5–8.
9. A. B. Christa Schwarz, *Gay Voices of the Harlem Renaissance* (Bloomington: Indiana University Press, 2003), p. 68.
10. David Levering Lewis (ed.), *The Portable Harlem Renaissance Reader* (New York: Penguin, 1995), pp. 261–2.
11. Locke (ed.), *The New Negro*, p. 143.
12. Nathan Irvin Huggins, *Harlem Renaissance* (London: Oxford University Press, 1971), p. 68.
13. Rochelle Smith and Sharon L. Jones (eds), *The Prentice Hall Anthology of African American Literature* (Upper Saddle River: Prentice Hall, 2000), pp. 444–5.
14. Lee M. Jenkins, *The Language of Caribbean Poetry: Boundaries of Expression* (Gainesville: University Press of Florida, 2004), p. 67.
15. Henry Louis Gates, Jr et al. (eds), *The Norton Anthology of African American Literature* (New York: W. W. Norton, 1997), pp. 986–7.
16. Lewis (ed.), *The Portable Harlem Renaissance Reader*, p. 296.
17. See De Jongh, *Vicious Modernism*, p. 16.
18. Lewis (ed.), *The Portable Harlem Renaissance Reader*, pp. 294–6.
19. Locke (ed.), *The New Negro*, pp. 138–41.
20. Lewis (ed.), *The Portable Harlem Renaissance Reader*, pp. 282–3.
21. Jean Toomer, *Cane*, ed. Darwin T. Turner (New York: W. W. Norton, 1988), p. 29.
22. Toomer, *Cane*, p. 5.
23. Locke (ed.), *The New Negro*, p. 130.
24. Smith and Jones (eds), *The Prentice Hall Anthology*, pp. 448–51.
25. Lewis (ed.), *The Portable Harlem Renaissance Reader*, p. 244.
26. Gates et al. (eds), *The Norton Anthology*, pp. 1314–15.
27. Maureen Honey (ed.), *Shadowed Dreams: Women's Poetry of the Harlem Renaissance* (New Brunswick: Rutgers University Press, 1989), p. 1.
28. Gloria T. Hull, *Color, Sex, and Poetry: Three Women Writers of the Harlem Renaissance* (Bloomington: Indiana University Press, 1987), p. 10.

29. Smith and Jones (eds), *The Prentice Hall Anthology*, p. 414.
30. Smith and Jones (eds), *The Prentice Hall Anthology*, p. 415.
31. Gates et al. (eds), *The Norton Anthology*, p. 945.
32. Gates et al. (eds), *The Norton Anthology*, p. 944.
33. Lewis (ed.), *The Portable Harlem Renaissance Reader*, p. 276.
34. Lewis (ed.), *The Portable Harlem Renaissance Reader*, p. 277.
35. Lewis (ed.), *The Portable Harlem Renaissance Reader*, p. 274.

# 12

## JAHAN RAMAZANI

# Caliban's modernity: postcolonial poetry of Africa, South Asia and the Caribbean

Readers of a book on modernist poetry may be surprised to find in it an essay on the English-language poetry of the so-called developing world. W. B. Yeats, T. S. Eliot, Gertrude Stein, Mina Loy, Jean Toomer – yes, no doubt. But the Jamaican Louise Bennett, the Nigerian Wole Soyinka, the Kashmiri Agha Shahid Ali? Surely to call these poets 'modernists' would be to commit what philosophers call 'a category mistake', to misattribute properties, to confuse classifications? Or perhaps, as Monsieur Jourdain in Molière's *Le Bourgeois Gentilhomme* didn't realise he had been speaking *prose* all his life, have these 'Third World' poets been modernists all along without being noticed?

Geography helps explain this appearance of a category mistake. Anglophone modernism – conceived as a literary response to the anonymity, stress and speed of modern life – is usually attributed to 'First World' cities from London and Dublin to New York and Chicago. Way off the canonical map of English-speaking modernism are the colonial outposts of European empires, except as sites from which adventurous poets and artists are seen as importing primitive or exotic materials to shore against their ruins.

A second reason for the seeming oddity of critically conjoining modernism and postcolonialism is historical. Most period-based conceptions of literary modernism locate it in the first half of the twentieth century, and postcolonial poetry, so called because of its emergence during and in the aftermath of European colonialism, flourished for the most part in the second half, post the post-Second World War decolonisation of these regions. Like novelists Chinua Achebe and V. S. Naipaul, poets such as Derek Walcott, Wole Soyinka and A. K. Ramanujan cut their literary teeth in the 1950s and 1960s, after the death rattle of high modernism. Their contemporaries were not T. S. Eliot and Ezra Pound but a generation usually seen as rejecting modernism, including in the USA poets sometimes labelled 'postmodern' – confessionals such as Sylvia Plath, New York poets such as Frank O'Hara, Beats such as Allen Ginsberg, and Black Arts poets such as Amiri Baraka.

A third and final reason for this apparent incongruity is stylistic. Modernism is often understood, by analogy with other 'isms' such as communism and feminism, as espousing form-shattering newness and radical experimentation in the arts: witness Gertrude Stein's *Tender Buttons*, Mina Loy's *Anglo-Mongrels and the Rose* and Pound's *Cantos*. Under this definition, early twentieth-century writers who composed formally patterned verse, such as W. B. Yeats, Robert Frost, Wilfred Owen, Langston Hughes and Hugh MacDiarmid, might qualify as 'modern', but not 'modernist'. Yet this view of modernist style would likewise leave aside the work of most postcolonial poets, whether metrical or unmetred, monoglossic or heteroglossic, realist or Surrealist.

These and other objections to calling postcolonial poetry 'modernist' are sufficiently forceful that a critic might be tempted to pack up his paragraphs and conclude. Instead, as you will have guessed from the fact that the paragraphs continue, I propose another option: neither to elide the differences between modernism and postcolonialism, nor to quarantine them in disciplinary isolation from one another, but, by identifying a transhemispheric and transhistorical common ground, to explore significant points of intersection between them. After all, many renowned postcolonial poets, including the Caribbeans Derek Walcott and Lorna Goodison, the South Asians A. K. Ramanujan and Agha Shahid Ali, and the Africans Wole Soyinka and Christopher Okigbo, have testified to the role Euro-modernism played in the formation of their aesthetics. Kamau Brathwaite's claim that T. S. Eliot helped Caribbean poets forge a vernacular poetics based in the region's speech rhythms is but the most famous example.[1] Despite the widespread critical assumption that postcolonial writers have rejected literary modernism, they have indigenised such modernist structures as translocal geographies that layer the local and the foreign, heteroglot vocabularies that creolise standard and dialectal registers, syncretic fusions that counterpoint diverse religious and mythical systems, and apocalyptic imaginings that conjure violent cultural transformation.[2] Yet perhaps more important for a reader of this volume than the question of influence – after all, many postwar poets of the 'developed world' were also influenced by the modernist generation but are not covered in this volume – is whether a primary historical paradigm for modernism can also be used to shed light on the distinct but related historicity of postcolonial poetry.

Let us return, then, to the three principal objections to claiming postcolonial poetry as modernist, reconsidering them in reverse order: can we acknowledge their force, avoiding a collapse of the postcolonial and the modernist into a 'postcomodernist' soup, while still bringing these poetries into overlapping, if not identical, critical frameworks? Regarding a definition of modernism based on formal experimentation, one danger of narrow-ing the criterion of genuinely 'modern' or 'modernist' to 'open-form' or 'avant-garde' poetries is obscuring the various shapes that innovation can take. A more porous yet still period-based conception allows for the impor-tance of modern Irish and Scottish poets' breakthroughs in reimagining both national and transnational identities (e.g. Yeats and MacDiarmid), Harlem Renaissance poets' ingenuity in infusing literary verse with the blues and jazz, among various oral and musical forms (e.g. Langston Hughes and Sterling Brown), and other examples of the hybridisation of distinct aesthetics and discourses, of the poetic re-creation of cultural and cross-cultural paradigms. This broader conceptualisation makes recognisable the analogous 'experi-mentation' of postcolonial poets.

As for historical or period boundaries, while we need to grant the centre of modernist and postcolonial gravity in different halves of the last century, this line should not be drawn too neatly, lest it obscure shared terrain. Just as modernist mastodons – Pound, Marianne Moore, Wallace Stevens, Langston Hughes, W. H. Auden – still trod the earth in the second half of the century, so too a few influential poets of the colonised world, such as the Bengali Rabindranath Tagore and (especially important for the present discussion of Anglophone poetry) the Jamaicans Claude McKay and Louise Bennett were publishing significant work in the first half of the twentieth century. McKay's publications are contemporary with those of the first-generation modernists, such as Eliot and Marianne Moore, and so the poetry of this writer working in the shadow of British colonialism can be considered, like that of Yeats and other Irish poets, both 'modern' and 'postcolonial'.

Last, but far from least, as for the assumption that literary modernism represents a response to the pressures of technological and social modern-ity, particularly in western cities, rich evidence of a complex encounter with modernisation – accelerating after the Second World War in the 'developing world' – can also be found in postcolonial poetry. Since this is the most widely recognised historical feature of modernism – after all, giving the aesthetic its name – the rest of this essay is devoted to the question of its possible relevance as well to postcolonial poetry. This approach may seem peculiar, since critics including Kwame Anthony Appiah, Linda Hutcheon and Fredric Jameson have more often explored the affinities between post-coloniality and postmodernity.[3] But to characterise the historical experi-ence of the postcolonial world as postmodern may be premature, when in these countries traditional agricultural forms of work still coexist alongside industrialisation; millions of subsistence farmers and day labourers along-side a tiny elite of knowledge workers; donkeys, camels and horse-driven carts alongside cars and aeroplanes. The shock of new technologies and new transportation systems, newly intrusive bureaucracies and newly murderous instruments of warfare has been fresh and vivid for writers of the postwar 'developing' world, as it was for writers in the early twentieth-century West, before this modernity could, in postmodern fashion, be taken for granted, as an always-already banality. For these reasons, and because the ongoing reaction against modernisation has emerged as one of the most volatile and dangerous features of the contemporary world, it behooves us to ask, as we do of modernist poetry, how does postcolonial poetry give aesthetic expression to the experience of trying to square tradition with the transforming effects of modernity? And how does this response to modernity compare with that of modernist poetry?

To borrow a critical template associated with western modernism is to raise the spectre of academically recolonising the ex-colonials, imperially subjugating an emergent alterity under Eurocentric dominion. Surely the differences between modernism and postcolonialism need to be granted and even emphasised. Yet, in my view, the still greater risk to postcolonial poetry as an academic subfield remains critical isolation and neglect. The institutionalisation of the study of postcolonial poetry remains uncertain: this poetry is regularly passed over in postcolonial studies for far more work on fiction and theory, and in modern and contemporary poetry studies for vastly more work on American, British and Irish poetries. Moreover, through its syncretic layering of mythologies, religions and cultural frames of reference, postcolonial poetry acknowledges that 'the foreign' can be approached only through inevitably distortive yet potentially illuminating parallels with the familiar. A transhemispheric (North/South) and cross-period (modern/contemporary) approach can help not only bring postcolonial poetry into more classrooms, anthologies and critical books, but also perhaps internationalise modern and contemporary literary studies, lessening its fragmentation along regional and national lines.

I have been referring to the early twentieth-century literary response to modernisation – urbanisation, industrialisation, technological and scientific advance, and so forth – as if it were unified. It wasn't. F. T. Marinetti's fire-breathing first Futurist manifesto (1909) famously glorifies the racing and roaring automobile and other aspects of the modern technological revolution. The Vorticist manifesto of Wyndham Lewis's London-based journal *Blast* (1914), while defensively mocking Futurist 'AUTOMOBILISM', is likewise intoxicated with machinery and mobility.[4] Yet, despite these initial cheers for early twentieth-century modernisation, most of the leading Anglo-modernists were less enthusiastic than the Futurists about smashing tradition and embracing new technologies. Indeed, western poetry in English of the first half of the twentieth century is rife with anxious and conflicted responses to modernisation, producing the notoriously paradoxical anti-modernity of the Anglo-modernists. Disgusted by the spectacle of modernity, Yeats decries 'that discordant architecture, all those electric signs', on O'Connell Bridge in Dublin.[5] Pound blasts the 'tawdry cheapness' of mass-produced goods; even beauty, he complains, has been reduced to a commodity in 'the market place'.[6] In the middle of Eliot's *The Waste Land*, a tryst is made to seem all the more mechanical and degraded because the typist pre-coitally 'lays out food in tins', or cans, and post-coitally 'smoothes her hair with automatic hand, / And puts a record on the gramophone'.[7] This vehement resistance to modernisation as mechanistic, cheapening and alienating softens among second-generation modern poets. Near the end of his life Auden looks back nostalgically to the industrial machinery of his youth, including parts of old steam engines and other 'beautiful old contraptions, soon to be banished from earth'.[8] Yet even Auden is hardly sanguine about the effects of mass-scale bureaucratisation on modern life ('The Unknown Citizen') and of anonymous, mass warfare on modern death ('Chinese Soldier'). Tortuously ambivalent, Hart Crane hails the Wright Brothers' first flight as the technological counterpart of imaginative flight into 'unvanquished space', even as his descriptions also hint at the constraints on merely physical ascent ('axle-bound, confined / In coiled precision').[9]

Also in the 1910s and 1920s, Harlem Renaissance poets rejoiced in, yet recoiled from, modernisation, as exemplified by Jean Toomer. On the positive side, in 'Her Lips Are Copper Wire', Toomer uses the electrification of cities – lamplights and billboards and a powerhouse – to metaphorise the connective energy of sexual love: a kiss removes the insulation from 'wires' and turns lovers' lips and poetic language 'incandescent'.[10] A similar exuberance, mixed with wry humour, marks the ironic conjunction in 'Gum' of large electric signs advertising Jesus Christ and chewing gum. Modernity thus avails a poet like Toomer of figurative leaps and ironic juxtapositions. Yet the lyric 'Reapers' evokes the horror of the machine's displacement of traditional agriculture. That poem begins with the sibilant-smoothed 'sound of steel on stones' and 'silent swinging' of black reapers' scythes, but ends – its syntax and rhythms and sonorities cut up – after a squealing field rat has been sliced by the indifferent force of a horse-driven mechanical mower, proceeding relentlessly on its brutally uncaring course: 'I see the blade, / Blood-stained, continue cutting weeds and shade'.[11] Not that the ambivalence toward modernity in Toomer's poetry and that of other Harlem Renaissance poets is identical with that of the white modernists. As Toomer indicates in 'Song of the Son', the early twentieth-century African-American poet mourns the passing of a rural black culture in harmony with nature and with the song forms born of slavery, such as the spiritual form he incorporates in his poem; yet the demise of a slave- and sharecropper-based economy and culture is not entirely to be regretted. Even as the speaker plaintively grieves that 'the sun is setting on / A song-lit race of slaves', he metaphorically recalls the violence and atrocity that have beset African Americans in lines that recall the spectacle of lynching: 'O Negro slaves, dark purple ripened plums, / Squeezed, and bursting in the pine-wood air'.[12]

Are technology and other forms of modernisation avenues to new promise, mobility and freedom, or are they new tools for containing and oppressing African Americans? Langston Hughes's early blues poems, especially in *Fine Clothes to the Jew* (1927), honour by their brevity and AAB stanzaic form the early blues recordings of the 1920s. Yet, if technology can be used to embody and transmit African-American voices, it can also be used to stifle them. In Sterling Brown's riotous 'Slim in Atlanta', the geography-traversing promise of the telephone morphs into its opposite – a tool of spatial confinement and incarceration. According to Georgia law, claims the speaker, blacks are forbidden to laugh outdoors and must 'do deir laughin / In a telefoam booth'.[13] When the trickster Slim Greer learns of this absurd Jim Crow law, he bursts into a phone booth, making hundreds of other African Americans wait as he laughs over and over at the spectacle of their effort to contain their laughter, his interminable anti-racist laughter – and the poem's – overbrimming such limits.

Against this backdrop of early twentieth-century western poetry, black and white, greeting, while grimacing at, the complex forces of modernity, how do we understand the similar yet distinctive response of postcolonial poets? Claude McKay, as a Jamaican-born immigrant to the USA and Europe, bridges the gulf between western and postcolonial poetic responses to modernisation, offering a first glimpse into the conflicted poems on modernity by 'Third World' writers born under British colonial rule. When the speaker of his Standard English poems looks upon the modern urban world, he is filled with a vitalising hatred. Racially marginalised in what he calls 'The White City', he watches 'The strident trains that speed the goaded mass, / The poles and spires and towers vapor-kissed'.[14] The speed of modern mass transport and the vertical sublimity that cheap steel has made possible are alluring, 'sweet like wanton loves', yet, shutting out the black immigrant, poison him with 'hate'. Alienated from 'the great western world', the speaker of 'The Tropics in New York' and 'Outcast' pines for the tropical fruits and pastoral landscape of his youth, the 'forgotten jungle songs' of his ancestors.[15] These poems aesthetically embody the ambivalences to which they give utterance by twinning traditional poetic form – sonnet, pastoral plaint, blazon – with the embittering torsions and distortions of a racially divisive and uneven modernity.

If the pace and effects of modernisation often struck white and black western poets as dehumanising and estranging, many post-Second World War poets of the subtropical south – with McKay straddling periods and geographies – describe even more jarring and rapid upheavals along these lines, even more startling juxtapositions of traditional custom and onrushing industrial and technological development. While the many faces of modernity – technological change, bureaucratic impersonality, capitalist entrepreneurship, disenchanting rationality, and so forth – often looked menacing to early twentieth-century writers, they have had a special significance for poets whose societies of origin are still recovering from the violence and exploitation of colonial rule. And, while the benefits of a Janus-faced modernity that enriches and impoverishes, empowers and enchains have long been evident in the West,[16] they have less often materialised, amid urban squalour, poverty and massive inequality, in much of the developing world.

The forcible and sudden colonisation of Africa brought native peoples into often alarmingly disjunctive contact with western development, beginning with the late nineteenth- and early twentieth-century scramble for Africa and continuing through the second half of the twentieth century. Kofi Awoonor of Ghana laments the upending of traditional economies and societies. The speaker of one of his poems feels dispossessed, like an unhoused wanderer amid the thorns or 'sharps of the forest' – an estrangement reproduced in the deliberate awkwardness of such literal translations of Ewe idiom ('sharps' for 'thorns'), discordantly joined to traditional songs.[17] Fracturing temporality, modernity and colonialism rupture the ties between generations. In the same poem, a parent attached to the traditions of his ancestors feels abandoned by his descendants, having no sons to mourn or daughters 'to wail when I close my mouth'. Postcolonial poets often experience the ongoing processes of modernisation as iterations of colonialism's fraying of the seams of traditional life. Lenrie Peters of Gambia allegorises this sense of sudden, jolting historical change: 'The violent arrival / Puts out the joint', he says of 'Parachute men', 'Jumping across worlds / In condensed time'.[18] The lacerating disorientations of modernity and colonialism, Peters's metaphor of parachuting suggests, dislocate peoples from one world into another, compress and conjoin discontinuous epochs.

Although the many-centuries-long history of European subjugation and settlement was less abrupt in South Asia and the Caribbean than in Africa, the poetry of these regions also figures modernity as entwined with the violence of colonialism, especially in tearing the fabric of traditional custom and community. Indeed, fabric is a locus of colonial violence in 'The Dacca Gauzes', a poem by Agha Shahid Ali.[19] The soft and seamless muslins once woven in Dacca, but now completely lost, are remembered through his grandmother as 'woven air, running / water, evening dew', the sequence of images and enjambments verbally evoking the flowing texture of the gauzes. But modernity, with its insatiable appetite for new spaces and new markets, dismembers: because Indian muslins threatened the sale of British fabrics in India, 'the hands / of weavers were amputated', preventing Indian weavers from competing with the British or passing on their skills to their children. Modernity severs thumbs from hands, parents from children, soft fabric from coarse. Recalling gauze so fine in texture it was like 'dew-starched' morning air, the verbal fabric of the poem – stitching together generations cut off from one another – attempts to redress these catastrophic losses; yet in remembering Bengali muslin-weaving as 'a dead art now, dead over / a hundred years', Ali's poem also acknowledges the impossibility of compensating for the atrocities it memorialises.

To reveal the full extent of the violence of western modernity, postcolonial poets must, as Ali's poem suggests, rewrite received dominant narratives of history, in which it is the non-West that is often figured as violent, cruel, barbaric. In 'The Fortunate Traveller', Derek Walcott disputes the 'imperial fiction' of Joseph Conrad's *Heart of Darkness*, declaring, 'The heart of darkness is not Africa', as Kurtz imagines it. Instead, 'The heart of darkness is the core of fire / in the white center of the holocaust'.[20] Strenuously reversing the ethical associations of dark and white, Walcott sees 'darkness' in Europe's systematically planned, bureaucratically managed and technologically enacted mass killing: 'The heart of darkness is the rubber claw / selecting a scalpel in antiseptic light' and 'the hills of children's shoes' that are left behind after Jews and others have been clinically slaughtered.

Dislocation and dispossession, systematic violence and colonisation, intergenerational and memorial rupture – modernity, it would seem, could scarcely be imagined more grimly. In some of the most chilling postcolonial representations of modernity, those violated by modernity in turn become strident violators. Satirising monomaniacal African modernisers, the Ugandan poet Okot p'Bitek bestows on his character Ocol a voice that eerily echoes the demolition plans of the Futurist and Vorticist manifestoes: 'To hell / With the husks / Of old traditions / And meaningless customs, // We will smash / The taboos / One by one, / Explode the basis / Of every superstition, / We will uproot / Every sacred tree / And demolish every ancestral shrine.'[21] Across the 'developing world', many supposedly forward-looking dictators, internalising colonial views as does Ocol, have called for the obliteration of tribal affiliations and backward-facing traditions, often with disastrous results. The Euro-modernist thrill in blasting the past becomes, in the African context, sadistic destruction and masochistic self-negation: 'Smash all the mirrors' of the 'blackness of the past', shouts the European wannabe Ocol.[22]

Whereas Euro-modernists such as Marinetti, Wyndham Lewis and Gertrude Stein, secure as inheritors of an officially sanctioned high culture, could glee-fully disavow traditions and libraries and museums, western colonialism threatened the indigenous cultural inheritances of Third World writers, as Frantz Fanon observes, with defacement, defilement and destruction.[23] Post-colonial poets such as Okot p'Bitek – deeply aware of their cultural riches and resources, both premodern and modern – satirise and lament the effects of such blindly modernising aggression, whether internally or externally afflicted. Like Harlem Renaissance poets such as Hughes and Brown, and like Irish and Scottish Renaissance poets such as Yeats and MacDiarmid, they champion subjugated cultural inheritances and identities that have been at risk of destruction. At the same time, unlike fundamentalist revivalists or reactionary terrorists, these postcolonial poets cast a wary eye on the fetishis-ing of an idealised precolonial past. Even the reputedly nativist Okot p'Bitek casts *Song of Lawino* and *Song of Ocol* in the form of an East–West dialogue, and these poems fuse such indigenous genres as the praise song, the insult and the funeral lament with the long western dramatic monologue. While resisting the obliteration of their cultural inheritances, such writers never-theless concede the inevitability of modernisation, working in hybrid forms, idioms and genres, acknowledging in their double-visioned sensibilities and language modernity's irreversible permeation of their world.

Both rooted and modernising, recuperative and hybrid, located and mobile, postcolonial poetry does not, in short, represent modernity unequivocally as a negative force. Take modern technologies of transporta-tion. Flight, travel, transport – these are the subject of an initial sequence of poems in Wole Soyinka's first book of poetry, *'Idanre' and Other Poems* (1967), where they evoke both the exciting speed and the unnerving colli-sions of development. The jet passengers in 'Around Us, Dawning' feel, like the flyers in Crane's *The Bridge*, helpless and alienated, 'bound to a will of rotors // Yielding' their will to an 'alien' mechanism. Yet, at the same time, they are availed of power, possibility, ecstatic movement – the sunlit speeding plane, hurtling into the dawn, is an 'incandescent / Onrush', the poem's surge of syntactically propelled and lightly punctuated exhilaration replicating the forward momentum of modern technology. In 'Death in the Dawn', another poem in the series, a driver en route to Lagos, Nigeria, encounters a car in which a man has been killed: 'Brother, / Silenced in the startled hug of / Your invention'.[24] In his apostrophe to the dead man crushed by his automobile ('Your invention'), the poet metaphorises the automobile as 'this mocked grimace / This closed contortion'. For Soyinka, technology both entraps and advances, both kills and empowers; in this regard, it almost seems a latter-day manifestation of the doubleness of Ogun, the Yoruba god of creation and destruction, as well as metallurgy, artisanship and the road. Here, the car speeds the speaker toward his destination, yet it becomes a death-dealing adjunct to the Yoruba mythologisation of the road as 'famished'. The poem ends with the question of whether this image of a man crushed within something of his own making is 'I', which would make the culturally and formally hybrid contraption of the poem itself a mechanism at once destructive and propulsive.

Indeed, for poets, the most immediate technologies are those of writing and performance, and in this respect, too, modernisation is imagined as a curse but also a potential blessing. On the verge of developing a highly visual style of poetry reliant on computer-generated fonts and spacing, Kamau Brathwaite acknowledges the western technology of the computer as a kind of 'muse', even as he worries about the word processor's origins in the scientific, capitalist, imperial culture resisted in his work. Addressing a poem to his mother, he confesses that he writes 'pun a computer o/kay? / like I jine de mercantilists! // well not quite!'[25] His pun on 'upon' verbally intimates the transformative reworking he hopes to enact with western technology, wringing from it unexpected possibilities, as a poet does with words. Invoking the Caliban/Prospero paradigm, Brathwaite affiliates himself with Caliban, since the Barbadian is also 'learnin prospero linguage', yet distinguishes Caliban's curses, seen as ultimately serving Prospero, from his own. Naming Chauncery Lane – as his note says 'not the London walkway, but downtown Kingston (Jamaica) reggae-making and recording centre' – Brathwaite places his transvaluation of technology within the context of a larger postcolonial transvaluation of the tools of modernity, akin to the postcolonial remaking of colonially named sites.[26] The resulting paradoxes for postcolonial poetry run deep. The 'dub' or performance style of poetry originated by Linton Kwesi Johnson, a black British poet of Jamaican origin who acknowledges Brathwaite as a precursor, is intimately bound up with technologies of electronic recording, staging and distribution. As with Brathwaite's visuality, the mechanisms of modernisation ironically enable the recovery and reinvigoration of a poetic orality that seemed endangered by the spread of print culture. For these writers, as for the Anglo-modernists, modernity and tradition become strange bedfellows in fashioning a new aesthetic.

Modernity is thus sometimes seen as rupture and dismemberment, eliciting postcolonial lamentation and anger; sometimes it is seen more equivocally as a set of tools at once repressive and enabling. At other times, the horror, violence and tragedy of modernisation are recast as postcolonial irony. The pre-eminent writer of Creole verse in the last century, Louise Bennett, even turns the distress and disorientation of modernity into a subject of considerable comedy. In a humorous variation on the motif of the country boy come to the city, 'Country Bwoy' is a dramatic monologue cast in the voice of a victim of a store elevator in Kingston. Mistaking one technology for another, a lift for an aeroplane, he pompously announces on arrival at the top floor, 'Dis is Cuba, I presume' – a wry turn, as editor Mervyn Morris notes, on 'Dr Livingstone, I presume', the remark attributed to Henry Morton Stanley, the late nineteenth-century white explorer of Africa.[27] While mocking the ignorant country boy's bafflement, this allusion also redounds on explorers in Africa, who are made to seem no less ridiculously displaced and disoriented. In other poems, Bennett's speakers are terrified by trams that speed too quickly ('Rough-Ridin Tram') or baffled by ballots that need to be marked ('Sarah Chice').

Although locals confused by the technology and the rationalising processes of modernity are often the butt of her humour, Bennett's irony cuts both ways: she is no less scathing in her ridicule of the supposedly advanced purveyors of modernity. The bureaucrat who maps and rationally administers modern society – for Max Weber, its mainstay – runs into considerable resistance in Bennett's verse. The speaker of one poem wards off the intrusive questioning of a census-taker, who pries into 'fimiliar tings', the intimate details of her family, property, marital status, even age: 'Me stare right eena census face / An tell him bans a lie!'[28] The modernity-thwarting speaker in 'Census' is, as often in Bennett's poetry, a female trickster whose resistant guile affords refuge. In the contest between a sly Anancy figure and a flat-footed, bureaucratic modernity, Bennett gives the advantage to Anancy's linguistic subterfuge and cunning, even as her doing so hybridises the mythical paradigm with a modern predicament. Bringing a robust Jamaican English into poetry and disseminating her verse in part through such media as newspapers, radio and TV, she refuses to be bound either by an infatuation with, or a traditionalist rejection of, modernity.

In another Anancy-spirited poem, Bennett juxtaposes Jamaican folk tradition and western 'development' to deconstruct the teleology of western narratives of modernisation. 'Jamaica Oman' takes to task the notion that 'Third World' women need to be liberated by the West: 'long before Oman Lib bruck out / Over foreign lan', she declares, 'Jamaica female wasa work / Her liberated plan!'[29] Questioning the developmental paradigm that casts the West as export model for other regions, Bennett shows Jamaican women to have modernised themselves long before the modernisation of western gender relations. Exemplifying an indigenous feminism, Jamaican women are presented as warriors (heroic Nanny, who is said to have made bullets ricochet off her buttocks to kill her enemies) and intellectual achievers (the spelling bee champion, who in the Caribbean gained access to further academic opportunities). Their strength and physical skill, their cleverness and intellectual resourcefulness, defy outside presuppositions that they are in need of liberation by the First World. While they may trick men into thinking they are demure, Jamaican women energetically guide and support, fearlessly push and prod men, even 'lick sense eena man head', says the speaker. This dramatic pile-up of verbs to suggest Oman's agency and her frenetic, varied activity recurs in a subsequent quatrain, where five transitive verbs appear in three lines – 'Ban', 'bite, 'Ketch', 'put', 'dig'. Playing on the biblical story of Eve's emergence from Adam's rib, Bennett vividly transforms a bone indicative of female subordination into an emblem of genuine strength: 'While man a call her "so-so rib" / Oman a tun backbone!' According to Bennett, Jamaican women need not look for salvation to 'Oman Lib', since they already control the finances, the social and familial life, and other aspects of the Jamaican 'yard'. The poem's verbal wit and rhetorical vigour are its most potent, immediate evidence of these claims.

As this and other poems indicate, 'Third World' poets cast doubt on the Western triumphalist narrative of global 'development', in which an exported programme of modernisation is imagined as helping 'developing' nations 'advance' and become more like 'developed' nations in economics, politics, social relations, technology and culture. Bennett's ebullient humour sets her apart from other poets, but her ironic and irreverent laughter in the face of the invasiveness, disruptions and velocity of modernity is the other side of the coin of the fear, grief and anger we have seen in the work of Soyinka, Ali, Walcott, Brathwaite, Okot p'Bitek and other postcolonial poets, as also in modern western poetry. The postcolonial response to modernisation is richly ambivalent, since laughter or anxiety combines with a readiness to indigenise modernity. Poets often represent their local cultural resources – myths and genres, an indigenous orality and the trickster's guile – as outlasting an externally imposed modernity by hybridising with, and thus transforming, it.

The postcolonial ambivalence toward modernity resembles but is not the same as that of the Euro-modernists. Because 'Third World' writers more often associate modernisation with the traumatic ruptures of colonisation, and because the geotemporal disjunctions between their experience of modernity and tradition are more acute, they sometimes represent modernisation as even more violent and disruptive than did the Euro-modernists. At the same time, like poets of the Irish Renaissance, the Harlem Renaissance, and the Scottish Renaissance, postcolonial poets link their desire to transvalue the forces of modernisation with the writerly effort to remake the master's verbal and formal tools. Because postcolonial poets encounter western modernity from across even greater social and geographical differences than do poets of the British Isles and African American poets, they tend to represent it as an even stranger and more estranging force, and they refuse to surrender 'native' forms, vocabularies and myths to a homogenising western modernity. Even so, they recognise that modernity cannot be naively screened out, without consigning their poetry to the nostalgic amber of nativism – itself, in part, a defensive reaction to colonialism and modernity.[30] So they respond to and harness the forces of modernity in fashioning a postcolonial poetics that includes discordantly literal translation (Awoonor), anti-compensatory elegising (Ali), mythical syncretism (Soyinka), cross-cultural genres (Okot), technically facilitated visuality and orality (Brathwaite) and comically updated archetypes (Bennett). Even as they refuse to let modernity erase their cultural traditions, even as they associate modernity with colonialism's violence, these poets modernise the indigenous and indigenise the modern, thereby giving expression to the disjunction and shock, humour and potentiality of postcolonial experience.

If one concept of modernist poetry is poetry that responds to modernity, then surely postcolonial poets of Africa, South Asia and the Caribbean belong in a collection of essays on modernist poetry in English, even though most of the major postcolonial poets emerged much later than the high modernists, did not write in what are usually seen in the West as 'experimental' styles, and explore in their verse sharply different geographic and cultural inflections of modernity. A comparative approach that straddles but does not erase the lines between North and South, coloniser and colonised, modern and contemporary, can help reveal these and other differences and resemblances between the poetry of the modernists and the postcolonials. Still, modernity makes it difficult to hold these lines securely in place, because its globalising acceleration of human mobility across national and regional boundaries has partly eroded them. The expatriation, exile and migrancy often associated with western modernists such as Eliot, Pound, Stein, Loy, H.D. and Auden – poets in search of aesthetic stimulation and publishing prospects abroad – is no less characteristic of postcolonial poets, such as McKay, Walcott, Brathwaite, Goodison, Ali, Ramanujan and Soyinka, who have traversed an even greater geo-economic divide for academic, economic and publishing opportunities in North America and the British Isles. Postcolonial poets have thus written out of the disjunctions and layerings of transgeographic experience, produced by migration, modernity and colonialism, even when they have been fiercely attached to the local soil. As such, they have created a poetry that is often a cacophony of discrepant idioms and genres, landscapes and images, gathered from local sites and from far-flung corners of the world. In its transnational reach, in its intercultural bearings, such poetry recalls the work of the Anglo-modernists, emergent during an earlier stage of globalisation. But, as in the poetry of the Irish Renaissance, the

Scottish Renaissance and the Harlem Renaissance, this transnational hetero-geneity has helped postcolonial poets fashion not discordant requiems for a doomed or dying elite culture, but nativity odes – however conflicted – to cultural identities still emerging and changing in the wake of colonialism and modernity.

## NOTES

The author wishes to thank the organisers of the Shannon-Clark Lecture in English at Washington and Lee University for the opportunity to deliver a version of this essay.

1. Kamau Brathwaite, *History of the Voice: The Development of Nation Language in Anglophone Caribbean Poetry* (London: New Beacon, 1984), reprinted and slightly altered in *Roots* (Ann Arbor: University of Michigan Press, 1993), pp. 286–7.
2. Jahan Ramazani, 'Modernist Bricolage, Postcolonial Hybridity', in Richard Begam and Michael Valdez Moses (eds), *Modernism and Colonialism: British and Irish Literature, 1889–1939* (Durham: Duke University Press, 2007).
3. Kwame Anthony Appiah, *In My Father's House: Africa in the Philosophy of Culture* (New York: Oxford University Press, 1992), pp. 137–57; Linda Hutcheon, 'Circling the Downspout of Empire', in Ian Adam and Helen Tiffin (eds), *Past the Last Post: Theorizing Post-Colonialism and Post-Modernism* (University of Calgary Press, 1990), pp. 167–89; Fredric Jameson, *Postmodernism, or, The Cultural Logic of Late Capitalism* (Durham: Duke University Press, 1991). On modernity and postcolonialism, see Simon Gikandi, *Writing in Limbo: Modernism and Caribbean Literature* (Ithaca: Cornell University Press, 1992).
4. Wyndham Lewis (ed.), 'Long Live the Vortex', *Blast 1* (1914), n.p.
5. W. B. Yeats, *Essays and Introductions* (London: Macmillan, 1961), p. 526.
6. Ezra Pound, *Hugh Selwyn Mauberley*, in *Personae: The Shorter Poems*, ed. Lea Baechler and A. Walton Litz (New York: New Directions, 1990), pp. 186, 187.
7. T. S. Eliot, *The Complete Poems and Plays* (London: Faber and Faber, 1969), p. 69.
8. W. H. Auden, *Selected Poems*, ed. Edward Mendelson (New York: Vintage-Random House, 1979), p. 300.
9. Hart Crane, *Complete Poems*, ed. Brom Weber (Newcastle: Bloodaxe, 1984), p. 87.
10. Jean Toomer, *Cane*, ed. Darwin T. Turner (New York: W. W. Norton, 1988), p. 57.
11. Toomer, *Cane*, p. 5.
12. Toomer, *Cane*, p. 14.
13. Sterling Brown, *The Collected Poems of Sterling A. Brown*, ed. Michael S. Harper (Evanston: Triquarterly Books, 1996), pp. 81–2.
14. Claude McKay, *Complete Poems*, ed. William J. D. Maxwell (Urbana: University of Illinois Press, 2004), p. 162.
15. McKay, *Complete Poems*, pp. 154, 163.
16. See Marshall Berman, *All That Is Solid Melts Into Air: The Experience of Modernity* (1982; New York: Penguin, 1988), p. 15.

17. Kofi Awoonor, 'Songs of Sorrow', reprinted in Gerald Moore and Ulli Beier (eds), *The Penguin Book of Modern African Poetry*, 4th edn (Harmondsworth: Penguin, 1998), pp. 103–4.
18. Lenrie Peters, *Selected Poetry* (London: Heinemann, 1981), pp. 25–6.
19. Agha Shahid Ali, *The Half-Inch Himalayas* (Middletown: Wesleyan University Press, 1987), pp. 15–16.
20. Derek Walcott, *Collected Poems, 1948–1984* (New York: Noonday/Farrar, Straus and Giroux, 1986), p. 461.
21. Okot p'Bitek, *'Song of Lawino' and 'Song of Ocol'* (London: Heinemann, 1984), p. 126.
22. Okot p'Bitek, *'Song of Ocol'*, p. 129.
23. Frantz Fanon, *The Wretched of the Earth*, trans. Constance Farrington (New York: Grove, 1963), p. 43.
24. Wole Soyinka, *'Idanre' and Other Poems* (New York: Hill & Wang, 1967), pp. 12, 10–11.
25. Kamau Brathwaite, 'X/Self's Xth Letters from the Thirteen Provinces', *X/Self* (Oxford University Press, 1987), p. 80. See Keith Tuma's reading of this poem in *Fishing by Obstinate Isles: Modern and Postmodern British Poetry and American Readers* (Evanston: Northwestern University Press, 1998), pp. 244–9.
26. Brathwaite, *X/Self*, pp. 84, 127.
27. Louise Bennett, *Selected Poems*, ed. Mervyn Morris (Kingston: Sangster's Book Stores, 1983), pp. 11–13, 125.
28. Bennett, *Selected Poems*, pp. 23–4.
29. Bennett, *Selected Poems*, pp. 21–3.
30. See Appiah, *In My Father's House*, pp. 47–72.

# PART III

# Receptions

# 13

JASON HARDING

# Modernist poetry and the canon

The process by which canonical reputations are made is more finely grained, subtly contextualised, and gradual, than many literary critics, with ideological axes to grind, acknowledge. The mechanisms of cultural influence that brought about the revolution of poetic taste associated with modernism were extremely complex and variegated: manifestoes, prefaces, introductions; vigorous and partisan debates in newspapers and literary magazines; selections in anthologies; pamphlets, essays and full-length studies; not forgetting the impact of modernist movements beyond the English-speaking world. The intellectual historian must seek to gauge the socioeconomic conditions in which modernist poetry was mediated and received, even the effects of intangibles (such as private conversation) that have now seeped into the shifting sands of canon formation. Taken together, attempts to reconstruct this intricate constellation of factors can leave accounts of the modernist canon a little under-explained. However, the main thread to follow does emerge clearly with the benefit of historical hindsight: it involves tracing the emergence of the new poetic in the avant-garde 'little magazines' established just before or during the First World War; the subsequent discussion of this poetry in the critical reviews of the interwar period; culminating in the institutional consolidation of a revolutionary poetic moment in university textbooks and syllabuses after the Second World War.

Modernism evolved in symbiosis with a rapidly changing literary marketplace, in fear of, and hostile to, the mass reading publics of Europe and North America. As Lawrence Rainey has shown, the commercial imperatives faced by modernist poets entailed new strategies of publicity and marketing, involving micro-economies of their own, heavily dependent upon patronage or patron-investors (for example, the New York lawyer John Quinn) who underwrote so much of the literature we now call 'modernist'. Slim, expensive deluxe editions of avant-garde poetry were not simply objects of aesthetic contemplation but commodities on a luxury market, possessing a 'cultural capital' upon which authors might advance their literary careers. Publishers and booksellers – the Egoist Press, the Hogarth Press, The Poetry Bookshop, Faber and Gwyer (later Faber and Faber) – targeted a tiny niche audience of poetry readers, often no more than a thousand strong, who wielded significant power as arbiters of cultural taste. These publishing institutions, then, began the work of shaping the lineaments of the modernist canon several years before university lecturers and their students were exposed to the startling innovations of the new poets. Modernist poetry was aimed at an unashamedly elitist or 'highbrow' readership of connoisseurs. Popularity was seen as a failure of nerve, rather than as a token of success.

Crucial to the cultural ecology of modernist publishing were the so-called 'little magazines' (including the *Little Review*, *Blast*, *The Egoist*) which not only served as showcases for poetry unsuitable for more commercial magazines, but as polemical forums stage-managing aesthetic controversy. Again, the readerships were exiguous (from a few hundred up to several thousand), but these unfolding debates were often noticed and taken up in more established periodicals, for example, the *Athenaeum* or the *Times Literary Supplement* in London, and in a variety of New York magazines, the *Dial* and the *New Republic*, even *Vanity Fair*. In such a manner, the audience for radical modernist poetry was broadened and fresh work brought into contact with the mainstream of literary discussion. The vitality and boldness of these little magazines and their significance in promoting new and experimental writers are striking features of the decade 1910 to 1920. Nonetheless, as recent scholars have demonstrated, the unacknowledged links, even complicity, between the avant-garde little magazines and the powerful forces of capitalist investment and speculation complicates the stridently oppositional jeremiads of modernist manifestoes. The formulation and marketing of a modernist poetic, the foundations of its later institutional canonisation, required subtle as well as less than subtle negotiations with, and interventions in, the dynamics of the cultural marketplace. It is no exaggeration to say that the 1929 Wall Street Crash had a sudden and profound effect upon the whole material economy of modernism.

The interwar period saw the appearance of a succession of monthly and quarterly magazines of a predominantly literary-critical nature (the *Criterion*, *The Calendar of Modern Letters*, *Scrutiny*, *Southern Review*). They were sober in style and format, demonstrating their continuity with the great Victorian reviews. Literary reviewing in these periodicals, the interpretation and evaluation of new works, had a vital role to play in the formation of the modernist canon. The distinctive profiles of these literary reviews of the interwar period, carrying critical articles of 2,000 to 6,000 words, reflected an important exchange between writers and overlapping, well-educated reading publics. The impact of these critical articles among networks of metropolitan intellectuals or university-based readerships was reinforced by republication in book form. This work did a great deal to establish the reputations of many poets first published in the earlier, more ephemeral little magazines. By the 1930s, then, a modern criticism had grown up to expound and explicate the new poetic. At this time, the custodians of the literary canon were social elites of publishers, editors, men of letters and university professors, over-whelmingly middle-class in background and usually cautious or sceptical in their response to the range and novelty of the new poetry. The struggle for the institutional recognition and acceptance of modernist poetry was a slow and controversial process, reflecting larger-scale transformations in the con-stituency of the audience for serious contemporary literature, together with the reform of university curricula.

Fundamental to this changing sociology, effecting the promotion and reception of modernist poetry, was the exponential expansion of univer-sity departments of English after the Second World War. Modernist poetry was earnestly incorporated into the woof and warp of American and British syllabuses. The intrinsic difficulty of this work could be used to justify the pre-tensions of 'professional' literary studies, armed with its own specialised, eso-teric terminology. Today, 'Modernist Studies' constitutes an enclave within the larger empires of literary and cultural studies: commitment to its fiercely contested canon of authors can seem like a conscious declaration of sociopo-litical, rather than aesthetic, allegiances. Yet, academics possibly overesti-mate their power to reconfigure a canon that was formed outside the uni-versities and extends beyond them, into the realms of literary journalism, of publishing and the media, not to mention the practices and preferences of poets and of readers. The modernist canon represents the consensus of institutional esteem in which some twentieth-century poets came to be held. Although this institutionalisation is authoritatively manifested in the secure position modernist poetry currently occupies in academic syllabuses, it is not identical with the profession of literary studies. As the following overview demonstrates, advocates of modernist poetry in Britain and America – univer-sity teachers or otherwise – faced distinct challenges in gaining acceptance for this work, especially during the crucial period from 1930 to 1950. In Britain, modernist poetry challenged the entrenched social mission to 'nationalise' literary studies. While in the United States, modernist poetry was reinter-preted in the light of liberal, instrumental imperatives designed to uncover a usable literary past.

It is hoped that this preliminary discussion dispels some of the misconcep-tions, and the mystique, that have clouded discussions of literary canons; a subject that has often generated more heat than light, more argument than insight. It is important to have a clear understanding of where the modernist canon originated and how it was transmitted through an interlocking set of institutional practices, before embarking upon a detailed examination of this ideologically charged terrain. The account that follows is organised into four sections: the successful overturning of nineteenth-century canons of poetic taste; the proliferating canon of American modernisms; the construction of alternatives to modernism as the predominant paradigm of early twentieth-century poetry; and postmodern attempts to diversify the modernist canon, or to dismantle it altogether.

## A revolutionary tradition

It is tempting to imagine that the modernist revolution in poetry might never have succeeded but for the noisy propaganda campaigns waged by Ezra Pound. By virtue of his connections with the little magazines – *Poetry* (Chicago), the *Little Review* and *The Egoist* – Pound was able to proselytise tirelessly on behalf of his friends. It was as one of Pound's protégés that T. S. Eliot burst upon the London literary scene. Pound's celebrated apologia ('Drunken Helots and Mr. Eliot'), his rude rejoinder to Arthur Waugh's attack on Eliot in the *Quarterly Review*, should be taken at less than face value. While it was true that many reviewers turned from Eliot's *Prufrock and Other Observations* (1917) in bafflement, Pound was not alone in discerning this volume's remarkable mixture of wit, technical innovation and urban disaffection. May Sinclair, for instance, championed Eliot's 'elusive' genius by suggesting his poetry required a different kind of attention.[1] In fact, Pound and Eliot sought to establish principles for reading modern poetry founded upon the presentation of concrete particulars, or the 'objective correlative' (in Eliot's once-famous phrase).

The publication of *The Waste Land* in 1922 made an immediate and important impact: it constituted a notable publicity and marketing coup for modernist poetry. The poem was awarded the considerable $2,000 annual literature prize from the *Dial*, largely thanks to the advocacy of Pound (he had emended it in typescript), who talked the poem up as the acme of the modernist movement in poetry since 1900. *The Waste Land* was discussed in the *Dial* in Edmund Wilson's perceptive article 'The Poetry of Drouth', which became the point of departure for an animated public debate about modernist poetry that ensued in the United States. The reaction of the English literary establishment was cooler, at times very hostile. In the *Times Literary Supplement*, Edgell Rickword acknowledged Eliot's sophistication, but he pointed out that *The Waste Land*'s discontinuities placed excessive demands on the general reader. The influential middlebrow critic, J. C. Squire, claimed the poem was incomprehensible: 'A grunt would serve equally well.'[2] No doubt such remarks enhanced Eliot's vogue among London's avant-garde circles. Appreciation of *The Waste Land* could serve as the cognoscenti's shibboleth.

Eliot's growing reputation as an avant-garde poet directed attention to his critical writings. *The Sacred Wood* (1920) was recommended by supporters as a demolition of Victorian and Georgian standards of taste. Although a provocative collection, it was widely admired by a generation of writers dissatisfied with prewar critical orthodoxies. These newer standards of criticism are on display in the trenchant articles and reviews Rickword printed in *The Calendar of Modern Letters* (1925–7). In *A Survey of Modernist Poetry* (1927), Laura Riding and Robert Graves tore up the unwritten contract linking the poet to the general reading public: 'The modernist poet does not have to issue a program declaring his intentions toward the reader or to issue an announcement of tactics.'[3] In effect, this combative criticism attempted to forcibly re-educate the audience for modern poetry. By 1932, Eliot's *Selected Essays*, opening with the key critical essay 'Tradition and the Individual Talent', staked his canonical claim to have renewed the English poetic 'tradition' with infusions from seventeenth-century dramatic verse and nineteenth-century French Symbolism. The magisterial tone of this essay cloaked an original polemical intent: it had first appeared in 1919 in the feisty little magazine *The Egoist*. The authority of his roles as editor of the *Criterion* (1922–39) and as a poetry director of Faber and Faber, could lead supporters to overlook the fact that Eliot approached his miscellaneous journalism as a programmatic defence of 'the sort of poetry that I and my friends wrote'.[4]

Equally significant was the use made of Eliot's work in the burgeoning world of academic literary criticism. An important pioneer was I. A. Richards, who employed Eliot's poetry instrumentally in his Cambridge lectures to exemplify modern critical theories. Richards's 1926 article on Eliot, which benefited from discussions with the poet (during Eliot's Cambridge visit as Clark Lecturer), characterised *The Waste Land* as symptomatic of an era bereft of all beliefs. In 1929, F. R. Leavis supported Eliot in the *Cambridge Review* against condescending reviewers. At this time, Eliot's poetry had an enormous cachet with Cambridge students; an indication that he had begun to gain a foothold in British universities. Leavis's *New Bearings in English Poetry* (1932) contained praise of Eliot's early work, crediting him almost single-handedly (qualified approval was accorded to Gerard Manley Hopkins and Pound) with reorienting the path of English literary tradition after the enervated dream-worlds of nineteenth-century verse. That Eliot was unquestionably the major poet of the age was a common refrain in Leavis's embattled quarterly review, *Scrutiny* (1932–53), which found little to celebrate in the poets of the Auden generation, or contemporary American poetry. *Scrutiny*'s austere judgements had a formative influence on generations of British university students. It should be noted that *Scrutiny*'s 'tradition' of twentieth-century poetry was unmistakably national in orientation, not internationalist.

Thanks to the so-called New Critics, modernist poetry acquired a considerable prominence in American universities. A diverse set of poet-critics (united chiefly by their rejection of the dominant trends in 1920s American criticism), the New Critics congregated around several spirited literary quarterlies: Robert Penn Warren's and Cleanth Brooks's *Southern Review* (1935–42), John Crowe Ransom's *Kenyon Review* (1939–59) and Allen Tate's *Sewanee Review* (1944–6). As theorists and apologists for modernist poetry, the New Critics paid particular attention to the formal complexity – paradox, tension and irony – of technique and metaphor. Tate was an early and partisan defender of *The Waste Land*. In a succession of original, penetrating essays published in the 1930s, R. P. Blackmur tackled the obscurity of modern poetry. This groundbreaking work was soon invested with a pedagogic intent. Brooks's *Modern Poetry and the Tradition* (1939) unfolded a canon of modernist poets underpinned by Eliot's precepts and example: he praised their rediscovery of seventeenth-century 'wit' and eschewal of romantic afflatus. Furthermore, the textbook anthology plus commentary, *Understanding Poetry* (1938), written by Brooks and Warren, gradually transformed college teaching of English poetry in America. The textbook focused on examples of critical practice, on formalist close readings or 'explications' of short lyric poems. In 1950, Warren joined Brooks at Yale University. The huge impact of *Understanding Poetry* demonstrated that the New Criticism had been transplanted from advanced, but relatively isolated, literary circles to prestigious centres of institutional power.

By the 1940s, then, Eliot's followers had been decisive in shaping the canon of modernist poetry. Ambitious academics earned their spurs with explications of opaque or allusive poems that had earlier been frustrating by their capacity to resist discursive exposition. The appearance of *Four Quartets* (1935–42) gave fresh life to the business of pedagogical elucidation. However, the sombre religious brooding of the *Quartets*, together with the expression of anti-democratic sentiments in Eliot's cultural criticism, harmed his standing with a younger generation of poets. Still, Eliot's reputation as the modernist poet and critic *par excellence* was enshrined in countless university English departments (particularly in the United States) throughout the 1940s and 1950s. On the other hand, Pound's declining reputation touched bottom when he was imprisoned in Pisa on the charge of treason in 1945. Surviving the possibility of execution, his poignant record of breakdown,

*The Pisan Cantos*, was awarded the Bollingen Prize in 1948, sparking a heated controversy, not just regarding its literary value, but over the manner in which *The Cantos* addressed the obsessive themes of usury, anti-Semitism and fascism.

In 1948 Eliot was awarded the Nobel Prize for Literature, confirmation of his ascent to respectability. Helen Gardner's study *The Art of T. S. Eliot* (1949) placed the emphasis on the *Quartets* and not the radical experimentalism of the early poetry. Thus sanctified, the Anglo-Catholic royalist poet could be laid to rest in Westminster Abbey. In 1965, *Life* magazine recorded his passing by drawing a line under 'the Age of Eliot'. Yet the inevitable critical reaction that gathered momentum after his death failed to overturn the centrality of Eliot's writings to the canon of modernist poetry. Influential critical histories, from C. K. Stead's *The New Poetic* (1964) to Michael Levenson's *A Genealogy of Modernism* (1984), took Eliot's oeuvre as the culmination of the development of the modernist movement in poetry. In *The Pound Era* (1971), Pound's most brilliant exegete, Hugh Kenner, made a stimulating case for viewing modernism as the 'Pound Era', thereby encouraging the rehabilitation of this poet's chequered reputation. Furthermore, the publication of *The Waste Land* manuscripts in 1971 served to reinforce a widespread assumption that the focus of modernist poetry should fall on the collaboration of Eliot and Pound: above all, on their forbiddingly elliptical, allusive and polyglot long poems. A large number of critical studies in the 1980s orientated modernism firmly along the Pound–Eliot axis, often marginalising the work of other poets, and treating the later poetry of Yeats as the unexpected flowering of a hitherto minor aesthete. Some critics even suggested that it had been the amanuensis, Pound, who had influenced the master, Yeats – not vice versa.

The ghost of Pound's reckless politics, however, continued to trouble his critics. Numerous scholarly monographs published in the late 1980s and early 1990s were preoccupied with Pound's fascism. In 1995, Anthony Julius's 'adversarial' study of Eliot – an approach employing the rhetorical methods of a lawyer – contended that previous critics had studiously failed to address this poet's anti-Semitism. Recent attempts to align Pound and Eliot's writings with the norms of postmodern culture have routinely arraigned them on the grounds of anti-Semitism, fascism and misogyny. This abeyance of sympathy marks the current unwillingness to read these poets any longer on their own terms, or in the light of the formalist and ahistorical terms laid down by the New Critics; although some opponents have arguably been too eager to unmask distasteful illiberal opinions before allowing the poetry to speak with its full complexity of tone and nuance. Eliot and Pound have always had detractors as well as admirers. Their place at the heart of the canon of Anglo-American modernist poetry will depend upon readers arriving at agreement about the existence of demonstrable merit in their works.

## American modernisms

Several strands of American modernist poetry developed in conscious opposition to the example of Eliot and Pound. William Carlos Williams, Wallace Stevens and Hart Crane, for example, all expressed misgivings or discontent about Eliot's pre-eminence. In a sense, modernism had a more fertile soil in America in which to flourish than in Britain. The dynamic growth of urban and industrial America (above all in New York and Chicago) antiquated for modern poetry readers the anaemic turn-of-the-century 'genteel tradition' (to use George Santayana's pejorative phrase) that emanated from New England high culture. The founding in Chicago in 1912 of the monthly magazine *Poetry*, followed by the stridently avant-garde magazine the *Little Review* in 1914, revealed the emergence of a metropolitan intelligentsia receptive to the new styles of advanced American poetry. In 1917, Amy Lowell's *Tendencies in Modern American Poetry* contained chapters on Edward Arlington Robinson, Robert Frost, Edgar Lee Masters, Carl Sandburg, and the 'Imagists', H.D. and John Gould Fletcher, but she paid scant attention to the American-born exiles Eliot and Pound. Eliot retaliated in *The Egoist* by suggesting the poets included in Lowell's new American canon were 'Laureates of some provincial Lycaeum'.[5]

Eliot's dismissal of contemporary American poetry was selectively reinforced by the New Critics. Blackmur rebuked E. E. Cummings for his 'sentimental denial of the intelligence'; he placed Marianne Moore as an 'idiosyncratic' poet and the poetry of Hart Crane as 'a great failure'.[6] Notwithstanding their close personal friendship, Tate condemned Crane for his 'insulated egoism'.[7] In a similar vein, the severe moralist Yvor Winters chastised Wallace Stevens as a 'hedonist'.[8] Behind these canon-making value judgements was normally the assumption that modernist American poetry should be grafted on to European high civilisation; to ignore this rich cultural tradition was to appear, as Eliot put it, 'provincial'. The search for a guiding 'tradition' aligned Eliot with the avowedly reactionary cultural politics of the Southern Agrarian poet-critics, who contended that modernist poetry must stand aloof from the vulgar materialism of contemporary American mass democracy. Brooks's *Modern Poetry and the Tradition* praised the Nashville 'Fugitive' poets – Ransom, Tate and Warren – for their urbane wit and refined ironies. Brooks largely ignored the New York-orientated modernisms of Williams, Stevens, Moore, Cummings and Crane. The interwar polemics regarding an emergent canon of modernist American poets reveals a conflicted and confused field. Tate looked in sad awe at Crane's tragic career. Blackmur could admire aspects of Moore's quaintness. Winters praised some elements of Stevens's poetry. Still, these poets all struggled to achieve a secure place in the modernist canon. In the foreword to the 1950 edition of his popular and catholic anthology, *Modern American Poetry*, Louis Untermeyer asserted: 'Old standards have tottered; no new certitudes have been established.' His collection sought to exhibit 'the rich diversity of recent American poetry' though he claimed the book's contents highlighted the 'important poets'. The twentieth-century poets accorded more than twenty pages were E. A. Robinson, Sandburg, Frost, Eliot and Archibald MacLeish.[9]

Donald Hall's introduction to *Contemporary American Poetry* (1962) showed that the times were changing. Until recently, Hall argued, American poetry had been under the 'benevolent tyranny' of an orthodoxy 'derived from the authority of Eliot and the New Critics'. Hall quoted Williams's lament in his *Autobiography* (1951): '[*The Waste Land*] wiped out our world. . . . Eliot returned us to the classroom.' Hall stressed instead 'the line of William Carlos Williams' in present-day American poetry, drawing strength from the colloquial idioms of *Paterson* (1946–58).[10] In *Poetry and the Age* (1953), the poet-critic Randall Jarrell had rejected academic 'orthodoxy' by championing the work of Frost, Williams, Moore and Stevens. One of the striking features of the 1950s was the rising reputation of Stevens, whose *Collected Poems* (1954) quickly attracted intensive attention. Roy Harvey Pearce's *The Continuity of American Poetry* (1961) attempted to take stock of the recent upheavals. Pearce concluded that the modern American poet had a choice between two modes of development: the 'Adamic' impulse to freedom, represented by Stevens, and the 'mythic' call to community, best exemplified by the theocentric Eliot. Although Pearce hinted at a synthesis between these traditions, the major trend in American academic criticism in the following two decades could be construed as a concerted reaction against Eliot, by a movement that exalted Stevens as the supreme poet of the century.

During the 1960s and 1970s, a new generation of critics associated with Yale and Johns Hopkins universities – Harold Bloom, Geoffrey Hartman and J. Hillis Miller – attempted to 'deconstruct' the hegemony of the modernist canon institutionalised by the New Critics. In a succession of dense theoretical writings, these critics approached Stevens as a philosophical poet, or perhaps as a philosopher of poetry, whose writings wrestled with the phenomenological and the existential dilemmas facing modern man. Bloom argued that Stevens and Crane were the 'inheritors and continuators' of a tradition of romantic visionaries and the truly canonical figures of twentieth-century poetry in English, unlike Eliot and Pound, whom he provokingly suggested might turn out to be the 'Cowley and Cleveland of this age'.[11] Hartman also extolled Stevens as the great romantic poet of the period. Hillis Miller brooded upon the responses of Stevens and Williams to the terrifying absence of God's apparent withdrawal from the world. Miller suggested that Stevens sought to recover a divinely immanent universe through his poetic fictions; the materiality of Williams's signifiers constituted a more radical gesture towards the end of ontology. The Yale critics consciously disregarded the postulation of authorial intentions if they appeared to contradict their speculative interpretations, a procedure that troubled more conservative critics, but was seen as liberating by fellow poststructuralists. It is very likely that the subtle commentaries of Frank Kermode and Helen Vendler have done as much to secure Stevens's canonical standing in Britain and the United States as the freer and more fugitive readings of the Yale critics.

It would be wrong to think, however, that Stevens's belated entrance to the canon of modernist poets had somehow supplanted Eliot, who continues to receive detailed and varied forms of canonical attention. Denis Donoghue resisted challenges to Eliot mounted by proponents of Stevens, by claiming that his academic colleagues betrayed in their critiques of Eliot an undeclared antipathy towards religious belief. According to Donoghue, Stevens's existential preoccupation with human consciousness was not *prima facie* raw material for a superior poetry. Beyond that, many serious readers of twentieth-century poetry have resisted a factitious either/or between Stevens and Eliot. Other critics – Hugh Kenner and Marjorie Perloff foremost amongst them – have argued for the continuing importance of the 'Poundian tradition' in American poetry, an inheritance transmitted to contemporary avant-garde poetics through the work of Pound's admirers, Louis Zukofsky and the Objectivists. The horns of Perloff's essay 'Pound/Stevens: Whose Era?' (1982) might appear as reductive and unhelpful as the binary opposition between followers of Stevens and Eliot, but it does bear witness to an ongoing debate about the relative importance of canonical authors.

## The road not taken

The contours of the canon we have been tracing can also be viewed from the outside; that is, in terms of the poets who have been excluded from it in the synoptic sweep of important studies of a modernist 'tradition' of Anglo-American poetry. It is worth recalling that, in the eyes of many contemporaries, the major English poets writing in the mid-1920s were not Pound and Eliot but Thomas Hardy, Yeats and Robert Bridges, along with those poets collected in Edward Marsh's popular anthologies *Georgian Poetry* (five volumes; 1912–22). Hardy and Yeats in particular were begetters of distinctive traditions which have proved, in many ways, as fruitful as the traditions originating from Eliot and Pound. The spectacle of Yeats remaking his poetic personae after the publication of *The Wild Swans at Coole* (1919), most notably in *The Tower* (1928), has attracted legions of younger enthusiasts. Whether or not this refashioning is properly called 'modernist' (Yeats described himself as one of the 'last romantics') is another matter. Yeats's lofty, mannered, anecdotal introduction to *The Oxford Book of Modern Verse* (1936) is a case in point – the prologue to its decidedly idiosyncratic contents. Yeats devoted more space to Dorothy Wellesley and Laurence Binyon than to Eliot and Pound. The principal torch bearers of the modern movement in English poetry in this anthology appeared to be W. J. Turner, Edith Sitwell and Herbert Read. At the same time, Eliot paid careful attention to the composition of Michael Roberts's *Faber Book of Modern Verse* (1936), a bold reordering of the landscape of contemporary poetry beginning with Hopkins (by contrast, Yeats had opened with Walter Pater), excluding Hardy and the Georgians, and printing substantial offerings from the work of Pound, Eliot, later Yeats, and Auden. Published simultaneously, the Faber collection soon eclipsed its Oxford rival, shaping (in the words of the poet Anne Ridler) 'the taste of a generation'.[12]

Though *The Faber Book of Modern Verse* laid out a canon there were dissenters. In a series of polemical studies published throughout the 1930s, 1940s and 1950s, the American poet and critic Yvor Winters bitterly berated the false turn taken by modern poetry. Winters excoriated the modernist poets for their obscurantism and irrationality, denoted by what he called 'the fallacy of imitative form': that is, the mistaken belief that a chaotic world can be mirrored artistically by chaotic form. Principal proponents of the fallacy – Eliot, Cummings, Stevens, and especially Pound ('a barbarian loose in a museum') – were scolded in Winters's sweeping and unsparing literary judgements.[13] Put bluntly, Winters abhorred the moral 'decadence' exhibited by modernist poetry.

Though the English poet and critic Donald Davie thought that Winters's valuation of Bridges, Thomas Sturge Moore and Elizabeth Daryush as the major poets of the age was quite eccentric, his own irascible brand of counter-modernism owed something to Winters's stern example. In *Articulate Energy* (1955), Davie stringently examined symbolist theory and practice, finding them both wanting. He warned of the dangers poets courted when they dislocated or abandoned conventional syntax. *Articulate Energy* closed with a plea for modern poetry to ground itself once more in human experience, or the 'reek of humanity'.[14] This devaluation of symbolist poetics, an implicit

JASON HARDING

defence of the British Movement poets of the 1950s, had consequences for
the redrawing of the map of modern poetry.

Perhaps the best of the revisionist literary histories published in the
late 1950s was Frank Kermode's *Romantic Image* (1957), a closely argued
attempt to trace the preservation of romantic concepts and motifs (the isolation of the artist, the image) in the theories of the avowedly anti-romantic
modernists. This study contended that T. E. Hulme's theory of the Image
revealed the complex interrelationship of symbolism and modernism. Kermode's analysis cast doubt upon Eliot's symbolist historiography, the 'dissociation of sensibility', which had been used to assail the reputations of Milton
and the romantic poets. Kermode's close reading of Yeats's 'Among School
Children' attended to the poem's 'romantic' elements and to its climactic symbolist images of tree and dancer. Drawing freely on historical scholarship to
support its conclusions, *Romantic Image* extended the insights of Edmund
Wilson, another appreciative but judiciously sceptical critic of the symbolist-
modernist retreat into esoteric artistic symbols. By the later 1950s, then, the
continuity of modern poetry was increasingly claimed as a romantic survival.
The case was put most forcefully in Graham Hough's *Image and Experience*
(1960). Hough claimed that Imagist principles had debilitated the work of
Eliot, Pound and Stevens by severing their work from a vital relationship
with a wider audience. With breathtaking audacity, Hough contended that
these poets had been a fascinating but ultimately fruitless diversion from the
central (romantic) tradition of modern English poetry: namely, Hardy, Frost,
Graves and John Betjeman. *Image and Experience* characterised modernist
poetry as an ill-advised 'détour, a diversion from the main road'.[15]

This critical reaction or 'counter-revolution' (as Kermode termed it) broadened the terms of the debate about the canon of modernist poetry. The publication of James Reeves's Penguin anthology *Georgian Poetry* (1962) hastened
a historically informed reappraisal of these poets. In *The Georgian Revolt*
(1965), Robert H. Ross sought to unsettle the 'ridiculously oversimplified'[16]
assumptions about the nature of Georgian poetry. He discovered that, far
from being mere pseudo-pastoralists, the Georgians had extended the subject matter and diction of modern poetry, especially in the years 1911 to
1915. But the harsh criticisms of Eliot and Leavis, allied to the disenchant-
ment felt by a postwar generation of British critics, inflicted lasting damage
on the reputations of the Georgians. Stead's *The New Poetic* gave serious
attention to the innovations of a few of the poets published in the Georgian anthologies (including Rupert Brooke, D. H. Lawrence, Siegfried Sas-
soon and Graves), yet the movement was essentially pigeonholed as prewar
and therefore outside the charmed circle of the 1920s 'high modernism' –
a term gaining increasing critical currency in American universities during

the 1970s – which had apparently descended from the Imagist movement. The privileged pre-eminence of modernism, let alone of 'high' modernism, was never unanimous and did not pass unchallenged by independent-minded critics and poets.

Davie's *Thomas Hardy and British Poetry* (1972) proposed Hardy (rather than Eliot, Pound or Yeats) as the most far-reaching influence on British poetry during the last half-century. Hardy and his heirs – Lawrence, Auden, Philip Larkin – represented a rejection of the eclectic internationalism of modernism, showing the divergence of British and American poetic traditions. This cultural chauvinism was reinforced by Larkin's *Oxford Book of Twentieth-Century English Verse* (1973), which reprinted twenty-seven poems by Hardy, followed numerically by Yeats (nineteen poems), Auden (sixteen poems), Rudyard Kipling (thirteen poems), Lawrence and Betjeman (twelve poems each). According to Davie, the ambition of American poetry since William Carlos Williams to sever all ties with English poetry accounted for the very different tastes of postwar readers of British and American poetry. Whereas post-Second World War American poetry has been self-consciously 'post-modern', that term has had a rather different resonance in the context of *English* poetry. The discrepancy begs a question about the appropriateness of the retrospective valorisation of 1920s 'high modernism' as the high-watermark of Anglo-American poetry. The term carries with it the implication that anything not classed as 'high' or 'modernist' is necessarily of inferior quality. Not so for Davie, who could combine an admiration for Pound with admiration for Edward Thomas; or for Christopher Ricks, a subtle exegete of Eliot's poetry as well as of the dissimilar talent of A. E. Housman.

Hardy, Frost and Yeats continue to attract supporters who argue for their place in the front rank of achievement in twentieth-century English poetry. Although it is sometimes proposed, it is debatable whether their prestige has been enhanced by academic critics who feel the need to bestow the honorific adjective 'modernist' upon them. Indicative of the complexity of the debates surrounding the literary history of modernism are the essays Blackmur contributed to the special issues of the *Southern Review* devoted to Hardy (1940) and Yeats (1941). Attempting to order Hardy's poetry into 'some sort of canon', Blackmur complained of a fanatical 'thicket of ideas, formulas, obsessions, indisciplined compulsions'.[17] Blackmur contrasted Hardy with Yeats, whose peculiar mythical paradigm – *A Vision* (first edition, 1925) – was absorbed into the texture of his poems. For all the occult byways, Blackmur still praised the iconoclast Yeats as 'the greatest poet in English since the seventeenth century'.[18] The quietly meditative poetry of Frost has been equally difficult to assimilate into tidy-minded narratives of modernist poetry. In his *A History of Modern Poetry* (two volumes, 1976 and 1987), David Perkins defended Frost against narrow modernist standards or norms. He claimed that Frost had written 'the finest short narrative poems yet written in the 20th-century'.[19]

## Opening up the canon

The modernist canon, like all literary canons, is open-ended and amenable to change. During the past thirty years or so, the most sustained assault on the canon has arisen from an accusation that the institutions central to canon-formation have deliberately privileged the claims of white, male authors while covertly excluding non-whites and female writers. The aggressively partisan 'culture wars' that have been fought in North American and British universities since the 1970s have attempted to 'open up' the canon to hitherto marginal figures, sometimes with the express aim of dismantling the cultural elitism implied by a select canon. The enormous expansion of university English departments after the Second World War has rendered undergraduate reading lists a revealing indicator of revisionist intentions. Academic syllabuses cannot dislodge an author from the canon; that is, unless a corresponding crisis of faith takes place in the interlocking institutional networks of publishing, scholarship, literary journalism and reviewing. Still, a core canon of white, male modernist poets has been most forcefully contested and unsettled by the revisionist zeal exhibited in (mainly North American) college classrooms, struggles reflecting larger sociocultural changes in the profile of instructors and students at institutions of higher education. This polemical intent was signalled in Houston A. Baker and Leslie Fiedler's *English Literature: Opening Up the Canon* (1981), a collection that sought to inaugurate a wide-ranging interrogation of the class, gender and ethnic identities of canonical authors. Habitually motivated by explicitly ideological agendas, attempts to preserve or to open up the modernist canon have been tendentious.

African-American poets participated in modernist movements, notably in New York throughout the 1920s, yet black poets were conspicuous by their absence from the modernist canon. Neither Geoffrey Moore's *Penguin Book of Modern American Verse* (1954) nor Oscar Williams's *Anthology of American Verse* (1955) contained a single black author among over a hundred poets represented. In 1969, Donald Hall observed pointedly: 'A world of black poetry exists in America alongside the world of white poetry, exactly alike in structure – with its own publishers, bookstores, magazines, editors, anthologists, conferences, poetry readings – and almost entirely invisible to the white world. Like the rest of the black world. The world of white poetry has practised the usual genteel apartheid of tokenism.'[20] Whether or not it is correctly described as tokenism, Untermeyer's anthologies of *Modern American Poetry* published work by three black poets from the modernist era – James Weldon Johnson, Langston Hughes and Countee Cullen. By 1977, Moore had added Hughes, Cullen and Gwendolyn Brooks to his Penguin anthology. In the wake of the 1960s civil rights movement, scholarly attention was directed to the work of black American writers, including the group of intellectuals associated with the literary salons and coteries of Harlem, New York. The epithet 'Harlem Renaissance' gives too strong a sense of uniformity to a disparate group of writers, but it does highlight the existence of lively and innovative circles of advanced black writing that interacted with American modernist poets. It does seem incontrovertible that black poets faced material difficulties that militated against the wider dissemination of their work, in forms that are quite dissimilar from the situation of white poets. As Gwendolyn Brooks remarked in her foreword to *New Negro Poets* (1964), black poets have 'spoken racially' and have 'offered race-fed testimony'.[21] The questions of race and ideology confronted by African-American poets in the interwar period has tended to, and may continue to, place their poetry in a different category from the rarefied, verbal icons celebrated as 'high modernism'. For instance, the experimental blues poetry of Langston Hughes – sometimes proposed as the most gifted of the Harlem Renaissance poets – is grounded in a social and political consciousness easily distinguishable from the modernisms of Eliot, Stevens or Moore. The appearance of *The Norton Anthology of African American Literature* (1997), edited by Henry Louis Gates Jr and Nellie Y. McKay, suggests a strenuous advocacy of autonomy, rather than a desire for inclusion within a multiethnic or multicultural canon.

Unquestionably the greatest restructuring of the modernist canon over the past thirty years has been the recovery of neglected women writers. Throughout the 1970s feminist critics attacked the gender bias of an elitist, restrictive, male-centred literary canon. In 1978, Elaine Showalter declared 'the lost continent of the female tradition has risen like Atlantis from the sea of English literature'.[22] The work of reclamation was undertaken in numerous revisionist accounts of modernist literary history. Sandra Gilbert and Susan Gubar's *No Man's Land* (three volumes; 1988, 1989 and 1994) launched a radical critique of the misogyny of a masculine literary tradition, championing instead the flowering of an oppositional, feminist modernist poetics. A critical anthology, *The Gender of Modernism* (1990), edited by Bonnie Kime Scott, attempted to reconfigure the modernist canon with chapters on some twenty-six authors, including the poets Djuna Barnes, Nancy Cunard, H.D., Mina Loy, Rose Macaulay, Charlotte Mew, Marianne Moore, May

Sinclair, Sylvia Townsend Warner and Anna Wickham. *The Gender of Modernism* usefully extended the breadth of the discussions over canonical modernism, preparing the climate for what Scott described as the goal of postmodern feminists to refigure or reweave a tangled mesh of modernists. Scholarly accounts of woman-centred publishing networks based in London, Paris and Chicago have added greatly to understanding the diversity and complexity of modernist literature. The debates arising out of this recent research have been fruitful, though the female poets discussed in *The Gender of Modernism* have, in common with their male counterparts, encountered resistance in gaining admittance to the canon.

An obvious candidate for canonical election is Hilda Doolittle or H.D., whose early Imagist poetry had received serious attention from Richards and Blackmur, and was included in the standard literary histories of Stead, Kenner and Levenson. After the publication of H.D.'s posthumous *Collected Poems* (1983), containing a mass of previously unpublished work, attention was directed to her longer, meditative poems. Critical monographs by Susan Stanford Friedman and Rachel Blau DuPlessis stressed H.D.'s difference from male contemporaries, viewing her writing as the articulation of the physical experience of women that has been marginalised in a patriarchal world of publishing; although Lawrence Rainey has disputed these claims by suggesting that H.D.'s aesthetic valuation would be considerably lower were it not for the patronage of her immensely wealthy lover, Winifred Ellerman, who enthusiastically promoted her work to a privileged coterie audience. Uncertainty about canonical stature has also accompanied the critical discussion of two female poets intimately associated with the avant-garde communities fuelling modernist experimentation in the arts – Mina Loy and Nancy Cunard. Loy has perhaps fared better of the two as a fellow traveller in Marjorie Perloff's prewar 'Futurist moment'. Cunard's *Parallax* was dismissed by Leavis in the epilogue to *New Bearings in English Poetry* as merely derivative of *The Waste Land*. Her reputation was further damaged in conservative circles by her political activism. Nevertheless, the inclusion of both Loy and Cunard's poetry in Rainey's Blackwell anthology, *Modernism* (2005), should help to ensure their continued attention before the broad conclave of canonical electors. On the other hand, Rainey omitted Laura Riding, an author who has done as much as any female writer to shape the reception of modernist poetry; though it is no longer true, as Martin Dodsworth complained in 1994, that this original poet endures an 'invisible status' in literary histories.[23]

A modernist canon forged in London and New York, then enshrined in the elite institutions of England and the United States, has been accused of being reluctant to acknowledge the merits of the Scotsman Hugh MacDiarmid, the Northumbrian Basil Bunting, the Irishmen Thomas MacGreevy, Denis Devlin and Brian Coffey, the Welsh poets Dylan Thomas and Lynette Roberts, and the Anglo-Welsh poet David Jones (Yeats's *Oxford Book of Modern Poetry* was unusual for the number of Celtic poets represented in its pages). In *Repression and Recovery* (1989), Cary Nelson argued that a traditional modernist canon had subjugated many American poets on the basis of their class, race or gender. Given the incompatible premises, values and requirements upheld by social institutions and pressure groups, attempts to formulate a select canon will inevitably be a contentious undertaking. It is natural that the reputations of writers should be pressed into the service of redirecting contemporary cultural debates. This *Cambridge Companion to Modernist Poetry* seeks to extend the boundaries of canonical modernism to the larger Anglophone world of Commonwealth and Caribbean poetry.

In an intriguing case of a canonical poacher turned gamekeeper, Harold Bloom deplored the Balkanisation of the western literary canon proposed by an egregious 'School of Resentment' (feminism, deconstruction, new historicism). Unresolved ideological competition or conflict, however, may be a healthy state of affairs in the cultural conversations of a democratic society, not necessarily a symptom of disabling instability. The establishment of the modernist canon in Anglo-American universities could never guarantee that it would be taught in a way that effectively or consistently transmitted the values of any monolithic institutional power – nor is it clear why the preservation (through the institutions of education, publishing and journalism) of what modern, pluralist democratic societies deem valuable can be clearly identified with a repressive, homogeneous 'dominant' ideology. On the other hand, egalitarian cultural politics runs the risk of endorsing what Tocqueville lamented as the undiscriminating 'hypocrisy of luxury' of affluent democracies. As systematic records of a discernible consensus about the assessment of achievement, a literary canon is a fundamentally inegalitarian concept.

The modernist canon of poets has shown itself to be dynamic and elastic enough to accommodate a new variety and proportion without sacrificing the hierarchical principle of judging the excellent from the less good. The specific sociohistorical forces shaping the story of this canon do not obviate the ongoing critical necessity to find strong arguments to uphold it as a set of institutional practices. As we have seen, proponents and opponents of modernist poetry alike have debated the literary *value* of individual authors with remarkable vehemence. These questions of interpretation, and of evaluation, are essential to the survival of the modernist canon. According to Kermode, since works of art cannot speak for themselves, cadres of commentators are required to disentangle knowledge from opinion and to recommend subtle distinctions between what ought and what ought not to be let go. Although these critical elites are increasingly to be found working in universities, it is salutary to close by reflecting on Samuel Johnson's celebrated dictum that 'after all the refinements of subtlety and the dogmatism of learning', the 'claim to poetical honours' rests ultimately upon readers 'uncorrupted with literary prejudices'.[24] It is sentimental and futile to wish away the specialisation of twenty-first-century intellectual life, yet 'claim to poetical honours' might indeed depend not solely upon an army of university specialists, but on the continuing human appeal of canonical works to a diverse corpus of poetry readers.

## NOTES

1. See Jewel Spears Brooker (ed.), *T. S. Eliot: The Contemporary Reviews* (Cambridge University Press, 2004), pp. 3–6, 10–13.
2. Brooker (ed.), *T. S. Eliot*, p. 115.
3. Laura Riding and Robert Graves, *A Survey of Modernist Poetry* (London: Heinemann, 1927), p. 124.
4. T. S. Eliot, *To Criticize the Critic and Other Writings* (London: Faber and Faber, 1965), p. 16.
5. T. S. Eliot, 'Disjecta Membra', *The Egoist* 5.4 (April 1918), 55.
6. R. P. Blackmur, *Language as Gesture* (New York: Harcourt Brace, 1952), pp. 318, 283, 316.
7. Allen Tate, *On the Limits of Poetry* (New York: Swallow, 1948), p. 228.
8. Yvor Winters, *In Defence of Reason* (Denver: Swallow, 1947), p. 445.
9. Louis Untermeyer (ed.), *Modern American Poetry* (New York: Harcourt Brace, 1950).
10. Donald Hall, 'Introduction', *Contemporary American Poetry* (1962; Harmondsworth: Penguin, 1972), p. 25.
11. Harold Bloom, *Yeats* (New York: Oxford University Press, 1970), p. v.
12. Anne Ridler, 'Introduction to the Second Edition', in Michael Roberts (ed.), *The Faber Book of Modern Verse* (London: Faber and Faber, 1951), p. 35.
13. Yvor Winters, *Primitivism and Decadence* (New York: Arrow Editions, 1937) and *In Defense of Reason* & *On Modern Poets* (New York: Meridian, 1959).
14. Donald Davie, *Articulate Energy* (London: Routledge & Kegan Paul, 1955), pp. 161–5.
15. Graham Hough, *Image and Experience* (London: Duckworth, 1960), p. 56.
16. Robert H. Ross, *The Georgian Revolt* (Carbondale: Southern Illinois University Press, 1965), p. vii.
17. Blackmur, *Language as Gesture*, pp. 51–2.
18. Blackmur, *Language as Gesture*, p. 123.
19. David Perkins, *A History of Modern Poetry*, vol. 1 (Cambridge, Mass.: Harvard University Press, 1976), p. 232.
20. Hall, 'Introduction', *Contemporary American Poetry*, p. 37.

21. Gwendolyn Brooks, 'Foreword', *New Negro Poets: USA* (Bloomington: Indiana University Press, 1964), p. 13.
22. Elaine Showalter, *A Literature of Their Own* (London: Virago Press, 1978), p. 10.
23. Martin Dodsworth, *The Penguin History of Literature: The Twentieth Century* (Harmondsworth: Penguin, 1994), p. 221.
24. Samuel Johnson, *Lives of the Most Eminent English Poets* (1781; London: Frederick Warne, 1872), pp. 501–2.

# GUIDE TO FURTHER READING

The following bibliographies consist of (1) anthologies containing modernist texts and related materials; (2) general works on modernism (with an emphasis on studies in whole or in part devoted to modernist poetry); and (3) suggested further reading for each chapter of this Companion. To avoid unnecessary duplication, anthologies and critical works cited in the Introduction and the individual chapters have not been included here.

## Anthologies and readers

Axelrod, Steven Gould, Camille Roman and Thomas Travisano (eds), *The New Anthology of American Poetry*, vol. II, *Modernisms 1900–1950*, New Brunswick: Rutgers University Press, 2005.

Brooker, Peter (ed.), *Modernism/Postmodernism*, London: Longman, 1992.

Caws, Mary Ann (ed.), *Manifesto: A Century of Isms*, Lincoln: University of Nebraska Press, 2001.

Cunard, Nancy (ed.), *Negro Anthology*, London: Wishart, 1934.

McAllister, Andrew (ed.), *The Objectivists*, Newcastle: Bloodaxe, 1996.

Rothenberg, Jerome and Pierre Joris (eds), *Poems for the Millennium*, vol. I, *From Fin-de-Siècle to Negritude*, Berkeley: University of California Press, 1995.

Taylor, Joshua C. (ed.), *Futurism*, New York: Museum of Modern Art, 1961.

## General works

Albright, Daniel, *Quantum Poetics: Yeats, Pound, Eliot, and the Science of Modernism*, Cambridge University Press, 1997.

Armstrong, Tim, *Modernism, Technology and the Body: A Cultural Study*, Cambridge University Press, 1998.

Bell, Michael, *Literature, Modernism and Myth: Belief and Responsibility in the Twentieth Century*, Cambridge University Press, 1997.

Butler, Christopher, *Early Modernism: Literature, Music and Painting in Europe 1900–1916*, Oxford: Clarendon Press, 1994.

Chabot, C. Barry, *Writers for the Nation: American Literary Modernism*, Tuscaloosa: University of Alabama Press, 1997.

Coughlan, Patricia and Alex Davis (eds), *Modernism and Ireland: The Poetry of the 1930s*, Cork University Press, 1995.

DeKoven, Marianne, *Rich and Strange: Gender, History, Modernism*, Princeton University Press, 1991.

Dettmar, Kevin and Stephen Watt (eds), *Marketing Modernisms: Self-Promotion, Canonization, Rereading*, Ann Arbor: University of Michigan Press, 1996.

DuPlessis, Rachel Blau, *The Pink Guitar: Writing as Feminist Practice*, Tuscaloosa: University of Alabama Press, 2006.

Emig, Rainer, *Modernism in Poetry: Motivations, Structures and Limits*, London: Longman, 1995.

Gray, Richard, *American Poetry of the Twentieth Century*, Harlow: Longman, 1990.

Harrison, Charles, *English Art and Modernism: 1900–1939*, Bloomington: Indiana University Press, 1981.

Hoffman, Frederick J., *The Twenties: American Writing in the Postwar Decade*, 2nd edn, New York: Collier Books, 1962.

Huyssen, Andreas, *After the Great Divide: Modernism, Mass Culture, Postmodernism*, Bloomington: Indiana University Press, 1986.

Kalaidjian, Walter (ed.), *The Cambridge Companion to American Modernism*, Cambridge University Press, 2005.

Keller, Lynn, *Re-Making it New: Contemporary American Poetry and the Modernist Tradition*, Cambridge University Press, 1987.

Kenner, Hugh, *A Homemade World: The American Modernist Writers*, London: Marion Boyars, 1977.

Krauss, Rosalind E., *The Originality of the Avant-Garde and Other Modernist Myths*, Cambridge, Mass.: MIT Press, 1997.

Lemke, Sieglinde, *Primitivist Modernism: Black Culture and the Origins of Transatlantic Modernism*, New York: Oxford University Press, 1998.

Lentricchia, Frank, *Modernist Quartet*, Cambridge University Press, 1994.

Mackey, Nathaniel, *Discrepant Engagement: Dissonance, Cross-Culturality, and Experimental Writing*, Cambridge University Press, 1993.

McGann, Jerome, *Black Riders: The Visible Language of Modernism*, Princeton University Press, 1993.

Matthews, Steven, *Modernism*, London: Arnold, 2004.

Montefiore, Janet, *Feminism and Poetry: Language, Experience, Identity in Women's Writing*, London: Pandora, 1987.

Motherwell, Robert (ed.), *The Dada Painters and Poets*, Cambridge, Mass.: Harvard University Press, 1951.

Naylor, Paul, *Poetic Investigations: Singing the Holes in History*, Evanston: Northwestern University Press, 1999.

Nelson, Cary, *Repression and Recovery: Modern American Poetry and the Politics of Cultural Memory, 1910–1945*, Madison: University of Wisconsin Press, 1989.

Perloff, Marjorie, *Poetic License: Essays on Modernist and Postmodernist Lyric*, Evanston: Northwestern University Press, 1990.

Perloff, Marjorie, *Poetry On and Off the Page: Essays for Emergent Occasions*, Evanston: Northwestern University Press, 1998.

Poplawski, Paul (ed.), *Encyclopedia of Literary Modernism*, Westport, Ind.: Greenwood, 2003.

Ramazani, Jahan, *Poetry of Mourning: The Modern Elegy from Hardy to Heaney*, University of Chicago Press, 1994.

Rifkin, Libbie, *Career Moves: Olson, Creeley, Zukofsky, Berrigan, and the American Avant-Garde*, Madison: University of Wisconsin Press, 2000.

Russell, Charles, *Poets, Prophets, and Revolutionaries: The Literary Avant-Garde from Rimbaud Through Postmodernism*, New York: Oxford University Press, 1985.

Stein, Gertrude, *Lectures in America*, New York: Modern Library, 1935.

Steinman, Lisa, *Made in America: Science, Technology, and American Modernist Poets*, New Haven: Yale University Press, 1987.

Thomas, Lorenzo, *Extraordinary Measures: Afrocentric Modernism and Twentieth-Century American Poetry*, Tuscaloosa: University of Alabama Press, 2000.

Tickner, Lisa, *Modern Life and Modern Subjects: British Art in the Early Twentieth Century*, New Haven: Yale University Press, 2000.

Timms, Edward and Peter Collier (eds), *Visions and Blueprints: Avant-Garde Culture and Radical Politics in Early Twentieth-Century Europe*, Manchester University Press, 1988.

Wilson, Edmund, *Axel's Castle: A Study in the Imaginative Literature of 1870–1930*, New York: Charles Scribner's Sons, 1931.

### Modernist poetry in history

Stead, C. K., *Pound, Yeats, Eliot and the Modernist Movement*, Basingstoke: Macmillan, 1986.

Williams, Louise Blakeney, *Modernism and the Ideology of History: Literature, Politics and the Past*, Cambridge University Press, 2002.

### Schools, movements, manifestoes

Blum, Cinzia Sartini, *The Other Modernism: F. T. Marinetti's Futurist Fiction of Power*, Berkeley: University of California Press, 1996.

Dasenbrock, Reed Way, *The Literary Vorticism of Ezra Pound and Wyndham Lewis: Towards the Condition of Painting*, Baltimore: Johns Hopkins University Press, 1985.

Gage, John T., *In the Arresting Eye: The Rhetoric of Imagism*, Baton Rouge: Louisiana State University Press, 1981.

Peppis, Paul, *Literature, Politics, and the English Avant-Garde: Nation and Empire, 1901–1918*, Cambridge University Press, 2000.

Puchner, Martin, *Poetry of the Revolution: Marx, Manifestos, and the Avant-Gardes*, Princeton University Press, 2006.

Robinson, Alan, *Symbol to Vortex: Poetry, Painting, Ideas, 1885–1914*, New York: St Martin's Press, 1985.

### The poetics of modernism

Schwartz, Sanford, *The Matrix of Modernism: Pound, Eliot and Early Twentieth Century Thought*, Princeton University Press, 1985.

Tashjian, Dickran, *Skyscraper Primitives: Dada and the American Avant-Garde 1910–1925*, Middletown: Wesleyan University Press, 1975.

## Gender, sexuality and the modernist poem

Dickie, Margaret and Thomas Travisano, *Gendered Modernisms: American Women Poets and Their Readers*, Philadelphia: University of Pennsylvania Press, 1996.

DuPlessis, Rachel Blau, *Genders, Races, and Religious Cultures in Modern American Poetry, 1908–1934*, Cambridge University Press, 2001.

Felski, Rita, *The Gender of Modernity*, Cambridge, Mass.: Harvard University Press, 1995.

Hogue, Cynthia, *Scheming Women: Poetry, Privilege, and the Politics of Subjectivity*, Albany: SUNY Press, 1995.

Izenberg, Gerald, *Modernism and Masculinity: Mann, Wedekind, Kandinsky through World War I*, University of Chicago Press, 2000.

Middleton, Peter, *The Inward Gaze: Masculinity and Subjectivity in Modernist Culture*, London: Routledge, 1992.

Miller, Cristanne, *Cultures of Modernism: Marianne Moore, Mina Loy, and Else Lasker-Schüler. Gender and Literary Community in New York and Berlin*, Ann Arbor: University of Michigan Press, 2005.

Stevens, Hugh and Caroline Howlett (eds), *Modernist Sexualities*, Manchester University Press, 2000.

## Pound or Eliot: whose era?

Chinitz, David, *T. S. Eliot and the Cultural Divide*, University of Chicago Press, 2003.

Coyle, Michael, *Ezra Pound, Popular Genres, and the Discourse of Culture*, Philadelphia: Pennsylvania State University Press, 1995.

Davie, Donald, *Studies in Ezra Pound: Chronicle and Polemic*, Manchester: Carcanet, 1991.

Ellmann, Maud, *The Poetics of Impersonality: T. S. Eliot and Ezra Pound*, Cambridge, Mass.: Harvard University Press, 1987.

Makin, Peter, *Pound's Cantos*, London: George Allen and Unwin, 1985.

Moody, A. D. (ed.), *The Cambridge Companion to T. S. Eliot*, Cambridge University Press, 1994.

Nadel, Ira B. (ed.), *The Cambridge Companion to Ezra Pound*, Cambridge University Press, 1999.

Schuchard, Ronald, *Eliot's Dark Angel: Intersections of Life and Art*, Oxford University Press, 1999.

Terrell, Carroll F., *A Companion to 'The Cantos' of Ezra Pound*, Berkeley: University of California Press, 1980.

## H.D. and revisionary myth-making

Chisholm, Dianne, *H.D.'s Freudian Poetics: Psychoanalysis in Translation*, Ithaca: Cornell University Press, 1992.

Collecott, Diana, *H.D. and Sapphic Modernism*, Cambridge University Press, 1999.

DuPlessis, Rachel Blau, *H.D.: The Career of that Struggle*, London: Harvester, 1986.

Edmunds, Susan, *Out of Line: History, Psychoanalysis, and Montage in H.D.'s Long Poems*, Stanford University Press, 1994.

Friedman, Susan Stanford and Rachel Blau DuPlessis (eds), *Signets: Reading H.D.*, Madison: University of Wisconsin Press, 1990.
King, Michael (ed.), *H.D.: Woman and Poet*, Orono: National Poetry Foundation, 1986.
Laity, Cassandra, *H.D. and the Victorian Fin de Siècle: Gender, Modernism, Decadence*, Cambridge University Press, 1996.
Morris, Adalaide, *How to Live/What to Do: H.D.'s Cultural Poetics*, Urbana: University of Illinois Press, 2003.

### Yeats, Ireland and modernism

Chaudhry, Yug Mohit, *Yeats, The Irish Literary Revival and the Politics of Print*, Cork University Press, 2001.
Cullingford, Elizabeth Butler, *Gender and History in Yeats's Love Poetry*, Cambridge University Press, 1993.
Diggory, Terence, *Yeats and American Poetry: The Tradition of the Self*, Princeton University Press, 1983.
Doggett, Rob, *Deep-Rooted Things: Empire and Nation in the Poetry and Drama of William Butler Yeats*, University of Notre Dame Press, 2006.
Foster, R. F., *W. B. Yeats: A Life*, vol. I, *The Apprentice Mage*, Oxford University Press, 1997.
Foster, R. F., *W. B. Yeats: A Life*, vol. II, *The Arch-Poet*, Oxford University Press, 2003.
Howes, Marjorie, *Yeats's Nations: Gender, Class, and Irishness*, Cambridge University Press, 1996.
Longley, Edna, '"Modernism", Poetry and Ireland', in Marianne Thormählen (ed.), *Rethinking Modernism*, London: Palgrave Macmillan, 2003, pp. 160–79.
Smith, Stan, *The Origins of Modernism: Eliot, Pound, Yeats and the Rhetorics of Renewal*, Hemel Hempstead: Harvester, 1994.

### Modernist poetry in the British Isles

Burke, Carolyn, *Becoming Modern: The Life of Mina Loy*, Berkeley: University of California Press, 1996.
Comentale, Edward P., *Modernism, Cultural Production, and the British Avant-Garde*, Cambridge University Press, 2004.
Crawford, Robert, *Devolving English Literature*, Oxford: Clarendon Press, 1992.
Dilworth, Thomas, *The Shape of Meaning in the Poetry of David Jones*, University of Toronto Press, 1988.
Makin, Peter, *Bunting: The Shaping of His Verse*, Oxford: Clarendon Press, 1992.
Schreiber, Maeera and Keith Tuma (eds), *Mina Loy: Woman and Poet*, Orono: National Poetry Foundation, 1998.

### US modernism I: Moore, Stevens and the modernist lyric

Bates, Milton, *Wallace Stevens: A Mythology of Self*, Berkeley: University of California Press, 1985.

Bloom, Harold, *Wallace Stevens: The Poems of Our Climate*, Ithaca: Cornell University Press, 1977.

Cook, Eleanor, *Word-Play and Word-War in Wallace Stevens*, Princeton University Press, 1988.

Costello, Bonnie, *Marianne Moore: Imaginary Possessions*, Cambridge, Mass.: Harvard University Press, 1981.

Filreis, Alan, *Wallace Stevens and the Actual World*, Princeton University Press, 1991.

Gelpi, Albert (ed.), *Wallace Stevens: The Poetics of Modernism*, Cambridge University Press, 1985.

Heuving, Jeanne, *Omissions Are Not Accidents: Gender in the Art of Marianne Moore*, Detroit: Wayne State University Press, 1992.

Holley, Margaret, *The Poetry of Marianne Moore: A Study in Voice and Value*, Cambridge University Press, 1987.

Miller, Cristanne, *Marianne Moore: Questions of Authority*, Cambridge, Mass.: Harvard University Press, 1995.

Schulze, Robin, *The Web of Friendship: Marianne Moore and Wallace Stevens*, Ann Arbor: University of Michigan Press, 1995.

Vendler, Helen, *On Extended Wings: Wallace Stevens' Longer Poems*, Cambridge, Mass.: Harvard University Press, 1969.

### US modernism II: the other tradition – Williams, Zukofsky and Olson

Ahearn, Barry, *Zukofsky's "A": An Introduction*, Berkeley: University of California Press, 1983.

Bremen, Brian A. *William Carlos Williams and the Diagnostics of Culture*, New York: Oxford University Press, 1993.

Clark, Tom, *Charles Olson: The Allegory of a Poet's Life*, New York: W. W. Norton, 1991.

Fredman, Stephen, *The Grounding of American Poetry: Charles Olson and the Emersonian Tradition*, Cambridge University Press, 1995.

Mariani, Paul, *William Carlos Williams: A New World Naked*, New York: W. W. Norton, 1981.

Maud, Ralph, *Charles Olson's Reading: A Biography*, Carbondale: Southern Illinois University Press, 1996.

Riddel, Joseph N., *The Inverted Bell: Modernism and the Counterpoetics of William Carlos Williams*, Baton Rouge: Louisiana State University Press, 1974.

Scroggins, Mark (ed.), *Upper Limit Music: The Writing of Louis Zukofsky*, Tuscaloosa: University of Alabama Press, 1997.

Scroggins, Mark, *Louis Zukofsky and the Poetry of Knowledge*, Tuscaloosa: University of Alabama Press, 1998.

Stanley, Sandra Kumamoto, *Louis Zukofsky and the Transformation of a Modern American Poetics*, Berkeley: University of California Press, 1994.

Terrell, Carroll F. (ed.), *Louis Zukofsky: Man and Poet*, Orono: National Poetry Foundation, 1979.

### The poetry of the Harlem Renaissance

Douglas, Ann, *Terrible Honesty: Mongrel Manhattan in the 1920s*, London: Picador, 1995.

Mishkin, Tracy, *The Harlem and Irish Renaissances: Language, Identity, and Representation*, Gainesville: University Press of Florida, 1998.

Nielson, Aldon Lynn, *Reading Race: White American Poets and the Racial Discourse in the Twentieth Century*, Athens: University of Georgia Press, 1988.

### Postcolonial poetry of Africa, South Asia and the Caribbean

Pollard, Charles W., *New World Modernisms: T. S. Eliot, Derek Walcott, and Kamau Brathwaite*, Charlottesville: University of Virginia Press, 2004.

Ramazani, Jahan, *The Hybrid Muse: Postcolonial Poetry in English*, University of Chicago Press, 2001.

### Modernist poetry and the canon

Doyle, Brian, *English and Englishness*, London: Routledge, 1988.

Gorak, Jan, *The Making of the Modern Canon*, London: Athlone, 1991.

Graff, Gerald, *Professing Literature: An Institutional History*, University of Chicago Press, 1987.

Guillory, John, *Cultural Capital: The Problem of Literary Canon Formation*, University of Chicago Press, 1993.

Harding, Jason, *The Criterion: Cultural Politics and Periodical Networks in Inter-War Britain*, Oxford University Press, 2002.

# INDEX

'Tempers, The' 182
'To a Poor Old Woman' 71
'To Elsie' 183
'Wanderer – A Baroque Study, The' 182
'Young Housewife, The' 72
Wilson, Edmund 228, 236
Winters, Yvor 232, 233, 235
Wintz, Cary D. 196
Woolf, Leonard 22, 69
Woolf, Virginia 22, 69
Wordsworth, William 20, 168

Yeats, Elizabeth 69
Yeats, William Butler 3, 5–6, 13, 20, 47, 52,
    53–4, 116, 117, 126–7, 128–44, 149,
    150, 153, 170, 171, 207, 208, 209,
    210, 215, 231, 234, 235, 236, 237, 241
'Adam's Curse' 133–4
'All Souls' Night' 137, 138, 142
'Among School Children' 142, 236
Autobiographies 132
'Black Tower, The' 144
Celtic Twilight, The 131
'Coat, A' 135
Collected Poems 137
'Curse of Cromwell, The' 144
'Dolls, The' 135
'Easter 1916' 135
'Fallen Majesty' 134
In the Seven Woods 133
Last Poems and Two Plays 129
'Leda and the Swan' 141–2
'Magi, The' 135
'Meditations in Time of Civil War' 138,
    140–1
Michael Robartes and the Dancer 135
'Mountain Tomb, The' 134
'Nationality and Literature' 131
New Poems 129, 143

'Nineteen Hundred and Nineteen' 138
'On Those that Hated The Playboy of the
    Western World, 1907' 134
Oxford Book of Modern Verse, The 53,
    126, 235, 241
Responsibilities 134–5
Rose, The 130
'Running to Paradise' 134
'Sailing to Byzantium' 137, 138
'Second Coming, The' 135
Secret Rose, The 139
'September 1913' 134
'Symbolism of Poetry, The' 53–4
'To a Shade' 134
'To Ireland in the Coming Times' 130
'To a Wealthy Man who promised a
    Second Subscription to the Dublin
    Municipal Gallery if it were proved
    the People wanted Pictures' 134
'Tower, The' 138–40
Tower, The 128, 135–42, 235
Vision, A 137, 237
'Wild Swans at Coole, The' 235
Winding Stair and Other Poems, The 128,
    135–6, 142–3
'Words for Music Perhaps' 143
    'Crazy Jane and the Bishop' 143
    'Crazy Jane Talks with the Bishop'
        143
Yriarte, Charles 103–4, 109

Zola, Emile 25
Zukofsky, Celia 188
Zukofsky, Louis 2, 6, 16, 116, 163, 172, 181,
    186–9, 192, 234
80 Flowers 188
'A' 186–8, 192
Bottom: on Shakespeare 187
'Poem beginning "The"' 186

# Cambridge Companions to . . .

## AUTHORS

## TOPICS